Same Sky, Different Nights

Nandasiri Jasentuliyana

The Journey of a Sri Lankan Barrister - *President Emeritus, International Institute of Space Law and Policy (IISL) from the chair of Deputy Director-General, United Nations Office at Vienna and Director, United Nations Office for Outer Space Affairs.*

A Memoir

authorHOUSE

AuthorHouse™
1663 Liberty Drive
Bloomington, IN 47403
www.authorhouse.com
Phone: 1 (800) 839-8640

Published by AuthorHouse 07/28/2016

ISBN: 978-1-5246-0042-6 (sc)
ISBN: 978-1-5246-0041-9 (e)

Print information available on the last page.

Dedicated to

SHANTHI
Amal, Chaminda, Janaka, Nina, Kara, Kai,
&
Family & Friends who are featured within these covers

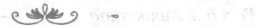

Prof. Ananda Guruge Writes....

Reliving my journey so far.....
Nandasri Jasentuliyana

Part 1 ... The small town boy

Part 2 ... The dream begins

Part 3 ... Halfway through

Part 4 ... Westward bound

Part 5 ... My own universe

Part 6 ... Awakening

Part 7 ... Ad Astra

Epilogue ... Glimpses of my untold story

Photographs:

Contents

Author's Note

"No man is an island, Entire of itself,
Each is a piece of the continent, A part of the main."
John Donne, Meditation XVII, Devotions upon Emergent Occasions.

The journey of my life is interwoven with the journeys of an uncountable number of others; family, teachers, colleagues, role models. Each place I travelled through, each person I met, perhaps by being at the right place at the right time, perhaps through sheer chance, molded me into the person I am today. This then, is as much their story as it is mine.

Initial inspiration to revisit my life came from my wife Shanthi and some close friends and colleagues. It was heightened by the hand of a journalist who traced my journey, and his story is the final chapter of this book. But in the end, the undeniable motivation is Bhava Thanha - the magnetism of the ego.

It is only a simple personal record with personal experiences, reminiscences and observations. Every aspect of such a document cannot be expected to appeal to or interest every reader. I hope that some find my story informative and even interesting and others a vehicle to reminisce with nostalgia, and possibly the young readers will be provided with some inspiration. To me, this personal narrative of my life celebrates my space age journey, which led me to a most fascinating career at the United Nations that made life worth living.

It has been over two years since I embarked on this personal voyage. Now it is my pleasant duty to acknowledge those who made it possible, in the interim, to complete this publication.

First and foremost, to my wife Shanthi for insisting that I write my story. Once I began, she was there to encourage me every step of the way. Mr. H.L.D. Mahindapala, by writing a brief biography covering my days at the United Nations, energized me to write my own story. I thank Dr. Ananda Guruge, for writing the introduction, and encouraging me to tell the story.

Most of all, I want to express my sincere gratitude to Ms. Aditha Dissanayake and Dr. Stephen Doyle, without whose encouragement and support, I would not have had the courage to bring this book to your shelf. Aditha who grasped every turn and twist of my story, helped me rearrange pages full of narratives which had no structure. She found just the right touch in helping me make this a better book, while always mindful that this is a personal story, and that it has to resonate in my voice. She nevertheless left a large editorial footprint over the entire text. I turned to her innumerable times for guidance on an assortment of matters that came up during the preparation of the final manuscript, and I thank her for her ungrudging response. My friend and colleague since graduate school, Dr. Stephen Doyle, went through the text meticulously to ensure it is readable and the language is precise. I am indebted to him for volunteering his valuable time so generously, and for providing me the confidence that the story is worthy of publishing.

Dr. Suneth Rajawasam, read the text and made useful suggestions. Reference has been made and extracts used from variety of popular sources instantly available on the internet, that are gratefully acknowledged. I am most appreciative of those who read the first print and made useful suggestions, particularly Mr. Douglas Pemasiri, Mrs. Ranee Gunasakera, and Dr. Nihal Jayawickrama, whose suggestions have been incorporated in the second print.

Ms. Cara Jayasekara, helped me with the initial formatting of the text and graphics. Dr. Lakshman Makandura graciously permitted the use of his facilities and offered the services of his associate, Dilip Niranjana, IT consultant, who volunteered to complete the final formatting of the entire text in a very professional manner with the able assistance of Mr. Manjula Kumara, displaying their skill and flair for desktop publishing. I thank Mr. Niroshan Kahawita, and the Sri Lanka Foundation in Los Angeles, for designing the cover.

The first print of this publication was launched at the Taj Samudra Hotel in Colombo, Sri Lanka, on the 28th of May 2013, sponsored by the Merrill J. Fernando Foundation. I wish to express my grateful thanks to Merrill, and his sons Malik and Dilan, of Dilmah Tea, for making it happen. It was later launched in Los Angeles, California, at the Royal Vista Golf Club, on 20th July, 2013, and it was yet another 'giving soul' present on that occasion that prompted the early publication of this second print. Shortly following the U.S. launch, Mr. Sathay Chandramohan, an oxford educated Sri Lankan entrepreneur, having read the book offered to publish 1000 copies for free distribution to schools and young people in the outstations of Sri Lanka. I am most grateful to him and his wife Geeta, for their admirable generosity.

Nandasiri Jasentuliyana
Los Angeles, California
njasen@hotmail.com

Introduction

My constant message to the youth of my Motherland has been that there is nothing in the whole world which could not be achieved through dedicated concentration on goals and well-directed hard work. Quite egoistically, I hold myself as an example. But far more poignantly does the author of this book, Nandasiri (Nandi) Jasentuliyana, stand out with an irrefutable claim to be a greater role-model. His achievements on the world scene are as wide-ranging as they are inspiring. It is his life and career that are presented in this delightfully readable volume, which I am privileged to introduce to the potential readers.

His is the story of a notable son of Sri Lanka who has brought significant fame and recognition to his Motherland. "Same Sky, Different Nights" is an apt title for his impressive autobiography, which he calls a journey. It began four minutes after midnight on the 23rd of November 1938 in his grandfather's home in Hirewatte. Thus born in Ambalangoda, his early childhood, school days and law education have much in common with that of Honorable C. W. W. Kannangara, the illustrious father of free education. They went to the same school, Richmond College in Galle, captained the cricket and soccer teams, and excelled in oratory and debating as well as theatrical acting. Nandi did even better in the field of athletics and both men became lawyers through a similar process. They shared a deep and abiding love for Sri Lanka and Sri Lankans.

Even today, as private citizens enjoying a well-earned retirement in California, Nandi and his charming and talented wife, Shanthi, are the most sought-after friends by the community. They are always there giving the best support, encouragement and leadership that one expects, whether it is in a religious function, a cultural performance, a social event or even a simple family celebration. The book throws much light on the background and the circumstances which shaped his most admirable character and personality.

Every reader, I am sure, will be glad that "after a decade of semi-retirement having reached the final stage of life," Nandi felt that time was ripe to revisit the people he met and the places he knew during the eventful journey covering over seven decades. It has been a journey of which only a very few people in the world could even dream. From Ambalangoda to Galle and then to Colombo and Montreal and thence to the wide world in a distinguished career in the United Nations, it took him all over the world until he retired after serving as the Deputy Director-General, United Nations Office at Vienna and Director, United Nations Office for Outer Space Affairs, New York and Vienna. Concurrently for fifteen years, he was the President of the International Institute of Space Law (IISL), with headquarters in Paris.

To most readers who have had the pleasure of knowing Nandi and his family, this volume brings to mind their own life experiences in Sri Lanka and abroad. The nostalgia that I personally experienced is ample proof of how his lively descriptive account will affect his friends and acquaintances. The first six chapters on his early years as a small town boy are replete with detailed information on a galaxy of relatives and family friends. What is really noteworthy is how he had been in touch with them all his life and recorded their and their progeny's achievements with up-to-date tidings on where they are now. His conclusion on his mother, whom he lost at the tender age of three, is a laudable expression of gratitude to those who took her place: "Yet, as if to make up for her early demise, in their own inimitable ways, my uncles, aunts, and cousins showered me with an infinite quantity of love and affection. I love them back with the same fervor."

Nandasiri's excellent first person presentation of his personal experiences, with candid details on where he excelled or otherwise, the challenges encountered, and the overall impact on his life is a veritable treatise on the country's education on the eve of

Independence. With my own formation in a similar process, I am grateful that this information is so lucidly and convincingly recorded for the future.

"Same Sky, Different Nights" stands out as a veritable literary masterpiece. It is a biography written in an innovative style. It is not the usual chronologically arranged narration of events and incidences in a person's life. With a deep love for people and appreciation of the beauty of the planet earth, Nandi embellishes the most intimate accounts of his life with graphic portrayals of people and places. He takes his readers to lives of numerous people who had influenced him or shared their experience with him in diverse ways. What a memory he has displayed to record even the most casual contacts so far back in his childhood and youth!

If a new word is to be coined, his story is full of "flash- forwards." For example: his baths in the river as a child of seven reminds him of the Island Hermitage where a host of foreign monks, led by the eminent Nyanatiloka Mahathera, disseminated the benign message of the Buddha to the world; his visit to the sacred cities as an adolescent enables to him to refer to the Cultural Triangle Project, which commenced in 1980; the Language Riots of 1958-61 give him an opening to document the origin and the denouement of the LTTE War to its very end in 2009; and a theatrical performance in the Law College is utilized to project the theatrical capabilities of Namel Weeramuni right up to his remarkably courageous production of "Madhyavedikayekuge Asipata" in 2007.

Of course, no opportunity is missed to digress into sociological explanations of the customs and taboos which govern the way of life of the people. This excellent account of Nandasiri's life is positively enhanced by its perceptive introduction to numerous aspects of the country's history, geography, government and society. It is a book to be read for pleasure and profit.

The thumb-nail presentation of Nandi's life and career in the Epilogue and the chapter preceding it by H.L.D. Mahindapala serve to rouse one's curiosity and interest on why and how Nandi's multifaceted life experiences are worthy of the highest attention. As Mahindapala says it, Nandi's journey from "an obscure Sinhala-Buddhist mixed school to the Office of Outer Space Affairs of the United Nations was inevitably long and arduous, with usual quota of diversions and pitfalls on the way." But this volume ends where his brilliant international career begins, creating within us the fervent desire to know more of this outstanding intellectual who, by his courage and perseverance, brought so much credit to his Motherland.

Ananda W. P. Guruge

Dean of Academic Affairs, University of the West, California, former Ambassador of Sri Lanka to UNESCO, France and USA, and former Senior Special Adviser to the Director General of UNESCO.

Reliving my journey so far.....

They marched up and down the Colombo Galle road; their cold, blank eyes staring straight ahead, the rifles on their shoulders gleaming in the light of the setting sun. These were the war years. Churchill had already declared his most famous war statement; "We shall not flag or fail. We shall go on to the end.... we shall not surrender".

Fascinated by this invasion of the outside world, I watched the British and African platoons marching down our street from the safety of my grandfather's lap, as he sat on the front verandah of his house in the quaint town of Ambalangoda.

Yet, even as I sought his protection to watch the marching troops, whenever I heard the sound of a Hawker Hurricane aircraft in the sky I would run out into the street pretending I did not hear Seeya's warning, "Don't run into the street, son". Standing by the side of the road, head raised high, one hand on my forehead to shield my eyes from the Sun; I gazed at the beautiful machines flying in the sky. I waved my hand and wondered if the pilot saw me, a three year old boy jumping with joy and waving madly, with his grandfather standing cautiously beside him.

More than 70 years later, I stared, presumably, at that same sky, now shrouded in darkness, from the deck of my house in Los Angeles. My wife Shanthi was seated beside me. A companionable silence had fallen between us; the silence of two people who had lived and loved and weathered bright sunshine as well as many a storm. Nursing a glass of cabernet as I gazed at the full moon and the stars in the sky it dawned on me, how vast the length and enormity of the journey was that I had travelled, from those early years when the sky had fascinated me, to the present when I had taken part in creating laws and regulations to tether the infinite plains of outer space.

It was as if the spotlight was on me. All the stars were focusing their beams on me. Looking up, I thought I saw a face on every star, the face of a loving, familiar figure that had molded me into who I am today. The way I think, speak, the way I stand, the subjects I had chosen to study, the games I had played, the tunes I had danced to, the girls I had known can undoubtedly be traced back to someone I had known in my past, someone who would have made an indelible mark on my journey so far.

After a decade of semi-retirement, having reached the final stages of my life, I felt the time was ripe to revisit the people I met, the places I knew during this eventful journey covering over seven decades.

A journey which begins four minutes after twelve midnight on the 23 of November in the year nineteen hundred and thirty eight in my Grandfather's house in Hirewatte, Ambalangoda.

Every journey, even if it is to travel back into the past can be better enjoyed if there is someone to share it with. I appreciate your presence as you join me in retracing these steps back into the mid-20th century.

Part 1

The small town boy

*"You don't choose your family.
They are God's gift to you, as you are to them"*

– Rev. Desmond Tutu

Chapter 1

Sriyagara

I remember vividly the water splashing onto my head from the clay pot in my grandfather's hands, as I stood knee deep in the gracefully flowing waters of the Madu Ganga, more than seventy years ago in the Southern coastal town of Ambalangoda. Eyes closed, hands clenched, I stood at attention till about the fourth dose from the Kale. "Brrrrr, brrrr" I rasped through the cascade of water. "Ekai, dekai..." (one, two...), counted grandfather. Once my body was accustomed to the cold, I jumped up and down gleefully, splashing grandfather as he bent down to fill the vessel again and again.

This was our daily routine. Everyday shortly after day break, Seeya and I made our way to the branch of the Madhu Ganga which flowed serenely to embrace the Indian Ocean, less than a kilometer away from Seeya's house on the Colombo Galle road. There were two bridges near the place we called our "special bathing spot" in the river, one for the railway line and a parallel one for the motor way. Those who travelled to and from Colombo either by train, bus or motor car would have witnessed this daily ritual between the old gentleman and the little boy. Seeya counted the number of times he poured the water over my head with meticulous precision. It had to be the same every single day. Half the number to be poured before he put soap on me to make sure I was wet all over, the other half, to wash the soap off me and make me sparkle with cleanliness. When the number reached a predetermined end, the bath too came to an end. It was much later, when he taught me to swim, that I really began to enjoy these morning trips to the river.

We usually walked along the railway line to reach the bathing spot and returned along the road which ran beside the beach. Often, Seeya would stop to chat with the passersby, for he knew them well.

In the evening I sat with Seeya on the porch of his two story house called Sriyagara, watching whatever was going on in the neighborhood. In the late thirties and early forties heavy traffic was unheard of even on the main roads and there were more pedestrians than cyclists on the Colombo Galle road.

From the porch, which ran the breadth of Seeya's house, one entered the small isthoppuwa (Portuguese word for an enclosed porch). The isthoppuwa led to the living room and the dinning room, which had two bedrooms on either side. One of these rooms was my mother's when she was growing up.

A narrow hall leading from the dining room led to two other bedrooms; one was Seeya's, the other was Achchie's, who regrettably was bedridden about the time I was born. Though the conversations I had with Achchie (known as Sauhamy), were monologues, from what I had heard about her I knew she used to pay particular attention to the cloth and jacket she wore, that was the customary dress at the time, and that, when she went visiting she made certain her dress and jewelry matched and were in place, by checking them several times in front of her wardrobe mirror.

Beyond the dining room was an open area with a half wall. It was here that the family spent most of their time, often observing whatever was happening in the pantry and the kitchen which had wood burning fires. There was an outhouse that served as a toilet. Those were the days when there were no attached baths and toilets except may be in the capital, Colombo. This also explains our daily trips to the river to bathe.

A staircase from the dining room led to an open hall and a balcony upstairs. On ordinary days, this hall upstairs with a door leading to the balcony which too ran the breadth of the house, was my favorite abode. The hall was mainly used when Seeya organized all night 'Pirith' ceremonies, followed by the noon time 'Dane' (offering of alms to Buddhist priests), that took place at least once every six months. Many relatives would gather in my Seeya's house on those occasions as he was the patriarch of the family.

Chanting of Pirith is a Buddhist Religious ritual. It deals with the chanting of selected "Sutras" loudly and ceremoniously. Sutras are a religious precept which is composed into Pali hymns with a story behind them. They can be sung in rhythm. The selected Sutras contain precepts that relate to needs and day-to-day affairs of both lay men and priests. As singing is done ceremoniously the preparation for it is important. An enclosure is built decorated with natural leaves or paper cuttings which are ensconced according to the traditional art of the island. A ceiling will be fixed above the enclosure with white cloths and it is decorated with flowers, leaves and young coconut leaves. I used to enjoy helping out in the process of decoration. In the middle of the enclosure there is a table and, around it, chairs placed to seat the monks who will chant Pirith. On either side of each gate 'Puncals', a kind of pots, are placed. On each pot there will be a coconut flower and a lamp. On the table decorated pots filled with pure water will be placed. And from the water a thread will be issued out. In Buddhism, alms or almsgiving is the respect given by Buddhists to Buddhist monks. Giving of alms is a step towards the beginning of one's journey to Nirvana through renunciation of worldly belongings and pleasures.

I enjoyed the ceremonies as many family members and friends brought their children and I had a great time with them. I was always grateful to Seeya when he organized such events, and I was also in awe of his imposing presence among such family gatherings. Ever since I could remember I was Seeya's little shadow. Wherever he went, if he allowed me to follow him, I went. This meant getting to know and love my hometown, Ambalangoda.

*　　*　　*

Situated fifty two miles south of Colombo, Ambalangoda to this day has a reputation for being a town of mostly Buddhist and many educated families, belonging to the fisherman's' caste known as Karawa. In the days I was growing up, the town itself was an extended family where family connections some close some not so close, bonded us together as one family. Good times and bad times were shared alike. It is heartening to note this special bonding of kith and kin has survived to the present, with those hailing from Ambalangoda helping each other, whether they are in Sri Lanka or distant parts of the world. There has been a disproportional amount of migrants from Ambalangoda, in contrast to other towns of the region.

It appears that Ambalangoda has its name because in that area there were many 'ambalamas' (traditional way side resting places for travelers in olden times). There are some who believe that the name has evolved from the fishermen's cry on seeing the land on their homeward journey. Looking at the land they cried, 'aan balan goda' which means 'look there you see the land'.

The town of Ambalangoda was built around the market that housed fish stalls, vegetable and fruit stalls, as well as sundry merchandize. The market served as the trading post during the Dutch and British trading period for Cinnamon, copra and other coconut products, rubber, graphite, and areca nut. It is recorded that coastal fishermen belonging to the Parava caste from Kerala, India, were frequent traders who visited the location where the market is built. They formed the origins of the Karava clan in Ambalangoda.

The trade grew with the building of the Railway Station near the market in 1893 when the Colombo to Galle railway line opened. By the 20th century a large majority of the merchants were Muslim and Tamil. As time went on, the Sinhala traders, particularly from three or four families, dominated the merchant houses in Ambalangoda. Trading stores were dotted along the Main Street extending from Seeya's house in the South to the house my father later built to the North.

The people of Ambalangoda and its environs are enterprising and adventurous. The town has a tradition of scholarship since early days and has nurtured more educated citizens than many other towns. We have a saying that "There is a university graduate under every coconut tree". As the natives advanced in education they were looking for new pastures in Colombo and countries abroad. It also meant that those left behind were also educated but in recent times they were not able to find suitable employment.

The people in the area were also largely radical with left leaning politics. In recent times it has even become a nucleus for youth uprisings and Rohana Wijeweera, the founder leader of the Jathika Vimukthi Peramuna (JVP), also had close family connections with Ambalangoda. He studied at Dharmasoka beginning in July 1959. The first three politburo meetings of JVP were held in Ambalangoda in 1970. Of the dozen politburo members half were from Ambalangoda.

Among the learned from Ambalangoda pride of place is taken by the great educators. While Ambalangoda produced many university and school teachers, three among them stand out for their significant impact on the education system of the country and the future of a whole generation of educated elite of my generation.

It so happened, that all three of them began their early primary education, as I did, in local vernacular schools and then had their entire school career at Richmond College, Galle; the oldest Wesleyan Missionary School in Asia. Though they were molded by a Christian missionary school all three rose to prominence for their unique contribution to Buddhist education system. The names of P.de S. Kularatne, C.W.W. Kannangara and L.H. Mettananda are etched in the educational history of the country as preeminent contributors to the modern indigenous education of the country.

They all served as teachers and principals of leading Buddhist schools. They are venerated by scores of students who had the privilege of their guidance and took advantage of the legacy they left in the educational institutions and systems they molded. Two of them served as ministers of education in successive governments for decades. They transformed the British education system that the colonists had left behind into a system that suited the local environment, able to lend itself accessible to the vast numbers of local students, particularly to the large rural population.

Having had the great honor of not only knowing them, but also meeting them when I was still a young man and gaining my education from the same school as they did, they served as inspiration to me, and I was very much influanced by their work.

Ambalangoda also produced a significant number of other educators, scholars and professionals who were prominent in their fields of endeavor. Among them were those who reached the pinnacle of their chosen profession such as cabinet ministers, chief justices and judges of the Supreme Court, heads of Armed Forces, heads of government departments, professors of medicine, engineers, accountants and professionals in other disciplines, as well as nationally recognized cultural leaders and sportsmen. Most of them were known to me through my own contacts or through my parents and grandparents. With few exceptions, I have had the good fortune of meeting them. Because Ambalangoda is a small town of closely connected families, almost all of them are my relatives by birth or through family marriages. As I grew up, I looked up to many of them. Because of the inspiration they provided, they are intrinsically part of what I am today. For that reason a list of eminent personalities of Ambalangoda is provided in the annex.

As for the origins of my maternal family name and its association with Ambalangoda, a reference to the name is made by the erudite Buddhist priest, Venerable Pollwatte Maha Paditha Buddhadatta, in an article written in the newspaper 'Lankadeepa' on 25 November 1958. He believes that there were Malabar fishermen who came from India and settled in an area identified as 'Nambimulla'. Among the names of the people who lived in Nambimulla was Rajapakse Manikunambi, the family name of my mother. Nambimulla is now known as 'Hirewatte' identified as my birth place and the residence of Seeya since the days when a prison was constructed in the area to incarcerate Dutch and later British prisoners.

* * *

While the beaches of tourist towns Bentota, Hikkaduwa, Beruwela and Unawatuna offer tourist activity and luxury, Ambalangoda has a gorgeous beach that provides a feeling of seclusion and an opportunity to explore its long stretch of undeveloped mass of golden sand.

The town is not only an important fish trading centre, but is also famous for its handicrafts: hand woven cotton, finely carved wooden doors and screens. But what are most synonymous with Ambalangoda are the masks and puppets. While the hand carved and hand painted masks in traditional dance dramas remain vibrant and colorful, the masks used for devil dance exorcism are so grotesque (ferocious faces with bulging, popping and staring eyes, a bloodthirsty carnivorous tongue lolling out of a wide mouth with a set of fang-like teeth, all topped by a set of cobra hoods) simply looking at them is enough to give you Goosebumps. The dance itself is utterly devilish, performed to the breakneck pace of the explosive drums; the whole exercise would halt the long strides of the devil himself. If so, the purpose is served.

Mask dances are now performed mostly for the entertainment of tourists, mainly in the beach resorts. For those who wish to delve further into the history of devol dances, the Mask Museum, named after one of the most prominent crafters of masks, Ariyapala who hailed from Ambalangoda, houses a wealth of knowledge. The museum displays masks symbolizing all the vivid characters, demons, gods, heroes and villains who appear in traditional mask dances and, illustrates the mysteries, legends, exorcism and psychology in the world of mask dances.

The fascination I have had for masks, begun in early childhood, continues to this day, so much so that the walls in my home today are decorated with Ariyapala's beautifully grotesque masks - conversation pieces that have helped overcome many a dull moment when entertaining visitors. I must admit though, that this fascination does not go beyond a simple admiration of exquisite craftsmanship. For I have never had any faith in exorcism. Such ceremonies around the world are vividly described, with the salutary effects they may have to the believers and the psychological benefits thereof, by the anthropologist Sir James George Frazer in his excellent study of magic and religion in the 'Golden Bough'.

*   *   *

I was lucky to be traversing the land I was born in, holding my Seeya's hand till I was seven, for there had been a time when Seeya had not lived in Ambalangoda. This was when many left their hometowns in search of greener pastures in the hill country towns where tea plantations had begun to flourish. Many towns of the hill country at the time were dotted with stores run by people from Ambalangoda and the adjacent towns and villages. Among them were also contractors who undertook the construction of tea and rubber factories and other buildings for the British planters.

My Seeya, Rajapakse Mannikudammi Jamis De Silva, was one such contractor, fortunate enough to make good in tea land. Nevertheless he returned home to roost and to build our ancestral home. It was located at the south end of the town in Hirewatte, a stone's throw from the beach. He invested his hard earned money in plantation land in the South. He also acquired a few acres of cinnamon in Karandeniya and rubber land near Hikkaduwa.

Hikkaduwa was my Achchi's hometown. The daughter of a landowner, she brought with her to the marriage cinnamon and paddy land in Meetiyagoda. It was when I visited these paddy fields in Meetiyagoda with Seeya that I saw the acre of land believed to have been blessed by the moon. It is here that the mysterious gem, called the moonstone is found. As captivating as a full moon gleaming in the night sky, the moonstone is considered sacred and has ornamented many a jewel since time immemorial. It is common knowledge that the most sought-after moonstones which have a haunting blue sheen, are found almost exclusively in the mines of Sri Lanka. The sleepy village of Hikkaduwa, which I used to visit in my youth, developed into an international holiday destination in the early 1960s. Today backpackers and package tourists alike favor the beautiful white sand beaches, colorful coral reef and the excellent surf. Travelers from all over the world are attracted to the beach party atmosphere created by the surfing and diving scene. Hikkaduwa also produced scholars and professionals most of whom had links through marriage to Ambalangoda. Several of my own extended family was married from Hikkaduwa.

My grandmother had a brother who lived in Hikkaduwa. A railway surveyor by profession, he lived in the ancestral house in the center of the village. In my young days I visited his home on several occasions particularly to attend religious ceremonies and later for sea baths with friends from Ambalangoda. His son, Terrance Warusawithana was a little senior to me but went to the same school as I did. Terrance became a lawyer and was later elected as the Mayor of Matale where he practiced his profession (my wife Shanthi's mother Margret Chandraratne too hailed from Matale). He is the only link I have from my grandmother's family.

Apart from visiting my grandmother's brother whom I called Podi Seeya, I was also in the habit of dropping into to see my grandfather's sister, Punchi Archie who lived with her family in a large impressive two storied house called Pulasthigedera, conveniently situated within walking distance of Seeya's house. I remember all the nooks and crannies of this house big enough to hide a five year old, as I spent most of these visits playing hide and seek with my kinsmen.

* * *

On Poya Days I visited the Sunandaramaya Mahavihara (known in town as the Maha Pansala-Big Temple) established in the Dutch period in 1753, with Seeya and the others in our household. It could be because the pansala is known to be one of the earliest Buddhist temples on the south coast, that its thorana (gateway), happens to be the largest on the island. On the outer wall of the shrine room are some rare murals depicting Jataka stories (stories from the previous lives of Buddha) which used to fascinate me as a child. Much later, in my late teens, we lived within a stone's throw of this "big temple" for about a year while my father built a new home in town. Not far from there is the Sundarama Viharaya, established in 1803 with its excellent wall paintings reputed to be drawn in 1805.

Another fascinating place that I have visited is in an inland suburb of Ambalangoda, Karandeniya, where the Galgoda Sailatalaramaya Maha Vihara Temple is situated. The temple houses a reclining Buddha statue, 35 meters long, in an unpretentious building. Made of wood and plaster, till recently this statue was the longest in the Buddhist world - now the title has been taken by the bronze Buddha that reclines in the middle of Bangkok.

I also remember visiting the 150 year old Kodawa Vihara Buddhist temple which is home to five monks in meditation. The temple is situated on the islands in the Madu Ganga which flows to the Randombe Lake that surrounds Ambalangoda. On a recent visit home I had the great pleasure of taking a boat trip with my wife and some friends through the rich mangroves of the wetlands of the area that took us to the temple on the islet.

* * *

To this day I vividly remember the Sinhala Tamil New Year celebration held in Seeya's house on the 13th and 14th of April, each year. This was a particularly enjoyable time for me and I looked forward with anticipation to celebrate the occasion with family, friends and the neighbors. Various beliefs, perhaps those associated with fertility of the harvest, gave birth to many rituals, customs, and ceremonies connected with the New Year. Sri Lankan traditional New Year begins at a time determined by astrological calculations.

I used to watch with fascination some of the older boys in the neighborhood playing a famous game called Guddu (similar to cricket or baseball). The open back veranda was where we played a New Year game called Panchi. I played the game with my cousins as well as adults. Seated in a circle on a mat, we competed with each other by throwing sea shells over a coconut shell (similar to snakes and ladders/crap). Yet, the most enjoyable moment for me was riding the swings specially constructed for the occasion by hanging two coir ropes from two coconut trees with a plank in the middle to sit or stand on, while swinging alone or with a partner.

Cultural rituals began shortly after the beginning of the New Year with Seeya lighting an oil lamp. Women folk led by my Singho Nanda congregated in the back veranda to play the raban (a type of a drum). They played very melodious tunes with vigor, announcing the incipient change in the year.

From lighting the fire for cooking, to making the Kiribath, (milk rice) exchanging money as a good omen, and eating the first meal, the family carried out a variety of rituals. The approach of each auspicious time for various rituals determined by astrological calculations was heralded by the unmistakable sign of very loud firecrackers which remains an integral part of the celebrations throughout Sri Lanka. Though I very much wanted to, I was too small to be allowed to light the crackers.

Once the important rituals were observed, the partying began with celebratory feasts of kavum (small oil cake) and kokis (crisp and light sweetmeat originally from the Netherlands) that were prepared by Singho Nanda and my Cousins Kusuma and Chulla.

We also observed the custom of offering betel chives to Seeya and the other elders as a token of love, respect and gratitude. Basking in the knowledge they are being loved and are cared for, by their children, the elders in turn showered blessings on the children. Presents were exchanged among family and friends usually in the form of clothing.

Each year the New Year celebrations came to an end with the anointing of the oil ceremony. In this auspicious hour, Seeya anoints the family members with herbal oil. Observing the tradition of going to work at a predetermined auspicious hour in the New Year, Seeya used to go to the town center to carry out a few business activities. My cousins would go to the temple, taking me with them, as it was customary for people to visit temples and engage in religious activities during the festive days.

* * *

Being Seeya's shadow, following him everywhere, had great advantages. It was with Seeya that I made my first visit to Colombo. Seeya and I arose very early in the morning to catch the early express train to the capital. By the time we got to the railway station (if I remember right we walked the distance of about a mile), the train was just leaving the station. Not deterred by this, Seeya went to the shop in the town center where he used to sell his rubber and cinnamon from his plantation. He knew there were lorries (trucks) that frequently transported the products to Colombo. We were fortunate that one lorry was just about to leave for Colombo. Lorries had a seat in front which accommodated the driver and the two helpers who loaded and unloaded the cargo. The merchant at the shop instructed the driver to take only one helper and asked the driver to assist with the unloading of the day's cargo, once they reached Colombo. Seeya promptly accommodated himself comfortably in the front seat. The helper hoisted me on to the load of rubber and cinnamon in the back of the lorry. There was no room to stand or sit as the lorry was loaded to the brim. I had no alternative but to lie down horizontally all the way to Colombo. Luckily the lorry had a small opening in the partition between the front and the back sections.

Peeping through this I somehow enjoyed the journey as we sped through the countryside along the southern coastal belt. The novelty of the wayside attractions kept me entertained as this was my first trip outside the immediate environs of my native town. Thus I entered Colombo, for the first time in my life, horizontally.

— ❖ —

Chapter 2

Amma

I watched Miss Laura's fingers holding a piece of chalk trace the first letter of the Sinhala alphabet on my black slate. She took her hand away and suggested I do the same. Breathing heavily as if I had climbed a mountain, holding the wooden frame of the slate with my left hand, I tried as best as I could to write the letter "a" in Sinhala. Here I was in the world of school and education, for the first time in my life at age of three.

Situated close to the railway station, an all-girls school named Prajapathi, which had two half-walled buildings, was where I learned the Sinhala alphabet. Miss Laura, the teacher of the kindergarten, was extremely kind and helped me trace over and over the Sinhala letters which she so beautifully wrote on my slate. I regret to say, her instructions were of no avail because though I learned the alphabet eventually, my handwriting was never legible. The first word I learned to write was Amma (mother).

These were the days when my parents lived in a house not far from the school in Maha Ambalangoda. The vague memories I have of my mother, Joslin De. Silva, belong to the time we lived here. Though she was very loving and kind, undoubtedly some of my pranks got on her nerves. One day in order to punish me she locked me up in a room. I remember yelling at the top of my voice hoping someone would come and rescue me from this temporary confinement. Luckily for me, my Uncle Martin who was passing by heard me screaming and came to my rescue. As soon as he opened the door I ran out of the room and out of the house straight into the house opposite ours searching for the company of my Cousin Chand.

This was the house of Uncle Jasenthuliyana, the most well known person who carried this name. He was an erudite teacher at Ananda College who later became the principal of Dharmasoka College, the leading school in Ambalangoda that has produced a great number of scholars and professionals. For some reason best known to him, he gave the name Ariyasinghe to his four sons while his name was retained for the two daughters (knowing perhaps that when they get married they will change their name). And so, most people mistake me to be his son.

I remember playing cricket with my Cousin Chand who is today, a retired gynecologist residing in Los Angeles. I also used to play with Uncle's other two sons Mitra who retired as a Deputy Inspector-General of Police and Vipula a leading Rheumatologist in Colombo.

Their mother was the best friend of my mother. Every time I met her till she passed away not too long ago, she used to tell me stories about my mother. According to Aunt Madura my mother was sweet and kind and always helped the needy. She told me about my mother's days at Museaus College which she too attended with my mother's elder sister. She remembered my mother as a quiet but sociable student always willing to help her friends.

Shortly after the lock-up incident my mother passed away from complications following the birth of my sister. I have heard that she eventually suffered from a disease in the gut complicated by pneumonia. I have also heard that her final demise was because she was given rice and curry while having very high fever as a result of pneumonia! Whatever the reasons, those were the days when there were no antibiotics and other medications which, if they had been available, would definitely have extended her short life.

She was admitted to the Galle Hospital which was considered the best hospital outside Colombo, but to no avail. I was not destined to enjoy the love and tender care of a mother as I grew up.

The last memory I have of my mother is seeing her in her coffin in the dining room of Seeya's house. Wondering what she was doing there, I remember going half way up the staircase to get a better look. Seeing her lying there, wanting to cuddle against her, feel her warmth, I promptly came down and tried to climb on to the coffin, nearly toppling it over. Someone picked me up and took me away. I do remember the funeral procession. Too young to understand the enormity of my loss, I gazed with fascination at the drummers who led the funeral procession. There ends my memory of her, except for the few occasions I have visited her grave in the public cemetery which was overrun by the tsunami in 2004.

*　　*　　*

One other person, who knew my mother well, was one of the nieces of Seeiya, Seelawathie Nanda. Being my mother's first cousin, she was my mother's bridesmaid at my parents' wedding. She was married to a Railway Head Guard. They were both close friends of my father and showed immense affection towards me. Their daughter Malini belonged to my generation, though she was younger than me. We have been in close contact through the years mainly because our paths often crossed in adulthood as well.

Malini married a highly respected economist at the Central Bank of Sri Lanka who also hailed from Ambalangoda known by the name of Uswatte-Aratchi. While working at the Central Bank he won a scholarship to the Cambridge University in the UK and obtained a PhD degree. When he was at Cambridge I visited him on my first visit to the UK. Later on he joined the United Nations as an economist and worked in Bangkok and New York. When they were transferred to New York I was asked to find an apartment for them and naturally I found one in the neighborhood where I was living. My son Amal and their son and daughter went to the UN school. Over the years our two families were constantly in touch with each other.

After he retired as Director, Social Development Division of the UN he and Malini moved back to Colombo. They continue to make annual visits to their children in the US and we have been visiting them whenever we are in Colombo.

Malini had a brother, Bandula who also worked in the printing section of the UN and was married to a senior secretary in the UN.

* * *

My mother had four siblings (three brothers, two elder and one younger, and one elder sister). Henry, the eldest of the brothers, died before I was born. I know nothing about him. Singho Nanda (aunty) is his wife and my Cousins Kusuma and Chulla are his daughters. They moved into Seeya's house after the demise of Uncle Henry, and looked after the household chores for Seeya, as well as taking good care of the bedridden Achchi (grandmother). They were extremely fond of me and I was spoiled by them. They looked after all my needs and even fed me my meals, telling stories or singing songs so that I would finish everything on my plate.

The elder of the two sisters later married Piyasena Jayasuriya who was the secretary of the Village Council in Batapola. She moved to Batapola where they acquired some plantation land in the village. Their son, a university lecturer with a PhD, now resides in the United States. His parents are now deceased and his aunt Chulla is residing in an elders' home in Maharagama where I visited her not too long ago, to our mutual delight!

* * *

My mother's second brother was Rajapakse Mannikkunambi Martin De Silva, (known as R.M.M. De Silva). He led a very colorful and famous life and is the best known in the family. He married Kusuma Mendis, from the Mendis clan that later established the brewery and liquor business with the well known brand of Mendis Special. The couple had no children and both, particularly my uncle Martin, were extremely fond of me. When my mother died he wanted to adopt me but my father summarily dismissed the proposal. My uncle was never too close to my father ever since the incident and the feelings were mutual as far as I know. No surprise, for they were poles apart in their demeanors.

Uncle Martin was educated at Richmond College, Galle and was an accomplished sportsman. He played in the College cricket team and was the captain in 1921 and 1922. His vice captain was V.T. Nanayakkara who later became a member of parliament from Matale. My uncle was an all-rounder and an outstanding left arm spin bowler who owned all the bowling records of the college. For decades he held the records in the Mahinda-Richmond (Big Match of the South) batting- 97 not out, and bowling-7 wickets for 6 runs and 8 for 29. His bowling record stood unbroken till Sirisena Ambewatte of Mahinda took all 10 wickets in 1950. In the four years he played (1919-1922) he had 9 five or more wicket hauls with a total of 59 wickets for 212 runs. There were occasions when he took five or more wickets with a best of 8 for 29. An astounding record by any standard! No surprise, therefore, that he went on to become one of the best all-rounder's of the Singhalese Sports Club (SSC). In 1934, he had the best bowling record for all clubs, and played in the All-Ceylon national team.

At the time he played for Ceylon only a couple of non Europeans played on the team. With his cricketing prowess he was able to secure a good position with the Ford Company which was run by Europeans. He was very successful and purchased a sizeable rubber estate with an attractive bungalow in Yatiyantota. He owned an *Austin* car. Naturally, working with Europeans meant he had to keep company with them, socially as well.

Eventually, he lost his job and moved back to Ambalangoda. At first he rented a fancy house with a large garden in Patabandimulla which was immaculately kept with fine furniture and decorative items. There he started living on his savings and took to politics getting elected as the Chairman of the Ambalangoda Urban Council (UC).

In due course he sold the rubber estate, exhausted his savings and moved in with Seeya. He brought with him Aranolis, his man Friday, who had been an orphan from his teens and was a good companion to me. Though my uncle loved me I was terrified of him. The others at home though, did not realize the depth of my anguish.

There were times he fought with Seeya and moved to the Rest House in town with bag and baggage including his almariya (Portuguese word for wardrobe). He would stay there for months until he decided to come back home. In the latter days when he had no funds Seeya had to pay his bill!

The Rest House was less than a kilometer from Seeya's house. It was located by the sea on a small picturesque hill. At the bottom of the hill abutting the sandy beach is an unusual formation of two huge rocks in triangular shape facing the beach. This enclosure was like a swimming pool that provided a safe place for sea bathing. Not only in my young days but throughout my visits to Ambalangoda, even in recent times, I have enjoyed bathing in the sea with friends at this inviting location.

The Rest Houses scattered throughout the country were built by the British for travelers, particularly officials on circuit. Those days they were upscale and rather expensive places in the towns outside the capital. Generally lawyers, doctors and other professionals congregated there in the evenings to relax and enjoy a drink with friends, and to catch up on the day's news and happenings. Regrettably, in more recent days, with the proliferation of star class hotels, Rest Houses have been neglected and have become rather seedy places.

I looked forward to the time when my uncle decided to reside at the Rest House. This was because he would treat me to a lunch of ham, bacon, porkies, and the like which were exotic food at the time. I particularly liked the sweetish British tomato sauce that came with it. This was a nice change from the usual pol sambal (delicious dish of grated coconut and chilies) and bala malu (tuna fish curry) at Seeya's place - the standard fare in any Ambalangoda house even to this day.

At the Rest House his wife would generally pass the day knitting, while he imbibed his whisky and arrack when the former was no longer affordable. Aunt Kusuma was very fond of me as he was, and whenever I came visiting accompanied by Aranolis, she would immediately stop her knitting and take me to the beach. With loving patience she explained all sorts of things to me or rather, answered many questions of no significance that I asked her.

Through all of the travails of my Uncle's life, she remained an unwavering support to him. He never raised his voice to her in anger even when he was dead drunk. He could not be without her beside him and she was though somewhat westernized, a very dignified and devoted lady. She remained so, to the end, through the good as well as the hard times.

Many years after the death of Seeya, my uncle occupied the ancestral house. By now his wife, who was very talented was working as a seamstress to make ends meet. Though times were very hard, she kept an immaculate house. It was then full of ebony furniture some of which my uncle had purchased during the good times. One of his friends from his Colombo days, Sir Cyril De Soyza, hearing of his plight, visited him and offered him a job as the manager of the regional office of Sir Cyril's bus company (South Western Bus Co). At the time, this was the largest operator of buses plying between Colombo and the deep south. The Regional Office was located at Ambalangoda, and therefore, this was a convenient offer. Yet, Uncle Martin's pride did not allow him to accept this offer even from a longstanding friend. After a second visit from Sir Cyril, however, he accepted the post. This was around 1955. Bus companies were nationalized in 1958 and he continued working for the National Transport Board, in the same capacity for a brief period before he retired. (Aranolis, who had been given employment in uncle's office, continued to work in the company and raised a family of his own).

In his seventies, Uncle Martin had taken up coaching cricket. He became cricket coach of Devananda College which had recently formed a cricket team. He molded the team to be very competitive in a few seasons so much so that the leading school in Ambalangoda found it fit to play an annual big match between the two schools. By then he had sold our ancestral house and moved to an upstairs apartment near the cricket grounds, where he lived with his wife and adopted daughter Emily. She remained a spinster and took care of the house in her foster parent's old age. I guess, perhaps, the adoption of Aranolis & Emily substituted, for my father's refusal of my Uncle's desire and explicit request to adopt me at the demise of my mother.

Once, my father, closer to his own retirement, offered to buy the ancestral house. It was of sentimental value to him as it was built by Seeya, and was the home of my mother. But Uncle Martin would have none of it. It was tit for tat for my father having refused his offer to adopt me on the death of my mother. Unknown to my father, the house was later sold and my father built a new house closer to the town center, on the same road known as Main Street. Over the years, I used to make visits to my uncle and his wife Kusuma Nanda whenever I was in town. He passed away in his early eighties I believe, as did his wife while I was abroad. On hearing the news a great sadness engulfed me which lasted for days as I recalled the fond memories I had of Uncle Martin, for he continued to be an influence on me in my youth as well. More about Uncle Martin will appear later in this narrative.

*　*　*

Mary was my mother's only sister. She, like my mother, was dark in color and attractive judging by her wedding photographs. She too was educated at Museus College, Colombo along with my mother. She ran a house full of children where I was a frequent visitor in my young days at Ambalangoda, and later, during school vacations. Loku Amma (big mother) as I used to call her, always welcomed me, and I suspect, she may have felt that I should be made to feel at home in her home empathizing with me as her departed sister's child.

She married Phillippu Hewa Lewis Don William De Silva of Kaluwadumulla, Ambalangoda (I called him Loku Thaththa). He was an apothecary who ran his own dispensary in the scenic sea side village of Dickwella, a few miles south of the town of Matara in the Deep South. As an apothecary (a person who prepared and sold medicine and drugs) he offered general medical advice to patients now mostly offered by doctors. He also dispensed medicines (now done in pharmacies) from his dispensary, which is a small outpatient health facility providing basic primary healthcare services in rural communities. I called him Loku Thaththa (big father) and remember visiting his Dispensary on several occasions while going on pilgrimages with my father to Kataragama, a journey I made several times later in life as well. Loku Thaththa's place was a convenient place to break journey.

Loku Thaththa was a kind man who always gave us a good meal accompanied by Kiri (curd) and Pani (treacle-honey) which Dickwella was well known for. Along with a few prominent residents in the area he was instrumental in establishing Vijitha Vidyalaya, which today is a fully fledged Central Collage. He was a very reserved introvert as I remember him. Nevertheless, he stood as a candidate for elections to the parliament from the area. I accompanied my father who went to assist him in the election over a week-end. He was contesting as an independent candidate and I remember the color of his banner was yellow. There were a number of candidates from different political parties and when the results were announced he had a total of a few hundred votes, placing him near the bottom of the list. The only other occasion I remember him was when he passed away. At the time his family was residing in Colombo. He died of jaundice and I remember seeing his body somewhat yellow in color, which I was told was due to his ailment.

Loku Thaththa and Loku Amma had five sons and a daughter. This though, was not an unusually large family at the time. As a child, I always enjoyed their company and I had the feeling they in turn were happy to have me around. I was very much younger than they. They lived in Kaluwadumulla in a big house with several rooms built around a central court yard. There was a very large garden as well. Being a family of seven they naturally, needed space. The house was purchased by selling a good portion of the land Loku Amma had inherited from my Seeya. I used to visit them there often.

Whenever I was with my cousins, I used to go from room to room and jump onto their beds to be cuddled or teased. They had a man who helped around the house and I used to hang around with him as well, particularly when he milked the family cows, which was an activity that fascinated me. Having one's own supply of milk was essential to feed a large growing family inexpensively.

My cousins began their schooling at Dharmasoka College, Ambalangoda from the mid thirties to mid forties. In 1947, as the children entered the university level education, the family moved to Kollupitiya, Colombo. Their house in Colombo was of medium size with several small rooms sufficient to accommodate the entire family. The house was to the east of the main Galle Road on the heavily built up Kollupitiya Lane.

A major city in Colombo, Kollupitiya (which can be directly translated as "playground of youngsters") comes from the name of a chief from Kandy who had unsuccessfully attempted to dethrone the last king of Kandy. During the period of British and Dutch administration, a brewery had commenced in Kollupitiya which converted coconut treacle into liquor. Nowadays the suburb is mostly a commercial area containing fashionable high-end shopping malls as well as several foreign embassies.

On my first visit to this house in Kollupitiya with Seeya, I stayed a few days and got to know a boy about a year or two my senior, who was living next door. He was a Jayasuriya and on my subsequent visits to Kollupitiya I used to hang around with him and play all sorts of games. One that I enjoyed playing was carom. My cousins too had a carom board. They were pretty good at it and taught me how to play. I mastered the game in a few days and still retain the skills learned at the time. Over the years, I used to frequent the

Kollupitiya house and whenever I went to Colombo, I used to stay there for the duration.

*   *   *

Growing up, I was close to the youngest of my cousins, Tissa who was about four or five years my senior. As the others were older than we were, often Tissa and I ended up in each other's company. He was born at his father's dispensary unlike the rest of the family who were all born at Seeya's house. He also was a frequent guest at Seeya's house which drew us closer. On many occasions he joined us on our daily baths to the river and later we used to take sea baths together and play in the upstairs hall of Seeya's home. As time went by, however, I lost close contact with him because he went to work as a planter in the hill country tea estates. He married there and had three daughters who were all educated at Visakha Vidyalaya. The elder Sriyanthi is married and has a son and a daughter. The middle sibling is Anoma who works at the Central Bank in Colombo. Anoma has two daughters and the youngest, Priyanthi also has two daughters. Members of the younger generation are all in school, but are not yet in their teens.

Elder to Tissa was the only daughter in the family, Hemalatha. I remember her as a very warm and happy person who welcomed my company. She married one Pieris who was a postmaster. I visited her in their Mount Lavinia residence where my Loku Amma (her mother) lived in her last days, loved and looked after by her only daughter. Such are life's travails, though Loku Amma lived to a ripe old age, my cousin Hemalatha passed away in mid life.

Cousin Hemalatha had three daughters and a son. Her son Hemantha had just graduated when he visited me in New York and spent a few pleasant days with us during his visit to the United States for postgraduate work. He is currently professor of bio-chemistry at the Jayawardanapura University, and holds a PhD (University of Queensland, Australia). He is married to Nandani Peiris a veterinary surgeon. They have a son Hasanka Peiris, a physician attached to

General Hospital, Colombo and a daughter, Ravindi Peiris, with a degree in banking and finance from Monash University in Australia.

Hemantha's eldest sister Lilani is a lecturer at the Dental Nursing School. The other sister Padmini is working in the Finance Branch of the Open University in Colombo. The youngest sibling, Thamara is a teacher at St Ann's College, Kurunegala.

Elder to my cousin Hemalatha was her brother Nagasena. He worked for the Ceylon Transport Board (CTB) which was an agency of the government. He lived in their house at Kaluwadumulla with his wife Sujatha and children. He was somewhat of an introvert and though friendly enough, growing up, I did not feel as comfortable in his company as I did with the other members of the family. When he passed away I attended his funeral at the Ambalangoda cemetery, and learned that he died of chicken pox, a rarity for an adult in the seventies. As this was the location of my mother's grave, I found myself thinking of her and recalling my childhood as I watched the funeral proceedings of my cousin's funeral.

Cousin Nagasena had three sons. The eldest Anura is a construction engineer currently engaged in the extension work of the Port of Colombo. The second is Ranjith who is a police inspector in charge of the Panadura Police Station. Ranjith has two young sons. The youngest of the siblings is Mahinda who is an area manager for the Nestle Company. He too has two young sons.

I have pleasant childhood memories of my Loku Thaththa, Loku Amma and cousins Tissa, Hemalatha and Nagasena, with only sporadic and brief contacts thereafter. I had close and somewhat extensive contacts, both growing up and as an adult, with the three other cousins, though they were several years my senior.

* * *

My cousin Dayananda was fun to be with, in my childhood visits to their home at Kaluwadumulla. During my visits to their Kollupitya house, however, I was warned not to exert him too much by physical contact as he was suffering from pleurisy (an infection of the lung). I was intrigued that he had what was called courses, a western diet that was different to the local rice and curry consumed by the rest of the family.

Later, my father used to visit him in the Government Rubber Control Department in Colombo where he worked, in order to ensure that my father received the government subsidy that was available for replanting of rubber saplings in unproductive rubber lands. He in turn used to visit my father from time to time and stay with us, over the weekend, so my contacts with him grew. He was a very caring person always ready to help anyone in need of his assistance, and was concerned with my wellbeing as well.

He married Lily Witharna of Manning Place, Wellawatte. She was an erudite scholar in oriental languages and Buddhist philosophy and was awarded a PhD degree for a dissertation interpreting a Buddhist text written in the Pali language dating several centuries back. Her thesis was published by the Pali Text Society, London in three volumes. Later, as a visiting scholar at the Center for the Study of World Religions at Harvard University, she published a seminal work on the Buddhist Ceremony for peace and prosperity known as Paritta (pirith), the stanzas of which were written entirely in Pali many centuries ago. It was a joint production with her husband who illustrated the publication.

Since she married my cousin she was known as Dr. Lily de Silva. She had a distinguished teaching career at the university in Sri Lanka, retiring as professor of Buddhist Studies. I began a close association with her in the early sixties when I was at her university quarters while studying for my law exams at the University of Ceylon, Peradeniya. She attended to all my needs including thoughtful gestures like providing a nightly flask of coffee to help me through the late night and early morning study sessions. There I also had occasion to meet her younger sister Chandra and built up a close relationship with her and some of her family at Manning Place; relationships that continue today. Ever since my stay at her residence at the University, my cousin and his wife Lily were always in contact with me.

I later had the occasion to be of assistance to them on their sojourns to the United States, including the time when she fell ill in Boston. During her sabbatical leave on three different occasions spent at Harvard University and Colby College in Maine in the United States, she and my cousin were frequent visitors to my home in New York. We had long and friendly discussions on these visits and I learned a lot from them, often about philosophy.

It was from her that I learned of the rationality behind the rituals in Buddhism, which indeed, the Buddha discouraged as a source of salvation from the sorrows of Samsara (cycle of birth and death). She explained to me the rationality behind the Pirith ceremony that had fascinated me as a child, at Seeya's house, which she later described in her book: *Paritta: The Buddhist Ceremony for Peace and Prosperity in Sri Lanka;* (published in 1981 by the National Museums of Sri Lanka, Colombo).

In theistic religions, man resorts to prayer and ritual when faced with life's crises, when human plans are thwarted by circumstances beyond rational control. Buddhism recognizes no omniscient all-mighty God who listens to man's prayers and whose good-will can be evoked by prayer and ritual. But within the framework of Buddhism a substitute for prayer and ritual had to be evolved, if Buddhism was to respond to religious sentiments of the populace; a substitute which was not contradictory from the philosophical stand point of Buddhism. Paritta is the most important ritual which evolved in response to deep psychological demand. And indeed it satisfies all the psychological and social functions that prayer and ritual achieve in other religions. Paritta text is composed of extracts from the Buddha's teachings in the Pali cannon. Therefore, unlike magical formulae, Paritta have profound meaning embodying ethical values and philosophical ideas without invocation of gods for help and favor. Though at present average layman has no knowledge of Pali, most Buddhist have a vague idea of the content and admonitions of the parritta suttas (stanzas), it exerts a mal influence upon the people and tries to uphold ethical behavior according to the norms and social philosophy of Buddhism.

* * *

My cousin Dayananda and his wife Lily had two sons and two daughters. The eldest son Deepthi (Deepa) came to the United States in the late seventies while his parents were on sabbatical leave to attend college in Boston on a student visa. He decided to remain in the United States hoping to obtain a working visa and eventually become a US resident. But, at the time immigration rules did not allow him to extend the temporary work permit issued for trainees. After many costly applications submitted through a lawyer to the immigration service, he was denied residency status. He did however continue to be employed, and therefore, dogged along in the hope that some relief would be available in the future.

Deepa was constantly in contact with me for advice and I did my best to console and encourage him in his pursuits. As the second term of President Ronald Reagan began, there were indications that immigration reform might be in the offing and I advised him accordingly. Eventually, after several years of ebbing hope, in 1986 the Congress passed and the President Regan signed the new Immigration Reform and Control Act tightening immigration control, but also granting amnesty to approximately 3 million immigrants whereby they received permanat resident staus, provided they had entered the United Status prior to a predetermined date and had been in the country for at least five years. Deepa fell within this category and having applied for residency was promptly granted legal status. Five years later he was granted U.S citizenship. He continued to work in the Boston area as regional manager for the McDonalds Corporation, and purchased a comfortable home where he continues to live. His courage and tenacity are to be admired and is a reflection of many of the 3 million others granted status with him, as well as those who obtained the same privileges after several failures, and went on to make a happy and comfortable life in the United States.

Quite a different path was followed by his sister Sumudu. She showed promise from her younger days and excelled in her studies obtaining a law degree from the University of Colombo, in Sri Lanka and became an attorney. She won a scholarship and went to Cambridge University in the U.K., and obtained a Masters degree in international law and a Ph.D. in environmental law. She was on the teaching faculty of the University of Colombo as an associate professor of law.

In 2000 Sumudu was awarded a Senior Fulbright scholarship and carried out research on environmental rights and human rights at the New York University and George Washington University law schools as a visiting scholar. She has been a consultant to the United Nations and other international organizations, and is the author of several scholarly publications.

She is now the Associate Director of the Institute of Global Legal Studies and lecturer in international environmental law, at the University of Wisconsin, Law School. She lives in Madison, Wisconsin, with her husband Dr. Dhammika Atapattu and their two children Praveena and Prasanga. Dhammika, who was a research scholar at the National Institute of Health in Washington DC., is now an associate professor at California North State University Medical School. The family visited me not long ago, in Los Angeles, and I have been in close touch with her over the years, particularly since her move to the United States.

I have had less contact with her younger two siblings. Brother Udan is in the Foreign Service of the U.K. and is married to Mihiri. Their daughter Sachini is named after the great Indian cricket player Sachin Tandulkar. The youngest is sister Nela who is in Melbourne, Australia, married to Shantha Subasinghe. She works at the University of Melbourne in the Departmant of Food Technology. They have three children Hiranya the eldest is an accountant. The other two are daughters, Amila and Aruni.

* * *

Other than Cousin Dayananda, I have also been in close contact with his elder brother Hemasiri throughout the past years. He was always ready to make a comment that would amuse me as a child visiting his family home in Kaluwadumulla. He entered the University of Ceylon as a science student and along with his brother Hemachandra. They were the first to enter the university from my family. Cousin Hemasiri was also the first to graduate from the family and be employed as a lecturer in the faculty of science at the university in 1953. He made personal scarifies at the time, by getting a much needed, larger house for the family, and looking after the family as his father was no longer alive, and no one else in the family was employed. I was a visitor to the house on a few occasions and enjoyed helping my cousin Hemasiri to wash his new Ford Prefect car that he had purchased on a loan, and took great care to keep immaculately clean. It was the first car owned by a member of my generation in the family. In due course, others in the family were employed, and my cousin Hemasiri went to the U.K. on a scholarship where he obtained a PhD degree from the Department of Zoology, University College of Swansea of Wales.

Later, he was employed at the Department of National Museum in Colombo. I visited him several times in his career when he was one of the two assistant directors. His colleague happened to be Dr. Ranjith Senarathna who had earlier taught at my school and had been the coach of my under 14 cricket team. This made my visits to the museum particularly interesting. My early exposure to the Museum in Colombo due to these visits somehow made enough of an impression, that I soon became a museum junkie, visiting all sorts of museums around the world. Later still, to my great delight and pride, my cousin was appointed as the Director of the National Museum, only the second Sri Lankan to hold this prestigious and responsible position.

The Colombo National Museum has celebrated its 130th anniversary. What began as a collection of antiques in a dilapidated old building that housed the Royal Asiatic Society's (Sri Lanka branch) library has today become one of South Asia's best museums. The credit for establishing the museum goes to Sir William Henry Gregory, who was the island's British Governor from 1872 to 1877. Looking for more space to keep their books, the RAS library authorities were trying to get rid of the old animal bones and other antiques in the building, when Sir William got wind of it. The Governor, a scholar of repute, realized the urgent need for establishing a museum and made the proposal to the Constitutional Assembly in 1872. Despite financial constraints, Sir William eventually succeeded in establishing the museum in a massive two storied building in Colombo 7, on January 1, 1877.

A well-known story related to me by my cousin on one of my visits to see him was about the museum's most prized possession, the throne of the last King of Ceylon Sri Wickrama Rajasinghe. According to my cousin, it was linked to an amusing incident involving a person of unsound mind. The man was among the visitors to the museum, several decades ago. Noticing that anybody could enter the glass enclosure where the throne is kept, he suddenly went and sat on the throne, claiming that he was its rightful heir. He refused to budge from it until the police forcibly removed him and packed him off to the Angoda mental asylum.

The early administrators of the Museum were all Europeans and the first Sri Lankan to hold the post was Dr. P.E.P. Deraniyagala, an anthropologist of great repute. In October 1965 (the year I began my employment with the United Nations), my cousin, Dr. P.H.D.H. De Silva became the director heralding in a new era in museum history. As an expert chronicler of artifacts, he arranged to exhibit all items, according to classification, thereby providing greater opportunities to access the information in the museum. He organized seminars and issued publications to educate school children and the general public. The museum publication 'Singithi' was especially meant for children.

Dr. De Silva also took steps to install an alarm system to provide security for the Kandyan throne. The establishment of the Anuradhapura Rural Museum and Zoology Branch and the

Natural History Section of the Museum are among his many other achievements.

When he came to New York to catalogue the holdings of Sri Lankan antiquities at the Natural History Museum, I picked him up along with his wife from the John F. Kennedy Airport, and drove them to my apartment in Manhattan in New York. After a few days, they moved to a spacious apartment next to the Natural History Museum on Central Park West. There I visited them frequently and became familiar with his work and the delicious cooking of his wife Chandra.

He ensured that every nook and corner of the museum was examined including hundreds of items stored away in the Museum basement. He visited 140 institutions in 27 countries to gather information on antiques and archaeological treasures taken from Sri Lanka.

On the basis of his arduous work, in 1974 he published an invaluable catalogue of all such items belonging to Sri Lanka abroad entitled: *A Catalogue of Antiquities from Sri Lanka Abroad.* These included an intricately carved cannon on wheels on display at the Amsterdam Museum.

This artillery piece belonged to Leuke Dissawe (local governor in the Kandyan Kingdom and a confidante of the King. Dissawe was left behind to meet the British when they came to negotiate a treaty in 1800, when the king fled Kandy temporarily). A miniature model of this gun is on display at the National Museum, Colombo.

In 1977, on the 100th anniversary of the Museum, He also published a catalogue of holdings at the Museum (he listed that it had 93,647 antiques and archaeological treasures and 2603 anthropological models and that the number of coins had increased from 499 (in 1877) to 83,405 while the number of books and other publications had risen to over 500,000). When he finally retired he left an indelible mark of his tenure, which is considered a high water mark of the history of the National Museum.

He married Chandra Silva from Matale. She was a cousin of my step mother and therefore my contacts increased with my cousin's family. She was a tower of strength to her husband and looked after his every need, providing him the freedom to spend long hours at work and on extensive research he carried out in a variety of fields from reptiles to fauna and the ecology of bees in Sri Lanka. He published extensively on these subjects and became a legendary herpetologist who was recognized internationally. On his retirement from the Sri Lanka Museum Dr. De Silva spent time working in Saudi Arabia and Libya enriching the museums in those countries. They have three sons. The eldest, Ranil is a cost accountant in a company in Melbourne, Australia. Ranil has a son who is an engineer. My cousin's middle son Prasantha (Raj) is a graduate of the Hotel's School in Colombo and has been a senior staff member at several four and five star hotels in Sri Lanka and the Middle East. Shanthi and I have stayed in a couple of hotels where he was working and naturally he made our stays very special. Currently he is the food and beverage manager at the five star Galle Face Hotel in Colombo. One of the most historic tourist establishments in Sri Lanka, the Galle Face Hotel is an impressive colonial building situated by the beach in Colombo. Following its inception in 1864, it soon became and continues to be one of the most exquisite hotels east of the Suez along with Raffles of Singapore. It has continued to host Royalty, world leaders and celebrities from colonial Ceylon to modern Sri Lanka. Raj has a son Suranga who is following his father's footsteps and is a trainee executive at Cinnamon Lake, another five star hotel in Colombo.

The youngest of the three brothers is Rukmal who is the chef at Capri Club in Colombo which is one of Sri Lanka's leading social clubs. The 57 year-old Club, located in Kollupitiya in the heart of Colombo has a wide cross section of members ranging from honorable gentlemen, professionals, businessmen, planters and the wealthy. The Officers of the club have been some of the most prominent members of the highest social circle of Colombo. I was pleased to be of assistance when Rukmal came to the United States for graduate training. I advised him to apply to the leading culinary Institute in New York. When he arrived he stayed with us for a few days in New York City, before I drove him to his College. He is married without children as yet.

Among the children of my mother's sister, the closest contact I have had over the years was with the eldest of the siblings Hemachandra (Loku Aiya-elder brother). Apart from being with him during my visits to their house and Seeya's house in our hometown Ambalangoda, I came in close contact with him while he was living at my father's rented house in Kandewatte Galle. He was attending Mahinda College and was preparing for the university medical entrance examination. He played cricket at Mahinda College with my father's brother who was also on the team. I was very fond of him as he was of me. I used to sleep next to him as a child. He would rise very early in the morning before it was daylight, and with my father's encouragement, though I was in grade one, wake me up as well. He saw to it that I learned my first words and numbers at this ungodly hour. Whenever I started to fall asleep he pulled me up by my ears!

My cousin Hemachandra later moved to Pembroke College, Colombo and entered the Medical Faculty of the University of Ceylon in 1947, which was when the family moved to Kollupitiya. He used to commute several miles back and forth to the medical school by bicycle. When he graduated in 1954, as a medical doctor, taking advantage of the financing facility provided by the government for medical doctors, he purchased a *Volkswagen* car, a model that had just come to Sri Lanka.

Following his training at the Colombo hospital, Dr. P.H.D.H. De Silva was posted to his first assignment at the Katukurunda Hospital as the anesthetist in charge (both he and his brother Hemasiri went by the same name Dr. P.H.D.H. De Silva - one a medical doctor, the other a PhD in zoology). It was a new hospital and he made certain that the operating theater was fully equipped in the best possible manner by getting all the necessary equipment from Colombo.

By this time, my father had remarried and was working in Kalutara, the main town that the hospital was serving. It was natural that my cousin would come to my home for lunch. He usually came with two other doctors who were also newly graduated - Dr. Ray Austin and Dr. Theva Buell. As a teenager I was fascinated by all three and looked up to them as my role models.

Little less than a decade later, I met Dr. Buell in Montreal, Canada when we were both at McGill University. He was a fellow at the medical research center named after Dr. Wilder Penfield, a world famous neurosurgeon who pioneered the techniques to unlock the mysteries of the human brain. Still later, Dr. Buell became a household name in Sri Lanka, as one of the leading cardiologists in the country. It is sad to note that he passed away when he was yet in his prime.

My cousin Hemachandra next moved to the Police Training School hospital in Katukurunda as the medical officer. From there he was transferred to Kotagala and Lindulla hospitals in the hill country of Sri Lanka, as District Medical Officer.

When I was in my last year at high school in Galle I visited him in Lindula during the school holidays. This was my first train ride upcountry and vividly etched in my memory is how I feasted on the beauty of the landscape as the train climbed its way up the mountains at a slow pace. The hill country is exceptionally beautiful, with crystal clear waterfalls and tea plantations dotted throughout. The highlands of Sri Lanka offer a salubrious cool climate throughout the year. Everything is green and lush in this god given countryside. The British who colonized the country in the nineteenth century knew its value and planted coffee and later tea, and today one can see miles and miles of 'green carpets' of tea bushes where tea pluckers are seen busily picking the 'bud and two leaves' that go to form the most popular brew in the world, 'Ceylon Tea'. My cousin picked me up at the station and we went to his British type bungalow which was provided to him by the government. As usual his wife was a great hostess, and during the weeks I spent there, I enjoyed fresh garden grown vegetables that she cooked. It was a memorable holiday.

Shortly thereafter, he was transferred to the General Hospital (now the National Hospital) in Colombo as a medical officer in the gynecology ward of Dr. A. Sinnathamby who at the time was the professor of gynecology and obstetrics in the medical college. Cousin Hemachandra lived in Horton Place in the comfortable annex at "Woodlands," an ancestral house of the second Prime Minister of Sri Lanka Mr. Dudley Senanayake. The main house was a massive building where the former Prime Minister had conducted many a political discussion including important negotiations with the Tamil leaders of the time. These were the years when I was at the Law College in Colombo and living at the Law Hostel at Barnes Place, a stone's throw from my cousin's residence. I used to visit him there particularly when I needed to borrow his car. He still had his *Volkswagen* and never hesitated to lend it generously to me whenever I requested it.

Later, he was awarded a scholarship and went to the UK. He qualified as a Member of the Royal College of Gynecology and Obstetrics (MRCOG) in 1966. While he was there I visited him twice in Hitchin, a small sleepy town in Hertfordshire, U.K. There, he was residing in very spacious quarters with his family. Also resident was his friend Dr. Gunasinghe who had preceded him to the UK and was working at Hitchin Hospital. He was twice unsuccessful at the MRCOG examination and therefore invited my cousin to reside with him for purposes of joint study. My cousin accepted the invitation though it was of some inconvenience to travel to London for lectures. Regretfully, while my cousin succeeded in the exam his friend did not, for the fourth time.

My cousin returned to Sri Lanka and worked as a consultant Gynecologist in the service of the government at the Galle Hospital. His children were admitted to local schools. Later he was assigned as Consultant to the Kegalle Base Hospital. He built a modern house in Nawala, Colombo for the family, so that the children could attend schools in Colombo. He visited the family on his off days. Living without the family gave him the opportunity for research and he collected a large body of material relating to uterine abnormalities with clinical complications. He was invited by the Sri Lanka Medical Association to make the prestigious 'Murugesu Sinnatamby Special Oration' presenting the results of his unique research. It was the first time a non academic had been invited to make the oration.

* * *

While he was still at Kegalle JVP activities began. Founded in 1965 by Rohana Wijeweera, with the aim of providing a leading force for a socialist revolution in Sri Lanka, this group drew on students and unemployed youth from rural areas, most of them in the sixteen-to-twenty-five age group. Many of these new recruits were members of lower castes, Karava and Durava from the south. They felt that their economic interests had been neglected by the nation's politicians, including those on the left, who were mostly from the majority Govigama caste, considered by those belonging to it, as the highest in the hierarchy of the caste system. Between 1967 and 1970, the group expanded rapidly, gaining control of the student socialist movement at a number of major universities and winning recruits and sympathizers within the armed forces.

The JVP drew worldwide attention when it launched an insurrection against the government of Mrs. Srimavo Bandaranaike in April 1971. The uprising led by the Sinhalese, People's Liberation Front, or Janatha Vimukthi Peramuna, was an unsuccessful Marxist youth rebellion that claimed at least 3000 young lives. Although the insurgents were young, poorly armed, and inadequately trained, they succeeded in seizing and holding major areas in Southern and Central provinces of Sri Lanka before they were defeated by the security forces. Subsequent insurgency took place during the UNP governments of President Jayewardene and President Premadasa (1987-1989), which similarly ended in absolute failure, leaving more victims in its wake.

The second insurrection was aimed at a protracted terrorist war to wrest the control of the government, unlike the first insurrection that was poorly planned attempt to grab power. Unarmed civilians suspected as non supporters of the JVP, were hacked to death or shot by death squads that roamed the towns and villages. Schools, government offices, Shops and other public places were subject to closure at short notice, at their will. The entire country was engrossed in fear. If the situation continued the country would have been thrown into such chaos; it would have taken decades to recover. But fortunately, with the political leadership of President Premadasa, the armed forces quelled the terrorist uprising particularly energized by a foolish move on the part of the JVP. It called on all security forces personnel to resign immediately or face the threat of their families being killed. It was a move that began the end of the movement. Much later, it surfaced as a Democratic Party advocating a socialist agenda. But it never garnered much support from the people to be an effective force, and now remains merely as a vociferous group against the policies of ruling parties. [1]

Their attempt to seize power in 1971 created a major crisis for the government and forced a fundamental reassessment of the nation's security needs as well as people's outlook towards the future of their own security. The local JVP activists visited the government bungalow of the hospital where my cousin was living, in Kegalle, which was a hotbed of the movement. My cousin was sharing the bungalow with Ana Seneviratna, the superintendent of police of the area. (He later went on to become one of the most admired police officers of Sri Lanka and retired as the Inspector-General of the Police Force). While he was an obvious target for the JVP, so was my cousin as the JVP had prohibited the hospital staff to work as they did with all public servants. It was obvious that my cousin was one of the targets. The rebels visited the residence at the time he would have returned for his mid day meal. They waited inside the house for him to shoot him as was the norm when the JVP targeted people. He was however held-up at the hospital delivering a baby (assisted with forceps) with no electricity, with the aid of his torch light, as the JVP had blown the electricity transformer of the Hospital. The baby girl who saved him from grave disaster is today, a medical doctor doing a fellowship in Los Angeles, USA. The visitors left behind two gunshot pellets and took with them the stereo and other goods they had found in the house, indicating that the motivations of the revolutionaries were not exclusively political. The experience however was not pleasant, as anyone who was one way or another victimized or terrorized by the JVP would know.

Shortly after this event, my cousin went abroad to work in Zambia. Being an expatriate, terms of employment were very much better for him there than in Sri Lanka, although this was not the sole motivation that made him leave his motherland. After his three year contract in Zambia, he moved to Malta on similar terms. While he was in Malta I visited him. It so happened, his son and wife who had just married in Sri Lanka came to Malta at the same time I was there, as part of their honeymoon. My cousin had been living with his wife and daughter in Malta while the son had stayed behind in Sri Lanka to complete his university education. For me, it was a very pleasant experience to tour the Island in their company. Malta is an archipelago of islands with two islands that are prominent above the others. The capital Valletta is in the main Island where my cousin and family lived. Though small in size (about the size of Colombo) with a population less than that of Colombo (about 3 to 4 hundred thousand at the time), Malta has a very rich history going back to Anceint Greece. Valletta itself is a peninsula with two harbors on either side. The Grand Harbor on one side is a panoramic place dotted with many cruise ships and private boats. With many palaces, churches and gardens it is considered an open air museum. The Parliament and the Court House of Greco-Roman architecture with tall columns and triangular roofs I saw in Malta were very impressive. The basilicas and churches with high domes added to the beauty of the panorama of the city. Walking near the harbor on narrow, mostly cobbled streets was very interesting.

One day we drove down for a day trip to the center of the Island towards Medina, where the Mosta Dome with its famous frescoes and the beautiful Rotunda are located. The Mosta Dome is a Roman Catholic Church. It is the third largest unsupported dome in the world. It is built in the 19th century on the site of a previous church. Its dome is among the largest in the world. During the World War II, on April 9, 1942, during an air-raid, a 200 kg Luftwaffe bomb pierced the dome and fell among a congregation of more than 300 people awaiting early evening mass. It did not explode. It is now on display inside the rotunda with a plaque reading in Maltese: The Bomb Miracle, April 9, 1942. One version of this event states that, upon opening the bomb, it was found to be filled with sand instead of explosive and contained a note saying "greetings from Plzeň" from the workers at Škoda Works in the German-occupied Czechoslovakia (who had allegedly sabotaged its production).

The drive through the narrow roads through immaculately kept small towns and villages was notable for the complete absence of pedestrians or indeed any life at all. It was altogether a very pleasant visit.

Once his assignment was over, Cousin Hemachandra moved to Tripoli, Libya on contract. I heard several stories of his experiences there particularly at the hospital. Though I had visited Tripoli, it was not possible for me to visit him during his stay there as this was an extremely busy period in my work. He and his brother were in Tripoli during the bombing of Libya by the United States, ordered by President Reagan following the terrorist bombing of the Pan Am aircraft over Lockerby. Fortunately they were not affected by the incident as the damage was done outside of Tripoli in sparsely populated areas of Libya. My cousin Hemachandra as a physician, though, was on twenty-four hour duty at the hospital on alert to treat any casualties.

Once he concluded his work there he returned to Sri Lanka. He built a house in Kotte and continued part time work with a clinic in the house and a practice at the Nawaloka Hospital (one of the biggest private medical facilities in Colombo). He travelled for extensive stays abroad to visit his children and grandchildren. On those ocassions he and his wife used to visit us, and on his last visit in 2006 they visited us in Los Angeles, California.

Every time I travel to Sri Lanka naturally I make it a point to visit him. When we meet we speak of cricket. Since his retirement a few years ago, he enjoys watching cricket on television, and of course, looks forward to the visits of his children and grandchildren who are all in the United States.

He married Dorothy, a nurse by profession while he was on his first assignment at the Katukurunda Hospital in 1955. They had two children. Son Padmalal (known as Lal) was born the next year, while they were still in Katukurunda. Daughter Amani was born six years later in 1961 while they were residing at Woodlands in Colombo. Over the years I have had close contact with both my nephew and niece due to the mutual fondness shared by their parents and me.

Lal even in his very young days struck me as a particularly brilliant person. He also turned out to be a very calm and collected young man, mature for his age. He had his early education in the U.K. and at Richmond College Galle, my old school. Later he attended Ananda College, Colombo. Dr. Padmalal De Silva graduated as a physician from the Medical Faculty of the University of Colombo in 1980 and carried out specialized training in anesthesiology at the General Hospital in Colombo in 1982. He proceeded to the U.K. and completed fellowships in anesthesiology at Ormskirk hospital in 1984. He moved to the United States in 1984 and completed a fellowship and was employed at the Beth Israel Medical Center affiliated with Harvard University in Boston, where he continues to work as an assistant professor of anesthesiology. He is also a consultant anesthesiologist with the Newton Medical Center in Boston.

Lal married his medical college classmate Nimmi Goonetilleke, who is a non- practicing physician with a great flare for gardening. Her garden was featured in a professional photography book *New Eyes* by Tilak Hettige. As noted earlier, I met them as a new couple in Malta. I have visited and stayed with them in Boston, whenever I was there for a lecture at the Massachusetts Institute of Technology (MIT) and for the Board meetings of the International Space University. They have visited me in Los Angeles. They continue to be attached to Sri Lanka and visit their motherland annually. They expect to live in Sri Lanka in their retirement and are just completing a residence in the town of Kandy, and will move there soon. There, he will indulge in his hobby of following the national sport-cricket. They have one daughter Sayumi. She has inherited the good genes of the family and after graduating from Brown University and University of Massachusetts Medical School, became a physician. Currently she, my grandniece, is completing her residency at University of California Los Angeles (UCLA), and although extreamly busy found time to see me when I visit her.

My cousin's daughter, my niece Amani was born in 1961. She had her education in Sri Lanka at Visakha Vidyalaya, Colombo. She spent her time growing up with her parents and so she had a varied and rich life going from country to country which has made her a cosmopolitan lady. I met her on occasions when I visited her parents. But my contacts became closer when she decided to have her university education in the United States. Around 1987 she arrived in New York with her parents. I picked them at the John F. Kennedy Airport and took them home. After a few days my wife and I drove them to Newark, New Jersey. She registered at the New Jersey Institute of Technology to pursue a degree in computer science. While she was there, living in the college dorm, she frequently came to visit us and often spent her holidays or weekends with us. Once she graduated, she obtained employment as a computer specialist with American Telephone and Telegraph Company (AT&T) in New Jersey.

Soon thereafter she decided to be married to Michael Luddy a classmate of hers at her university. Her parents came and stayed with us in preparation for the wedding. She depended on my wife and me to make the wedding arrangements, which we were delighted to undertake. After considering different options, she agreed to a wedding on a boat, anchored in the Hudson River in Manhattan. It is a special location for weddings with a wonderful view of the Manhattan skyscrapers and the two-level George Washington Bridge, with twelve traffic lanes connecting New York and New

Jersey. We took all the required paraphernalia and I built a 'Poruwa' (a platform where traditionally the couple alight to be married) for the wedding, constructed according to traditions drawn from the ancient Sri Lankan culture, and decorated with ample flowers. As the place was released to us only a few hours before noon the poruwa was completed by me just before the guests arrived. The main event in Sri Lankan weddings during the Poruwa ceremony is the signing of the marriage registration that legalizes the union. It is conducted at the end of the ceremony. At Amani's wedding these traditional customs were followed to the extent feasible, with the usual Sri Lankan sweetmeats. Yet, because the groom was of Jewish faith, the ceremony concluded in western tradition including music and dancing. It was a grand occasion with the friends of the couple in attendance.

Following the wedding the couple lived in a house that they purchased in New Jersey. They used to be visitors to our home frequently, particularly when there was any social occasion where friends and family gathered. Over the years the couple drifted apart with their own individual interests taking precedence. She continued to live in the house and continued to advance in her profession acquiring a Masters degree. When my wife and I had to move to Europe, we requested her to accommodate our son Amal, who remained behind to be employed in the New York area where he had grown up. Because she declined, even though unknown to us it may have been for good reasons; our contacts dwindled. It was a great disappointment to us. However, looking back today, it is quite possible that she had good reason under the pressures of the time to decline our request.

Many years later, she met and married a wonderful young man Niranjan Nugera also a information technology specialist. On that occasion she invited me to be the attesting witness to her marriage, and naturally I took that as a mutual opportunity to forget any misunderstanding we may have had. By that time she had moved near Princeton, New Jersey. Her parents had arrived for the occasion. My wife and I drove with friends to the marriage ceremony, which took place at the city hall, followed by a reception dinner with a close circle of friends and family at the spacious new home they had just purchased. I visited her later on occasions when I have been in the general vicinity. I also met her parents who were spending extended vacations, particularly after the birth of their only granddaughter Niraya.

* * *

The youngest in my mother's siblings was her second brother R.M. Piyadasa De Silva. In his young days he had played in the cricket team of Dharmasoka College, Ambalangoda. As a grownup he was a very quiet man, almost a recluse. Unless he was spoken to he would not speak. He would usually give a very brief answer to any question you put to him. These are the only memories I have of him, although he lived in Seeya's house where I spent my early years. Later on, he was ordained as a Buddhist monk and donned the saffron colored robe. During most of his life thereafter he spent his time in remote meditation retreats. I was told that he was quite an erudite Buddhist priest. I met him several times on my visits to Sri Lanka when he had been invited to religious ceremonies at my sister's home and the home of my cousins. On one such occasion I inquired about his wellbeing and learned that he had cataract surgery in his eyes and was in need of appropriate spectacles. I am very glad that I was able to be of some assistance to him by providing the spectacles. On one of my later visits I learned with sadness that he had passed away. I am however pleased that one of my own family became a member of the Buddhist Sangha; the order established by the Buddha to preserve and practice his teachings (Dharma) and provide spiritual support to the Buddhist community.

* * *

Growing up, there were uncountable number of times when I yearned for my mother; when I felt my whole life was a loveless void. Yet, as if to make up for her early demise, in their own inimitable ways, my uncles, aunts and cousins showered me with an infinite quantity of love and affection. I loved them back with the same fervor.

FOOTNOTE:

[1] The JVP and LTTE movements that originated about the same time in early 1970s stand out as the first terrorist organizations in the country. There had been several revolts of different forms in the country since the British began ruling the country. The struggles against British rule were different in the 19th century from those of the 20th century. A year after British Administration began one Sinngno Appu started a revolt against it in 1797. In 1815 the British annexed the Kandyan kingdom to its territory in the Maritime Provinces in the South. Preceding that, there were low level protest movements against the British from 1802 to 1815 in the Maritime Provinces, which were easily suppressed. Following the annexation a rebellion led by the Kandyan Chieftain Keppitipola was defeated by the reinforced British forces in 1817. A more widespread rebellion in 1848 led by Puran Appu and Dingi Rala in Kandy and Kurunagala Districts were ended with their death. These were armed insurrections doomed to failure against the superior British army. In the struggles for independence of the 20th century there were agitations mainly for constitutional reforms and self-government. They were led by the Ceylon Congress within the Legislative bodies. These were jointly led by the educated Sinhala and Tamil leaders who were mostly educated in England. There was also the Temperance Movement that affected the British rule. In May 1915 a religious clash occurred between the Buddhist and Muslims of Kandy. Soon it spread and became an ethnic riot between the Sinhalese and Moors. Serious clashes ensued in Colombo and its suburbs. But none of these rebellions and agitations manifested in the form of terrorism.

Chapter 3

Thaththa

A nine year old boy stands on the bank of the Dodanduwa Oya a few hours after the sun begins its journey westward. He stretches his arms in front of him, takes a deep breath and makes a clean dive into the crystal clear water. As graceful as a goldfish, he swims to the white hut in the distance, called the Poya Seemawa, touches its walls and swims back home. He is next seen on a catamaran mastering it across the same waters as the sun reaches its zenith in the sky. The boy feels the soft breeze caressing his cheeks, hears the soft splash as a kingfisher catches its midday meal, and finds an immense sense of peace entwined with a sense of adventure engulfing his heart. I know how he felt. Nearly seventy years later he still lives somewhere deep within me reminding me of those early years I spent in my Thaththa, Jasentuliyana Siripala De Silva's loving, protective shelter.

I have been told the words Jasentu Liyana mean 'Tombu Keeper'. I also know that in Spanish Jasentu (pronounced as Hasentu) is used in some contexts to refer to Jesus, and have often wondered whether it meant 'of Jesus'. The only other reference I have come across to this name is in a chapter of a book entitled "Lanka's Leading Poetess" where Gajaman Nona is referred to as the "daughter of the famous Headmaster and Tombu Keeper, Contagamage Jasentu Grero who taught Sinhala and Dutch languages." In recent times Jasentu Liyana written as one or two words referred to one single family in Ambalangoda. That family's offspring gradually spread all over the country and across the world.

At the beginning of the 19th Century the area to the north of Ambalangoda was known for Arrack renting. Arrack, a popular liquor in Sri Lanka, produced from coconut. From the days of the Dutch, arrack renting was controlled by the government through a licensing system and the fees provided an important source of income to the government. It also became an important source of income accumulation to the distillers, wholesalers and retailers involved in the arrack trade. The founders of some of the most prominent merchant families of later years such as, Rodigos, Soysas, Fernandos, and Silvas, of Moratuwa and Panadura in the western province were distillers in the years around 1830. These families much later had strong links to Ambalangoda through marriages.

In the southern province the arrack rents brought in only small sums, but there were wholesalers and retailers, who were mostly minor government officials, involved in the trade on a limited scale. In her brilliant book 'Nobodies to Somebodies', Kumari Jayawardane recounts the entire development of the trade, indicating that my greatgranduncle, Jasentu Liyana Samuel Silva of Ambalangoda was a renter in 1834. We derive the family name from him.

The link between the name Jasentuliyana and its association with Ambalangoda, has also been recounted by the Venerable Pollwatte Maha Paditha Buddhadatta. In the same article, he refers to my maternal family name written in the 'Lankadeepa' of 25 November 1958. According to him, an inscription on an ola leaf notes that, in 1400 A.D, king Veerabahu of Gampola presented as 'nindagam' the area including Ambalangoda to one of his brave Generals named Rajapakse Nambukara, who defeated a powerful enemy force. The place he lived in Ambalangoda has been identified through a stone inscription in the area by the sea known as Madampe. The same inscription notes that a group of carpenters came to Ambalangoda to construct the General's abode. Among them was one named Jasentu Andrawass. The learned priest believes the residents of Ambalangoda today are the decedents of the General and his retinue including carpenters. He has further recounted that the ola leaf inscription speaks of a Jasentuliyana Patabandi. Patabandi is apparently the name given to the heads of the fishing industry or those of the 'Karawa' caste.

*   *   *

Though I remember very little of my mother, of my father I have warm and vivid memories dating back to the days following my mother's demise. I remember snatches of conversation between my mother's brother, Uncle Martin, his wife, my Aunt Kusuma and my father, imploring Father to let them adopt me. There were others, relatives and friends who suggested he should remarry in the belief this would help him bring us up. My father stubbornly refused to listen to them, fearing we might be subjected to step-motherly treatment, and so decided to raise us himself from the day my mother passed away when I was three and my sister, an infant. He believed, with an Ayah (Nanny) at hand, he could take good care of us.

The first of them was employed right after my mother passed away because it was believed at the time that breast feeding was a must for a new born baby. In any event, options were limited. Milk powder and other alternative baby foods available now were very rare, particularly in towns outside of Colombo. It was therefore not an unusual practice to find a young mother to be the surrogate.

While we lived at the house in Kandewatte, Galle my father's mother and younger sister stayed with us helping father to take care of us, while an Ayah looked after the daily household chores. As we moved from place to place, father's youngest sister, Aunt Dotty, stayed with us until my sister completed kindergarten, and was admitted to boarding school. Thereafter, with domestic help my father was able to look after his family on his own. Much later, when we were both teenagers and in boarding schools, my father remarried.

*   *   *

As a young man my father was very handsome. Fair in complexion for a southerner, he was of medium height and was known as the

Prince for his looks and for the immaculate way he dressed. Born in 1909 he was educated at Dharmasoka College, Ambalangoda where he played in the cricket team. He married my mother when he was in his late twenties.

They met and fell in love at the beach. My mother, who was dark in complexion and very attractive, was in the habit of going for long walks on the beach, enjoying the sea breeze and the dramatic performance of the sun as it bid farewell to the sea. Undoubtedly, my father watching the blue sky turn into many hues of red would have found the brilliant gleam in my mother's eyes, and the sheen of her dark stresses combed into a tight knot at the nape of her neck, far more alluring than the evening sky. He would have fallen in love not only with her gentle loving temperament but also her radiant good looks. She was always ready to help others and never thought twice before she parted with anything she could afford to give away. There were many in the neighborhood who needed help and she was ever willing to assist them in anyway she could.

I am told the love affair which started to bloom on the beach faced opposition from my mother's side. In those days, towns such as Ambalangoda offered very little by way of entertainment particularly for the young. As with other young people it had been my mother's habit to go for long walks on the beach, often with family members, and sometimes with friends. It was also pleasant to meet friends and acquaintances for a chat as one walked along the beach, for almost everyone in town was somehow familiar with each other. There were also pleasant activities to observe. Kite flying was certainly one.

I learned from my Cousin Hemachandra, who often used to accompany my mother and grandfather on the visits to the beach, there apparently came a time when my grandmother started to lose her temper whenever my mother returned from a walk on the beach. She would scold my mother, throwing a tantrum, and finally retiring to her room till she calmed down. This ritual, which had baffled Cousin Hemachandra, was explained when a formal marriage proposal was received by my mother's parents from my father's parents sent through a Kapumahattaya (a marriage broker) as was the custom at the time. My mother's parents were not happy with this proposal, perhaps because they did not see it as right that the two young people should have fallen in love without seeking the consent of their elders and perhaps because they were a much better off family than my father's. But, as if to prove true love triumphs all obstacles, "the Prince" took the hand of his Princess in the presence of the two families in 1936.

At about the same time he was married, my father joined the government service and was assigned to the Ceylon Government Railway (CGR). He told me that at the government service entry exam one of his assignments was to write an essay on the topic of "The Coconut Tree" (unbelievably simple topic in today's terms)! His first post was in Colombo. My mother continued to live with her parents and my father came home on his off days. This was so until I was born after which they moved to a separate house in Maha Ambalangoda. When my mother died, my father moved the family to a rented house in Kandewatte, Galle. He continued to work in Colombo and come home on his off days.

Like most officers and clerical persons of the time, my father used to wear what was called a full suit consisting of trousers, coat, shirt, and tie and sported a handkerchief on his breast pocket. On most occasions he wore a waistcoat as well. He also wore a Prince of Wales hat with a round brim that resembles what policemen wear in some countries, including Ceylon till recently. While the hat was meant to provide protection from the hot sun, it is impossible not to wonder how my father and his contemporaries managed to wear a full suit and keep themselves cool in a country that is just north of the equator.

When he was at work, my father dressed in immaculate white attire with black or brown shoes. At other times, he wore beige or checkered suits with two tone shoes which had brown and white tips or the other way round. Like most people those days, for quite some time, he wore a round pocket watch with a gold chain that went to the left lapel of the coat while the watch remained in the inside coat pocket. In the few photographs I have of my father he was dressed in this attire, except for one, where he is wearing a sarong and standing in front of the house he built in Ambalangoda, when he was quite advanced in age.

He was a smoker for a very long time (most people were at the time) and carried a tin of Gold Leaf or Navycut cigarettes in his hand. When I was in my teens he gave up smoking and the occasional drink he imbibed. I am told by others that he did so to set an example to me. He was quite unaware that by then those habits, though secretly indulged in, had already caught up with me as well as many of my friends. Whether or not because of his example, smoking mercifully never took hold of me.

* * *

From Kandewatte we moved to Kalegana, Galle. The house was owned by friends of my father who belonged to an extremely well to do family. Modest in size with three small bedrooms, living and kitchen area it had an open verandah and a very large garden as it was part of a large land owned by the friends next door. They had even a larger garden with a luxurious house as well as a guest house. Both lands were part of a rubber estate. The houses were situated at the bottom of a hill abutting the main road that connected Galle and Gintota via the interior of the land passing Kalegana. The hill itself was the rubber land. The two houses were separated by an unusually large pool built for bathing and washing.

I enjoyed the outdoors very much, often going up the hill to observe the workers at the rubber factory. [1] Sunil a young lad who was helping around the house was my constant companion on these explorations. He taught me a trick or two. The one I remember well is how he taught me to walk on two stilts. He cut two rubber branches and made make shift stilts on which I would tie my legs. He then, taught me how to walk on those stilts. In the beginning they were about two feet tall but gradually Sunil raised them up to double the height. First I had to crawl along holding on to the wall of the house. Then I learned to walk holding on to two sticks as if they were crutches. Gradually I became quite proficient and throughout the time we lived in that house walking on those stilts was my main occupation. There was a lovi (cherry) tree in the garden and for a while we had fun climbing it. But once the stilts were mastered, fruits were easily accessible during the season without having to climb the tree.

It was while we were living in this house that the respect and awe I had for my father increased twofold. This was the day my Aunty Dotty, who lived with us and attended Rippon College, a girl's school on nearby Richmond Hill, suddenly went missing. My father looked for her everywhere he could think of and eventually thought she may have accidently drowned in the pond like structure that was our bathing spot. He dived to the bottom of the pond many times looking for her. His efforts were in vain, and he grieved for her till it was discovered that she, having got miffed by some admonition or the other made by my father, had decided to go to a distant relative's place in Gintota and wanted to be incognito.

Before, during the time and after we were at Kalegana, my father, used to take me to the movies on his off days. He loved to see movies whenever he had the free time. I loved those trips with him because I got to sit on his lap not only at the movie, so he did not have to buy a ticket for me, but also in the Rickshaw that transported us to the movie and back. The Rickshaw was the main mode of transportation for those who did not own a car. Rickshaws were aplenty and available at all public places like the taxis and three wheelers of today. The Rickshaw was drawn by human power and the carriage was large enough to accommodate one person. This meant a child like me would be accommodated on the lap of the person seated. It had a hood that could be raised when the sun was strong or as protection against the rain. We used to take a Rickshaw when we visited the doctor or on other important visits which were not within ready walking distance. Rickshaw pullers, though not necessarily strong, had the knack of pulling this contraption for considerable distances, and in some instances even across the entire town.

When Albert Einstein visited Ceylon for a day in 1928 en route to Japan, he and his wife Elsa had ridden rickshaws to tour Colombo. Not surprisingly they had profound reflections to record on this unique form of transportation. It is reported that Einstein's diary dated 28 October 1922 read "We rode on a small one man carriages drawn at trot by men of Herculean strength, yet of delicate build. I was bitterly opposed to be a party to the abominable treatment accorded to fellow human beings, but the circumstances did not permit me avoiding it." However, Einstein's wife, being pragmatic is said to have remarked "for these men to earn a living, they need our patronage".

At the time motorized vehicles were not available as transport except for the wealthy. Rickshaws were accepted as a necessity and as a means of earning a living for part of the population. But later the rickshaws succumbed to motorized forms of public transportation. It could also be in part that because they were considered as inhumane they became obsolete.

*   *   *

While we were at Kalegana I used to attend the same vernacular school near St. Aloysius College that I used to attend while at Kandewatte. But now it was quite a distance that I had to travel. My father's friends next door had two bullock carts. They were two-wheeled vehicles pulled by cattle used as a means of transportation since ancient times in Sri Lanka and in many parts of the world. One was pulled by a single oxen and the other by two. Jamis, the carter (driver) sat on the front of the cart, while passengers sat in the back. I used to ride on the bullock carts back and forth with a couple of ladies from next door, friends of my father, who at the time attended the Galle Convent which was adjacent to St. Aloysius Boys College.

Jamis' employers had a magnificent house filled with beautiful furniture and other trappings, with a staff of three or four to cook, clean and help around the house and the carter Jamis, who was my special friend. There were five in this family of Fernandos: Mother, three daughters Muriel, Hilda, Nora, and two brothers Victor and Stanley. I used to call them Akkas (elder sisters) and Aiyas (elder brothers). They were in my father's generation though somewhat younger than he, and I was a small child. I recieved their full adulation on which I feasted. Being rich, they led luxurious lives. Having grown up in the lap of luxury this was nothing special to them and they were all very modest in demeanor though stylishly dressed.

The village of Kalegana had four huge houses and all four belonged to four brothers of the same family. They were merchants with shops in the Galle town and owned tea and rubber estates. They were the first to have motor cars in the area.

Once, when there was a fear of Japanese bombing during the war, my neighbors built an underground bomb shelter, as did many others at the time. This shelter was an impressive one covering a good part of the upper garden. It was stocked with a several months' supply of food and other necessities. Though no one ever took cover in this shelter, I spent many a happy hour playing inside this underground hideout.

As time went on I became a part of the family. They always had Alsatian dogs. At the time there were two named Raja (king) and Rani (queen). Though they were very friendly with the family, they were ferocious to outsiders. One day Raja bit me on my right calf and I was rushed to a clinic. I had to have rabies shots for a week and as a result ran a high fever. My neighbors kept me at their place and tended to me in the best possible manner. I still carry the scar both physically and mentally. Somehow since then I have been mortally afraid of any dog, bigger than a cat. I continued to be close to the family, and treated them as my extended family as I grew up.

*   *   *

Shortly after the incident of the dog bite, my father was transferred to the Station in Polgahawela. The railway had a system that its staff was transferred every three to four years alternating between what was then called non congenial or hardship stations and those that were not considered as such. Many of the non-congenial stations were those rampant with Malaria. Polgahawela, though not too far north east of Colombo, was considered a non-congenial station. Coastal stations along the western coast, north and south of Colombo, were considered desirable stations.

As my Aunt Dotty by then was completing her education at Rippon Girls School, my sister was sent to the boarding school at Visakha Vidyalaya, Colombo. I was sent to live with my father's other sister Amy, for about a year. While in Polgahawela, my father was infected with Malaria and was hospitalized in Galle. I well remember the day he was admitted to the hospital. I thought I would never see him again. Malaria of course was a very dangerous disease at the time. My father recovered in due course and went back to his station after a short period of rest at his sister Amy's house.

My father was next transferred to the railway station at Dodanduwa as Officer- In- Charge (OIC). Dodanduwa is a fishing village with several interesting sites located half way between Ambalangoda and Galle. Looking back now I see the three years I spent in Dodanduwa, from the age of seven to ten, as the most carefree and happy days of my life.

We were provided a railway bungalow as our residence and finally, my father, my sister and I were together as a family. We had Manike from Ukuwela, Matale, as our housekeeper, cook and a sort of guardian for me and my sister. We also had Jagath, a lad from the family estate in Karandeniya to help with the cleaning and the gardening. Jagath who was a lover of street poetry was also our playmate. My grandfather was a welcome visitor from time to time and stayed with us for a few days on each visit until he could no longer travel by train from Ambalangoda to Dodanduwa.

Our bungalow home was quite spacious and had a large garden with a deep well that supplied the water for our use which included bathing. There was no plumbing in those days in most towns and villages outside of the capital Colombo. Water was also manually drawn to water the many plants we had planted all over the spacious garden.

My father enjoyed gardening and this was his preferred recreation. He planted vegetables (chilies, tomatoes, pumpkin, beans, okra, tomatoes and the like) on specially prepared plots (Paththi). All over the garden he planted banana and papaya trees and a few pineapple plants. Jagath and I were his helpers. We were well trained in the work and I immensely enjoyed helping my father, even though the assignment of carrying water from the well was rather tedious. Most of the fruits and vegetables we consumed were home grown.

The back garden of the bungalow abutted the scenic Dodanduwa Wewa (lake), a salt water lagoon and an important ecological site, with mangroves that provide breeding grounds for shrimp (prawns) and other brackish water fish. Also called Rathgama Lake this was a retreat of peace and tranquility for me. A familiar and distressing sound we heard a couple of times a day from a distance was the sound of dynamiting for fish.

Dodanduwa Wewa is also home to the famous Polgasduwa Island Hermitage - a Buddhist forest monastery founded by the Venerable. Nyanatiloka Mahathera, a German national, in 1911. He was a learned German priest who founded a dynasty of foreign monks including the Venerable. Nyanaponika, he was a Jewish German who, having read Buddhist literature and being impressed with the Dhamma, managed to escape the Nazi rule. He came to Sri Lanka to be ordained by the Venerable. Nyanatiloka. The Hermitage has an excellent English and German library and is a secluded place to live the life of a monk, study and meditate in the Buddhist tradition. The Island Hermitage was the first centre of Theravada Buddhist study and practice set up by and for Westerners. Its many prominent residents, monks and laymen, have progressed from Buddhist studies and Pali translations to actual meditation practice; from merely hearing and knowing about Buddhism to actually living and experiencing the Dhamma. Thus the Island Hermitage forms an essential link with Theravada Buddhism in the West. Today, however, there are no Western monks in the hermitage, which now has only Sri Lankans.

Among the foreign monks that had resided there was the Venerable. Mahinda. He was from Sikkim, a small state bordering Tibet. His elder brother was the Prime Minister to the King of Sikkim and his next brother was a monk with whom he was living. The monk and Rev. Nanatilake brought him to the island hermitage where he was later ordained as a Buddhist priest in 1930, and named S. Mahinda (Sikkim Mahinda). He became a scholar in Sinhala, Pali and Sanskrit. His love for the adopted country was expressed in his poetic works infusing vigor into the struggle for independence that had been initiated by the national leaders. Nidahas Mantaraya (Independence Chant), Nidahase Dahana (Gift of Independence), and Siri Lak Amme (Mother Lanka) are some of his famous poetic compositions rekindling the patriotic fervor of the nation.

The hermitage consists of two islands: Polgasduwa and Meddeduwa. Characterized by rich jungle vegetation and abundant bird, animal and reptile life, and despite being infested with mosquitoes and snakes, the hermitiage is a place filled with tranquility. Since it is situated as an island in a lagoon, the climate is quite hot and humid. The island is overrun by a jungle of scrub and thorn-bushes with creepers growing over the palm-trees at the water's edge. The few paths that are cut through the island are arched with wild creepers. The kutis (lodges) are basic, the sanitation primitive, and the lifestyle of the priests, modest (they sew their own robes and dye them in the boiled juice of the bark of trees).

Devotees visit with alms (lunch) for the incumbent priests daily. They come by boat in the mornings and prepare the mid- day meal. Just before 11am the bell in the hall with half walls, where the priests congregate for the mid-day meal, is sounded by the devotees indicating that they are ready with the meal. The priests make a slow and deliberate walk to the hall in silent meditation, one following the other with downcast eyes. Once the alms are offered the priests recite Pirith and make a short sermon. Then they carry their meal with them to the Kutis and consume their only daily meal. The rest of the time is spent in meditation, reading and writing.

* * *

I spent most of my spare time on the lake. Just across from the bungalow was a *Poya Seemawa*, a little one room cottage built on stilts on the lake, used for the ordination of Buddhist priests. I used to swim back and forth to the mostly abandoned Poya Seemawa. There were a couple of times when I had scary experiences with cramps, but I was young and nothing dissuaded me from doing what was fun. Eventually I became a good swimmer.

I also used to roam the lake in a catamaran borrowed from the neighboring coir factory. The catamarans were used to carry the cocoanut husks soaked in the lake which were then beaten hard with wooden machetes and spun into coconut fiber strings or into loose strands of fiber used for coir mattresses and other products.

Of course my mentor in all these activities was Jagath. Whenever my relatives or family friends brought alms to the resident priests on Polgasduwa, we used to arrange the catamarans to ferry the family friends and the alms across the lagoon. I enjoyed those visits immensely because I was able to show off my boating prowess to family and friends who were mostly new to the experience. Eventually, I became quite good at handling the catamaran and up to this day will not avoid an opportunity to be on a boat of any kind wherever I go.

Ironically, it so happened as a child Shanthi too visited Polgasduwa carrying alms to the priests there with her family. The catamaran she was on toppled leaving her with harrowing memories which lasted till she met me. I finally managed to rid her of this fear of boats.

In front of the bungalow was the train yard which fascinated me as it did most children. It was the train that brought Seeya whenever he came to visit us. And it was by train that I went to visit Seeya during school holidays. I particularly looked forward to visiting him during the Vesak festival.

Ambalangoda was reputed at the time as the place that celebrated the occasion in the grandest manner. Vesak is celebrated commemorating the birth, the enlightenment and the death of Lord Buddha. In Ambalangoda, as in the rest of the country, temples are filled with pilgrims. The beautiful decorations of lanterns in Ambalangoda are more intricate and larger than elsewhere. They are made especially for the occasion, and the large pandals adorned with thousands of colorful lights, depicting Buddha's life, were unique in Ambalangoda. People from several towns in the south of the country congregated to watch the festivities in my hometown. The center of attraction was the 'pererhera,' a procession of hundreds of dancers, drummers and attractively decorated elephants with one carrying the religious relics. The procession begins and ends at the Mahapansala temple and winds its way through the entire town over several hours during the nights of the week of Vesak celebrations.

The Perahera in Ambalangoda is no longer so elaborate, while the ancient Maligawa Perahera in Kandy, Duruthu Perahera in the Kelaniya temple and more recently the Gangaramaya Temple's Navam Perahera in Colombo have become very much more elaborate than they used to be. They are now events well patronized by foreign tourists.

The best vantage point to watch the Ambalangoda procession was the upstairs balcony of Seeya's house. Many family members and friends gathered to witness the procession from Seeya's balcony. I revelled in being the center of attraction as Seeya's youngest grandson and, of course, thoroughly enjoyed the sweetmeats that Singo Nanda had prepared for the occasion.

The trains fascinated me for another reason. Each time the trains passed by I would watch and wave at the passengers who on and off, would wave back. After a year or so of this I became more adventurous and used to ride the footboard of the trains as they started off from the station and jump off them just when the train started picking up speed. This was more fun than simply watching the trains and of course like other boys my age, I was oblivious to the dangers involved in the practice.

Each time I jumped off a train, I waited a little longer than the previous time, testing my skills. Mounting a slow moving train and jumping off is quite an expertise that one cultivates through practice and, I guess, with some daring.

All this started after I had seen others, kids and adults out of necessity, perform this routine. Once, my father was on an express train that had no scheduled stop at Dodanduwa. He had arranged with the driver at the earlier stop to slow the train down at Dodanduwa so that he could get off and be on duty in time. I was very impressed by my father's skills as he alighted from a train that was moving at tremendous speed. This was the clincher for me to try. Luckily I survived the railway tracks in front of the house, just as I did the lake behind. These were glorious days.

* * *

It was while we were still in Dodanduwa that the first parliamentary elections were held under a new constitution for the now independent Ceylon. This was quite a learning experience for me. My father was a strong supporter of his old mentor who was a candidate for the Ambalangoda- Balapitiya multi member constituency which included Dodanduwa. P.de.S. Kularatne, my father's mentor and a distant relative, was the candidate of the United National Party (the right wing party). He was a distinguished educationist having served as the principal of Ananda, the leading Buddhist school in the country, founded Nalanda College and several other Buddhist schools. Opposed to the UNP were the leftist parties of different shades of socialists. The most prominent was the Lanka Samasamaja Party (LSSP), a party of Trotskyite orientation led by a highly educated lot some of whom were schooled at the London School of Economics (LSE) of the London University in the UK. The

Communist Party and the Bolshevik Party of Leninist orientation were the others. In addition there were the ethnic oriented parties, The Federal Party and the Tamil Congress.

My father, as a government officer, was not permitted to be directly involved in the election campaign. He more than supported his candidate behind the scene. Having got a good dose of the UNP literature around the house I was also a UNP supporter just because my father was one. The election was won by William Silva (also a distant relative) who was the LSSP candidate.

The 1947 election campaign and the aftermath sharpened my interest in politics, which I carry to this day. My allegiances changed over the years. As an adult I became a neutral observer, keenly interested in politics both national and international.

Though a representative form of government began in Sri Lanka more than a century ago, with the introduction of universal franchise, the first Multi-party general elections were held in 1947. D.S. Senanayake head of the UNP became the first Prime Minister of Ceylon. On February 4, 1948 Ceylon became an independent country within the British Commonwealth of Nations. My father took me to observe the first Independence Day celebrations (parade and fireworks) at the Galle Face Green in Colombo. I have vivid memories, particularly of the fireworks display, which was mostly in green, the color of the UNP. Maybe because of this experience, fireworks are something that I do not like to miss whenever the opportunity presents itself.

* * *

Not long after the election, my father's term ended in Dodanduwa and he was transferred to Ganewatte, which was considered a hardship station. The Railway Department had generous arrangements for such transfers. The household goods were moved via the goods train and the entire household members traveled by train on second class railway warrants.

In Ganewatte my father was provided with sumptuous railway quarters. The bungalow that was provided to us was situated opposite the station on a small hillock. I started a pen with two pet rabbits. Nearby was a small water tank, which was mostly muddy. It served as my swimming pool. Ganewatte was far interior from the sea, which I had been used to swim in up to that time. Not far from the bungalow was a government farm which produced vegetables and fruits including passion fruit, which provided the base for jam produced there. On the farm there was a tennis court where I used to play tennis with the son of a colleague of my father who lived in the bungalow next to us.

Elmore Perera was about three years older than I, but we kept company as there was no one else our age in the area. He studied at St. Aloysius College Galle where the family had been before their transfer to Ganewatte. He came home only for the school holidays - a routine that I was to follow in the next three years. His elder brother, who was much senior to us, befriended an engine driver operating a local train from Maho to Kurunegala on either side of Ganewatte. Whenever he operated the train my friend's brother got onto a train at the station prior to Ganewatte and his friend the driver would allow him to operate the train to Ganewatte from the previous station. After a while he would kindly take me along and I enjoyed the sojourns immensely. I would help the fireman shovel the coal to the firebox of the train, which was quite an accomplishment for me. This was the life in Ganewatte which was far different to that of Dodanduwa. But I was only there during the school holidays.

* * *

After his term in Ganewatte my father served as the Station Master in Kalutara. Here the bungalow was in front of the Kalu Ganga, in a picturesque setting where the river was separated about a mile away from the sea by a sand bank. I used to swim in the river almost daily and looked forward to it each day. In later years, as I became a reasonably good swimmer, I used to swim across the river to the sand bank and take a dip in the sea with some acquaintances from the neighborhood, whenever they were in the mood to do so.

I also used to roam the back roads of the entire Kalutara area on a bicycle. The Kalutara Sports club was next to the railway station and I used to watch club cricket matches. I saw some famous cricketers of the day playing whenever the Colombo Cricket Clubs came for games. I enjoyed thoroughly my holidays in Kalutara.

* * *

It was while we were at Kalutara that my father decided to remarry. On one occasion he took me to Colombo and introduced me to a lady who by my next holidays had become my stepmother.

My stepmother, Soma, hailed from Unawatuna, a suburb of Galle. She came from a well known family of Amarasuriyas. Her mother was the first cousin of Henry Amarasuriya and it was at his house, off Flower Road that I met her in Colombo on that first occasion.

My stepmother was an accomplished homemaker excellent at keeping house, cooking, sewing and everything else related to running a household. She was a devoted wife who catered to every need of my father. She was extremely close to her own family. The brothers and sisters were close to each other particularly because many of them were not married. My father liked them equally and they respected him and were ever ready to reciprocate his love and friendship. This I feel was partly due to the fact that they wanted to tend to their sister's family and welfare. However, as time passed, her devotion to her own family led to disagreements, which eventually turned to periodic arguments and quarrels, particularly after my father retired. But they both continued to look after each other to the time my father passed away.

When she came into our family I was fourteen and my sister eleven. At first everything worked smoothly and we were happy together as a family. But by the time my sister entered her teens she and my stepmother started to have disagreements often on trivial matters. They never argued in the presence of my father, and the way I saw it the problem was that both of them wanted to have the last word.

Still, in spite of these constant arguments they continued to look after the welfare of each other, as well as the families of each other until my stepmother passed away.

Somehow, I managed to be out of the fray perhaps because my stepmother liked me very much. It may have been a mutually reinforcing situation. In any event, she catered to my every need as well as a surrogate mother could. She prepared my favorite dishes, washed and ironed my clothes and entertained my guests with excellent hospitality. This was not easy as I had many friends who often dropped in for a meal or stayed with us for several days during the holidays. I also used to entertain my cricket teams at home. She did everything for me that a mother should do. In return, there was little I could do for her except to give her the sense of security that I would always be there for her if she ever needed support.

Of course, at the time, I took all this for granted. But, today, in retrospect I realize how lucky I had been, particularly in my teenage years to have had my stepmother in my life. The time I spent with my family in Kalutara was limited to school holidays. I received my stepmother's full attention once my father was transferred to Galle and I moved in with them for the last two years of my school days. My sister continued to stay in Colombo, at the Viskha Vidyalaya hostel and came home only for holidays. Those brief visits were enough to trigger a series of quarrels with my stepmother.

The transfer to Galle was my father's choice. My stepmother's first cousin Samarapala Amarasuriya was a deputy head of the Ceylon Railway Department. He was a mechanical engineer who later became its head as the General Manager of Railways. He was close to my family as were his other siblings. The youngest Kithsiri Amarasuriya was practically brought up by my stepmother after the death of his mother (my step grandmother's sister-in-law). Kithsiri became a planter and was a regular visitor to our home. My stepmother always had the best of meals prepared for him. I was close to the family growing up and kept contact with all the siblings during my entire adult life.

My father not only arranged to be transferred to Galle but also arranged to be in charge of the railway goods shed, where the goods transported by the railway are stored for collection by the consignees. They could also deposit goods for onward transport by the railway. The reason my father requested this assignment, rather than a more prestigious position, was that the work was light with little responsibility. His assistant did the bookkeeping. But what he liked most in this new designation was that he had a nine-to-five job, something hard to find in the Railway Department. The railway works twenty-four hours as trains run round the clock. My father had gone through the drudgery and done more than his share of night duty for many years. Station staff works on weekly eight hour shifts with plenty of overtime to cover the shifts of those who are on leave. I saw my father work twenty four hour shifts during Christmas or New Year holidays when the Christian staff and others were on holiday. He was without a wife and often without us because we were away in the school hostels. My father was ready to oblige when necessary, for which he was handsomely compensated with double pay. When I was young, I used to visit him when he was on duty, and mess around with the contraption that communicated the Morse code. At the time the telegraph was a prevalent means of communication in officialdom.

The real reason for his wish to have more freedom from official duties was that he wanted more time to devote to the property he inherited from my mother. By then he had somewhat expanded this property but wanted to do more in terms of expansion and upkeep. His reduced responsibilities at work freed him from working on weekends, and the two day break gave him enough time to travel to the properties and give them the attention required.

Since we moved to Galle he also started to plan for early retirement so that he could devote his time entirely to the land he owned. Being in contact with nature and planting things was something he enjoyed tremendously. Over the years he became somewhat of an expert planter, having picked up several tricks of the trade.

It was with these intentions in mind that after a few years in Galle, when I had left home to study in Colombo, he arranged with Uncle Samarapala to be transferred to Ambalangoda, also in charge of the goods shed. By this time he had already planned to build a house to live in, in his retirement. His choice naturally was our hometown of Ambalangoda at close proximity to the properties he wanted to maintain. My father was a very hard working person simultaneously holding two full time jobs. In later years he devoted his time entirely to his family, his work at the office and to the plantations.

Today, on reflection I realize the enormity of the sacrifices my father made, widowed in his early thirties on behalf of his two young children by bringing them up on his own. Even today, well past the age of seventy, there are still moments when I miss him.

FOOT NOTE:

[1] Rubber tree initially grew in the rain forests of South America. The history of Sri Lanka's rubber industry began way back in 1876 with the planting of rubber trees in Henerathgoda near Gampaha. Henerathgoda Botanical Garden contains the first ever rubber seedling to have been planted in Asia from a Brazilian seedling. Natural rubber is derived from latex, a milky substance from the rubber trees. The trees would be 'tapped', that is, an incision made into the bark of the tree and the latex sap collected and mixed with acid. When the liquid is set in trays, they are rolled through a press to remove excess water and made into thin sheets. They are then dried in smoked stacks. The dried rubber is then compacted into bales and crated for shipment. While the latex is used in the manufacture of various rubber products, even the timber is used, in treated form for producing furniture and other timber based products. The rubber industry generates employment to a vast number of people in the country mainly from rural areas, where the estates are. It has been a major export and a prime foreign exchange earner for Sri Lanka, in spite of the increase of worldwide production of synthetic rubber in more recent times.

Chapter 4

The Jasenthuliyanas

I gazed, long and hard, at the framed certificate hanging on Aunty Amy's sitting room wall. At first, as a child, I neither could read nor understand the significance of that piece of paper. But as I grew older, I gradually managed to read the words and realized the certificate was awarded to my Uncle Piyasena for obtaining a Bachelor of Arts (BA) External degree from the University of London, UK, which was still rather rare in the late thirties. I felt overawed by his achievement. To this day I can still recall clearly the wording on that piece of paper. Such was the enormous influence it had on my psyche. I believe this certificate was one of the reasons that pushed me towards academic achievement in my own career.

Though I was familiar with my father's siblings, I know little of my father's ancestry. My grandfather died before I was born. My paternal grandmother lived with my parents till her death, which regretfully I am unable to recollect. It occurred when I was very young. I do remember that my father, even as an adult, married and employed, was nevertheless subjected to her incessant directions and criticism, which my father never quite appreciated or followed. She was very loving and kind to me.

My father's sister, Aunt Amy and her family lived in Talapitiya, a distant suburb of Galle. She was married to Naddy De Silva of Nupe, Matara. He was in the service of the Ceylon Government Railway as a train head guard (officer-in-charge). I called him Guard Mama (Uncle Guard). A man of very few words he would come home from work, go to his room and was never seen till he left home for work the next day. He cycled back and forth to work; a distance of several miles which I guess kept him in good health.

He liked and was good at playing cards. Once every two to three months, on a weekend, he organized all day and night card games at his home. He had a group of regular players. My father and his two younger brothers joined him whenever they were available. Usually two, sometimes three tables full of players amounting to 12 to 18 were in attendance. They played a game called *Ajutha and Hath Wasi* (7 chances). They played for stakes. After every round the winner contributed a specified amount to the kitty (joint pool). The funds in the kitty went to my uncle Naddy and were used to cover the expenses such as meals. There was good camaraderie between the players and they enjoyed each other's company as much as the game. This was a fairly frequent happening in many middle class houses those days, prior to the era of television and other forms of adult entertainment.

All the meals were provided by my Aunt Amy with the help of her staff. The house had a festive atmosphere when the games were on and we kids loved it, enjoying the good food and the activity in and around the house.

Aunt Amy's house was relatively large with five bedrooms, living and dining rooms and two porches on two front sides of the house. It had a cemented mada midula (court yard) and around it a washroom with a tank for washing and bathing, a second dining room or pantry, and a kitchen. There was an attached garage, first used for the bullock carts and much later for cars. The toilet was an out-house built away from the main house as modern toilet facilities were not then common in provincial towns.

The front room was generally occupied by one or more semi-permanent or visiting family members, and close and distant relatives. The four rooms around the dining room were occupied by other family members including me. The house also had a very large garden and abutted the Galle to Matara railway line. It faced the level crossing at Thalapitiya, where local trains stopped to pick-up passengers.

Aunt Amy and Uncle Naddy had a son, Sarath, a year older than I, and a daughter, Chandra, about four years my junior. The first time I was sent to stay with them Aunt Amy. I called her Loku Nanda (elder aunt), was in the Galle Hospital where she had given birth to her second daughter Indra. Later, a third daughter, Neela was born. They were my playmates as we grew up.

While I was there on that first extended stay, I attended a vernacular school with my Cousin Sarath. The school was part of the Gangarama Buddhist Temple about a mile from the house. The principal of the school was Uncle Jayawickrama from Matara who was a relative of Uncle Naddy. He was one of the semi-permanent lodgers in the front room of Uncle Naddy's house. A serious but kind man he was later transferred to a school close to Matara and left us, but continued to visit on important family occasions. Throughout my school days, I used to spend a part or most of the holidays at Aunt Amy's house. She treated me as if I was one of her own sons. Hers was one big family and I used to look forward to my visits as this meant playing from morning to night. The visits were made during the school holidays when I had no school studies to be done. In addition to my Cousin Sarath, who was my constant companion, there were his three sisters and two girls Mallika and Anula from the house next door that formed our group of playmates.

This was where I first began to play soft ball cricket. We also played many board games like snakes and ladders. As the house was next to the railway line we were fascinated by the passing trains. It was natural that we played also a game simulating the trains. Each of us took turns running around the house which had two or three train stations manned by the others. We built signal posts for trains with ropes pulling the signals up and down. We made train tablets by pushing the two ends of an eakle on a *gobolla* (small young coconut, size of a tennis ball). Of course, we used to fight as often as we played, but these quarrels were short lived and lasted only till we wanted to play again.

Even when we were in our teens Sarath and I continued to fight, often very ferociously. Sometimes he won and at other times I won. This was good combat training, and came in useful when later I had to actually fight someone other than my cousin, for the first and last time in my life!

My Cousin Sarath was later educated at St Aloysius College Galle and Ananda College Colombo. He was determined to enter medical school and made several attempts at the medical entrance examination. It was during this time that we shared a room for a year in a Colombo boarding house at Kattawalamulla Lane, Maligawatte, close to Ananda College. This was the last year he tried the medical entrance exam and my first year in the Law College, Colombo. Not having succeeded in his ambition Cousin Sarath entered the Technical Training College in Amparai, in the east coast of Sri Lanka, set up by a German Foundation. This institute trained junior level engineers in all fields of engineering. Once graduated the alumni filled many engineering positions in the government service to augment the cadre of engineers produced by the university. Our engineering population at the time was not sufficient for developmental and other projects undertaken by the government in the fifties, shortly after independence.

Cousin Sarath specialized in civil engineering and worked for the Ceylon Transport Board (CTB). He was involved in the construction and maintenance of the CTB buildings. He married and had a son. One fateful day very early in the morning his *Volkswagen* met with a head on accident on the Galle Road, at Mount Lavinia. His wife died on the spot but the baby son, who was thrown out of the car, survived. My cousin escaped relatively unhurt. Thereafter, he went to the Middle East and worked in the civil engineering field for about two years.

Cousin Sarath left his son with his younger sister Indra, who was married and had no children of her own. After his contract expired he returned to Sri Lanka and built a large two storied house on a sea side lane in Wellawatte. He remarried and started working as a building contractor but soon migrated to the United States. Since the early eighties he has been in Washington D.C., working for a civil engineering company engaged in building highways in the Maryland area. My wife and I visit them from time to time, whenever we are in the Washington area.

Cousin Sarath and his present wife have two grown children. Their son Sandhi is a psychologist who undertook his graduate work at University of California at Davis. I was able in a small way to be of some assistance when he was initially settling down in California. His son Dumindra from the first marriage continued to be brought up by his sister whom he called Amma (mother). Much later he came over to the United States and joined the United States Marines. In 2008 he was married. My wife and I were invited to attend the wedding at the Marine Academy in Baltimore. We could not make it to the wedding. I very much regret this failure, because my cousin has not taken it lightly and has somewhat distanced himself from us since the wedding.

Aunt Amy's eldest daughter Chandra was educated at the Sacred Heart Convent in Galle, along with her two younger sisters. She married fairly early in life. Her husband Amaradeva Perera was a businessman from the merchant family of Pereras in Wadduwa. They also owned agricultural property and led prosperous lives. In due course she became a knowlegdable business person assisting her husband. They moved to a spacious house they purchased on Galle Road near the clock tower in Moratuwa. There, not far from the house, they purchased a building with the Square Deal Pharmacy (drugstore). They ran an extremely good business until her husband passed away rather prematurely.

They had two daughters and a son. The eldest daughter Harsha married Thusitha, a police officer at the Police Headquarters in

Colombo and established a family in Moratuwa. The second daughter married a businessman and settled in Ambalangoda. The youngest in the family is son, Nalin Perera, who assisted in the business and became a leading race car driver in Sri Lanka.

Unfortunately, there was time of sadness and concern to me personally, and to those around her, when after her husband's untimely death, Chandra went through a difficult period where her interest in her business, properties and even the home she help establish was under challenge. But she showed her resilience in working her way back to relative normalcy, to the relief of everyone concerned. During those trying days I had visited her with a heavy heart, but I am now pleased to be informed that she is back to her usual self, and happily enjoying the company of her grandchildren.

My cousin Indra became an English teacher at St. Johns College, Moratuwa. She married Sarath Fonseka a tea taster and now a senior executive at Jafferjee Tea Traders and Exporters. They live in Sarath's ancestral house in Moratuwa and have no children of their own. But they were foster parents to Indra's brother Sarath's first born, whose mother died in a car accident. Indra is now retired but is in demand as a private tutor. I have been in touch with her whenever I visit Sri Lanka. She has visited the United States on a few occasions. The boy they raised is now a married man living in the United States. The youngest in the family is Neela. She married Dharshan De Silva from Ambalangoda. They both worked in the Middle East for some time and returned to Sri Lanka and established the Lanka Pharmacy (a drug store) at Mount Lavania. During the nineties, on several occasions when I visited Sri Lanka, I used to stay at the Mount Lavinia Hotel. As the Pharmacy was just down the road from the hotel I used to see her on those occasions.

They have a daughter and a son. The elder, daughter Surangi, was educated at the Medical College in Kathmandu in Nepal and is now working as a medical doctor. She married a doctor and the couple is working in the Government Hospital in Kandy. Their son Udara is studying Marketing and conducting outsourced online business in medical billing for a group of doctors in the United States.

* * *

My father's eldest brother was Sumanasena. I called him Loku Thaththa (elder father). He was the person in the family I had least contact with. I saw him only on the few occasions he visited Aunt Amy's place. He married a lady from Batapola very late in life and they had no children. I remember visiting his house only once.

Like Guard Mama, he was also in the CGR working as a train head guard (ofiicer-in-charge) and, like Guard Mama, he was a man of few words. He was also a man with limited patience, particularly where he saw injustice of any kind. An incident that illustrates his temper, which made him somewhat famous, also cost him his job.

The Ceylon Government Railway department was headed by a British citizen until the first Ceylonese to head the Department, Mr. Kanagasabai, was appointed in the late forties. He was a Tamil and apparently there was a feeling among some Sinhalese staff that he was favoring the Tamils for promotions and transfers. Loku Thaththa was incensed about it. His colleagues who considered him to be a strong nationalist, true or not, informed him he was soon to be a victim as well. One day he happened to see the General Manager, Mr. Kanagasabai, at the Colombo Fort Railway Station and instinctively slapped him. Loku Thaththa then explained why the General Manager deserved the slap.

Loku Thaththa was dismissed from service, but considered what he did, was right. He did it in the interest of those he thought were being victimized (whether in fact there was the perceived discrimination and whether his actions had any salutary effect thereafter is a matter of conjecture). He pursued the matter in courts for awhile to no avail, and went back to live with his wife at the Batapola residence. His wife owned the house as well as some property, so he was able to spend the rest of his life in leisure, and passed away I believe in his late fifties.

* * *

While my father's elder brother was hot-headed, his younger brother, Piyasena, was a very thoughtful, collected person. He was the first to graduate with an academic degree among the members of my parental families.

Up to the time of Independence from colonial rule, university education in Sri Lanka was reserved for the wealthy and well-connected upper class families mainly in Colombo. Most of them were educated in the U.K. until the forties, when the University of Ceylon was established. Until then the University College established in 1921 had prepared students for examinations in the U.K. Yet, at the early stages, admission to the University of Ceylon was reserved to those from elite Colleges in Colombo. It was, not very common for people from outstations to attend university or obtain academic degrees. If one was not wealthy enough to go to the U.K., one could pursue self-education to obtain a degree as an external student of the University of London, which held exams in Sri Lanka.

My Uncle Piyasena (I called him Punchi Bappa-small uncle), was one of those committed people who wanted to gain a higher education. Of course, those days under the colonial regime there were enough jobs in the government and the colonial mercantile sector, which paid a decent salary with many perks and good retirement benefits. This meant there was no need to obtain academic qualifications to obtain a decent life. For many young people, like several in my parental families, education beyond the level needed for governmental or mercantile sectors was not an imperative. Uncle Piyasena, however, pursued further education and earned a Bachelor of Arts (BA) External degree.

External degree from the University of London. The framed certificate was proudly displayed on the living room of his sister

Amy's house, which at the time was his home. That was also what intrigued me as a young boy and perhaps some way fueled my own academic pursuits later in life.

After he obtained his degree he entered the teaching profession as a member of the Department of Education and was posted to Rahula College, Matara, a pioneering Buddhist school (made famous by the cricket legend Sanath Jayasuriya and a host of high government officials produced in more recent times).

I once visited his class, and was in awe of the aura created by him standing with a long wooden pointer constantly directed at what he wrote on the blackboard. He taught a class of senior level students who looked to me as if they were even more grown up than they in fact were. This was on a trip to Matara with my Aunt Amy's family to attend a religious ceremony at Uncle Naddy's ancestral house in Nupe, Matara. In retrospect, I feel he may have deliberately taken me and my Cousin Sarath, who by then was under his wings, to the class he was teaching that day, in order to impress upon us the importance of education. The visit, left an indelible impression on my mind.

Uncle Piyasena used to travel to Aunt Amy's house for weekends and was one of those semi-permanent occupants of her front room. While my cousin had grown up seeing him constantly I saw my Uncle Piyasena only when I was at my cousin's house on weekends. Somehow, on Fridays when he came to stay for the weekend, I was terrified of him. It is difficult to explain why. He looked very serious and I felt he was not the kind of person who would understand a small boy like me, who was bent on playful behavior. I had the impression intuitively that he expected us to do nothing but study. That was a time when studying was the last thing on my mind.

While my father was resident in Kalutara, Uncle Piyasena married Sumana Punchihewa from Wadduwa (I used to call her Sumana Nanda-Aunt Sumana). I remember attending the wedding in the bride's ancestral home in Wadduwa. It was a small Walauwa (manor type) house at the main junction on Galle Road in Wadduwa next to the Police Station. She had a brother, Kamal Punchihewa, who later became a well-known industrialist heading United Motors Company and Coca Cola (local company). Kamal married Yaso Fernando a left wing politician. Their son Ana Punchihewa was the President of the Sri Lanka Cricket Board (the premier sporting organization in the country).

It was at this wedding that I became familiar with the traditional Sri Lankan marriage ceremony. All the necessary steps that should be observed at a wedding were followed to the letter. I still can see in my mind's eye the couple standing on the traditional 'poruwa' and being blessed with the customary ceremonial gestures, a tradition that has been followed from before the 3rd Century B.C.

In recent times, during the 'Poruwa' ceremony, the couple is symbolically married, with the signing of the marriage registration that legalizes the union done separately. The 'poruwa' itself is a small, raised platform with a canopy above it, constructed according to traditions drawn from the ancient Sri Lankan culture, and decorated generally with flowers including four coconut flowers.

The traditional drumming and music (chanting) are part of the ceremony led by a person who chants 'Slokas' or blessings, which are the primary verses from Mahabharata and Ramayana, the great epics of Indian Mythology. They are offered to deities representing knowledge, wisdom, beauty and opulence, invoking their blessings for the happiness of the couple.

During this ceremony the bride's father symbolically hands over the bride to the groom by the gesture of helping her to mount the 'poruwa' and placing her right hand over that of the groom. Also during the ceremony seven sheaves of betel leaves are dropped on the 'poruwa' by the couple, symbolic of remembering seven generations of relatives and seeking protection for the seven generations to come from the union. The bride's uncle unites the couple by tying their fingers with a golden thread and sprinkling water on the nuptial knot. That is considered an absolute symbol of marriage, while water poured on the earth and the earth symbolize lasting witnesses to the union. The groom places a necklace on the bride, symbolizing that he will provide for her from that day on. The couple feeds each other with milk rice, 'Kiribath', specially cooked for the occasion by the bride's mother, symbolic of a pledge to take care of each other for life. The couple offers betel sheaves to their parents and immediate family, symbolically expressing their gratitude to the elders for the love and guidance provided to the couple during their upbringing. Finally 'Jayamangala Gatha' (stanzas of victory from Buddha's preaching) is sung by four young girls to offer blessings to the couple.

At the time of his marriage, Uncle Piyasena had been transferred from Rahula College to Ruwanwella Central College and the newlyweds took residence there. Shortly thereafter, he secured a scholarship and went to Australia for his graduate studies. When he returned with a Diploma in Education (ED), I was at the Katunayake airport in great awe to greet him, along with the other members of the family. He was posted to the Teacher Training College in Katukurunda. This was the next township from Kalutara, where my father was residing and working. On weekends he used to visit us on his bicycle. Even when he was a teacher at Matara he used to ride the bicycle from Nupe to Rahula College where he used to teach. He was constantly going about on a bicycle till very late in life. Naturally that may have kept him fit because he was always a wiry, tall and handsome man and like my father, was quite fair in complexion. He passed on his good looks to his two sons.

After many years in Katukurunda, Uncle Piyasena was transferred to the Teacher Training College at Balapitiya. It was a few kilometers from Ambalangoda, our hometown. He moved to a spacious house with an ample garden in Maha Ambalangoda. He travelled to work from there. His bicycle was still his preferred mode of transportation. I used to visit him there almost every school holiday at least for a week or so if not more. I had become quite close to him and his wife, and lost the childhood fear I had of him. I also got to know his children more closely. Once he retired he moved to a smaller house in Patabandimulla. By then his children were grown up. In his retirement he became an avid card player, and of course his bicycle was always at hand. Later he purchased a nice home in Moratuwa and moved there. His younger son secured admission to the University of Moratuwa in Katubadde, and the move helped his son to commute to the university from home. He also purchased an automobile and said goodbye to his bicycle leaving it behind in Ambalangoda. He spent a rather sedate life in Moratuwa where I used to visit him whenever I was in Sri Lanka.

On one occasion when I happened to be in Sri Lanka on vacation at my Aunt Dotty's place in Colombo, a telephone call was received by my Aunt quite late in the night. This was during the JVP uprising and a curfew was in effect after dark. We heard that my Uncle Piyasena was taken ill. His elder son was at his uncle Kamal's residence in the outskirts of the city of Colombo. A cousin of mine and I, after securing an emergency permit from the local police, went to Uncle Kamal's place. It was a large mansion with locked gates. We jumped over the wall and contacted Uncle Piyasena's son. Together we arranged an ambulance to take Uncle Piyasena to Durdans (a private hospital in Colombo). The reason for his hospitalization was complications from diabetes. After a couple of days his condition became complicated and he was moved to the General Hospital in Colombo (a government establishment), which was the premier place of treatment in Sri Lanka. There he went into a coma and remained in that state for about a week.

I arranged for the consultant neurosurgeon at the hospital to see him. The surgeon was the brother of a lawyer friend of mine. The medical staff did their best to treat him. One of the prime diagnoses was that my uncle was suffering from cerebral malaria. Quinine, the drug of choice for malaria was intravenously administered.

One day when I came to the hospital to see him in the afternoon, I found him reading the newspaper. On inquiry I learned that he had awakened that morning and after a wash had wanted *Indiappa* (local version of pasta) for his meal. A family member had promptly arranged for the meal as he desired with all the accompaniments. By the time I arrived he had had a good feed of 'Indiaapa' and was happily reading the news of the day. I was most pleased and told his wife that because he was now fully recovered, I would be attending to other affairs I had put off during my visit to Sri Lanka. That night he went to sleep happy, never to wake again.

He and his wife had two sons. Susil and Upul and both went by the name Jasenthuliyana (though their father went by J.L.P De Silva (Jasenthuliyana Piyasena De Silva). They were much younger than I, by a decade or so, and growing up I used to observe them playing with each other though there was also a fair gap of about six years in their own ages. They were perhaps more studious and somewhat more sedate than I was at that age. This was perhaps due to the way their father conducted himself and the academic environment of the household. They both had their early education at Dharmasoka College, Ambalangoda.

Susil entered the Dental School at Peradeniya University from Aquinas College Colombo, and graduated as a dentist. Following his training he joined the army as a dental surgeon. He served at the Army Headquarters at Pannipitiya. It was during this time that his parents learned that he was in love with a girl from Ambalangoda who was at the university with him. Susil's parents Who had great expectations of finding a partner for their son from a well recognized family of wealth, vehemently objected to him falling in love with a girl of his choosing and depriving them of making the choice. This was the norm of the day, when parents expected their children to enter into proposed marriages and not love marriages. Susil was equally adamant. Slowly they drifted apart. In due course he married Indra Kalaptha from Ambalangoda without his parent's presence.

Indra was an Arts graduate from Peradeniya University. I was appraised of the situation during one of my visits to Sri Lanka. As usual I made a visit to my Uncle Piyasena and his wife at their Moratuwa residence. During the course of the visit I inquired about Susil and I got an unusually cool response, which clearly indicated to me how things stood between the parents and the son. Nevertheless, knowing that they had a soft spot for me, I told them that I would bring Susil, his wife and the newly born baby with me when I would visit them next. They vehemently opposed the idea.

Regardless of their opposition, I arranged for Susil to visit his parents with his wife and baby. Following a very reluctant welcome during the first visit, where I was practically having a seperate dialogue with each of those present, as time passed the contacts increased and the family was back together.

In due course, Susil left the army and established a dental surgery in Panadura opposite the bus station, and built up a very successful private practice. He built two spacious residences where I used to visit him off and on at Panadura. Susil's daughter Shamika Jasenthuliyana studied in the United States and since graduation continues to work in New Jersey. His son, Shashika Jasenthuliyana, also studied in the United States, and is completing a Ph.D. in Information Technology in Northern Texas.

Susil's brother Upul entered the Moratuwa University in Katubadde from Royal College, Colombo, and graduated as an engineer. He was also musically-talented and played in a band that he and his engineering friends formed during their undergraduate days. Shortly after graduation he immigrated to Australia and established himself in Sydney, Australia. By then he was married to Dushani, daughter of Bandu Manakulasuriya from Dehiwela, who served as deputy secretary in the Ministry of Industries and later as general manager of the Steel Corporation. Unlike his brother, Upul had the blessings of his parents and his mother became close to Dushani. I have visited them at their Dehiwela house and whenever we are in Colombo he never fails to visit me and invite me to his home. Dushani worked for a Finance Company in Colombo. Later, she was employed at the City Bank in Sydney.

Shanthi and I visited them in Sydney at their house on Fifth Avenue in Camprise. When we went there they had a five year old son, Tharaka, who was very smart. I have pictures of him in a cute cap taken with me. Aunt Sumana was there when we visited them. She used to make frequent visits and later lived there until she passed away, struck by cancer. Son Tharaka studied at the Kingsgrove College in Sydney and currently he is at the Australian National University (ANU) in Canberra completing a combined degree in Finance and Economics. His other son Lasika is studying at the Asian International School in Colombo. Upul continues to commute between Colombo and Sydney where the two sons are based, and also continues his musical interests by playing with his musician colleagues in bands in both cities. Just as I have been, he is interested in family relationships. He was most helpful to me in writing this book by providing me with whatever information that I requested him to gather on recent developments in the family.

* * *

The youngest brother of my father, Dr. J.C. De Silva (Jasenthuliyana Chandrapala), was known as J.C. and I called him Podi Bappa (small uncle). He had the good looks of his brothers and his bluish green eyes stood out (much more prominently than in my father and his other brothers). He was educated at Mahinda College, Galle and played in the cricket team in the late forties. He first qualified as an Apothecary and later worked in several rural hospitals as the physician in charge.

He had a long stint at Welimada hospital in the hill country, where most of the patients were maternity cases. Whenever he was not delivering babies he was dispensing medicine and advice to patients in the outdoor clinic. He had a government bungalow just outside the hospital compound. It was a comfortable building with a large garden where his wife was fond of cultivating vegetables, for which the area is well known.

I visited him there during two of my school vacations in the mid fifties. He welcomed me with open arms, particularly as I was a cricketer like him. We had common interests in sports. We often played badminton in his backyard. He used to drive down to the Bandarawela club in the late afternoons whenever he was able to get away from the dispensary. The Bandarawila Club, like those in similar towns, is synonymous with colonial hill country towns. It is a living monument to an exotic past and is tied up with the living spirit of the European tea planters and the railway staff of Bandarawila Railway Station. Without doubt one of the oldest surviving sports clubs in Sri Lanka, the Bandarawila Sports club was first begun in 1897 by sports enthusiasts comprising European Tea Planters and railway staff from the Bandarawila Station. It was then known as the Railway Sports Club. It had only one tennis court and the seats were made of wooden railway sleepers. By 1948 modest improvements were made to the club and since then it has become known as the Bandarawela Tennis Club. The present management, Aitkin Spence Company, has made all necessary additions and renovations to sustain the Bandarawela Tennis Club as one of the enduring institutions of a living past.

It was at this club that I used to play table tennis and billiards with my uncle, Dr. De Silva. The drive was about ten kilometers along a narrow winding and scenic route. On our way back and forth to the club we used to chat mostly about sports or family. He was a very amiable person although he flared up when he considered anything or anyone to be unjust or unfair. He married Stella Fernando from Beruwela, who came from a well to do family of land owners in the area. She had a brother, Linton, who became a lawyer rather late in life. Another brother was an executive in the commercial sector. The wedding took place while my father was resident at Kalutara, a short distance from Beruwela. Our home was the base for my Uncle on his wedding day, because he was resident at the time in a faraway town.

I enjoyed attending the very festive marriage ceremony at the bride's residence. Even more so the Home Coming (commonly known then as 'At home') that took place at our home in Kalutara. I had the pleasure of helping in the decorations, particularly with the colored lights that illuminated the home. This was when I learned a lot about electricity. Since then those bulbs have been used to decorate the house during the period of annual 'Wesak' Celebrations. I continued to enjoy setting the lights each year wherever we lived. Through trial and error I learned a few tricks, in the course of which I experienced a few electrical shocks as well. I had not realized then how lethal this could have been considering the high voltage used in Sri Lanka (220 volts, double that of the United States).

After my uncle received his license as a medical doctor, they moved to Ambalangoda and established a private clinic at Urawatte, a suburb close to Ambalangoda. There he did not have the burdens of hospital administration. He made his way to the Ambalangoda Club almost daily to play card games. The Ambalangoda Sinha Club is where the towns' lawyers, doctors and other professionals meet mainly to play cards or billiards. The people in Ambalagoda knew one another and often were related by blood or marriage, so there was a great camaraderie, which attracted the regulars to the club. My father also was a patron, though not as regularly as my Uncle J.C.

Whenever I was in Sri Lanka I never failed to visit my Unle J.C. and his wife. Aunt Stella was a very friendly person. She was very attached to my uncle and looked after all his needs. She was very kind to me and treated me very well during my visits to them. Today she is the only surviving family member of my parental families.

They had three daughters, much younger than me. I used to carry them when they were babies during my visits to their Welimada home. Sometime in the seventies my uncle wrote to me in New York, informing me of the possibility that his middle dauhter, Vajira, might be coming to the United States on a scholarship to study. She had completed her studies at Visakha Vidyalaya in Colombo. He had wanted her to visit me in New York to be acclimatized before proceeding to Greensborough, North Carolina to the campus of Bennett College. Bennett is a unique institution with a century of history. Having had its beginnings in the unfinished basement of a Methodist Episcopal Church in 1868, within five years a group of emancipated slaves purchased the present site for the school. In

1926, the formerly co-education institution became a college for black women and has remained so to date.

I met Vajira on arrival at the John F. Kennedy airport and she stayed with us for a couple of weeks. Thereafter she visited us during her college vacations, which she spent with us. She was a good student and graduated with a degree in biochemistry.

She worked at the prestigious Oak Ridge National Laboratories as a research trainee in molecular biology. Born as part of the Manhattan Project in 1943, Oak Ridge National Laboratory was established in the dark days of World War II when American scientists feared that adversaries were rapidly developing new nuclear weapons of unimaginable power. Built seemingly overnight on isolated farm land in the mountains of East Tennessee, Oak Ridge became the "secret city" which, within two years, housed more than 75,000 residents. Oak Ridge developed the world's first sustained nuclear reaction, leading to the atomic bomb that ended the Second World War. Today, Oak Ridge National Laboratory is one of the world's leading scientific research centers and supports a peacetime science and technology mission that is very different from its role during the Manhattan Project.

Following my Sri Lankan ways of thinking in those days, I had written to her father that she should return home now that she had completed her studies in the United States, explaining the trials and tribulations that a young pretty Asian girl with no family roots in the U.S. might be subjected to. Indeed, unknown to her I had looked what possibilities would be there for her which will entice her to go back home, and applied on her behalf, for three research posts that were advertised in the local papers. She had two offers available to her and her father by then had written to her in no uncertain terms that she should return home.

At the end of her assignment at Oak Ridge, Vajira returned to Sri Lanka and worked as a research officer at the Tea Research Institute (TRI) for some time (one of the posts I had applied on her behalf).

She had since then also acquired professional qualifications in the accounting area, and later worked at the Development Finance Corporation of Ceylon (DFCC). She married Gihan, son of P.A. Silva, a senior civil servant, who later became Chairman of C W. Mackie Limited, a commercial establishment dealing with trade and export of rubber and coconut products. Vajira and Gihan built a house in Kohuwela, a suburb of Colombo, and moved there from Gihan's parent's house on Flower Road. They had two children, a son and daughter. Shortly after the second child was born Gihan died of a sudden, massive heart attack at a very young age - in his early thirties. Vajira continued to work as a consultant to commercial enterprises.

In view of my close association with her while she was in the United States, where I had provided her with help and guidance she needed in her studies and training, I continued to be in close touch with her whenever I visited Sri Lanka. On these occasions, she made certain that my wife Shanthi and I were invited to dinner at her home.

Her daughter Nadisha earned her Ph.D. in Bio-Science at Texas A & M University in the United States. She married Chris Schwedes, a fellow student at Texas A&M who also earned a Ph.D. and works in an engineering firm in the Los Angeles area. They gave us a delightful gift when they visited Shanthi and me in the company of her mother and grand mother, who is the only surviving family member from my father's generation. They had traveled to the U.S.A. to attend Nadisha's graduation. Vajira's younger son Dimitri is a financial analyst working at Alliance Bernstien, a US based global asset management firm in New York. The Alliance was founded in the late sixties, during the time I was living in New York. He married Anna an American lawyer, graduate of Rutgers University in New Jersey, working as an assistant to a Judge in the New Jersey Court.

I had less contact with Vajira's two other sisters. They were also educated at Visakha Vidyalaya. The elder of the two, Indira, is also a lawyer. She married Gamini Wijesuriya, a chemical engineer. They both worked in Dubai for many years and recently moved to Africa. They have two daughters and both are medical doctors having earned their degrees from Cambridge University in the UK.

The youngest in the family is Inoka, a medical doctor. She works as the Consultant Anesthetist at the Negambo Hospital. She married Priyath De Silva, who obtained a Masters degree in Economics from a US university, and is a high-ranking government official in an important ministry in Sri Lanka. They have a daughter who is attending the International School in Negambo.

*   *   *

The youngest in my father's family is Aunt Dotty. I called her Punchi Nanda. She lived with us constantly during my young days. During a couple of our school holidays I and my cousin Sarath were invited by one of her cousins, Jasenthu Liyana Sirisena, to visit his coconut estate. Known as J.L. Sirisena, I called him Sirisena Mama (Uncle Sirisena). We were teenagers and Aunt Dotty went along with us to visit the estate in Dummalasuriya near Madampe in the North Western Province. Madampe is considered a part of the coconut triangle of Sri Lanka, which produces the largest commercial quantities of coconut. [1]

Sirisena Mama was the Superintendent in Charge of the Heemaliyagara Group (very large extent of land comprising multiple estates including several hundred acres of coconut). It was owned by the famous De. Mel family and the area was known as Malsiripura, a prime coconut area. Aunt Dotty, my cousin and I spent about a month with him on the estate during each visit.

My uncle lived in a very spacious two storied estate bungalow. It was in the center of the large estate and we had plenty of space to play cricket and other games or just wonder around. It is here that I first learned to ride a bicycle. Between the playing and riding, my cousin and I had our usual fist fights, which mostly ended as a wrestling match on the ground. We also learned much about the coconut industry simply by watching what went on around us. Sirisena

Mama had a large staff both indoors and outdoors to care for the premises. We were served with good food and drink. Whenever my uncle was in attendance, both breakfast and dinner were somewhat formal. Western food was served by the staff at a well laid out table with crockery, cutlery and white linen. Thus, I was exposed to the refined life and western ways at a fairly young age, a glimps of which at that stage was indeed helpful later.

Sirisena Mama and Aunty Dotty were married and went to live on the estate. In the end, they had a life that most can only dream of.

Sirisena Mama and Aunt Dotty were very fond of me and somehow or other kept in touch with me. When their two eldest daughters approached school age they rented a house near Visakha Vidyalaya on De Fonseka Place, Bambalapitiya in Colombo. My aunt and the two daughters were resident there with uncle visiting them on weekends. During the weekends and during the school holidays the family was together at the estate.

I used to visit them at home whenever I went to Colombo. I used to give the news of my visits, particularly regarding the two girls which were of some interest to the rest of the family. As Aunt Dotty's family grew with the arrival of three boys, they moved to a nice two story modern house on Lauries Road Bambalapitya, just off Galle Road. Uncle continued to be mostly at the estate although he had senior assistants which allowed him to make more frequent visits home. He had established a successful commercial establishment in the Dummalasuriya town, and at the time, was also dabbling in local politics in the area, which subsequently took him to greater heights in national politics, as noted in the narrative later. My association became even closer with the family after I moved to Colombo to attend the Law College.

Their eldest daughter, Pushpa Jasenthuliyana attended Visakha Vidyalaya along with her younger sister Saroja Jasenthuliyana. They were both adorable as they grew up. I was very fond of them from their young days. They grew up to be well mannered young ladies.

Pushpa entered Medical College and graduated as a physician. She was assigned to the Government Hospital at Kohuwela, Colombo. She married Jayantha Jayawardane. The couple later proceeded to the UK on scholarships and obtained specialized qualifications. On return, Jayantha was attached to the Peradeniya University hospital teaching faculty in gynecology and obstetrics. Pushpa worked at the Kandy Hospital. They were occupying a university bungalow and I visited them there off and on when I was in the area. Later, they moved back to Colombo and Jayantha is now a professor in the Department of Gynecology and Obstetrics and Dean of the Faculty of Medicine at the Jayawardanapura University Hospital. Pushpa is attached to the Colombo North Teaching Hospital, (Ragama hospital) in the suburbs of Colombo.

They have two children, a son, Tharinda, who is married, has earned a management degree and currently works for the Carsons Group of companies as a financial stock analyst. Their daughter, Thanuja, having completed studying at the University of Jayawardenapura in Colombo, is working as a financial analyst. During a very recent visit to Colombo I was happy to have attended her wedding at the Mount Lavania Hotel, when she married Dasun Mendis, an accountant. I was particularly pleased to attend the wedding because Pushpa had been a bit peeved that I was not able to spend enough time with them when her father passed away during one of my previous visits to the Island.

Saroja entered the Law College and on completion of her studies took oaths as an attorney-at-law. For some time she worked as a lawyer at the Insurance Corporation of Sri Lanka, the National Savings Bank and the Bank of Ceylon. Once she had children, she became a homemaker taking care of the family. She married Anil Silva from Katana, a law graduate from the University of Colombo and an attorney-at-law. He served as a senior state counsel at the attorney general's department in Colombo.

This is the department responsible for all legal action taken by the State including the prosecution of anyone accused of a crime. He takes action on behalf of the State, or defends it in civil proceedings, and he is responsible for providing legal advice to all entities of the government. It is considered the star institution of the State service and the most brilliant young lawyers are selected to serve that department. The institute provides the best training ground for young lawyers. Consequently most of the lawyers who serve there leave the service after a decade or two and establish a private practice of their own. In due course, they often become the most successful lawyers among the members of the unofficial bar (practicing lawyers representing clients in courts). Those who remain in the department are often appointed to the Court of Appeal or the Supreme Court as judges.

After a decade of service in the department, Anil established his own criminal law practice as a defense attorney in 1987. He was extremely successful as a practicing lawyer. He was elected Secretary of the Bar Association of Sri Lanka (the association of practicing lawyers) for a two year term in 1995. He was the pride of the family when he was appointed as a President's Counsel in 2010. It is the highest recognition that could be bestowed upon a lawyer. Historically, following the practice of the United Kingdom and many Commonwealth countries, the title was Queen's Counsel. That was localized in Sri Lanka in recent years as President's Counsel.

Anil and Saroja have built a very attractive home in the suburbs of Colombo where I have visited them most times I have been in Sri Lanka. They have two children. The older, Maheshika Silva is also following her father's footsteps and is a lawyer in the attorney general's department. Maheshika studied at St. Bridget's Convent in Colombo and was a brilliant student at the Law College. She passed all her law exams with First Class Honors and graduated third in the order of merit. She won several awards including the Gold Medal for oratory. She was a member of the team that represented the Law College and became the international runner-up at the SAARC Law International Moot Competition held in Delhi, India in 2005. Maheshika also holds a law degree from Open University of Sri Lanka and completed the final exams for CIM (Charted Institute of Marketing). She is married to Asela Serasinghe, who is also a lawyer and a member of the attorney general's Department. He was a student at my old school, Richmond College, Galle, and later studied at the Royal College, Colombo.

Son Arindra Silva studied at St. Joseph's College, Colombo and completed IAB finals (International Association of Book Keepers) and CIMA (Chartered Institute of Management Accountants) and is working as a finance executive at the Dilmah Tea Company while pursuing a law degree at Open University in Colombo. Dilmah Tea is an international conglomerate which has captured major market shares in Australia, Canada, the U.K. and the Middle East, supplying major chains such as Safeway Supermarkets in the U.K. and McDonalds in Australia. Dilmah Tea has remained a family concern since its establishment by my friend Merrill Fernando. An entrepreneur par excellence, he heads the company with his two sons Dilan and Malik, who are excellent managers. It is an extremely socially conscious enterprise which has established a privately funded foundation (Merrill J. Fernando Foundation) that carries out considerable charity work. Dilmah also sponsored the Sri Lanka national cricket team to the tune of three million Sterling Pounds. Dilan & Malik's mother Devika (nee Jayawickrama) is a relative of my stepmother, and she has been in contact with me visiting us in New York, Vienna and Los Angeles.

Aunt Dotty's eldest son is Shantha Jasenthuliyana. He and his brothers were educated at the Royal College, Colombo. Following his father's example, Shantha served in the plantation sector of Sri Lanka and is currently serving as an executive in the Janatha Estate Development Board in Colombo (a State Corporation managing the tea estates owned by the State). He married Ramya, a lawyer who, prior to her retirement worked as a legal officer in the Sri Lanka Air Force. They have two daughters Asangi, working for Singapore Airlines and Anjali, studying at a university.

Shantha's younger brother, Channa Jasenthuliyana, works in the Information Technology (IT) section of the Development Finance

Corporation (DFCC), a bank funded by the International Monetary Fund (IMF) in Washington, D.C. He married Thushara De Silva, a distant relative of mine and daughter of S.G.A. De Silva, former Chairman of the Ambalangoda Urban Council (UC). She works as a senior executive at Ceylinco Group of Companies. They have a son, Kalana, who is finishing his education at Royal College.

The youngest in the family, Lalith Jasenthuliyana, settled in Madampe and took over the management of the business enterprise established by his father. He married Deepika from Badulla, a trained English teacher who is working at J.L. Sirisena Madya Maha Vidyalaya (Central College) in Dummalasuriya, which is named after my uncle, her father-in-law. They have no children.

Punchi Nanda and Sirisena Mama had a considerable impact on my life. I looked to them for advice and support, and they extended their unresrved as I grew-up. I fondly remember how I was permitted by Sirisena Mama to take his car when ever I needed it, and indeed, it was his *Ford Consul* that I drove to and from my wedding. Even before that he had given me his *Bug Fiat* when he bought his new *Ford Consul*. I drove that for a while until it broke-down too many times and I decided to abandon it. You will meet them throughout this narrative.

* * *

After my father remarried, my stepmother's relatives too became a part of my extended family.

My stepgrandmother had married a Weeraratne and they lived almost next door to her cousin's well known Amarasuriya Walauwa (mansion) in Unawatuna. My stepmother, Soma, had three brothers and three sisters all of whom never married, except for one sister. The eldest was a sister who was fairly advanced in age by the time I knew her as was my step grandmother. Both passed away when I was quite young and therefore I had limited contact with them.

The next was her brother Weeraratne whom I called Loku Mama (Big Uncle). He was an executive at Roseugh & Company, a British trading concern in Hunupitiya, Colombo. He used to enjoy a couple of arraks after work and, as a law student; I would join him for banter over a drink. This made me familiar with a few notable watering holes (bars) in Colombo particularly the Globe Hotel and his favorite - the Bristol Hotel in Colombo Fort. He passed away in his mid fifties suffering a sudden heart attack.

Following him was Sumanapala Weeraratne whom I called Punchi Mama (Small Uncle). He was an accounts executive at Baur & Company, a Swiss mercantile company on Chatham Street, in Colombo Fort. He rose to the position of Chief Accountant. He lived to a ripe old age. The last time I visited him at the ancestral home in Unawatuna, where he spent his retirement, he told me that he was "in the waiting list in the departure lounge." Both uncles were fond of me and in later years, as a law student, most of my pocket money (expense allowance) came from them. Consequently I had a fairly enhanced allowance. They both were very caring people, particularly looking after the welfare of their family and neighbors.

The youngest of my stepmother's brothers' was Jayatissa Weeraratne. He was an executive in the family firm Amarasuriya & Co., managing the large family holdings of tea, rubber and coconut lands. Although he was a friendly person, he was an introvert and very religious. I had little contact with him.

The elder of the two younger sisters of my stepmother was Bandu, who married a Jayasuriya, a very reserved person who was working for a commercial establishment in Colombo. They resided at Kawdana Place, Dehiwala in a very spacious house. It was there that my uncles also lived, because they were lifelong bachelors and it was a close knit family. I was a frequent visitor there in later years. The couple had two sons, Kanishka and Upul. They both studied at nearby St. Thomas' College Mt. Lavinia and played for the College Cricket Team.

After Kanishka left school he became an ardent supporter of a political party, the U.N.P. It was mainly because Punchi Mama, (Uncle Sumanapala) also supported the same party, being part of the Amarasuriya clan, that were stalwarts of the U.N.P. This led to a tragic event during the time of the JVP terror campaign, when Kanishka was caught with U.N.P. propaganda material and banners in his van while he was on his way to a U.N.P. rally. The JVP thugs promptly executed him and set fire to his van. After the parents passed away, the younger sibling, Upul, took residence at Kawdana Place and continued to prosper as a businessman.

The youngest in my stepmother's family, with a considerable age gap from the rest, was Chulla. She was the prettiest of them all but the one who was not able to find a suitable husband in spite of incessant attempts by the family. She looked after both her mother and her eldest sister and nursed them when they were confined to bed as they advanced in age. Eventually she did the same for my stepmother in her old age. She continued to reside at the ancestral house and tended to all five as the younger of the two uncles (her brothers) retired and took residence in the family home in Unawatuna. Many years after, she herself was confined to a wheelchair. The house was passed on to Upul and in recent years it has begun to show its wear and tear. I had good relations not only with my stepmother, but with her brothers and sisters as well. They loved me as if I were their own flesh and blood.

FOOTNOTE:

[1] Cultivation of the coconut palms in Sri Lanka existed for more than twenty two centuries. According to historical records cultivation of coconut palms in home gardens has been done since the second century BC. It developed into a plantation crop early in the twentieth century. It was reported by Marco Polo in 1300 AD that some Sri Lankans were even at that time, drinking toddy (a popular local brew) from the coconut tree. During the British colonial times, local entrepreneurs received a large extent of land in the North Western Province for coconut cultivation in the period between 1860 and 1893. As a result the areas under cultivation increased rapidly. Sri Lanka is the largest consuming

country (nearly 80% of coconut used for domestic consumption). It is called the Tree of Abundance with every part of it utilized in the form of tender nuts and dry fruit as food, drink, oil, milk and liquor; the leaves and trunk for construction of houses. Under British rule, its products have been put to commercial use and became a principal export commodity (fresh coconuts, arrack, coir, jaggery, copra, coconut oil, reapers and rafters were exported). Over the period of the last three decades, there has been a considerable decrease in coconut area, production and productivity because of conversion of coconut lands for the purpose of construction of buildings, a consequent of increased population and urbanization. This leaves a dearth of coconut products even for local consumption.

Chapter 5

Nangi

It is said that "brothers and sisters are as close as hands and feet". This is probably true. Although we loved each other, my only sister, Premalatha Pemasiri (nee Jasentuliyana), and I were as close and yet as far apart as two siblings could ever be. My sister, whom I called "Nangi", was three years my junior. In my eyes she was never my playmate but my kid-sister when we were young. After my mother passed away she grew up in the company of my father's youngest sister, Aunt Dotty, who lived with us and kept a constant eye on my sister until she entered Visakha primary school and took residence in the school hostel.

By the time she became a teenager my father had remarried. While they both cared for each other there was also constant friction between my stepmother and my sister when my father was not around. Although my stepmother was very attentive to my needs and our relationship was most cordial, it was not the same between her and my sister. In later life, however, particularly after my sister's marriage, they became close and my sister was quite concerned for the welfare of our stepmother.

In contrast, my father adored my sister, and to my resentment she was identified as the role model for me, because she used to do well in her studies, while I was more inclined towards sports. In later life, this changed as the roles were reversed. As adults we were both extremely close to our father and attentive to all his needs.

One of my sister's closest friends from young days in school is Manil Jayasuriya (nee Pieris). Through my sister I knew the entire family very well. Mani's mother was a very close friend of my mother. The Pieris family was dear to us and it was at their place that I happened to see Douglas. On that occasion I thought to myself, "Here is someone who would make a good husband for my sister."

The Pieris family was distantly connected to our family. They had four daughters and a son and we continued to have close contact with them through the years. All four girls went to Visakha Vidyalaya, where my sister studied. The eldest, Manil (Mani), was the same age as my sister and thus was the closest to us. She married Sam Jayasuriya, a relative of Douglas. He was known as 'Tripa' at the university because he was ready to join any one going on a trip. He was an accounts executive in Colombo until he migrated to Canada. There he worked as an accountant in a Canadian Bank in Toronto for several years. He then worked as an accountant for the International Criminal Tribunal for Rwanda (ICTR), which is an international court established in November 1994 by the United Nations Security Council, to prosecute people responsible for genocide and other serious violations of international law in Rwanda. Just on the verge of retirement from his United Nations service he passed away due to a sudden heart attack.

They had two daughters Champa and Samanthi, both married to IT specialists and living in San Jose, California where Mani joined them after Sam passed away. Mani's second sister Lakshmi (Lachchi) married a physician, Dr. Chandrasena, and migrated to Australia. Shanthi and I have visited them in Melbourne on a couple of occasions while I was on official duty. They had two sons, Dilan and Dehan, who became physicians and married also to two doctors. Their sister, Tammie, is a lawyer who works for the Foreign Ministry of Australia.

Mani's second sister Indra also migrated to Australia with her family following her only brother and his family. The youngest of Mani's sisters, Mala, married to Naomal Perera and migrated to Canada with her family. She lived in Toronto till her untimely death. Her other sister Indra and brother Tharin, an accountant, also live with their families in Australia. All of them were in contact over the years with my family and have been close friends.

*   *   *

On one of my frequent visits from New York to Colombo, as usual, I visited our friends the Peiris' who, at the time, were living on Fife Road, Colombo. There I happened to notice a young man of my age and inquired who he was. Learning of his background, he happened to be related to Mani's husband Sam (Tripa) Jayasuriya, I suggested to Mani that he might make a good partner to my sister, and she agreed. I conveyed the news to my father who at the time was actively engaged in looking to find a suitable partner for my sister.

Shortly thereafter the two of them had an opportunity to meet, as Mani was a mutual friend and her home was a perfect place for chance meetings. I am told that they hit it off from the day they first met, and six months later, they were married. The wedding took place in the premises where the five star, Taj Hotel now stands facing the Galle Face Green. It was then run by the Hotels Corporation and had premises where weddings were hosted.

I was the groomsman at the wedding, and the bestman was K.H. J. Wijayadasa, a classmate of the bridegroom at the sniversity. He later became the Secretary to two Presidents of Sri Lanka. What I took away most from the wedding was the beaming happiness of my father at seeing his only daughter happily married and with his complete blessings.

When my sister was married my father handed all his property over to my sister. He did so, after inquiring from me what I would wish to have of his property, and I told him that my wish was for him to pass on everything to my sister. By that time I had completed my education and was settled with an attractive job at the United Nations. When it comes to marriage, the wealth in any form offered to a bride by her family, (known as a dowry), would always attract a more suitable partner for her than otherwise. In my time, dowry system was a part and parcel of marriages arranged by the parents of a couple. It is less so now, in the era of abundant love marriages where the couples fall in love and marry irrespective any other consideration. That was a rare exception in my time. Hence, in those days it was important for a girl of marriageable age to have access to some form of wealth either being part of a wealthy family, through inheritance, or being a member of a recognized profession with the potential for a high income.

Years after my father's inquiry, I learned that my father had given five acres of paddy to me. Upon inquiry why this was so when we had agreed, that he would give everything to my sister, his response was "it was not possible for me, because I had no reason to disinherit you completely".

After the demise of my father, this land was looked after by our close family friend Sujatha Bandularatne. She ensured that the paddy from the field was used for annual almsgiving on the death anniversary of my father, and for other charitable work. I had not visited it since I was a teenager and on a recent visit with Sujatha we agreed that the land should now be given away to charity, as she herself is no longer able to properly look after it. Today, the land is cultivated by Lionel, who was a young boy at my father's home when I was young, and served as a playmate and my constant companion. Later, Lionel was employed by my sister in her household as one of the two employees that her husband was entitled to, while serving abroad on his diplomatic assignments.

*   *   *

My sister's husband Douglas Pemasiri, the person I happened to meet by chance when I visited Mani at Fife Road, hailed from the remote village of Hathagala in the deep south of the Island. Hathagala is a village just outside of Hambantota the area where President Mahinda Rajapakse hailed from. The President is in the process of transforming the wayward town in to a modern metropolis with an up-to-date harbor, an international cricket stadium, and a state of the art airport.

Douglas was the second of three sons of the Village Headman of Hathagala. His eldest son, Danister, was a government official. His son Chandana Liyanapatabandi became a lawyer with a successful practice and was a Board Member of Mihin Air and other corporations. He was interested in aviation and I invited him to several United Nations workshops I organized in the field of aerospace law. This gave me the opportunity in Dubai and Bangalore to get to know him well as a modest but devoted servant of the law. It is a matter of great pride that as of this writing I learned that Chandana had been appoited as a Presdential Counsel, the highest honor bestowed on a practicing lawyer. His younger brother, Vipula, was educated in the United States and is employed in the private sector located in the suburbs of Los Angeles where I see him from time to time.

Douglas' younger brother Nanda is a well known broadcaster in Colombo who spent a time in the Middle East. Douglas's sister Kusum entered the Medical College. My father was delighted to help her in her studies. He asked me to send a stethoscope to the young medical student and I promptly sent it from New York. She graduated as a physician and married her batchmate Dr. Nyanis Subasinghe. They migrated to London where both had successful medical careers. They had two sons who also became doctors and are married to two lady doctors. I have kept contact with the family and we have visited each other, the most recent occasion being when they visited us as a family in Los Angeles.

The youngest in the family, Daisy, was in the Sri Lanka Diplomatic Service and later joined the United Nations agency for Trade GATT (now known as the World Trade Organization WTO), based in Geneva. She married Walter Perera a functionary of ILO (International Labor Organization, Geneva, predecessor of WTO), whom I used to visit during my visits to Geneva for United Nations meetings. He always had an excellent rice and curry dinner ready for his guests. They had a daughter who graduated from a British university and works in the UK.

Douglas also has an elder sister Harriet who was married to a businessman and another younger sister Asida, who was government officer at the Rubber Control Department as was her husband Bernard. They were all very cordial to me, but regretfully, I have long lost contact with them and their children who all remained in Sri Lanka.

Douglas had his education at Dharmapala College and graduated with a degree in economics from the University of Ceylon, Peradeniya. He later obtained a Masters degree in economics from the same university. At the time he married my sister he was a Land Development Officer (LDO) in the government service. He was then serving in Anuradhapura. Since obtaining his Masters degree he joined the Department of Trade and Commerce in Colombo. Shortly thereafter, he was posted as the Consul and Trade Commissioner in Karachi, Pakistan. By then his son Waruna had been born and they all traveled together to Karachi. There they had a very large house leased by the government with two domestic helps, the local gardner, and security officer posted at the residence by the Pakistan authorities. They spent three comfortable and happy years in Pakistan before returning briefly to Colombo to serve two years at the home office. It was during their time in Pakistan that their second Son Nuwan was born. I visited them in Karachi each year on my way in and out of Sri Lanka for my annual vacations. My father too visited them in Karachi.

Thereafter, Douglas served three years from 1978 at the Embassy as the senior diplomat in charge of trade and commerce portfolio. During those years we had more frequent contacts due to the relative proximity of New York and Ottawa. It was also during that period that our father visited me in New York and visted with my sister's family in Ottawa and toured the east coast of North America.

Douglas was next posted as the Consul and Trade Commissioner at the Consulate in Bombay (Mumbai). There they had a wonderful apartment on the 21st floor of a highrise facing the Bombay harbor and I loved to visit them there just to sit on their verandah and watch the ocean and the ships come and go. After four years in Bombay he once again returned briefly for a stint at the home office. He was then posted as the Consul General and Trade Commissioner to Copenhagen, Denmark with responsibilities for all Nordic Countries.

My wife Shanthi and I took several vacations there and traveled with my sister and her family to Sweden and Norway. On one of those tours we were driving on the high mountainous road from Bergen to Oslo through the most exotic scenic area dotted with the World famous Norwegian fjords. Shanthi and Nangi were seated in the back of the car while Douglas drove along the extremely curvy and narrow road. The scenery is so enticing it is hard for any driver not to glance around, which makes the drive even more treacherous. Suddenly, a car appeared around a blind elbow bend at quite high speed. Obviously, it was someone familiar with the area to have driven in that fashion, leaving no margin for error by unfamiliar tourists. In order to avoid him, Douglas had to wear to a side and we ended up in the ditch. Luckily, the ditch saved us from toppling down a seven to eight thousand foot precipice. It is a miracle that we lived to tell the tale. Douglas was so shaken up he immediately asked me to take over the driving, although after the harrowing experience, I was in no better shape than he was.

Once when we were in Denmark my wife had a slight case of food poisoning and as a precaution we took her to the nearest hospital. They wanted to keep her overnight for observation. In the morning we learned that nothing was wrong with her. We wished to take her home because we were on our way to Moscow in a few days to attend a United Nations meeting. The hospital would not discharge her until further tests were done. They did several tests and several specialists such as gastroenterologists and gynecologists kept on checking her, keeping her in the hospital for about four days until they had done detailed and comprehensive tests and were able to rule out any serious ailments. This was the dedication that the medical staff paid to their patients. The hospital itself and the food were as good as any found in a five star hotel. The hospital had several wings in its four towers and although half were empty, they were ready to accommodate large numbers in the event of a disaster or medical emergency of any kind. At the end of the stay we received a bill with the amount due as nil. We were surprised and inquired who had paid. The response was that as we were visitors to Denmark all services were free.

At the end of his term of three years, once again Douglas returned to base and worked as Deputy Director of Foreign Trade in the Ministry in Colombo. Thereafter he was posted as Trade Commissioner at the Sri Lanka Embassy in Ottawa and finally at the Mission to the United Nations in Geneva. There he had major responsibilities to cover the organization for the General Agreement on Tariff and Trade (GATT), United Nations agencies including the U.N. Conference on Trade and Development, the International Trade Center and others. I used to visit them often because I used to travel to Geneva several times a year on official United Nations work. After a three year term there he returned to Colombo as Director of the Department of Commerce.

By then, my sister had disposed of some of her inherited properties because it was not easy to manage them from abroad. With the proceeds and ' help, she built a large and attractive residence in Nawala, Colombo. Whenever they were in Colombo they occupied it and when they went abroad it was rented. So during Douglas's final years of service when he served as the Director of the Department of Trade and Commerce, they were well settled at their home in Nawala.

* * *

My sister while abroad had acquired an interest in cosmetics and had qualified as a hair stylist. She established a small scale business in hair styling using part of the residence. By then, their two sons were at universities abroad. Waruna was in the United States, and Nuwan in Switzerland. As before, they used to visit us from time to time in New York, particularly during those years when Waruna was at U.S. universities. Whenever I went to Colombo I stayed with my sister until they went abroad.

The elder son Waruna Liyanapatabandi, after finishing his secondary education at the International School in Geneva, Switzerland, graduated with a physics honors degree from Franklin and Marshall University in Pennsylvania in the United States. He then followed an MBA course at Columbia University in New York City. While at Franklin and Marshal, he was a regular visitor to our house in New York and stayed with us while attending Columbia. Thereafter he entered the financial world in Wall Street working for Merrill Lynch as a stockbroker.

After a few years he started his own brokerage firm in Long Island, New York. He began with only an assistant and it grew to a firm that employed about twenty brokers. With the boom in the United States stock market in the late nineties he made a substantial amount of equity. He then purchased an apartment at the newly built Trump Towers adjacent to the United Nations Headquarters in Manhattan, New York. He used it as a second office and residence. In due course he sold his firm in Long Island as well as his residence there and moved to Trump Towers. This was when the Market boom was cooling. He began other ventures including an internet publishing company - New Novel. Com. He himself authored novels including one based on the famous murder case of Jon Benet Ramsey entitled 'Quiet, Samantha Foster'. They were written under the name Warren Patabendi.

Later, he was amicably separated from and divorced from his first wife, Isadora. A pretty damsel, half Swiss and half Honduran, she worked for Waruna in managing his brokerage firm and was very pleasant and close to us. We enjoyed her company whenever they visited us. Isadora later remarried and remained a close friend of Waruna. Once I asked her why they separated and she politely explained to me "Mami (uncle) we were lucky and for quite some time the marriage worked for both of us and now it is time for us to move on".

At some point after 2000 Waruna completely left the brokerage field and moved to Miami, with a very substantial amount of capital in hand. Ironically, when he wanted to enroll at Columbia, I asked him why he wanted to move from science to study business, and he responded by saying he wanted to make a sufficient amount of capital to be able to retire and play golf by the time he reached his mid forties. I said, "That sounds fine," and of course did not take him seriously.

Shortly after moving to Miami he met his second wife Sirlena Vieira, who is a Brazilian. He purchased a large apartment overlooking the ocean and settled there with his wife and their daughter. He also continued to spend substantial amounts of time in Rio de Janeiro, the hometown of his wife Sirlene, and established a small import export business there.

My sister's younger son, Nuwan, graduated from Webster University in Geneva after completing his secondary school at the International School in Copenhagan, Denmark. By the time he completed his education with a BA degree In international relations, his father, Douglas, had just retired as Director of Commerce. By then my sister, Prema had become a U.S. Immigrant and settled in New York along with Douglas and Nuwan. Her elder son, Waruna, who was by then well employed in New York.

In due course my sister established a hairdressing salon in Queens in New York City, near a residence she had purchased. Nuwan too lived with the parents and worked at Staples, a commercial enterprise in their photo and duplicating department, and eventually became a manager. Douglas helped out in the management of my sister's hairdressing establishment but generally led a retired life.

After Waruna moved to Miami, my sister and her husband followed him and moved to Miami to be closer to their elder son and the granddaughter Morgan. Nuwan remained in New York but in due course my sister arranged a marriage for him and he went to Sri

Lanka to get married. After a few years he too moved to Florida to be near his parents.

For much of our adult life, my sister and I were extremely close. We used to visit each other on every possible occasion and I spent a good part of my vacation each year at her residence. Yet, it was always a hot and cold relationship, and sadly, in our later life, we drifted apart with our contacts being more infreequent. As fate would have it, we now live in opposite coasts of the United States in our retirement. I am glad though, that I continue to have a warm relationship with her husband Douglas, his family and of course her children Waruna and Nuwan.

Chapter 6

Under the Bo tree

The next step in my education, after I mastered the Sinhala alphabet under the kind tutelage of Miss Laura at the all girls' school in Maha Ambalangoda, began when I was enrolled in grade three at the Buddhist Mixed School in Dodanduwa.

It was about this time that my Uncle Martin, who unsuccessfully sought to adopt me, made the proposal to my father that he would arrange for me to study at his old school in Galle: Richmond College. My father had other plans. He believed that I should have a good grounding in the Sinhala language and Buddhism before embarking on a western education. In retrospect, I am grateful to him as his decision helped me gain a better appreciation of my culture and strengthened my links with the country where I was born. This helped me form a bond which has survived half a century of life abroad.

I do not recollect much from the first year I spent in the village school except that my students in my class used to recite poetry and sing songs which we were supposed to memorize. This happened under a large shady tree in the garden of the school as our loud singing ensemble would have disturbed the students in other classes.

The school was located a mile or so away from my father's official bungalow by a branch of the Dodanduwa Lake. That lake was connected to the sea, flowing under the railway line and highway bridges. I used to walk back and forth along the railway line to school, first with Jagath (household help and my playmate), and later, with the other students who also walked on the track to school and back.

The school premises consisted of two half walled rectangular buildings and two small rooms with thatched roofs. The former were used as classrooms, the principal's office and the staffroom while the latter were used for the kindergarten. In the center was a large garden with a big tree. The shade of the tree was always used as a classroom for singing and the garden was used for physical training. The principal was a kind man but the students feared him, because he was the one who gave a caning whenever one misbehaved. In those days misbehavior was not seen that often in village schools.

I enjoyed my days there and hung around with an amiable bunch. Most of all what I remember of this phase in my life is the two amazing teachers: Kithsiri Kumarasinghe and Amaris, who I feel had quite an influence on me. They both belonged to the 'Hela Havula' (Association for purity in the Sinhala language) which promoted 'Helabasa' (pure Sinhala) led by Munidasa Kumaratunge, a nationally revered person. They travelled by train daily from Mihiripanne, a village about an hour south of the school and within the immediate domain of their mentor and leader of the movement. They wore the national dress (white tunic and sarong). In certain ways they were indistinguishable, like twins, particularly when it came to their enthusiasm for teaching, and the way they dealt with discipline. Yet, they had different techniques and interests that made them complement each other. I consider it a great fortune to have been nurtured by these remarkable people during my formative years.

This also meant that we students received a good grounding in Sinhala and an exposure to 'Helabasa', which enhanced our appreciation of and our ability in Sinhala. They were both poets and were able to compose poetry at will, a trait that they readily imparted to their students. By the end of my days there I had become quite good at writing poetry and enjoyed it immensely.

It was with Jagath that I honed the skills my great teachers imparted to us in school. Jagath had a natural talent for poetry, which he had picked up from his village. He used to guide me as we had much fun conversing in impromptu poetry ('Hituwana Kavi'). I carried the ability of composing poetry for a while, and wrote a poem when I went to my next school. That work was published in the College Magazine.

I still remember a poem I wrote in Sinhala on another occasion thanking my grandfather for sending me a fancy box of color pencils as my tenth birthday present. My Uncle Piyadasa, who remembered the incident, got me to recite it on the day of Seeya's funeral and it went as follows:

iS;, iq<x yukd .Õ wi,
.f,a uf.a fmdä is;;a ke<ùhhs
nf,a fmïnr uf.a iShd tjQ ;E.s nf,a
,efïjd iSfha Tng ksjka
nf,a

As the rock by the river is swept by the cooling breeze
My childish mind too lullabies with that cooling breeze
By the power of the gift my beloved Seeya sent my way
May my Seeya be blessed to traverse the 'niravanas' way

These two emminent teachers also sacrificed their time selflessly after school hours to train the talented or the interested students among us in traditional dance and drama although this meant they had to take the long train ride home quite late in the day. They put on two variety shows each year to which parents and neighbors were invited. I remember acting in the play 'Vessanthara' a story from Lord Buddha's life; I had two small roles: as the drummer carrying the Royal message to the villagers, and a role of one of the king's attendants.

They also trained us for the area schools annual dance competition. I learned the Kandyan dance form and performed at the annual show held that year at the Devapathiraja College, Ratgama. We performed the 'Gajaga Wannama', in full costume and 'pantheruwa' (Tambourine) in hand, to the tune of 'Thanath Denam Thana, Denath Thanam Dena'. These baby steps in dance, theater, and other cultural activities became lifelong interests, and without the enticing manner in which these two rare teachers inculcated an interest in these activities, I doubt very much that I would have gone on to hone these skills in my later years as a student and cultivate an abiding interest in the performing arts.

The other lingering impressions at the school in Donanduwa relate to learning arithmetic from Mr. Amaris. My father was very keen that I memorize the multiplication table (chakkare). He considered it a vital aspect of learning and not surprisingly, as he worked with numbers quite a bit in his profession-which included balancing accounts of ticket sales, making charges for transported goods and payments to employees at the railway stations he managed. He also kept elaborate books on produce, income, expenditure and payments of workers in the rubber, cinnamon and paddy lands he had inherited from my mother and grandfather. He used to wake me up at the crack of dawn and make me learn the multiplication tables, because he considered early morning the best time for studies when one's mind is fresh.

I did not relish this early morning drudgery. Perhaps as a reaction to this I became a nocturnal person, who worked by night and slept late throughout my life. I only awakened early for reasons beyond my control.

My homework and reading were always done in the late evenings and at night. In those days electricity was not easily available even in towns and consequently the railway bungalows had none. So the premises were lit by oil lamps and my studying companion was a kerosene oil lamp with a wick that had to be delicately handled due to the potential fire hazards involved.

I also enjoyed participating, for the first time, in competitive sports. This was seasonal and restricted to the annual sports meet. At the time, being at a provincial school, the events held at the sports meet were mostly village games; the Sack race, where competitors got into a gunny bag (large sack) and hopped along as fast as one could. The tug o' war, and the Banis race, where competitors eat banis (buns) and the one who eats fastest is declared the winner. But there were also 50 and 100 yard sprints and the quarter and half mile races, high jump and long jump. I never won the under 10 sprints as we had among us Jayawickrama, a well made boy who dominated the dashes. A competitive spirit was inculcated in me at an early age through the participation in the annual sports meet, to which we always looked forward to.

I also played cricket with friends on and off. This was mostly at the home of Ranjith Weerasekara who lived not far from the school. He had several brothers senior to him who often played soft ball cricket in their large garden. I also visited friends of my father who lived near the railway station and who had a tennis court. The players were much older than I and were not attending our school, but I did learn to handle a tennis racket playing with them.

It was with my classmates Ranjith, Jayawickrama, Yapa and Hemachandra that I mostly hung around in school and after school. Jaya and Hema were the best students academically in our class while I was an average student.

They are the only students I remember from those days except for M.D.H. Jayasekare, who later went along with me to Richmond College. His father was Peter Silva an oriental scholar and lecturer at the Peradeniya University. My friend became a graduate teacher and spent his teaching career in the Maldives. After his retirement he returned to Colombo and took residence in Maharagama. A few years back on hearing that he was not well, three other friends from Richmond days and I visited him. We learned that he was suffering from Parkinson's disease. He was pleased to see us and we were happy to visit him and reminisce about the old days. He is the friend I have known the longest in life and with whom I still have contact.

Yapa joined the Postal Department and once I visited him while he was functioning as the Postmaster in Bandarawella. I have lost track of the rest, and remember no other boys but the five mentioned here.

Many years later, when I was in New York, Ananda De Silva who had come to the United States on a Fulbright Scholarship, called me up and apparently was rather miffed that I had no recollection of him from the school days in Dodanduwa. While I do not remember the incident, he branded me as a proud person and was offended enough to relate the story to others. I learned of his reaction years after the incident. Later I came to know him because, ironically, Shanthi was married to him before I met her.

There were also several girls in our class. I remember two. One was the daughter of a friend of my father, Doreen Sumanaweera, whose family lived near the school, by the railway tracks. The other was Yasomali Rodrigo from Panadura, niece of a teacher who lived with her aunt and was in the class ahead of us. They were both very attractive. Sweet Doreen, glowing with youths' effervescence, had flock of ashen hair that framed her pretty face. Yasomali was an ebony skinned beauty who could sing like a lark.

Doreen became a trained teacher and I later visited her once as her family was known to my father. I last knew her many years ago when she was a teacher at Christ Church Convent in Baddegama. I completely lost track of Yasomali after leaving the Dodanduwa School.

* * *

While living in Dodanduwa, school was not only the place of learning for me because my father insisted that I visit the priest at Shailabimbarama Viharaya (Buddhist temple) every other day to learn Buddhism and the Pali language. I did not like being asked to learn Pali (a dead eastern language) by copying the alphabet over and over but I did enjoy visiting the temple. This was mostly because the priests were kind and on the way to and from the temple

I played marbles and climbed fruit trees to pluck fruits on the temple premises. There was one other student who visited the priest to learn from the priest as I did. I am not sure I learned much, except for cultivating some sort of an appreciation of Buddhist culture. This might very well have been my father's intention when he arranged for me to go through the drudgery. In retrospect, I feel privileged to have walked the hallowed and historic premises of Shailabimbarama Viharaya established in 1802.

Less than a kilometer from the railway station, the temple had a memorial complete with a statue of Bhikku, Ven Sasanalankara Vinayacharya Siri Piyaratna Tissa Nayake Thera (known as Dodanduwe Piyaratna Nayake Thera), who placed Dodanduwa in the annals of our country's education history. He was a pious and erudite monk whose efforts to revive Buddhist education resulted in the establishment of the Piyaratna Vidyalaya, the first Buddhist school established almost one and a half centuries ago in 1869. It reminds one of an age of prosperity and bygone resurgence during the latter half of the 19th century when Buddhist leaders like the Most Venerable Hikkaduwe Sri Sumangala Nayake Thera attracted Western intellectuals like the American theosophist Col. Henry Steele. Steele came to the Island to learn the rich cultural and religious heritage of our country. He later became the leader of the Buddhist revival in Sri Lanka, and his leadership was followed by Anagarika Dharmapala and other national leaders in continuing the resurgence of the Buddhist educational system in the Island. A marble image of the Buddha was found at Kaveripattanam in India, and the French Governor of the district, who was approached by the Venerable Sasammatha Dhammasara Thera, chief incumbent of the temple at Dodanduwa at the time, gifted the statue to the temple. Later a second image of the Buddha, which was found at the same site, smaller in size, was offered to the temple by the residents of this Indian port town.

This was possible because Dodanduwa had its own port, an inlet formed along an outcrop of rocks at Dodanduwa, adjacent to the Rathgama lagoon. Its location made it an accessible place for religious resurgence in the 18th and 19th centuries. In 1808 the Most Venerable Kathaluwe Gunaratana Tissa Nayake Thera and his lay followers set sail from Dodanduwa in a local vessel for Myanmar (Burma) to bring back the tradition of *Upasampada*, (higher ordination) from that country to Ceylon. Unfortunately, Buddhism and ecclesiastical development were under continuous onslaughts of the Portuguese, Dutch and later the British and they continued to suffer and decline. There was an even earlier visit to Myanmar by the Venerable Kapugama Dhammakkanda Thera from Dadalla, and Ven Bopagoda Sirisumana Thera of Rathgama, who also left by a sailing vessel from Dodanduwa in 1786. These devoted theras set up the Shailabimbarama Vihara in Dodanduwa in 1802.

The harbor at Dodanduwa had been a small port of call for sailing vessels in the past centuries even before the Portuguese set foot in the country. It had brought prosperity to the adjacent villages. The fishermen of Dodanduwa were famous for their salted fish, which found a ready market all along the western seaboard and abroad. Local, Indian and Maldivian sailing vessels called at this port, as well as at Beruwala, Weligama, Devinuwara, Colombo, Chilaw, Mannar and even as far away as Trincomalee and Batticaloa.

Trading was done with vessels that came from the Indian port of Trichinapoly, Nagapattanam and Kaveripattanam and the goods that changed hands ranged from the famous salt fish (Jaadi) of Dodanduwa to clay roof tiles, clay pottery and handloom textiles. People of the area were prosperous and the fish caught in the locality were either salted or sold fresh. When the sea became rough during the southwest monsoon, they sailed to fish in the seas off the east coast. The sailing craft were as large as 60 or 70 feet long, forming a veritable fishing and trading fleet, sometimes drawn up on the beach like the wall of a fortress. I and my friends looked forward to the Maldivian sailing boats that brought seasonal bulto (a hard but tasty candy) and other sweetmeats known as' bondi- haluwa. We also always enjoyed the Jaadi with most of our meals at home.

The port was also a natural swimming pool for us, where we spent numerous hours enjoying the fresh blue waters of the Indian Ocean.

* * *

Though I did not know it at the time, I would soon be stepping out of this enchanting "garden" of my childhood to discover wider, greener pastures. But return I would, in my mind's eye, again and again throughout the years, to these carefree innocent days of my life in Dodanduwa.

Part 2

The Dream Begins

*"All our dreams can come true,
if we have the courage to pursue them"*

– Walt Disney

Chapter 7

Nisi Dominus Frustra

On a cloudless, sunny morning in early January my father dropped me with a trunk full of clothes, at the hostel of Richmond College, Galle. I was eleven years old. The year was 1949.

My father's decision that the time was now ripe for me to move on in my education was made after he was transferred from Dodanduwa to Ganewatte. His choice of a new school was Richmond College, one of the best schools in the country and undoubtedly a premier school in southern Sri Lanka.

The history of Richmond College, which was to be not only my school but my home as well in the years ahead, is connected with the pioneer Wesleyan Missionaries who landed in Ceylon on the 29th of June 1814. On the sailing ship in which they came was the Rev. Benjamin Clough, who remained in Galle and opened the first Wesleyan School in all Asia in the home of Mr. E. R. Gunaratne on Dickson Road, Galle. In 1857 the Rev. Joseph Rippon, who was then stationed in Galle, with daring foresight persuaded the Mission to purchase 17 acres of land for the school. Rev. Rippon had his theological training at Richmond College in Surrey in the UK, situated on the banks of the famous Thames River. Either out of love for his former college or because of the scenic splendor of the local counterpart, which was undoubtedly similar to the grandeur of the Thames, he renamed the place where the school now stands as Richmond Hill. Later, a girl's school established on the same location was named Rippon after Rev. Rippon.

The Wesleyan missionary, Rev. George Baugh is credited with changing the name of the school from the 'Boys' Anglo- Vernacular School' to Galle High School, which was later renamed in 1876 as Richmond College because it was located on Richmond Hill.[1] Rev. Samuel Langdon was its first principal. He is also credited with organizing a proper school program. In 1878 a Wesleyan Church was built at the entrance to the school property at the foot of the hill. The new church had a Victorian architectural style with stained glass windows that still shines in all their glory. The School began with a staff of 8 and 104 pupils on the roll. Nisi Dominus Frustra, the motto of Richmond College is a Latin phrase which means "If not the Lord, [it is] in vain".

When I entered Richmond the principal was Mr. E. R. De Silva O.B.E., a former student of the school, who had the distinction of becoming the first Ceylonese principal of Richmond in 1940. This was a period which saw major changes in the educational structure of Ceylon. The Free Education Scheme, which was devised by the then Minister of Education Mr. C. W. W. Kannangara, another illustrious a former student of Richmond, was being implemented at the time.

After I had left the school, in 1962, Richmond College, which had been owned by the Methodist Mission, was nationalized. Mr. D. G. Welikala, the first head of Richmond under state management, was also its first Buddhist principal. With the takeover, the Methodist Vernacular School on Richmond Hill was amalgamated with the Richmond College.

The last two British principals at Richmond were Rev. W J T Small (1906–1922) who returned from the UK during my years at Richmond to spend his retirement, and Rev. Alec A Sneath (1922–1939). I still can picture the day when Rev. Small was welcomed with garlands and walked up the hill with a parade of students, teachers and alumni following him.

There followed a welcome reception to which the parents were invited. My parents were there. I still have a picture of the reception with my stepmother seated among the audience that was published in the school annual magazine.

Following Rev. Small and Rev. Sneath, there were six alumni who became principals of Richmond: Mr. E.R. De Silva (1940–1957), Mr. A.S. Wirasinghe (1957–1961), Rev. Claude Ivor de Silva (1961), S. Kariyawasam (1973–1977), Mr. B. Suriarachchi (1979–1986), and Mr. S. Illaperuma (1986–1994). The first two were my principals, the third my vice-principal; and the last three were fellow students of mine at Richmond.

The school has produced many notable alumni, including Presidents, Prime Ministers, Cabinet Ministers and Prominent Legislators. Among them are His Excellency Mahinda Rajapaksa, the current President of Sri Lanka and former Prime Minister; Hon. Dr Wijeyananda Dahanayake, former Prime Minister of Ceylon; Hon. Dr. C. W. W. Kannangara, former Minister of Education and the "Father of Free Education", in Ceylon; and Hon. P.de S. Kularatne, also a former Minister of Education. They are the shining stars among many cabinet ministers, including half a dozen that were in school during my time. My close friends Vasudewa Nanayakkara, Minister of National Integration; and Chamal Rajapaksa, former cabinet minister and currant speaker of the parliament are currently functioning at those levels. Former students of Richmond adorn every profession in the country. A full list of those up to my days at Richmond is provided in the Annex.

I grew up knowing the great heights these and other prominent alumni had reached, and I had a great desire to emulate them. Without doubt, they provided the inspiration to persevere in the pursuit of excellence even though this seemed as elusive as a mirage on the Colombo-Galle road on a hot April day.

I cannot but note some semblance of similarities, if there were any, during the early years of my life and the life of one of the greatest of Richmond alumni, Hon. C.W.W. Kannangara. He was born in Randombe, Ambalangoda not far from my home. He attended the local school as I did, and went to Richmond at the age of 12. At Richmond he showed an interest in a variety of subjects and activities in addition to academics. He was a good sportsman, played cricket and football. He was the captain of the college cricket team, a member of both English and Sinhala debating teams, and took part in drama, as I did. While at Richmond, he showed an interest in law and entered the Law College. There end the similarities. Unlike me, he excelled in academics at Richmond and earned the highest marks for arithmetic and mathematics in the entire British Empire at the Cambridge Senior Examination in 1904. Later in life, he became a national leader in the independence movement of the country. Still later, as Minister of Education in 1944, he introduced free education to all Sri Lankans, from the cradle to the grave, providing many of us with the key to prosper in and out of Sri Lanka.

In January 1949, when I entered Richmond, the home to such luminaries, I was assigned to the Lower Lincoln dormitory which was the one next to the kiddies' dormitory. It was a long dormitory with the top half of the wall on one side covered with wooden trellis work that gave it ample light and ventilation. The dorm accommodated perhaps thirty students who were mostly in grades four and five.

I had taken the entrance exam to enter Richmond Collage before leaving Dodanduwa. When the time came for me to enter the new school in January 1949, my father took me to see the principal. Although I had taken the exam I had little knowledge of English, and the principal having seen the results, recommended to my father that I should be entered to grade four as the medium of instruction in grade six at the time was English. This was a shock to me as I had just completed grade five at the school in Dodanduwa and was looking forward to entering grade six. My father readily agreed with the principal, and I had no choice whatsoever regarding the matter. A factor that the principal took into account in his recommendation was that luckily, I was young enough to be in grade four. Once my father agreed to his suggestion, we were escorted out of his office with the principal wishing me well in my school career at Richmond.

*　*　*

From the main street level of the Richmond Hill junction a driveway winds its way up past the other school buildings a distance of a little over a kilometer, eneding at the playground at the very top of the hill. Adjacent to the playground is the hostel. The hill is perhaps the highest point in the Galle area and provides dazzling vistas. On a clear morning looking northwest, one can see as far as *Sri Pada* (Adam's Peak - Sri Lanka's holy mountain sacred since ancient times to Buddhists, Hindus, Muslims and Christians), the second highest mountain in the country, located about 100 miles inland. On the opposite side are scenic vistas stretching towards the ocean, only about three to four miles away. In view of the elevation the climate is most agreeable, although seasonally somewhat cool in the mornings.

Richmond was a serene place disturbed only by the hustle and bustle of the children moving around in the school or playing on the fields. The hostel was a conglomeration of ten buildings and a chapel. Except for two buildings, a junior dorm and a sickroom, the others were long hall-like buildings with covered corridors around them. They were built to connect each other through covered walkways. The sickroom is built about one hundred yards away from the rest of the structures. Two of the interconnected buildings were used as a study hall and the dining room respectively. The rest were dormitories. There was an out building with toilets and another for washrooms and showers, which were also connected through a long covered walkway.

On one end of the Lower Lincoln dorm where I lived during my early days at Richmond, was the room of the dorm master, Mr. Dunstan Fernando. He was an old boy of Richmond who later became vice-principal at Richmond and principal of Wesley College. He was a teacher of English literature and mathematics. Having studied in the U.K., he was quite well schooled in western ways and western music.

We were mortally afraid of him as he was quick to resort to the cane at the slightest misbehavior, as his preferred form of discipline.

At the other end of the dorm was the cubicle for the prefect-in-charge, Mr. Elmo Perera, who was an accomplished sportsman at Richmond. He later became the Surveyor-General of the country and on retirement, a lawyer who championed human rights causes and argued many fundamental rights cases before the Supreme Court. His vigor elicited the chagrin of the judges. Elmo was a very warm person with a great sense of humor but equally fast at disciplining his boys. I had a good relationship with him over the years and was fortunate to know someone as principled as he was, even at great cost to him. On one occassion, he was reprimanded by the Chief Justice and the Supreme Court for having vigorously challenged their authority while arguing a case of fundamental rights before the court.

I was happy to have had M.H.D.H. Jayasekare as my neighbor at the Lower Lincoln dorm, for he too came from the Dodanduwa School. I found a certain amount of security in his company in the new environs. On my other side was Munidasa Abeywickrama, a talented sportsman and a happy-go-lucky fellow who did not take life too seriously. He was the son of Mr. Henry Abeywickrama who became a minister in the cabinet of Sri Lanka and served in many portfolios over a long period. Although Jayasekare and I maintained contact, I lost touch with Munidasa shortly after I left school. Along with them were Ranjith Mendis, Wilfrey Rodrigo, the Kahingala brothers, Freddie Armstrong, Senarath Mendis, S.L. Amarasiri, and Dayananda Jayasuriya. We all basically associated together throughout our Richmond days.

After I left school, I lost contact with Mendis, Rodrigo, and the Kahingalas. Freddie became a planter and I used to see him on and off. Senarath Mendis entered the Law College a couple of years after me and we continued to have close contacts after he became a lawyer and set up practice at the Balapitiya courts. His house abutted the Galle-Colombo road in Ahungalla near my hometown of

Ambalangoda. I used to stop there when passing by, even briefly for a chat, and I continue to do so to the present. Amarasiri graduated with a degree in chemistry and had a long technical career ending up as head of the country's Tea Research Institute and the Coconut Research Institute. Although I did not see him for long periods I met him whenever I visited the Kandy area where the institutes were based.

Dayananda Jayasuriya (DJ) was from an illustrious family in Walasmulla deep in the south of the country. He was a lanky, handsome individual. DJ was the most talented of all the boys of our age both in academics and sports. He was a brilliant student and an outstanding sportsman to whom academics and sports were second nature. We were competitors throughout our sports career with one of us becoming team captain and the other vice captain of cricket, soccer and athletics at different age levels. While I had to work hard to achieve success in sports, everything came naturally to DJ. He later graduated with a degree in English and taught at St. Thomas' College, Gurutalawe, and at the university preparatory level at Aquinas College in Colombo. Then he went into private sector management.

When I saw him last he was functioning as Personnel (human resources) Manager of the prestigious State Trading Corporation. I telephoned to say I was in Colombo and he promptly asked me to come and see him late in the morning in his office. As soon as I walked into his office he told his assistant to mind the shop and went out with me to Nippon Hotel, a Japanese establishment nearby. I thought by then he was sober and settled down in a comfortable job, and that we were going to have a cup of tea and chat about our schooldays. I ordered a cup of tea as it was about ten in the morning, but to my surprise he ordered double arrack (the local brew). We chatted for a while and it was with some regret and difficulty that I managed to leave. He seemed to need company in order to enjoy his drinks. During our conversation he told me briefly about his health problems in the past. I was struck especially by the request he made as I got up to leave. As he patted my back, he said: "I hope you will place a red rose on my coffin when I pass away." I laughed, and took it as a statement made in jest.

A few days later, I happened to be at the Central Bank of Ceylon and dropped by to see his elder brother Cyril, who was working there. He had played cricket for our rival school (Mahinda) during my time and I knew him quite well. It was then that I was informed of the full extent of his delicate health situation requiring several hospitalizations. I failed to notice this when I met him bcause he looked quite healthy. He passed away not too long thereafter, at the very young age of about forty. Regrettably, I was not there to place a red rose on my childhood friend's coffin.

* * *

In the hostel, life began with the ringing of a bell at six in the morning. Immediately after the bell everyone had to gather at the playground for PT (Physical Training). After twenty minutes of stretching, sit ups and slow jogging, everyone was sent off for the morning ablutions. At the time the toilets were bucket latrines and to use one you had to wait in line amidst good humored banter. There were no wash basins and everyone ended up at one of several outdoor taps which were the locations for cleaning and washing. Towards the end of my days a new building with modern amenities was finally completed at the school.

The scene at the time in school hostels is well depicted in the recent autobiographical novel *Cat's Table* by Michael Ondaatje (a canadian of Sri Lankan origin). He recounts the pranks of one of his schoolmates at St. Thomas' College Mount Lavinia, Ceylon, as follows: "he was especially celebrated after he managed to lock our boarding-house master in the junior toilet for several hours to protest the revolting lavatories at the school (you squatted over the hole of hell and washed yourself afterwards with water from a rusty tin that once held Tate & Lyle golden syrup 'Out of the strong came forth sweetness,' I would always remember). He was whipped and expelled from school for a week, and Warden gave a stirring speech that morning at the chapel that damned him. Of course, no lesson was learned from the episode-by anyone. Years later, when an old boy of the school donated funds to St. Thomas' for a new cricket pavilion, my friend Senaka said, "First they should construct some decent bogs".

Until I read Ondaatje, I had assumed we in the provincial towns were damned to such conditions while the Colombo colleagues enjoyed the luxury of more modern facilities. Even at this late stage it is some consolation to know that most in our generation suffered the same fate.

At seven, the bell rang for the study hour and everyone was at his desk in the study hall, silently engrossed in his work. The master-in-charge for the week, and a prefect, were on supervision, but this did not deter the courageous from indulging in other forms of activity such as writing letters or playing 'book cricket' (an imaginary game of cricket with the score kept by turning over pages in a book and adding up the random page numbers that turn up). Whenever someone was caught, he was 'put on the bench' (made to stand on his chair for the rest of the time) so everyone could observe the delinquent. After the study hour, the bell rang for breakfast that was waiting in the dining room. Breakfast was usually *indiappa and kirihodi* (string hoppers and white-curry-gravy) or bread, butter and jam, along with tea and milk. Those who paid extra were served eggs or a glass of milk. Some of us who were into sports thought that it was essential to have an egg and glass of milk in the mornings to perform at optimal level on the playground, for which the parents had to meet the bill. Of course, no one told us then that there is something known as cholesterol that will require you later in life to take a daily tablet to unclog the arteries that the ample eggs and milk helped clog.

After breakfast we descended the hill to get to the classroom. The school began with an assembly in the College Hall. The school uniform was blue shorts and white shirts at the primary level, and white shirts and long white trousers at the secondary levels. During the assembly the juniors occupied the front half and the seniors the back half. While more than eighty percent of the students were Buddhist, there were a few Muslims. The rest were Christian, mostly Methodists. The Buddhists had to stay in silence, gathered in the hall until a short service was conducted for the Christians in the adjoining premises. Once that was done and assembled in the hall the teachers gathered on the podium followed by the principal with great dignity, with his black cloak draped over his immaculately pressed full suit.

Assembly formally started with the vice-principal playing a record of a classical instrumental piece on the gramophone which in retrospect looked a monstrosity with the horn-like contraption bulging out and the records, the size of a large pizza, turning round and round. At first, I was flabbergasted by the pomp and pageantry, and the classical music was strange to my ears (which till then was attuned to only 'Kavi'-Sinhala poetry). The music was followed by a brief presentation by a teacher, usually on good morals. Often the lesson was offered by reciting a story or an example of a well known person or incident. Among a few that stuck in my mind was the example of how Demosthenes got over his disability of stuttering and became a great orator by perseverance. Several years later, I would write an essay on perseverance in the college magazine. Naturally, I referred to the example of Demosthenes. The principal closed the assembly with announcements such as welcoming and introducing new staff members, important upcoming events, and results of exams and sports events. Then the students would file out to their classrooms.

* * *

My first year in grade four was rather strange for me. Mainly because English was liberally used except for the Sinhala language class. I was in some ways lucky to have had Mr. M.T.S. Fernando as the class teacher. He was one of the teachers who taught Sinhala language. At the time and for a long time thereafter, he was the only teacher dressed in the national dress (white kurutha and sarong). The class teacher had limited functions, mostly administrative such as marking attendance and ensuring that the records of the students were maintained so that the end of term reports could be prepared. But I felt a little secure knowing that I could speak to him, if need be, in Sinhala. We were taught arithmetic (mostly addition, subtraction and multiplication), English, Sinhala, music and art. It was not too difficult to follow the classes. Arithmetic was mostly numbers, and I knew the subject better than anyone. I had already done more advanced work in grade five of the vernacular school. music, art and Sinhala did not require much understanding of English either. Music was the most English oriented course and it made me uncomfortable.

My first challenge at Richmond was to learn English. This was important because I was to live in the school hostel where the practice of charging five cents each time anyone spoke in Sinhala had just been lifted when I joined. Almost all the other students spoke English well enough, although some occasionally used a generous sprinkling of Sinhala as well. For a while I struggled with this alien language but with the help of 'broken English' (a mixture of English and Sinhala), I eventually managed to get along with the boys in the dorm and in grade four.

Grade five was exactly the same and during those two years I caught up with most of the students as far as English was concerned, particularly as most of the conversation in school and at the hostel was in English. Of course, I had trials and tribulations as I tackled conversational English. I was one of those identified as someone 'who murders the king' (*raja maranawa*), a phrase attributed to those who abused the King's English. Occasions that led to such comments included a moment when, because of the lack of the right vocabulary, I happened to refer to someone who was walking towards us by saying "look at that chap he is coming yellow, yellow" (meaning he was scratching as he walked). Kaha in Sinhala has two meanings; scratching and the color yellow and I had thought scratching in English was called yellow.

Thus, the days spent at Richmond began with slight hiccups. My time there was almost a decade of carefree fun and frolic mixed with a first rate, all round education acquired in the wonderfully homely and historic city of Galle. Those were some of the best years of my life.

FOOTNOTE:

[1] There is some conjecture concerning the early history of Richmond College in the period prior to 1882. Some have noted that the school started in 1814 and became Richmond Institute for some and the Richmond Hill Anglo-Vernacular School to others in 1858. With the addition of the foundation classes in 1876 it became a collegiate school and renamed The Galle High School, while others point out that the latter was established as a separate institution in May 1876, and the former was amalgamated as its primary school in September of the same year. In 1882, on a suggestion by the Rev. Samuel Hill, The Galle High School was renamed as Richmond College. Since the publication of this memoire, the origins of the school has been researched meticulously, based on available historical records, and the findings have been published in a seminal work authored by Ananda Dias Jayasinghe titled, *The Forgotten History of Richmond College: A Documentary Survey.*

Chapter 8

College maketh a man

Strange as it seems now, unknowingly, at the age of twelve as a student of grade five I had already mapped out my future in an essay I wrote for a class assignment. Describing what I would do when I would be a man, I wrote:

> When I am a man I wish to be a proctor. I like to wear long white trousers, black coats, and black ties. I will earn as much as I can and build a grand house for me to live in, and buy a car. But I will not be proud. I will go to the Courts every morning and do my best. Till I am too old to work I shall serve there.
>
> If I earn enough I will use some of my money to make a big bridge in the village where I live. I shall help the poor people in my village as much as I can. I will write letters to the Newspapers about them.
>
> After some years as a proctor I will try, to enter Parliament. If I become a member I will do my best to serve my people.
>
> After that I will sell all my lands and house in Ceylon and go to England. I will live there till I die. I feel happy when I think of my future. The only thing I am sad about is that I may not always speak the truth when I become a proctor.
>
> [Richmond College Magazine, 1950]

Undoubtedly, although there were moments when I had been reticent during the initial two years of my life at Richmond, I enjoyed the great excitement of being in a new environment that offered many new experiences. By the time I moved on from the primary school to Form 1 (sixth standard) I had picked up enough English not to be out of place among my classmates. This was the result of the life in the hostel and the extracurricular activities that I participated in.

By the time I was in grade five I was bold enough to begin writing articles, prodded to a great extent by teachers who encouraged the students to contribute to the annual school magazine. "When I am A Man", written when I was still in primary school was the first essay my English teacher chose to recommend for publication. It is worth recalling that instinctively, and perhaps prophetically, I had written of becoming a lawyer and living abroad, possibly more because I was attracted to outward trappings than for thought out reasoning!

In form IV (senior prep), I wrote an article on perseverance using Demosthenes to illustrate my thoughts on the subject. In form V (senior class), I wrote a satirical essay on fashions of the day, and still later a satire in Sinhala that is contained in the annex. They were all selected for publication in the annual school magazine.

Next, I took a foray for the first time into political issues, writing in the Richmond College Magazine about the need for the newly decolonized Asian countries to forge ahead with an agenda of peace to confront the tensions of the cold war. The Five Principles or *Pancha Sila* elaborated by the Asian Heads of State led by Jawaharlal Nehru in June 1954 formed the basis of the article. The principles dealt with the concepts of territorial integrity, non-aggression, non-interference, equality, and peaceful co-existence. I used them as the essential elements for my argument for a peaceful world that assures economic and social development for all nations. It was also my first written reference to the role of the United Nations, referred to then as the U.N.O. My final article was in the 1957 issue of the magazine, titled "Ends and Means." It dealt with the means necessary to reach in the end-- a better world which offers every one equality of opportunity free from the fear of war and want, devoid of nationalistic passions and power politics, nurtured by international cooperation, and governed by principles of international law. The essay concluded as follows:

> We must come to realize the absurdity of today's civilization based upon nationalism, power politics and its consequent militarism. The future world let us hope will be based not merely upon economic and political competition and exploitation but upon world-wide social cooperation and spiritual ideas of give and take. If that becomes our motive, the end in view will not remain an ideological utopia. If pessimism is banished and universal cooperation established, we can reach that advance in society during our life time—when each of us will be able to live in comfort and take pleasure in our work; when we could have a world in which not guns, but the bells shall sound, where love and affection will reign, and where joy and happiness will be not the exception, but the rule.

Though some of the writings may very well be characterized as idealistic, they nevertheless surprise me to the extent that they dealt with international affairs, international law and cooperation, subjects that were the center of focus in my adult career.

At Richmond, apart from the academic activities, everyone was encouraged to participate in the theater and the choir. With great tepidity I ventured slowly into these extracurricular activities. I first ventured in to this realm by playing a minor role in the primary school play 'Snow White and the Seven Dwarfs'.

Both the primary school and secondary school plays were produced mostly in English, but included at least one Sinhala play. By the second year, I was a keen participant in the Sinhala play as I was chosen for a major role at the audition by Mr. P.D.O. Christopher, who produced almost all the Sinhala plays throughout the years I was at Richmond.

Mr. Christopher was not only an outstanding teacher of arithmetic in the primary school, but also the Cub Master. He was a "no-nonsense- type" of teacher who nevertheless attracted the respect of his students. Both in class and during extracurricular activities conducted by him, we learned many of life's lessons; such as what it means to be honest, courageous, and meticulous. Though these moral lessons were a part of the education of cubs, what was special was that even in class and in other activities too, he inculcated in us a great sense of responsibility and concern for your own welfare and that of others. He was a teacher's teacher who taught by example rather than by articulation. I have often thought of him in many situations throughout my life, and felt grateful to him for having imparted such great gifts to me during my formative years.

An outstanding producer of Sinhala plays, Mr. Christopher wrote his own scripts for the school productions. His characterizations were unique.

Through the years I learned a great deal from him regarding theater. I took part in almost all his semiannual plays.

The Sinhala plays of the Senior School were produced by our senior geography teacher Mr. P.J.H. Gunasekara, who went on to become the principal of our rival school, Mahinda. In 1956 I took part in his play Dittha Mangalika, a Jataka story.

It was around this time that I came under the influence of Gamini Hattatuwagama (G.K.), who was in the university entrance class and was the lead actor in the senior school productions. Even though G.K. was not living in the hostel (he was living with his parents just across from the College), he helped my dorm to stage two plays for the annual theater day in two consecutive years. It was an informal event at the hostel, when each dorm put up a play with the help of prefects and senior students. G.K. graduated with a degree in English, as an outstanding student under the highly respected professors E.F.C. Ludowyck and H.A. Passe. Both of these professors had been teachers at Richmond. G.K. later came back temporarily to teach at Richmond. While on the staff he produced plays in English and Sinhala for a year or two during my senior years. That was when I highly benefited from his guidance. He inculcated in me an abiding interest in theater of all forms. G.K. went on to become a university lecturere at Peradeniya and Kelaniya universities. He became a nationally recognized writer, producer, director, actor and critic, but was most famous as the father of the 'street theater' that he introduced to the country.

Mr. Shelton Wirasingha, the vice-principal at Richmond, was also an exponent of theater. He produced the senior English plays in which GK had taken leading roles. GK is said to have noted that the role of Shylock in the Merchant of Venice, which he played at Richmond, made a lasting impression on him. I used to often sit watching the seniors rehearse, while my classmates might have been in the library studying, and I was deeply impressed by Mr. Wirasingha as director, and G.K. and colleagues as actors in the English plays.

Theater unarguably was an important part of the education at Richmond. Not only GK, but both Prof. E.F.C. Ludowyck, who gave form to modern English theater in Ceylon, and Prof. Ediriweera Sarathchandra, who gave birth to modern Sinhala theater with his productions of *Maname* and *Sinhabahu*, were old boys of Richmond. I carried this interest in theater that was nurtured by GK and Shelton Wirasingha beyond Richmond. Though living abroad I made it a point to see almost all well known productions during my many visits to the Island. I also feel privileged to have seen more plays around the world than someone born in Sri Lanka could ever imagine. We will offer more about that later.

I consider G.K. a mentor not only in drama but also in public speaking. I used to admire him and his colleagues in the debating team, which at the time was exclusively in English. It gave me a thrill to watch GK with his enormous vocabulary handle many national and international debating issues with such ease and poise. Among his colleagues in the debating team I remember Prassana Dhanayake, who went on to become a Major in the army commanding the Singha

Regiment; Lynton De Silva, an executive at the Bank of Ceylon; J.L.A. Mendis, an academic; Kingsly Wickramaratne, head of a large commercial establishment; and Turin Abeyratne, a school principal. Also John Dhanapala who after graduation came back to teach on the Richmond staff and became my soccer coach. Their speeches were well prepared, full of substance, and well delivered. The impromptu responses with flights of oratory, and often laced with humor and sarcasm were even more enjoyable and instructive to admirers like me.

It was this experience that prompted me to take part in elocution. In the beginning Richmond conducted only English elocution, but by the mid-fifties Sinhala elocution was also offered. I took part in annual elocution contests and progressively did reasonably well in both competitions.

By the time I was in form five, at the end of which one takes the Senior School Certificate (SSC) public examination, I was quite competent. In 1956 I won the English Elocution Senior Contest. As the winner's award, I received the Tudor Edition of the *Complete Works of William Shakespeare* edited by Professor Peter Alexander. The beautifully bound volume was in a casing embossed with the College crest. It was presented to me at the annual prize giving celebrations by Lady Syres the wife of the High Commissioner (Ambassador) of the United Kingdom to Ceylon at the time.

The book still remains with me as a cherished possession. Though the sixteenth century Shakespearean English was not my cup of tea, I got through reading *Hamlet* and *Romeo and Juliet*. Later in the English literature classes we had the opportunity to read in modern English some of Shakespeare's plays, like *The Merchant of Venice*, *As you Like it*, *Macbeth* and *The Taming of the Shrew* under the guidance of wonderful English teachers Mr. Shelton Wirasingha and Mrs. Florance Jayawardane. But my favourite book among the text books used in class was *A Tale of Two Cities*, read in the class of Mr. Walter May in form four (Senior Prep). The novel by Charles Dickens, set in London and Paris before and during the

French Revolution, depicted the plight of the French peasantry demoralized by the French aristocracy in the years leading up to the revolution, and the corresponding brutality demonstrated by the revolutionaries toward the former aristocrats in the early years of the revolution. Shelton Wirasingha was a first rate motivator, always making suggestions whether in class or on the field of sports. I remember how he encouraged us to read books such as *Walden,* by the famous American writer Henry David Thoreau, a novel based on life in the woods that inculcates in one a deep appreciation of the environment; and *Brave New World*, a novel on societal change by the British writer Aldous Huxley. Many of us did not immerse in those classics at the time. But we carried with us an inquisitiveness, which lingered long enough for a few of us to indulge in reading them later with great rewards.

Among the finalists in the English elocution contest were Vasudewa Nanayakkara (Vasu); Lalith Edirisinghe, who became an editor of the leading national paper *The Sunday Observer;* Tyrone Jayawardane, who became an executive at Richard Pieris & Company, a well known commercial establishment; and Lakshman Wickramasinge, who became an executive at the Central Bank of Ceylon and later a Scout Commissioner at the Headquarters of the Scout Movement in Sri Lanka.

In the Sinhala contest I was a finalist on most occasions. The year I won the English contest the Sinhala contest was won by Sena Nanayakkare, who became a physician and settled down in the UK with a successful practice in medicine. For many years he was the President and the live wire of the Richmond College Alumni Association in the U.K. I was very pleased to have been invited to be the Chief Guest at their annual Dinner Dance in London. None of us was any match to Vasu, who was far ahead of the rest of us in his oratorical prowess. Those abilities took him to the highest levels of oratory, which he displayed in abundance both in our country's parliament and on the political stage. He had over half a century as a preeminent politician in Sri Lanka. During the course of his career he has been a parliamentarian, a cabinet minister and a presidential candidate. It was a privilege to have matched skills in elocution and debating with such a naturally gifted orator.

Having honed our public speaking skills in elocution contests, we also became members of the college debating teams. I was a member of both the English and Sinhala debating teams. G.K. again was my inspiration and guide as I tried to emulate his incomparable debating style. My teammates were Punya Ilayperuma, who became a leading lawyer and regretfully passed away at his prime; Neil Dias, an outstanding lawyer who contested parliamentary elections; Vijaya Dhanayake, who became the mayor of Galle and a Member of Parliament, and he was a nephew of the former Prime Minister Wijayananda Dhanayake; and Tissa Wirasinghe, who became a principal of a leading Kandy school and later a respected educationalist. In retrospect it is interesting to note that most of them became lawyers or politicians. Their debating skills would have served them well in either profession.

We debated international issues such as 'Nuclear War', 'Regional Cooperation', and national issues such as pros and cons of the 'Death Penalty', the 'Dowry System', and 'Free Education'. In view of later developments arising from ethnic issues that led to a terrorist war in the country, it is ironic to note now, that among the topics we debated in the mid-fifties was the question 'Whether an Army is Necessary for Ceylon'.

The highlight of our debates was the debate with Mahinda College. During my time members of the Mahinda debating team included Dharmasena De Silva, now professor of management at Wichita University in Kansas, USA; Leelananda De Silva, former Permanent Secretary, Ministry of Planning and Senior Economist United Nations, Geneva; Nalin Samarasinghe, Senior Economist, Asian Development Bank, Manila, Philippines; Chandra Wickramasinghe, former Permanent Secretary, Ministry of Housing; Dr. Upali Manakulasuriya, Physician in New Zealand; and Dr. Nandi Wijesinghe, Gynecologist in the United Sates and now a neighbor of mine. We debated on such subjects as 'whether western influence has done more harm than good to Ceylon', and 'Pros and Cons of the Free Educational System.' I am glad I had continuing contacts with all of them during our adult lives long past school days. Along with G.K., the other staff coach for the debating team was Mr. Ananda Wijesekara our history teacher, who later became a prominent lawyer and Presidents Counsel, and who, I believe ironically, was a student at Mahinda College.

* * *

Among the other extracurricular activities that I took part in, scouting was the one that took a fair amount of my time, particularly on weekends. The World Scout Movement founded by Lord Robert Baden-Powell, a decorated soldier, talented artist, actor and free-thinker, was established in 1907, The movement has its headquarters at Geneva, Switzerland. The movement's mission is to contribute to the education of young people, through a value system to help build a better world, where people are self-fulfilled as individuals and play a constructive role in society.

Scouting provides structured settings where young people can learn new skills and develop habits that will help them succeed. scouting has offered youth a concrete program of discovering, sharing, and applying knowledge and skills to develop academic skills, self-confidence, ethics, leadership skills, and citizenship skills that influence their adult lives. Most of all scouting encourages youth to achieve a deeper appreciation for service to others in their community.

The National Scout Movement of Sri Lanka, was founded in 1912, and became a member of the World Organization of the Scout Movement in 1953. As Sri Lanka is a multireligious and multiracial country, scouting has been a great unifying force among school children.

The Scout Troop at Richmond was led by our math teacher Mr. H.D.A. Gunasekara, a devoted teacher and a demanding leader. He had the assistance of Mr. Gunasoma Nanayakkara, our geography teacher, who was the predecessor to Mr. Gunasekare but continued to assist the Troop along with Mr. Ranjith Senaratna, who later became the Director of the Colombo Museum. With time and some hard work under the excellent direction of our scout masters, I became a Queen's Scout, the highest level a Scout can achieve. I was also awarded the College Scout Prize for the Best Scout. It was handed to me at the annual college prize giving by Mrs. A.G. Ranasighe wife of the Chief Guest at the Prize Day. At the time, Mr. A.G. Ranasinghe was the Permanent Secretary to the Minister of Finance, the head of the Treasury and Secretary to the Cabinet who later became Governor of the Central Bank of Ceylon.

In order to progress through the scout movement one had to master an assorted set of knowledge and skills such as recognizing and appreciating fauna and flora, map reading, hiking, camping, swimming, life saving, marching and parading, cooking, sewing, carpentry and the whole gamut of life's skills. Each time you complete the requirements of a given skill you are given a badge that you wear on your uniform indicating your mastery of the discipline displayed on the badge.

One has to progress through the lowest rank of tenderfoot to second class and first class scout, and eventually, when all requirements are satisfied for recognition; one earns the Queens Scout badge. This is comparable to the Eagle Scout in the United States. One of the last requirements is a grueling full day hike carrying with you a tent for an overnight stay in the open air. You also have to carry your provisions and prepare your own meals. I trudged from Galle to Baddegama for a weekend to complete the requirement for my badge. Most of the required skills were mastered at scout camps, which were conducted usually over long weekends.

One of the popular places for camping by the Scout Troop was *Rumassala Kanda* (popularly known as *Buona Vista*) in Unawatuna - a large mound-like hill, which forms the eastern protective barrier to the Galle harbor. Tradition associates this hill as a piece of the Mt. Himalaya brought by Hanuman the monkey general of Rama, the Indian king in the epic *Ramayana*. Legend has it that Rama was at war with Rawana, the Raksha king of Lanka, after the latter abducted Sita Devi, wife of Rama. During the battle when Rama was injured Hanuman is supposed to have brought medicinal plants from the Himalayas to treat Rama. He is also supposed to have brought a chunk of the mountain along with the plants he brought. At *Rumassala*, a variety of medicinal plants are still believed to be extant, having sprung from that chunk.

Bouna Vista affords a magnificent view of the Galle harbor, the Fort and the surrounding area. We used to camp on the grounds of the Bouna Vista College, mostly a vernacular school which had given early education to such luminaries as Sir Senarath Paranavitana, the first Sri Lankan Archeological Commissioner. He is venerated as the pioneer promoter of the great archeological sites of Sri Lanka. Other teachers there included Martin Wikcramasinghe, the doyen of Sinhala literature; and A.T. Ariyaratne, who is the founder of the *Sarvodaya* (self help) movement, considered internationally as one of the most successful organizations of its kind. In recognition of his unique work, he was awarded the prestigious Magsaysay Award honoring greatness in public service and leadership in Asia.

The other location where we camped out was the abandoned Royal Air Force airport in Koggala. Prior to the Second World War, the lake at Koggala was used for seaplanes. After the outbreak of war, a water runway was demarcated and a flying boat base, the largest in the east, was established. After the Japanese occupied the Malay Peninsula in 1942, the QEA/ Imperial Airways flight from London to Sydney lost Singapore, which had been its refueling point between Calcutta and Perth, Australia. It was vital to the British/Australian war effort that the flight be maintained at any cost, so an alternate route was established through Koggala. From 1943 to 1945 QEA Imperial Airways flew Consolidated Catalina flying boats from Koggala lake to the Swan River at Perth. It was at the time the world's longest non-stop air route. At 28 hours, the flight was so long that the passengers saw the sun rise twice, and it came to be called the 'flight of The Double Sunrise'. After the war, Air Ceylon operated services to and from Koggala by Dakota aircraft till 1964 and thereafter by Avro aircraft. These services were terminated following the closure of Air Ceylon, the national carrier in 1978. Koggala, however, continued as a Sri Lanka Air Force base.

Koggala was also the hometown of the famous writer and novelist Martin Wickramasinghe of *"Madol Duwa"* fame which describes and brings to life so vividly the environs of Koggala. The museum of Folk, Art and Culture built in his honor at his old residence, has an excellent display of local folk items depicting folk life of the times gone by.

We made numerous boat trips in the lagoon and the Koggala Lake to see many a small island and to study the ecosystem with hundreds of varieties of indigenous trees and shrub in which bird life abounds. The ability to identify various species was one of the skills to be mastered for a scout badge. At these camps we learned endurance activities, cooking, cleaning, singing and outdoor fireside group entertainment, as well as an assortment of other skills. The camaraderie at these camps, which were educational as well as entertaining, was excellent.

There were also intercollegiate gatherings of Scouts and we used to attend what was known as the Southern Corroboree, where the Scout Troops from the schools in the south of the Island competed with one another in the various skills that scouting taught. In the United States these competitions are held at Annual Jamborees.

The essence of the Scout Law, which we learned during our scouting days: "to help other people at all times, to keep physically strong, mentally awake and morally straight," served us well throughout our lives.

Chapter 9

Passage through India

I am grateful to the Scout movement at Richmond College for opening the doors of the outside world to me; grateful that this world happened to be the land, Mark Twain described as "the most extraordinary country the sun visits on his rounds." In 1956 Bertie Gunasekara and I were selected from Richmond as members of the national scout contingent to the Second All-India Scout Jamboree, where several regional countries from Asia participated. The sad news that Bertie has passed away reached me as I was writing these pages. The Jamboree gave me my first opportunity at the age of 18 to go abroad and visit another country, and ever since then, to be bitten by the travel bug.

The Ceylon Contingent to the 2nd All-India Jamboree was composed of 15 keen scouts and 10 scouts masters from various parts of the island, as well as a few others who accompanied the contingent.

When we assembled at the Scout Headquarters by the Beira Lake in Colombo, we were given detailed instructions of the tour and its complete programme. We had already been advised about prior preparations regarding what to carry with us and other essential pre-trip information.

In the afternoon we were given a send off at a garden party hosted at the compound of the Queen's House - the Governor's residence (now *Janadhipati Mandiraya*) on Prince Street near the Chatham clock tower in Colombo Fort. The Governor-General H.E. Sir Oliver

Goonetileke gave an inspirational pep talk wishing us well and reminding us that we were going as 'Ambassadors of Goodwill' to a country which for the last 2,500 years has had very close ties – religious, cultural and social- with Sri Lanka. We were overawed by the entire event graced by high-level personalities, including the Chief Scout Commissioner E.W. Kannangara, and a senator who handed us letters of appointment signed by the Commissioner. It was an honour to take part in the group photo with such eminent figures of the time.

On the night of 17th December 1957, we boarded the train from the Fort Railway Station to Talaimannar. Uncle Sumanapala (my stepmother's brother) was there to see me off. He generously handed me a couple of hundred rupees, which were very handy during the tour. By morning, we reached Talaimanner. Hauling our bag and baggage, we trudged to the dock and boarded the ferry to Dhanuskodi, a town in the middle of the wasteland of the southern coast of India.

The ferry ride started with good cheer. Excited over the opportunity of sailing off in the Indian Ocean everyone started to sing and have a good time. But, alas, the merry-making did not last for long. One by one we became seasick. The rickety old ferry that had been plying up and down for decades was not really seaworthy for an entertaining trip across the open sea. It was, in the end, a horrific journey with a boat full of people throwing up, resulting in a stench that made everyone even more sick.

Needless to say we were relieved when we finally saw land, on the distant horizon. The excitement of seeing our giant neighbour India for the first time was a tranquilizer that made us forget the bad experience of the ferry ride. We alighted in Dhanuskodi, where the Indian Southern Railway line had its last stop. I do not remember seeing anything in the vicinity except the railway station. It was a long trudge to the station from the boat and quite taxing in the hot sun even for the young Turks. There awaited two especially reserved railway compartments for our contingent. One for the scouts and the other (a first class cabin) for the officials who accompanied us.

Our contingent was led by the Deputy Commissioner C.M.P. Wanigatunga. He was a very polished man, a part of the aristocracy of Sri Lanka. We were also accompanied by his wife Manel, who was the bridesmaid at the wedding of Mr. Solomon West Ridgeway Dias Bandaranaike, who was the Prime Minister of Ceylon at the time of our Indian trip, and Mrs. Sirimavo Bandaranaike (nee Ratwatte), who later became Prime Minister of Sri Lanka. The gracious demeanour of the Wanigatungas and the professional way they lead the contingent certainly rubbed off on many of us, who were grateful to have had such exposure. The experience undoubtedly had a positive influence on us in our later years.

The Troop Leader was H.S. Embuldeniya from Trinity College Kandy, a good boxer who later joined the Police Force. Others who took a prominent part among us were L.W. Rasiah from St. Thomas' College, Mount Lavinia, who was my Patrol Leader (I was his deputy); H.F.R. Sithamparam from Jaffna College, Jaffna; H.Y Sally from Zahira College, Colombo; and M.P Radhakrishnan from Christian College, Kotte. Along with Bertie, we were a clique who generally associated with one another as a group, and ended up sharing a tent at the Jamboree. In retrospect, I note that the clique included members of every community in the country, but at the time it was a given and every one enjoyed each others friendship.

* * *

The train journey was very long but enjoyable thanks to the company and the new vistas we were passing through.

For several hours we went over a desert like landscape, till the train reached Madras (Chennai). In Madras, we walked around the town and stayed at the Central Y.M.C.A. There, for the first time, we were exposed to a level of poverty and disease that we were not quite accustomed to, despite coming from a poor country to the south of India.

Our next destination was Sanchi – though not directly related to the Buddha's life, it had become a pilgrim site since Emperor Asoka erected a stupa there in the middle of the 3d century BC. It is also the place from where Arahanth Mahinda, son of the Emperor Asoka, departed from India to bring Buddhism to Sri Lanka. Later rulers enlarged the complex. After the decline of Buddhism in India, the ruins lay neglected until the 19th century, when they were despoiled by treasure hunters.

Restoration activity commenced in the early 20th century, with the rebuilding of the principal stupas and the creation of the Present Park and museum. A UNESCO World Heritage Site, today Sanchi stands in testimony to the golden Buddhist age of Emperor Asoka. It has become a shrine for the followers of Buddhism owing to the several structures and sculptures that illustrate the Buddhist legends. Of the total of eight Stupas built by Emperor Asoka in the 3rd century B.C., only three Stupas remain.

A resident Buddhist priest from Sri Lanka, who was at Sanchi, explained to us in detail the history and significance of the site, and I believe he later became the Chief Incumbent.

Our next stop was Agra, where the local Scout Association took care of us. While in Agra we visited the Taj Mahal, the mausoleum of Shah Jahan's favorite wife Mumtaz Mahal, which is considered today as one of the New Seven Wonders of the world, and a World Heritage Site.

Finished in marble, it is perhaps India's most fascinating and beautiful monument. It took 22 years (1630–1652) of hard labour and 20,000 workers, masons and jewellers to build and set it amidst landscaped gardens. Built by the Persian architect, Ustad 'Isa, the Taj Mahal is on the bank of the Yamuna River. It can be observed from Agra Fort from where Emperor Shah Jahan gazed at it, for the last eight years of his life, a prisoner of his son Aurangzeb. This perfectly symmetrical monument is an acknowledged masterpiece of symmetry. Verses of the Koran are inscribed on it and at the top of the gate are twenty-two small domes, signifying the number of years the monument took to build. Built on a marble platform that stands above sandstone, the most elegant dome of the Taj Mahal has a diameter of 60 feet (18 m), and rises to a height of 80 feet (24 m). Directly under this dome is the tomb of Mumtaz Mahal. Shah Jahan's tomb was erected next to hers by his son Aurangzeb. The interiors are decorated by fine inlay work, incorporating semi-precious stones.

We also visited the Agra Fort (also known as the Red Fort). The great Mughal Emperor Akbar commissioned the construction of the Agra Fort in 1565 CE, but the red sandstone fort was converted into a palace by his grandson Shah Jahan, being reworked extensively with marble and pietra dura inlay.

Notable buildings in the fort include Jahangir's Palace, and the Shish Mahal (mirrored palace). The fort is crescent shaped, has a total perimeter of 1.5 miles, and is ringed by double ramparts of red sandstone punctuated at regular intervals by bastions. A 30 foot wide and 33 feet deep moat surrounds the outer wall. The fort is a typical example of Mughal architecture, effectively showing how the North Indian style of fort construction differentiated from that of the South. It too faces the river Yamuna.

From Agra, our journey continued to Delhi. The first afternoon we were in Delhi happened to be Christmas Eve 1956, and Sir Edwin Wijeyeratne, High Commissioner (Ambassador) of Ceylon in India, together with Lady Wijeyeratne entertained our contingent with a garden party at their residence. The party concluded with a sing song. With several leading Indian Scout and Guide Officials and State Officials, as well as some ambassadors of the countries attending the Jamboree present on that occasion, it gave me my first glimpse of the diplomatic world.

In Delhi, the local Scout Association had made arrangements for our visit and organized a comprehensive programme for which we were most grateful. Delhi is a city that bridges two different worlds. Old Delhi, once the capital of Islamic India, is a labyrinth of narrow lanes lined with crumbling hovels and formidable mosques. In contrast, the imperial city of New Delhi created by the British Raj is composed of spacious, tree- lined avenues and imposing government buildings.

Although Calcutta was the capital of India until December 1911, during the British Raj, Delhi, constructed by the Mughal Emperor Shah Jahan, had served as the political and financial centre of several empires of ancient and medieval India; most notably of the Mughal Empire from 1799 to 1849. Delhi has been the seat of power for several rulers and many empires for about a millennium. Many times the city was built, destroyed and then rebuilt. Interestingly, a number of Delhi's rulers played a dual role, first as destroyers and then as creators.

Little did I know, when we visited the magnificent Rashtrapati Bhavan, home of the President of India (formerly the British Viceroy's House), that many years later, I would visit the same precincts and meet the glorified incumbent of the place. Yet, on this occasion too, I did meet the President, though not at the Rashtrapati Bavan, but at the adjacent Secretariat, which houses various ministries of the Government of India. This also turned out to be a place to which I would make several later visits during my working life.

I scarcely remember nor cared much for the fleeting handshake when I met the first President of India, Dr. Rajendra Prasad, at a reception offered to the scouts attending the Jamboree. I now see the visit as a good omen. As a young student I never even dreamed that I would have the honour not only to revisit the place, but to meet in somewhat more meaningful contexts, several presidents, heads of government, cabinet ministers, diplomats and other high officials of India throughout nearly four decades of my working career at the United Nations.

Of all the Presidents (with whom I came in contact, it was Dr. Abdul Kalam that I was most familiar with, the reason being that as a young man he spent decades working for the Indian Space Research Organization (ISRO). I had long and continuous contact with ISRO during my working life because I was engaged in space related activities.

Our scouting contingent also visited the nearby Parliament House, as well as, the stunning Jama Masjid mosque - the largest in India and the final architectural magnum opus of Shah Jahan completed in 1658 after fifteen years of construction. We next saw the imposing buildings in the Qutb Minar, which dates from the onset of Islamic rule in India, including fine examples of early Afghan architecture. It is a soaring tower of victory that was started in 1193, immediately after the defeat of the last Hindu kingdom in Delhi. It is nearly 73m high and tapers from a 15m-diameter base to just 2.5m at the top. The tower has five distinct levels, each marked by a projecting balcony.

Today, this impressively ornate tower has a slight tilt, but otherwise, has worn the centuries remarkably well. It reminds one of the leaning Tower of Pisa in Italy. We wandered around the Red Fort. One phenomenal testament to the once-mighty Mughals was the palace of Emperor Shah Jahan's new capital, built when he moved his capital here from Agra to Delhi, to bring prestige to his reign.

Next we saw the *Yantra Mantra* an Observatory consisting of 13 astronomy instruments, built in 1724 by Maharaja Jai Singh II of Jaipur, for the purpose of revising the calendar and astronomical tables; and also to predict the times and movements of the sun, moon and planets. The tallest of them is 90 feet high. The term *Yantra Mantra* or *Jantar Mantar* though literaly translated as the calculating instument is associated with the magical art of astrology, which also benefited from the calculations made by these wonderful devices. Looking back, I can but wonder how I presaged my long association with renowned astronomers from around the world in my later life, with visits to the most modern astronomical observatories with unimaginable capacity. It all started at the foot of this ancient astronomical centre 'Yantra Mantra'.

Our final stop was at the India Gate the national monument of India, originally known as All India War Memorial, built to commemorate the 90,000 soldiers of the British Indian Army who lost their lives while fighting for the British Indian Empire (After India's independence, India Gate became the site of the Indian Army's Tomb of the Unknown Soldier).

* * *

After a wonderful tour and a great learning experience we made our way finally to Jaipur in Rajasthan, the location of the Jamboree on the 26th of December 1956. Jaipur, the capital of Rajasthan was given a colour coat of pink a century ago in honour of a visiting British Prince. It has ever since retained this colour. Built by Maharaja Jai Singh, the notable astronomer, this 260 year old city has been a capital of royalty, and the first planned city in India. The very structure of Jaipur resembles the taste of the Rajputs and the Royal family.

As we approached the camp site in Jaipur we began to have grave doubts if the Jamboree would ever be a success. Our eyes met a handful of tents pitched in a desert where 12,500 campers (10,000 boy scouts and 2,500 girl guides) would soon be arriving. It was early morning and the cold wind was unbearable. As the day passed the sun began to worry us with its intense heat and we began to wish everything would soon be over so that we could head back home.

The next morning we had to rally round the arena for the flag break, during which the Jamboree was officially inaugurated by the Governor of Rajasthan. It was a very impressive ceremony and Ceylon had the honor of leading the March Past. The sixteen thousand boy scouts, girl guides and officials then marched past the saluting base. Each day, the salute was taken by a prominent personality and it made us proud one day when it was the High

Commissioner for Ceylon in India who rode in an open jeep, with a large Ceylon (Sri Lanka) flag fluttering in the air, carried by the Standard Bearer of the Ceylon Contingent, Rasiah. It was really a heartening sight to see thousands of young lads and lasses including the Ceylon Contingent marching past on the old battlefield of those men of chivalry, the Rajputs.

The dust and cold were now only a memory, with everyone happy to be enjoying the company of comrades hailing from different nations. Apart from the busy schedule of competitions, conferences, camp-fires, networking and other scouting activities, there were cultural programmes as well. The grandest of all was the Festival of Folk Dance and Music. During the six mile route march which was part of the closing ceremonies, we were astonished by the rousing welcome given us by the citizens of Jaipur, men women and children perched on what remains of the great Mogul architectural edifices of Jaipur, making the Jamboree an event which would remain indelible in the minds of all who attended it.

During our stay in Jaipur we also had the opportunity to visit the city. We saw the Nahargarh Fort, which encloses (Hawa Mahal), the sprawling palace complex, formal gardens, and a small lake. Having had a wonderful time it was with deep regret that we left Jaipur.

On our return, we broke journey in Bombay (Mumbai) and toured the city. We were fascinated by two sites: The Gateway of India, built to commemorate the visit of King George V and Queen Mary to Bombay in December 1911. This was designed to combine both Hindu and Muslim architectural styles (the arch is in Muslim style while the decorations are in Hindu style), standing impressively by the sea and rising to nearly one hundred feet from street level. We also visited the Hanging Gardens on top of the Malabar Hills laid out in 1881 over Bombay's main reservoir, possibly to cover the water from the nearby potentially contaminating activities.

Our sojourns in Mumbai also included a visit to a university, which I particularly welcomed because I was making contingency plans for my future education. Although the primary purpose of our trip to India was to attend the Jamboree, we were able to tour a good part of India covering nearly 5000 miles, and visit many historical and religious places of interest. We had carried with us a colour film entitled *Ceylon My Home* which was shown on many occasions at the Jamboree and at social events, such as the Garden Party given by the High Commissioner, providing good publicity for our country. At all such occasions Ceylon Tea was always served to popularize it. Over all, it was an amazing experience at a very young age that gave me an exposure to the outside world, broadened my horizons, and helped me in later years. As an adult, I have had several opportunities to visit most places that I visited during my maiden trip to India in 1956. Each time, I have looked back with nostalgia on my first experiences in those locations.

Among the many friends I made at the Jamboree, was a particular Indian lass who drew my special attention during the course of the camp in Jaipur. After I returned to Richmond, we wrote to each other as pen pals, and whenever I pondered my future after Richmond, I began to consider the possibilities of entering an Indian university. But, as with all infatuations, our passion, hampered by distance and time, was short lived. In retrospect, it seems probable that the visit to the Bombay University would have been more of an incentive for my consideration of an Indian education, than the deep black eyes of the beautiful Indian girl I met in Jaipur. An issue, that is open for debate, I suppose!

Chapter 10

Taste of Glory

I stood in front of the wicket, bat in hand, waiting for the flash of the red leather ball. In the slightest fraction of a second the ball came towards me – wood touched leather. I ran down the pitch, my eyes on the red dot rising, rising towards the sun as if it had no intention of returning. Then the fall began. Silence reined the grounds. Thump! The ball landed well over the fine leg boundary. The crowd went wild. The umpire signaled six runs.

With beads of sweat running down my forehead, heart thumping fiercely, I raised my bat to salute the cheering fans. For a moment I felt as if I was Sir Garry Sobers, Peter May, Collin Cowdrey all rolled into one. Then I heard the chants of my friends; "Well done, Nandi!" And I was back where I belonged; on the Galle cricket grounds playing as the Captain of the Richmond team.

I confess, during my school days I paid scant attention to my studies. To my father's great disappointment cricket, soccer, and athletics were the centre of my world.

My first foray into organized sports at Richmond was when I dared to attend cricket practice for the under 12 team. Up to then I had never played with a proper cricket ball made of hard leather. We had used a soft tennis ball in the games we played with friends at one or the other's home garden during my days at the vernacular schools. It was again a tennis ball or a 'kaduru bole' (fruit of a tree resembling a cricket ball) that my Cousin Sarath and I played with, in his home compound.

Our coach was the vice-principal Mr. Shelton Wirasingha, an accomplished cricketer who had played on the Richmond College Team. He was an exacting teacher who conducted every activity he was involved in, in a wellplanned, methodical manner. His first priority was fielding and it turned out that for a while I was best at this, mainly because the other skills - batting and bowling - needed some training. Fielding (to be catching a ball hit at you either along the ground or in the air) did not call for that much trained skill, except perhaps a good eye to track the trajectory of the ball and good hand- eye coordination. Of course, even fielding was a challenge at Richmond, where the playing grounds were very uneven and a lesser area was covered in grass than gravel.

With the excellent training of the basics given by Mr. Wirasingha I eventually became good at batting and was able to be recognized as a part time bowler as well. Mr. Wirasingha believed in training the right skills when one were young, and once properly mastered, honing these skills could continue throughout the player's career.

At first we played little competitive cricket except for a few practice matches. After two years I had mastered the batting skills and was playing on the under fourteen team. In 1952 I became the captain of the team. We used to play inter college cricket matches with St. Aloysius, Mahinda and All Saints Colleges, which were all boys schools in Galle. That year, I was good enough to be selected to play in the under sixteen team as well in the additional match played by the under sixteen team against Dharmasoka College, Ambalangoda.

Most of these matches were played at the Richmond College grounds because none of the other colleges had their own grounds. All the other Galle schools played at the Galle Cricket Club grounds, The Esplanade. But this was mostly reserved for the College senior teams because it was costly to play at the club grounds. This meant that when the other schools played junior level matches with Richmond it was always on our home grounds.

One incident that is etched in my mind occurred during our match against St. Aloysius College. My Cousin Sarath Parakkrama played for the St. Aloysius team and was fielding at silly point when I was batting. I had driven the ball hard and it hit him on his forehead. He had to be taken to hospital where he received a few stitches. He never continued competitive cricket after that mishap.

* * *

After a time, we had a closely knit group of players who generally graduated from one level to the other almost in a pack. The group included some players from our competing schools as well. Again, in my final year in the under 16 team I was the Captain. Toward the end of the season the vice captain, DJ and I were called up for cricket practice along with the College team. I was once again selected to play in the College First Eleven Team in 1954, while still a member of the under sixteen team. That year the College senior team played two third term matches against St. Thomas' College, Mount Lavinia, and Royal College, Colombo (cricket is played in the first of three school terms, except for a couple of games played during the third term, which is reserved for track and field which has limited amount of competitions). I was a reserve for the Royal match. I played on the team for the first time in the match against St. Thomas' College. As my first game for the college team, it was a memorable one.

We took the train to Mt. Lavinia on a Friday afternoon and played the game over the week-end returning to Richmond on Sunday evening. We were hosted in the College Hostel for the duration. As all the others were senior in age, and more experienced, I was somewhat overwhelmed and felt out of place as the baby of the team on the weekend sojourn.

Our team was captained by Ranjan De Silva, an all-round sportsman, only son of the principal Mr. E.R De Silva. Among the players was

Wilmot Samarasinghe, another all-round sportsman who won the four hundred meter race and long jump event at the Public Schools Athletic Meet. He became a well known planter with a successful career as Regional Manager of tea plantations managed by the George Stewart commercial establishment. Rajah Wickramasinghe, also an athlete who won put shot and discus at the Public Schools Meet. He later joined the Air Force and became a high ranking officer and a sports administrator at the national level. In retirement, he served as the Scouts Commissioner. The other was Vernon Wambeck was a superior sportsman who won discus and javelin at the Public Schools Meet, and went on to represent the country in javelin, having held several records at the national level.

The St. Thomas' team was a much superior team, being one of the two or three best teams in the country at the time. During the period I played in the team Don Piachaud, a fast bowler, and Lariff Idroos the leg spinner famous as a googly bowler, were in a class by themselves for speed and guile. The first occasion I played at St. Thomas' I was all at sea facing the fast bowlers on their turf pitch (a novelty at the time, as most matches were played on matting wickets).

I remember the sea breeze blowing all over the pitch with only the railway line between the pitch and the sea. I made a handful of unintended sneaky runs before I got bowled out. The next time we played there (the annual encounter alternated between Mt. Lavinia and Galle) Idroos bowled me out for a duck.

During my playing days St. Thomas' team had P.I. Pieris, Buddy Reid, Neil Chanmugam and Idroos; all of whom played later on the national team. Michael Tissera captained the team the same year I captained Richmond (1958). He went on to captain the national team. Idroos became a physician and lives in Los Angeles. Time to time we reminisce about the past. Only recently he reminded me how time has moved on and things have changed. When his college team visited us in alternate years, we played on what is considered today as a pristine world class cricket grounds in Galle. But back then, there were cows grazing around (natural lawn mowers that kept the grounds in good order), and all sorts of other distractions, which of course, never bothered us and were considered as part of the normal scene.

Playing the other third term match on a matting wicket against Royal we were more competitive although we never got the better of them. During my time Royal had Darrel Livers, Michael Wille, F.R. Crozier who later played on the national team, and Lorenz Pereira who went on to play for Cambridge University in the UK. He captained the Royal team the same year I captained Richmond.

1955 was my first full season playing for the college team. We played several club matches including the Galle Cricket Club; and college matches in Galle, Matara, Kandy and Colombo. Our team was captained by Douglas Gunawardane, who later entered the Peradeniya campus of the University of Ceylon and obtained an arts degree. He was a member of the university cricket team. He and J.N.A. Gunawardane the vice captain, a stylish batsman, were the stars on our side.

Regrettably, both had very short productive lives. Douglas met with an accidental death and J.N.A. suffered several medical setbacks throughout his life shortly after he left Richmond. Hillman Kulasooriya, who became a planter, and Keerthi De Silva, an engineer, were the others who scored runs during the season, while Vernon Wambeck was the star spin bowler who took wickets constantly.

The *Richmond Cricket Review* for 1955 states that I "contributed useful scores". One I remember was the match against St. Aloysius which we won by innings when I made 40 odd runs not out. We played against Wesley College and Zahira College, Colombo; Prince of Wales College, Moratuwa; Kingswood College, Kandy; Dharmasoka College, Ambalangoda; and St. Thomas' College, Matara, in addition to the third term matches against Royal and St. Thomas' Colleges. The Dharmasoka match was special to me as it was played at the grounds of Ambalangoda, my hometown. This was the first time I had played there, and I was happy to have fared reasonably well when my town folks were spectators, although cheering the home team.

The highlight that year was the 50th anniversary encounter against Mahinda College. The Richmond-Mahinda match was known as the big match of the south, and dubbed the "lover's quarrel", which reflected the close and friendly interaction between the two schools. The first "big match" in the country was played between Royal College and St. Thomas' College in 1879 in Colombo.

During the big match special enclosures are erected around the Galle Esplanade cricket grounds to accommodate many students, parents, alumni, well wishers and those simply interested in cricket. These observers throng to Galle for the two day encounter. Bands play and the spectators cheer loudly, almost non-stop, for one side or the other.

Being the anniversary match, it was a very special occasion for the entire town of Galle. The Mahinda team was captained by D.H. De Silva (Hemachandra), who entered the university and graduated with a degree in arts and captained the university team. He later played for the national side along with his brothers D.P. (Premachandra) and D.S. (Somachandra) De Silva who were in the Mahinda team. His youngest brother D.G.(Gunachandra) also played later for the Mahinda team.

D.H. went on to become the charity commissioner in the local government service, and served the Municipal Councils of Colombo and Kandy. His brother D.S. later became a cricket administrator, ending up as the Chairman, National Cricket Board. D.H. was a brilliant batsman while his two brothers were outstanding spin bowlers who were also good batsmen.

The vice-captain of the Mahinda team was G.M.S. De Silva (Sumanatilaka), a stylish batsman who went on to become the Chairman of the Ambalangoda Urban Council and a recognized politician in the area. He was also a successful businessman operating a gem and jewelry establishment. Being also from Ambalangoda, I was in constant contact with him whenever I was in Sri Lanka, and he and his wife, Nirmalee, have visited us in New York and in Los Angeles for vacations. He is highly respected in the area as an honest and principled politician who is dedicated to improving the quality of life for the people of Ambalangoda. Also in the Mahinda team were four Amendra brothers and Cyril Jayasuriya, brother of DJ, who went on to serve at the Central Bank of Ceylon.

Going into the final part of the game, Richmond had the upper hand and declared its innings while I was still not out. The match ended in a draw when the rains intervened, towards the end of the second day, when D.H. De. Silva and G.M.S. De Silva were in the midst of a healthy partnership for Mahinda. As evidenced the draw, the teams were equally matched. With the fluctuating fortunes, all the spectators witnessing this significant sports event enjoyed the occasion.

In 1956, Richmond played against the same teams with the addition of Aluthgama Vidyalaya. We fared badly that year. The worst came at the hands of Prince of Wales' College, Moratuwa. I was involved in a substantive partnership with the captain in a desperate effort to save an innings loss, but that was in vain. We received a true drubbing. That year also the team was captained by Douglas Gunawardane and J.N.A. Gunawardane was his vice-captain. They both contributed with good scores and bowling performances throughout the year. I am recorded in the annual college cricket review as having made several useful scores and was awarded college colors along with the captain.

The most memorable match that year was once again the Big Match against Mahinda. The teams had not changed much from the previous year, with the same captains. The only notable change was the absence of G.M.S. De Silva in the Mahinda side. In the first innings Richmond was bundled out cheaply. I was the highest scorer with 36 runs. Mahinda replied with a massive score of 276 runs with Captain D.H. De Silva just missing out on a century with

93 runs. But Richmond was up to the task with Captain Douglas Gunawardane also missing out on a century with 94 runs, and I was the next highest scorer with 38 runs, having had a partnership of 88 runs with my captain. Mahinda had only twenty minutes left before the end of play to score 30 runs. They made a spirited effort, but were able to make only 25 runs for the loss of three wickets. Richmond was lucky to escape with a draw, saved by the clock, to the great disappointment of Mahinda.

Our coach was Walter May who had played cricket for Richmond and later St. Thomas' College Mt. Lavinia and held an opening record in the Island's Big Match – 'Royal Thomian' in Colombo. He now lives in Perth, Australia.

* * *

The following year, 1957, I had the great privilege of leading the team as captain. Ours was a young and inexperienced side but we did well to win six matches, draw four, and lose only one. We managed to draw the game with the formidable Zahira College, Colombo team, which had done extremely well in the intercollegiate cricket circuit that year. Zahira team had Devraj and Nawaz who later played in the national team.

The big match fever affected our young side when we played against Mahinda. The Mahinda team was led by Sisira Amendra and it included five Amendra brothers (Sisira, Rajah, Stanley, Percy and Tissa). Five brothers on one team is a record that appears in the Wisden Cricketers' *Almanack* and has not been matched for over half a century. They had a large compound at their ancestral house where the family lived. They played cricket in all their spare time with each of them challenging the other. I had played soft ball cricket with them at their compound. Although we were rivals on the field when playing for our school teams, off the field we were close friends.

The friendship continued long after leaving school and is maintained up to this day, particularly with Stanley who now occupies the ancestral house where I have had the pleasure of visiting him on my visits to Sri Lanka. I had also seen him and his family in India during a visit to Prasanthi Nilayam. The ancestral house where he lives with the family is the main Sai Center in Galle. He had a career in the Railway Department, where his father had also been employed. He is now retired and devotes his time to social work.

Stanley's brother Percy immigrated early to Canada and I have been in touch with him from time to time. I had a very pleasant reunion with him when I went to Toronto to witness the first international cricket tournament in Canada, where the Sri Lanka team won the trophy. Percy is a cricket historian

who has a good collection of memorabilia. He gave me a copy of the photograph of the two teams taken at the Galle International Cricket Grounds in 1955, on the occasion of the diamond jubilee cricket encounter between Richmond and Mahinda. I have it proudly placed in my office.

The match itself was a draw. Richmond batting second was left to score over 200 runs to win. We lost several wickets and were saved only by some stubborn batting, particularly by our excellent wicket keeper, Bertie Gunasekara.

That year the highlight was when we defeated Wesley College, Colombo after 27 years in a series that began in 1900. Our bowlers, particularly Hamilton and Benjamin, did very well. The result was headlined in the *Daily News* paper the next morning in bold letters. It read: "Richmond brought off a magnificent victory over Wesley College, Colombo by 7 wickets-their first in 27 years". It went on to record that "Set with 107 runs to make for victory Richmond lost 2 wickets for 24, but skipper J.L.N. De Silva(name by which I was known in school) 50 and Chitral Jayawardane 49 not out, figured in a bright partnership of 78 runs. When they had seen the century mark passed and were within sight of victory the gallant skipper was out, but Richmond went on to hit off the runs and win with time to spare."

I believe the Wesley team that year, had several who played club cricket later, such as Abu Fuard, who eventually played in the national team and went on to become a highly respected cricket administrator, and the Claessen brothers, at least one of whom played later for the national team. While in the process of writing this manuscript I happened to see the national team playing a match against India and the Sri Lankan team was wearing black arm bands. The commentator explained that it was to honor Abu Fuard, the revered cricket administrator who had passed away the day before.

The year after, in 1958, I was still the captain of the team. This was the last year when a player could captain multiple years. Thereafter captaincy was limited to a single year. Since 1900, before I did, only five had captained the team for two years: R.D. Jayasinghe 1908/09; P.S. Tuduwewatte 1917/18; G.S. Weerasooria 1935/36; C. Nijuki 1940/41; and Douglas Gunawardane 1955/56. Four had captained for three consecutive years: D.M. Rajapakse 1913 to 1915; D.A. Jayasinghe 1928 to 1930; Christie Karunaratne 1944 to 1946; and during my early years at Richmond, Arnold Adhihetty 1948 to 1950.

D.M Rajapakse, who later became a respected parliamentarian, was the uncle of the President of Sri Lanka, Mahinda Rajapakse. When Mahinda was at Richmond hostel, Mahinda was a youngster along with his elder brother Chamal, who became a cabinet minister and speaker of the parliament. In fact their father D.A. Rajapakse and two cousins (sons of his uncle D.M.), George Rajapakse and Laksman Rajapakse, had also played in the Richmond cricket team, and later, became cabinet ministers prior to the days of President Mahinda Rajapaksa.

The school magazine records that Mahinda Rajapaksa won the upper kindergarten class prize in 1952, the same year I won my first Prize (Scout Prize). A chronicler of fame, Buddhika Kurukaratne, in a newspaper article quotes Daya Fernando, a retired director of education who was a Richmondite, narrating the schoolboy pranks of Mahinda Rajapaksa while he was at Richmond. He notes that once Mahinda climbed a signal post by the Richmond Hill Railway Station in protest against the older boys, who were playing cricket and not giving him a 'batting chance'. On another ocassion, his brother Chamal related how Mahinda climbed the top-most branch of a 'kadju' tree and threatened to jump down because his father had come with the cane to punish him for some mischievous act. Fernando goes on to conclude that even as a boy Mahinda was totally unpredictable. He left Richmond at a young age to study in Colombo about the same time that I left to enter Law College.

*   *   *

Among the captains of Richmond was my maternal uncle Martin (R.M.M. De Siva) who captained the team in 1921. The centenary publication of the college magazine in 1976 describes him as probably the best all-round cricketer Richmond has produced. He made 97 against Mahinda College, the highest score in the Big Match; a record that was not broken even up to my time. In the same game, he took 15 wickets for 25 runs.

Richmond won by a big margin. The match was witnessed by an English M.P., Sir John Randles, who gave two prizes for the best batsman and best bowler. Both were won by my uncle, R.M.M. De Silva, who handed the bowling prize to his Vice Captain V.T. Nanayakkara, who also bowled well and later became a member of parliament for Matale. After leaving school, Uncle Martin played for the Sinhalese Sports Club (SSC) with success and for the national team. He remained the only Richmond cricketer to play in the national team for a considerable time. In his retirement he coached the Richmond team, daily travelling from Ambalangoda to Richmond by train. Among those he coached were Jayantha Bandaranayaka and Prasad Kariyawasam.

Jayantha captained a decade after me in 1968, when he made a century against Mahinda, in the Big Match, bettering the mark set by his coach in 1921. That was also the first century by a Richmond cricketer in the series. Next year, he scored another century, setting a new record for the series of two successive centuries. Prasad was a good all-rounder taking 7 wickets for 30 runs in the 'Big Match' in his first year in 1969; and in 1972, as captain, he scored 156 not out, breaking the record for the series set by H. Sirisena for Mahinda in 1939. He later joined the foreign service of Sri Lanka and served as Ambassador at the United Nations in both Geneva and New York. Prasad presently occupies the key diplomatic post of Ambassador to India. While he was serving in his UN capacities, I had the opportunity to be associated with him, and I consider him to be among the best diplomats that the country has produced.

*   *   *

Let us go back to the 1958 season, my last season at Richmond. We had mixed results that year. We did well against the good sides, narrowly losing a few and narrowly winning with the weaker teams.

The game with St. Aloysius was one of the close games we won. St. Aloysius was captained by Michael Roberts, who was about the most consistent scorer for St. Aloysius during my time. He had captained the junior teams along with me, and we knew each other well. He was the son of T.W. Roberts; a District Judge who resided within the Galle Fort. He had siblings who were also talented. His sister, Norah Roberts, published an exhaustive but very readable work on Galle titled *Galle: As Quiet as Asleep,* which was republished as a second edition in 2005, edited by Michael.

An alround sportsman and a brilliant student, Michael graduated specializing in western history and became a Rhodes Scholar, earning a Ph.D. from Oxford University. After returning from England, he joined the university faculty at the Peradeniya campus. Later he immigrated to Australia and became a professor in the department of anthropology at the University of Adelaide. He has published extensively on the history and anthropology of Sri Lanka, including several well regarded texts on the subject in general. He has retained his deep interest in cricket and is a leading commentator on the world cricket scene. In 2006 he published an extensive work titled

Essaying Cricket: Sri Lanka and Beyond and continues to be a regular blogger on cricket and other topics. He has also published on a wide variety of socio-political subjects related to Sri Lanka, including a recent publicatin *Potency of Power & People in Groups*, where he generously notes that I had been one of those providing information for the publication. I am privileged to continue our childhood friendship and I follow his many-faceted writings thanks to the internet.

One of the not so close games that we lost was to Prince of Wales College, Moratuwa, which was captained by Lasantha Rodrigo, an excellent batsman. That team featured Anurudha Polonnawita, a fabulous left arm bowler. Both went on to captain club sides and play in the national team. Polonnawita had played for the Ananda side but in his last year of school he joined Prince of Wales. He later went on to become a cricket administrator and presently he is the national curator of the cricket grounds shouldering the enormous responsibility of preparing pitches for international cricket competitions.

During 1958, good scores were made by the vice captain Newton Pinnaduwa, who also bowled well as a pace bowler, along with Monty Austin. Newton served the Peoples Bank in Colombo and passed away when he was in his early fifties. Useful scores were also made by Chitral Fernando, Lalith Fernando and Tudor Jayasuriya. Lalith was a stylish left hand batsman. He later became a medical doctor and immigrated to the United States. There he has a successful practice in mental health in Kansas. He is a distant relative of mine, also hailing from Ambalangoda. He visited me in Los Angeles not long ago along with his wife, who is a physician as well.

Tudor captained the team later, and went on to become a lawyer with a successful career, ending as a senior partner of the leading law firm in Colombo F.J. & G. De. Sarams. During a recent visit to Sri Lanka, I had invited him and his wife to join me at a reunion of our mutual friends, where we began the evening with the staging of the latest Sinhala play written by our friend Namel Weeramuni. During the play, Tudor had left and was not present at the revelries that followed. When I telephoned next day to inquire as to what happened he revealed that he is a cancer victim and could not last the evening though he tried to. I was most grateful that he did attend and we had a long conversation about our days at Richmond. Regrettably, shortly after I returned from Colombo, I heard the news that, Tudor, a good sportsman and admirably principled person, had succumbed to the fatal disease.

In addition to Tudor and others, during my last year as captain in 1958, success of our team rested upon the trio of great bowlers: Hemasiri Fernando the pace bowler, Hemasiri Hettige an excellent off spin bowler, and E.V.G. Hamilton, who had a vicious off cutter as the two spin bowlers. We also had a leg spin bowler in G. Benjamin, who contributed well when called upon, thus providing great variety in our bowling side. All three, except Benjamin, joined the Air Force and played cricket for the Air Force team.

Hettige left the Air Force and joined the Central Bank, and served as the Head of its security force before retirement. He married a distant relative of mine and I used to see him often at the Bank during my visits to Sri Lanka. Hemasiri Fernando continued in the Air Force up to his retirement. Hamilton, who was a good rugby player as well, once received a blow to the head from a boot while playing rugby for his club. After a bad concussion his short life reached an untimely end.

Geo Weerasooria became an ordained priest and was the coach of the team during the two years of my captaincy. He was a gentle soul who knew exactly how to coach a team to be a winner. More than that, he taught how to play the game in the right spirit, win or lose. Later, he went to Manchester University in the UK on a scholarship from the World Council of Churches to do postgraduate studies in Theology. I have met him only once since we both left Richmond.

* * *

1958 also saw the first school boy team from Australia touring the Island. They played five matches in five provinces, which were popular cricketing areas of the country. Two were played in Colombo, one each in Kandy, Jaffna, and Galle.

I had the great honor to captain the combined schools team that played the Galle match. We did quite well, and as the game drew to a close we had a reachable target to win the game, although within a short time-frame. I went to bat at the fall of a few wickets, but just as I had settled down and tried to hurry the scoring, a vicious full ball landed on my face dislocating a couple of teeth. With a mouth full of blood I was taken to the hospital. I later learned that we failed to reach the target and the match was drawn.

I have not been able to find the score card anywhere. I have a picture of the two teams pausing in front of the pavilion in which I am proudly seated at the center next to the Australian Captain. It is of course a valued memento that hangs in my office along with pictures of my Richmond cricket teams.

The occasion of this particular match reminds me also the important difference in the attire, or should I say, the equipment we used then compared to the present. Basically, we played in tennis shoes with pads on, with a bat in hand and a flimsy cap to shield us from the hot tropical sun. We were exposed from head to toe and prone to every injury imaginable. We knew no better, and played on merrily. Though the protection was sparse, they were the days when the bodyline bowling was quite rampant, and even became a scandal during the coveted Ashes tournament between England and Australia.

As a memento of the risks taken on the field, I still sport a cut below my chin and a missing tooth from the injury I sustained from a ball to my face during the match against the visiting Australian Combined Schools' team. That injury required a few stitches and a visit to the dentist. If we had had the luxury of the helmet and other body armor with which present- day cricketers are protected, we would not have had such permanent scars to show off.

As time went on, we began playing in boots that not only gave a better grip, particularly during inclement weather, but also protected the feet from injury. As my father was not inclined to help me in any way in the field of sports, for some time, I was one of the few who continued to play in tennis shoes. It was even scarier to think that for a long while I played the game of soccer in bare feet. During the early days we all played soccer barefooted, but by the time we played in the senior team, there were only a very few who were not in boots. But again, without much thought those who did not have boots, or could not afford them, played barefooted. It was through the generosity of my uncles that I eventually acquired the necessary paraphernalia to protect myself.

* * *

The venue of the match against the Australian team as well as the Richmond-Mahinda big match of course was the Galle Cricket Grounds. It is considered to be one of the most picturesque cricket grounds in the world nestled against the ocean with the Galle ramparts providing the backdrop. This staging is highlighted by the massive clock tower that stands atop the Dutch Fort and the butterfly bridge, which enhances the already beautiful landscape. Before being brought up to international cricket standards, the venue was known as 'The Esplanade'. It was the home ground of the Galle Cricket Club. Built in 1876 as a race course, the ground was used for cricket matches after the racing ceased. In 1927, it was officially declared as a cricket stadium. A turf wicket was introduced to the stadium in 1945 under the guidance of Mr. D.L Hewa, who was then secretary of the Galle Cricket Stadium. Later, when I played for the club, he was the captain of the Galle Cricket Club (Galle CC). The turf was used only for club cricket except for the the Richmond Mahinda Big Match. As the pavilion, it had a quaint old two storied circular building resembling a tower.

The Galle Cricket Club pavilion was opened in 1955 during the time I played there, and just ahead of the 50th anniversary Richmond-Mahinda match. On the day after Christmas 2004, the ground was devastated by the tsunami resulting from a quake in the Indian Ocean, off the coast of Java, Indonesia. It was rebuilt with modern facilities and opened for international matches when the stadium hosted the last match played by perhaps the greatest cricketer produced by Sri Lanka, Muttiah Muralitharan, who reached the mark of 800 test wickets, the highest in the cricketing world.

This brings to mind the first ever international cricket match I witnessed in Galle. I was new to the game, being only twelve years old. I saw the visiting legendary cricket team from the West Indies playing our national team in a friendly encounter on their way to India. The team included the famous trio of W's, Worrell, Walcott and Weekes, along with the famous spinners Ramadhin and Valentine. It was a run-fest from the three Ws and a scintillating exhibition of bowling. The West Indians played against the Galle Cricket Club with some national players added to the side to make it competetive. There were flashes of brilliance from M. Sathasivam, F.C. De Saram, and cricketing brothers C.H. and C.I. Gunasekare, who were national players included for the occasion.

The legendary cricketer Dr. W.G. Grace, who made cricket a popular sport in England, was the first of many illustrious players to visit the country en route to or from Australia to play at Galle Face Green, in Colombo in 1891. Other fleeting appearances of great cricketing figures invigorated the local game and inspired many in the country, just as much as it inspired me when I saw the visiting West Indian team in Galle, and later the Australian team in Colombo, en route to England.

Apart from cricket, the grounds in Galle are used for soccer and athletics as well as the Independence Day parades and other festivities. Having participated in events that took place over a span of half a dozen years on the Galle Cricket Grounds, I carry very pleasant and nostalgic memories whenever I witness on television an international cricket match being hosted on this esplanade.

After the cricket season in my last year at Richmond I joined the Galle Cricket Club and played a few matches. The team was captained by D.L. Hewa, who had previously played for Mahinda. Playing in the national Daily News Trophy tournament, I opened batting for the Galle Cricket Club with veteran George Fonseka another Mahinda College cricketer, and made a few scores which were not that significant. The most memorable was the 97 that I made to win the match against Matara Cricket Club at Uyanwatte grounds in Matara, home ground of the cricketing icon Sanath Jayasuriya. The Galle club later produced world class cricketers who played in the national team, such as Lasith Malinga, Nuwan Kulasekara, Romesh Kaluwitharana, Champaka Ramanayake, Jayananda Warnaweera and Malinga Bandara.

Later, in Colombo, I joined the Bloomfield club and played at the Bloomfield grounds where we used to play school cricket against Wesley College. This was Wesley's home ground. I played a few matches in the Daily News Trophy tournament without any notable performances. By that time, I had realized that it was not possible for me to commit the time necessary for any organized sports at the club level. After the first season I did not continue.

* * *

The highlight of the season of that last year I played for Richmond was of course the Big Match. After six consecutive years of drawn matches, Richmond won in 1958. The Mahinda team was captained by Stanley Amendra and three of the brothers were still in the team along with brothers Sriman and Nethiya Jayawickrama. Nethiya later became a medical doctor and immigrated to the UK.

I opened the batting for Richmond and had the ignominy of being bowled out for a first ball duck by the youngest brother of D.H. De. Silve, Gunachandra De Silva. But Newton Pinnaduwa, the vice captain, and newcomer Tudor Jayasuriya made half-centuries. Hemasiri Fernando, the pace bowler, took 11 wickets for 65 runs to enable Richmond to win by 4 wickets. This was considered a great victory after all the draws in the series.

The second day of the game was rather tense as much of the town had turned up to watch the game and cheer Mahinda College knowing that, being behind, they needed the support. These were the days when most common folk turned up to support Mahinda, which was the leading Buddhist school in the area. A rumor started to spread in the pavilion that people from the fish market were turning up to watch the match with their fish knives in hand. If the intention was intimidation, it was a most un-Buddhist gesture!

This was when we were living in walking distance to the grounds. My father was working at the Galle Railway Station at the time. Yet, however close the grounds were, my father would never walk the short distance to watch me play, so as not to encourage my participation in extracurricular activities, which he firmly believed would make me neglect my school work. He feared that I might become a sportsman following the footsteps of my uncle R.M.M. De Silva, who in my father's eyes, wasted his adult life engaged in sports and indulging in excessive drinking which stood in the way of his success.

My uncle was a great admirer of his nephew, and the day after we won the big match, he invited the whole team to lunch on his account at the New Oriental Hotel (NOH). The Oriental was the grand old hotel built in the colonial days within the premises of the Galle Dutch fort. The hotel building, which dated back over 400 years, was used as the headquarters of the Dutch commandeer and his officers and later, as a billet for British soldiers. In 1865, the buildings were combined to create the NOH. It is the oldest registered hotel on the island, and was run by the Dutch Burger Brohier family from its inception until it was refurbished in 2002, when it was reopened as the new boutique hotel, Amangalla.

It was a great delight for us teenagers to be entertained at this historic venue, which was nearly a century old at the time. This experience during my young days remains vivid in my memory and I have made it a point to visit the place at least for a cup of tea, on every occasion I have been to Galle.

My father was so adamant on his stance regarding my involvement in sports, once when I was injured at the Galle Esplanade at an athletics meet, dislocating my knee, I was taken to hospital for treatment, and I told the coach that I would not like to go home and face the music from my father. I therefore requested that he take me to the College sick room instead. When the coach did as I had requested and informed my father accordingly, my father did not bother to show any concern, obviously hoping this would be a good lesson for me to put an end to my sporting career. I later learned from my stepmother that he had lost many nights' sleep over the incident although he was careful to remain cold and aloof in my presence.

On the occasion of the Big Match, hearing that the people of the town were congregating to the Esplanade, he too had come to see the final hours of the match. My joy would have doubled had I known he was there watching me leading our team to victory. It was only much later that I learned that he had seen his son, the captain of the Richmond College team, raising the winner's trophy.

The honor of leading the combined college team against the Australians, and captaining the College team that recorded victories against Wesley in 1957, and Mahinda in the Big Match in 1958, remain unforgetable as the highlights of my college cricketing career.

Chapter 11

Goals and Hurdles

I received two souvenirs from cricket and soccer during my school days. Cricket gave me the scar under my chin; soccer the scar on my forehead.

Soccer, or football as we used to call it, followed the cricket season which was played during the first of the three school terms. Richmond had taken part in organized soccer even earlier than 1900. Rev. W. J. T. Small a former principal, in an article written on the occasion of the centenary of the College in 1976 states, "One of my earliest memories after coming to Galle in 1906 is acting as referee in a match between Richmond and St. Aloysius which was won by the latter. They were certainly Champions in Galle in my time and I believe they have generally maintained their prominence up to the present day". He was so right; St. Aloysius maintained dominance even during my time.

I began to play soccer with the under-14 team, then joined the under-16 team, captaining each of them in due course. In 1954 I played only two under-16 matches. We won both - one against St. Thomas' College, Matara, the other against Mahinda College. After those, I was promoted to the senior team.

I played in the College team for five years beginning in 1954, the year I captained the under-16 side. In one of those five years we did not play any intercollegiate matches because our practice grounds were being redone. We played most of our matches at the

Galle Esplanade. I captained the side in 1958. We were not a great soccer playing school and played against only one Colombo school: Wesley College. We were lucky to draw that match once. The only other matches played out of town were against St. Thomas' and St. Servaitius Colleges in Matara.

The match against Mahinda College attracted much attention, but the match of the season for us was the one against St. Aloysius College. St. Aloysius was a football power house and they won against St. Josephs' and St. Benedicts' Colleges in Colombo, which were considered the best of the soccer playing schools in the country. During my time we did not win any matches against St. Aloysius.

A memorable occasion for me was when I headed in a goal against them and fell to the ground with a concussion, following a collision with an opposing player who had gone up with me to defend the goal. The goal was good and equaled the score at one all. Richmond lost the game in my absence by two to one. I was happy the goal counted, but it left me with a gash next to my eyebrow that needed a few stitches. I carry the scar to this day, along with the scar under my chin from cricket.

Among my teammates, those who stood out were Wilmot Samarasinghe and Keerthi De. Silva (former captains), Gemunu Amarasinghe and his brother Sanath Amarasinghe, Dayananda Jayasuriya (DJ), J.N.A Gunawardane, Tarzan Diaz, Sarath Boralessa, Douglas Gunawardane, Newton Pinnaduwa, and Walter Gurusinghe.

The reasons for our mediocre performances during my time were twofold. First, we used to play soccer in bare feet with no boots, unlike the schools in Colombo and a few players in the south. We were introduced to boots in my second year on the senior team. This turned out to be a handicap, because we found them rather awkward and it took time to get used to playing in boots. Second, we lost a year of practice and experience because we did not compete that year, while our play ground was being repaired. That meant only a few experienced players were left on the team in the following year.

Our team was coached by Mr. G.W.S De Silva and in the final year by Mr. J.H. Dhanapala, who were both outstanding players for the Richmond team during their playing days. While Mr. Silva had been long time on the staff in charge of the boarding and head of the administrative staff, Mr. Dhanapala, who was a prefect during my junior days, had just joined the teaching staff, after graduating with an arts degree from Peradeniya campus of the University of Ceylon.

* * *

I spent much time practicing track and field events as well. We had an excellent coach in Mr. Gunasoma Nanayakkara, our geography teacher. I took a particular liking to geography simply because of the manner in which he taught the subject. As an athlete from under-14 days to the senior years I spent much time under his guidance. Not only did I admire him as a coach who made us master basic skills, but I also learned much from his ways of organizing and conducting sports events. Once I became a senior, he allowed me to organize much of the primary school annual sports meets. This taught me good organizational skills, which I was able to hone to my great advantage in my adult years. Regrettably, Mr. Nanayakkara left us and joined Trinity College, Kandy. He became Trinity's sports master and also took a prominent part at the national level as an official. His two sisters Kamala and Leela Nanayakkare were also my teachers that I respected a great deal.

In later years, I was fortunate to have as our athletic coach two prominent athletes who represented the country at international competitions. First was Walter May, an alumni of Richmond, who had won the inter-university competition in India and represented the country in 400-meter hurdles, the event in which Sri Lanka had won the only Olympic medal, when Duncan White bagged the silver medal at the Olympics held in Melbourne, Australia. I was particularly lucky to have had Walter May as coach, because I specialized in the shorter version of the same event. He was a very relaxed coach who knew how to impart the essential skills needed to be a winner, without worrying over every single detail. I owe much to him for my technique of hurdling. Apart from being our coach, he was in consecutive years, our English, civics, and history teacher as well. His manner of teaching attracted me to both history and civics as subjects. It certainly was the reason that I chose those as two of my four subjects for the Higher School Certificate (H.S.C.) examination that selected students for entry into the university. This exam was later replaced by the G.C.E Advanced Level examination. Mr. May left us and later migrated to Australia and lives today in Perth.

The coach who took over from him was K.L.F. Wijedasa, the national sprint champion who represented the country in the 100 -and 200-meter dash. He was our history and government teacher. He went on to become the doyen of coaching in the country at the national level. He left us and became the coach of Ananda College, there after at the University of Ceylon, Peradeniya, and finally honorary coach at Royal College. A highly respected sports official, he coached national champions. I used to keep in touch and occasionally visited him in my adult life.

Both Walter May and K.L.F. Wijedasa were not only outstanding teachers and coaches, but also perfect gentlemen who set high standards of conduct for us to emulate with great respect.

I was a good athlete from my primary school days. At the college sports meet, one of the fist events I won was the under-14 Pole Vault with a height of 6ft 3 ½ inches in 1951. The following year I came second in the Paul Vault and won the 75- yards Hurdles event. I also took part in the relay team.

The college athletic competition was an Inter House Meet. I belonged to Hanover House, which won the champioship that year. The other three houses were Cambridge, Windsor and Winchester (names of British towns). In the mid-fifties, the names were changed to Darrel, Langdon, Small, and Sneath (names of prominent British principals of Richmond). Four of the six dormitories in the College Hostel were named after the House names. I was the captain of the Sneath House in 1956. In 1953, I won the under-16 Hurdles, Pole Vault and came second in the High Jump to Wickramapala Samarasinghe, who later became a physician and migrated to the U.K.

That year, 1953, for the first time, I was a member of the College Athletic Team and participated at the junior level in the Southern Province Inter-Collegiate Meet, as well as the Public Schools Meet (open to all schools in the country for participants who had won at the provincial level meets). The Public School Meet was begun in 1930 by Sir John Tarbat an Englishman, who had attended the Annual Schools Meet in Melbourne, Australia, and thought of doing the same in Ceylon. Championship Cups are now named after him. He attended the first twenty-five meets.

At the Southern Group Meet, I came third in the Hurdles event which was won by Christo Pannambalana of St. Aloysius College, Galle and his school-mate K.M. Nelson, who came second. The following year he entered St. Josephs' College Colombo and went on to shine in the event at the Colombo Schools Meet and the Public Schools Meet. Later he migrated to the U.K. but in his retirement has returned to Sri Lanka. Today he manages and lives on a rubber plantation near Kalutara. I had the pleasure of meeting him on social occasions during my recent visits to Colombo.

I also came third in the junior High Jump event, which was won by Oswald Rajapakse from Dharmasoka College Ambalangoda. That year he transferred to Ananda College and went on to shine in the High Jump, Pole Vault and Long Jump events. Later he went on to become the Public Schools Champion, National Champion and won the High Jump event at some international meets representing his country. Along the way, he set records at every level, and became the first in the country to clear 6 feet in the High Jump event. He joined the police and later immigrated to the United States with his wife Paisley, a fellow athlete at the national level.

Nearly half a century after our encounter at the Southern Province Meet, I reconnected with Oswald when I moved to Los Angeles, where he is resident. He was a native of my hometown, Ambalangoda, and we visited each other several times and reminisced about the days gone by. Memories were refreshed of life in our hometown, our sporting days, and of his father, who was the marquee tailor in town - himself an eminent athlete, having set the Long Jump and Hop-Step and Jump national records.

The second place in the Southern Province meet in High Jump that year was taken by Nandi Wijesinghe of Mahinda College, Galle. He later became a medical doctor and married his classmate Nilakshi. They immigrated to the United States. There he became a specialist in gynecology and obstetrics. His wife became a pathologist. By the time I came to Los Angeles, half a century later, Dr. Wijesinghe also was there as Head of the Department of Gynecology and Obstetrics at the Anaheim General Hospital, Los Angeles, California, as a reowned specialist in high-risk pregnancies. As he lives only a few minutes away from my house we visit each other occasionally.

*   *   *

That year, it was quite exciting for me to have joined the team to the Public Schools Meet. From the time I was 12, I had been travelling to Colombo to watch the Public Schools Meet. I would get a train warrant from my father and travel on my own to Colombo. These were my first ventures alone, apart from travelling back and forth from home to school during the holidays. The independence my father inculcated in me from my younger days, by allowing me to venture out on my own on many such occasions, was admirable. The result was that I was fortified with tremendous experiences that allowed me not only to travel the world uninhibited, but also it taught me many lessons that stood me in good stead when I had to face challenging situations, both in my personal and working life.

I would get off at the Kollupitya station in Colombo and go to my cousins' place on Kolluptiya Lane. They would welcome me there and the next morning I would take the double decker bus to Borella. From there, I walked to the Oval (now the P. Sara stadium) a hallowed venue of sports at the time.

Established in 1864, the world-famous ground is the country's biggest cricket venue. It hosted its first cricket Test Match between India and England in 1934. The first match I watched there was in 1953, when Lindsey Hassett's Australian team was on route to England, and played a one-day game at the oval against Ceylon, led by F.C. De Saram. Among the team was the all rounder C.I. Gunasekae, stylish bat, his brother C. H. Gunasekare, and the wicket keeper opening bat Mahes Rodrigo. I missed seeing them on the earlier visit in 1948, when Bradman's team visited and M. Sathasivam, who was known as the Black Bradman, captained the Ceylon side. The oval is now used for cricket, but in the fifties and even sixties, it was a multipurpose ground including being used as the venue of the premier athletic event, the Public Schools Meet, where the Governor-General Sir Oliver Goonetillake was the chief guest.

The trips I made as a member of the athletic team to this hallowed grounds were far more enjoyable and memorable than my solitary trips as a spectator when I was young. The reason is we sang, joked and played pranks with each other and teased the members of the girls teams from Galle schools that travelled up on the same express train. I was accused of high-pitched singing, as was another member of the team Walter Gurusinghe, who imitated film stars of the day.

We travelled on Thursdays, competed on Fridays and Saturdays returning on Sundays. We used to be hosted at the Carey College hostel and walked to the Oval leisurely carrying our gear and the College flag. There, the scene was one of great excitement and splendor. The stands were crowded and usually a number of well-known athletes from previous Richmond teams and other alumni living in Colombo turned up to greet us.

The following year, 1954, was the best year for me in many ways. I won the Junior Hurdles event breaking the ground's record at the College Meet. I won the High Jump Event and won the Cup for Best Performance. At the Southern Group Meet I won the Junior Hurdles event equaling the Group Meet Record of 12.3 seconds set the previous year by Christo. I was also tied for the first place in the junior High Jump with Nandi Wijesighe of Mahinda College, at a height of 4 ft 8 inches. At the Public Schools Meet, I secured the second place in the junior Hurdles event, which was won by W.D.M. Abeysekare of Royal, who was the leading hurdler among us, as we advanced from junior to senior levels. I also ran a leg in the 4x110 yards relay event. We came second in the heat but fourth in the final with Dayananda Jayasuriya (DJ) and G.H. Amarasinghe, two excellent Richmond sprinters, and Sarath Balapatabandi, another fine all-round athlete. DJ came in second in both 100 yards and 200 yards events to W.D.M. Abesekara of Royal. The following year, G.H. Amarasinghe won both events.

In 1955, I competed at the senior level (under 19), and had a good year at the College Sports Meet, winning the 120 yards Hurdles and High Jump events, and coming second in the Pole Vault event. My House (Sneath) carried away the Championship Cup. At the Southern Group Meet, having won the heat, I came in third in the senior hurdles event. I also ran a lap in the senior 4X440 yards relay team and we came third. The meet was held at the Boossa race course where we ran on the cinder track, which was new at the time. It was much faster than grass tracks. That was the beginning of artificial surfaces for track and field competitions, which today have completely replaced grass tracks. The performance of the senior team as a whole was not satisfactory, but the juniors won the Championship Cup.

Rarely has Richmond achieved success as a team in the field of athletics outside the Southern Province, though we had many individual winners at the Public Schools level. But, in 1955, on the 25th Anniversary Silver Jubilee Public Schools Meet, Richmond won the Junior Championship and the Outstations Championship, a distinction that no other school had achieved at that time. We were awarded the Junior Tarbat Challenge Cup, edging Royal College, Colombo which they had won on four previous occasions. We were also awarded the Outstations Tarbat Challenge Cup which had been won by St. Anthonys' College, Kandy in the two years since it was first awarded in 1953. It is not often that an outstation college can seriously offer competition as a team to the well coached and funded athletes of the Colombo colleges, all of which had excellent facilities. For that reason, we were truly proud.

I was happy to be a member of the team that year, although I met with no success. That was my first year at the senior level. The historic successes were due to the grand achievements at the Colombo Oval by G. H. Amarasinghe, who won both 100-and-200 meter races, and R. L. de Silva, who won the junior Hurdles event, improving on the time he established with a new record surpassing the mark that I had held at the Southern Group Meet. They also combined with Sarath Balapatabendi, who had been placed second in the long jump event, to be second in the 4x110-yards relay event. We were a close knit group by then, and RL and Amarasinghe continued to be a close friends of mine in and out of school.

RL was the nephew of the former Prime Minister Wijeyananda Dhanayake. He was from Matara and he lived at his uncle's residence near the school. Amarasinghe was the son of a very successful merchant in Galle, who owned the leading clothing and textile store 'Silvas' in the heart of the shopping district on the Main Street in Galle. While I was living in Galle with my parents, he often used to give me a ride in the *Hillman Minx* car in which he was chauffer driven back and forth from school. After the demise of his father he took over and ran the establishment with success. Much later he moved to Colombo and continued his business from there.

The following year, in 1956, we had a mixed year with the outstanding juniors from the previous year moving up as freshman seniors. The College Meet was held on the cinder tracks of Boossa and R.L De Silva emerged as the best athlete winning three events. Greatly improved as a hurdler, he beat me in the Hurdles event for the first time since we started competing at the junior level. At the Southern Group meet R.L. once again beat me in the hurdles event and we came first and second. G.H. Amarasinghe won both sprint events 100 and 200 yards. Newton Pinnaduwa and Sarath Balapatabandi were placed first and second in the Long Jump and Triple Jump events respectively. That was quite an achievement for a young team, most of who were competing at the senior level for the first time. At the Public Schools Meet we were not so lucky. R.L. had an injury preventing him from competing and I was disqualified for beating the gun at the start of the Hurdles event.

The following year in 1957, I had the honor of being the captain of the College Athletic team. Both at the College Meet and the Southern Group meets, the results of the Hurdle event were the same, with R.L. beating me and winning the event and this time smashing all the records set before him. He also won the Hop-Step and Jump event.

At the Public Schools Meet, Ananda College produced two excellent hurdlers, Vijitha Wijesekara and Palitha Wanasundara, who edged R.L. to the second spot and knocked me out of contention. In the previous year, as juniors, R.L. in a record breaking run had beaten them both. Palitha later became a close friend at Law School, and we have continued our friendship through the years. When I visit my homeland, frequently I visit him at his home in Rathnapura, where he is a very successful lawyer and one time Mayor. He also visited me recently in Los Angeles. Vijitha immigrated to Australia.

Other notable hurdlers during my time in the junior and senior levels were Lalith Athulathmudali (Royal, Colombo), Luis Adhihetty (Wesley, Colombo), C.E. Scherranguvial (St. Thomas' Mt. Lavinia), S. Chinniah (Hartley College, Jaffna), H.M. Fuard (Wesley), and Ranjith Malawana (St. Josephs', Colombo).

R.L., a brilliant sportsman, went on to become the national champion. He joined the Police Department and, not too long after his marriage, he met with a tragic death at a very young age.

At the Southern Group Meet we had emerged as easy winners. It was a particular pleasure for me to collect the winner's trophy from then minister in the cabinet Hon. D.A. Rajapakse, father of the current president of the country Mahinda Rajapakse. I also relished the honor of carrying the College flag during the march-past of athletes both at the Southern Group and the Public Schools Meets.

* * *

Swimming was an activity that took place throughout all three school terms. When cadeting was discontinued at Richmond in 1935, the idea of holding aquatic sports was revived. Mr. A.F de Saa Bandaranayake, the cadet master organized the swimming classes and every year about 50 boys were taught to swim. Boys were also prepared for the examination of the Royal Life Saving Society, which awarded medals and certificates to those who were successful. Mr. Shelton de Silva, vice-principal, was our swimming coach and organized Inter- House Swimming meets.

During my time there were no inter-collegiate Aquatic Meets, and Richmond was the only school in Galle that had an organized swimming program. As Richmond had no pool, swimming practices and Aquatic Meets were held at the No. 1 Jetty in the Galle Harbor.

The splendid natural harbor of the port of Galle was in use in pre-Christian times, but gained in importance much later and by the 14th century it was arguably the most important port in the country. It retained this preeminence until 1873 when an artificial harbor was built in Colombo. The great Chinese admiral Zheng commemorated his visit by leaving a trilingual inscription in 1411; the three languages were Chinese, Tamil, and Arabic, implying that a cosmopolitan trading community used the Galle harbor. The Portuguese arrived in 1505, and later built a small fort adjoining the harbor. But it was after Galle was captured by the Dutch, in 1640, that the fort and the harbor were expanded and became a very profitable center of trade in cinnamon, pepper, cardamom, other spices and precious stones. The English took over in 1796 but made few changes to the infrastructure. Among the Asian ports of the United Dutch East India Company (VOC), Galle was second only to Batavia (now Jakarta, Indonesia).

The Court of Arms bearing the insignia VOC adorns the entrance to the fort facing the jetty where we had our swimming classes and aquatic meets. It was a bit of a drudgery to go back and forth to the jetty from Richmond. It took about 45 minutes each way, by bus or train, and walking to them at both ends. But we enjoyed each other's company and the outings. Once we reached the jetty and started swimming in the scenic harbor, we felt quite elated.

After a lapse of a decade of inactivity, the swimming program came to life once more in 1954, resuscitated by Rev. Shelton De Silva. We had a large number of boys in the program, displaying the enthusiasm of the students of the time. We were trained for the Royal Life Saving Society examinations. Two of the outstanding senior swimmers, Dayananda Aeywickrama and Sarath Boralessa, obtained the Silver Medal and the Instructors Certificate. Trevor Roosmale-Cocq, Osmond Jayawardane, a couple of others and I obtained the Bronze Medals and Intermediate Certificates.

Sarath joined the police. Trevor, after graduating from the Peradeniya University, had a successful career in the commercial sector, rising to be a Director at the mercantile concern Carsons. I had contact with both for a while as adults, but not in recent times. Osmond lived with his family in their ancestral home near the College. It was a large walauwwa with an equally large garden, which came in handy because he had at least five brothers who were all accomplished sportsmen at Richmond. Osmond, who was the youngest, in addition to being a good swimmer, was an outstanding athlete who won the Pole Vault event at the Southern Group Meet. He later immigrated to Australia. We were close friends in school although he was a class ahead of me. Recently I made contact with him when he visited his sister in Vancouver, Canada.

The following year, 1955, the progress in swimming was rapid with a larger number of boys; nearly one hundred, in the program. For the first time, a swimming Gala was organized as an Inter-House competition with a Challenge Cup offered to the winning House. It was a colorful event at the Galle jetty with a fair number of spectators present.

I won the open 60 yards back stroke event that year and continued to do so in the ensuing competitions. I finished third in the breast stroke event and took part in the winning relay team. I also won the Silver Medal in the Royal Life Saving Society examination.

By then Rev. Shelton De Siva had left, and after the interim swimming master, Berti Wimalasuriya, joined the staff of Dharmaraja College, Kandy, Elmore Perera took over. Elmore Perera returned to the staff of his alma mater, soon after graduating with a degree in mathematics. Elmore was a very versatile person. He was the Prefect in charge of the young kids dormitory when I was there, a great sportsman and an intellect.

Elmore later joined the survey department and retired as the Surveyor-General of Ceylon, and joined the Law College as a student. He studied law as an adult and became a well-known lawyer. He took up unpopular causes and appeared at the highest courts, defending fundamental rights cases. He was a champion of human rights, and stood up for integrity in public service. His great enthusiasm for such causes did not allow him to compromise at any cost. His uncompromising integrity led to his being admonished, and eventually being punished, by the Supreme Court and the Chief Justice. Elmore challenged the court's impartiality. Today, he is spending his retirement championing the causes he fought for. Often his articles on those topics appear in the daily press.

That year the Inter-House Competition had to be postponed because of the extensive loading and unloading of ships in the harbor. In my final year in the program, I was awarded the Distinction Award of the Royal Life Saving Society, their highest level. Among the others who also received the same awards were Shelton Jayasekara, who became premier magician of the country and President of the National Magicians Circle; and B.H. Jayaratne, who became a banker. He was most helpful to me on occasions when I had to transact business at the Bank of Ceylon during many visits back home.

Berti Gunasekara, Walter Gurusinghe, Susantha Gunawardane, N.R. Dhanapala, Ananda Manawadu, and T.R. Rajawasam were also outstanding swimmers who won competitions and life saving medals. While I have lost contact with many of them, I have met Ananda and Rajawasam, who were close friends in school, whenever I was on visits to Colombo.

* * *

Season after season, one sport followed the other. We were there to face the challenge of excelling in the field of sports; whether it was cricket, soccer, track and field or swimming. We were there for the glory of the school and seeking personal achievement. No gashes or scars ever deterred us, for as the College anthem aptly puts it; "Never mind a knock or two never fear the fight". That spirit from the field of sport carried us through our adult lives with ample rewards.

Chapter 12

Marx and Engels

Sports apart, my interest in elocution and debating led me to a greater interest in politics of the country, to which I had been exposed in my youth through my father's support of political candidates.

Richmond was an active place for political awareness. At the hostel many debates took place on political issues at the monthly, formal, Sunday night debates, and more often, in informal discourse among friends. Naturally, when I entered Richmond, due to my father's influence, I was a supporter of the right wing United National Party (UNP). However, soon my views evolved and drifted toward Socialism, and I became an admirer of the Lanka Sama Samaja Party (LSSP) with Trotskyite leanings. I read Marx and Engels and was an admirer of the leadership of the party, partly due to their intellectual prowess, and their concern for the working class and the poor.

My friend Vasudewa Nanayakkara, on the other hand, was a firebrand UNP supporter, mainly because his family was the main benefactor of the party in Galle. His father was a wealthy businessman running one of the most successful wholesale and transport business in the southern part of the country. His fleet of lorries (trucks) transported much of the goods back and forth from Colombo to the southern cities. The lorries were painted with the name of the business: Vasudewa & Company, which was well known in the south. The company was named after the eldest son of the owner (Vasu). His father was also a landed proprietor, owning tea estates in the southern hills in the Akurassa region. He also was an ardent supporter of the UNP. So, coming in to Richmond, it was natural for Vasu to be a UNP supporter.

At the 1952 general elections in the country, riding the wave of sympathy in the wake of the death of the first Prime Minister of the nation, D.S. Senanayake, the UNP, led by his son Dudley Senanayake, won the elections. In the ensuing celebrations Vasu led the UNP group in the school demonstrating around the school grounds. He was head to foot donned in green (the color of the UNP) with a green shirt, cap and flag in hand. He was carried on the shoulder of others as their leader.

Having been an admirer of socialism for a while, in my senior years at school, a few like-minded friends and I formed an informal socialist group. I had detected some vulnerability in the compassion displayed by Vasu towards the minor staff of the school, and so I decided somehow to rope him into our group. I knew it would be a daunting task. An occasion presented itself when I invited Tissa Vitharana, a senior medical student at the Medical College, who happened to be the nephew of the leader of the Lanka Sama Samaja Party (LSSP), Dr. N.M. Perera, to address our group. One Sunday he motored down from Colombo in his Vespa scooter, and gave a very succinct lecture to about fifteen of us, including a few friends whom we had invited to the lecture.

Vasu was among the reluctant invitees. Prior to the lecture I had been working on him, mainly on his conscience, preaching socialist dogma, which I hardly understood myself. To my joy he was mesmerized by Tissa's lecture, and slowly but steadily drifted towards socialism. By the time the 1956 general Election arrived, which was won by the newly formed Sri Lanka Freedom Party (SLFP), led by Solomon Dias Bandaranaike, Vasu was a true socialist, who was more conversant with socialist philosophy and its demagoguery than the rest of us. Although we had banded together to study the subject before he did, he became more committed than us.

Vasu became such an ardent supporter that he organized a strike among the workers of his father's tea estate. The leaders had thought they were immune from any consequences, because the proprietor's son was leading their cause. His father promptly sacked one of the leaders and ordered the workers back to the estate. The employee who was sacked wanted to regain his employment, and sheepishly went to Vasu's father and spilled the beans. Vasu's father was so incensed that he nearly disinherited his son!

In spite of his father's admonitions, Vasu remained a socialist, and over the years went on to lead many strikes and demonstrations that were considered major trade union activity in the country. He was the youngest of the recognized stalwarts in the LSSP, which was led by several political legends of the country.

* * *

The Lanka Sama Samaja Party, considered the oldest political party in the country, was founded in 1935 with the broad aims of achieving Independence from Britain and propagation of Socialism. It was led by a group of young Trotskyites motivated by Philip Gunawardena. The LSSP grew out of the Youth Leagues, in which a nucleus of Marxists had developed. The leaders were mainly educated returnees from London; youth who had come into contact with the ideas of the European Left and were influenced by Harold Laski. Dr S.A. Wickremasinghe, an early returnee and a member of the State Council from 1931, was part of this group. Its original members were Philip Gunawardena N. M. Perera, Colvin R. de Silva, Leslie Gunewardene, Robert Gunawardena (Philip's brother), and Vernon Gunasekera, the Party Secretary. Edmund Samarakkody and V Karalasingham joined them later.

Prior to the formation of the LSSP in 1933, the youth group was involved in the 'Suriya-Mal' movement, which had been formed to provide support for indigenous ex-servicemen by the sale of 'Suriya' (Portia tree) flowers. The 'Suriya-Mal' movement surged as a reaction to the fact that at the time Poppy Day funds went solely to British ex-servicemen. The LSSP had its beginnings in this movement which was an early anti-colonial movement.

In 1940 the LSSP split from of the pro-Moscow faction led by S. A. Wickremasinghe, M. G. Mendis, Pieter Keuneman and A. Vaidyalingam. The expelled members formed the United Socialist Party (USP), which later evolved into the Communist Party of Ceylon (CPC). At the outbreak of the Second World War the CPC was forced to go underground because of its opposition to the British war effort. The two State Council members of the party, and others on its Central Committee were arrested and jailed. On 20 April 1941, a secret conference was attended by 42 delegates. Leslie Gunewardene, who was in hiding, attended this conference at which the new CPC program and constitution were adopted. An openly functioning section of the party was established, led by Robert Gunawardena, S.C.C. Anthonipillai, V. Karalasingham, K.V. Lourenz Perera and William de Silva. The 'open' section of the party led a wave of strikes in 1941, 1942 and 1944.

During the 1940s the most powerful trade unions in the country supported LSSP politics. Bala Tampoe was the LSSP mastermind leading the union activities, along with the head of the then powerful Mercantile Union (CMU) headed by I.J. Wickrama (Bala Tampoe at age 92 as current head of the CMU, is almost certainly the oldest trade union leader in the world today). Other prominent members of the party were Vivienne Gunawardane (wife of Leslie Gunawardane), who was later a member of parliament, Wilmot Perera, Reggie Siriwardane, D.G. William, P.D. Wimalasena, Wilfred Senanayaka, Prof. Osmond Jayaratna, Dr. Tissa Abeysekara and Prof. Carlo Fonseka.

Vasu became active in the LSSP beginning in the mid-sixties, about the time when the LSSP joined the coalition government of then Prime Minister Sirimavo Bandaranaike (first woman head of a government in the world). Three of its members were ministers in the cabinet: Dr N. M. Perera (Finance), Cholomondely Goonewardena (Public Works) and Anil Moonesinghe (Communications). The Coalition Government fell in 1965, following the desertion of several members. However, the number of votes won by the LSSP increased at the general election held that year.

In 1970, the United Front, of which the LSSP was part, was elected to power in a landslide victory. The LSSP had 18 MPs in the House of Representatives, including Vasu, entering parliament for the first time representing the Kiriella electorate which he won by a large margin. Dr N.M Perera, Dr Colvin R de Silva and Leslie Gunewardena became Ministers of Finance, Constitutional Affairs, and Plantation Industries and Transport, respectively. The Party was able to advance parts of its program considerably: foreign-owned plantations were nationalized, democratically elected workers' councils were established in state corporations and government departments under the purview of its ministries (and of that of a sympathizer, T.B. Subasinghe of the SLFP), and measures were taken that narrowed the gap between the rich and poor.

Several LSSP members were appointed to important posts in which they could press the party program forward: e.g. Anil Moonesinghe became Chairman of the Ceylon Transport Board, theoretician of the party, Hector Abhayavardhana, was made Chairman of the People's Bank, and Prof. Doric de Souza was appointed as Permanent Secretary to the Ministry of Plantations. Dr Seneka Bibile, a member of the LSSP, became the founder Chairperson of the State Pharmaceuticals Corporation (SPC), which distributed drugs at affordable rates, by generic name instead of the trade name, and that became a model for the Third World.

The 1950s and 1960s were in many ways the "Golden era" of the LSSP. At the time the most powerful trade unions in the country supported LSSP politics. It peaked in political strength in the 1970s, but has declined gradually during the last 30 years.

In 1975, the United Front broke up with the expulsion of the LSSP ministers. There followed a period of wilderness for the party. In 1977 disaster struck. The LSSP and CP lost all their parliamentary seats, and the Left was unrepresented, something that had not happened in the 46 years since the introduction of universal suffrage. The same year the LSSP suffered another split. A group led by the then youth leader, Vasu, broke away and formed the Nava Sama Samaja Party (NSSP) with a non-communal socialist agenda.

In 1994 the LSSP joined the People's Alliance (PA), the front led by the SLFP. It had three members elected to parliament that year. Bernard Soysa, Minister of Science and Technology in the PA Government, on his demise was succeeded by Batty Weerakoon. Vasu had by then returned to the LSSP from the NSSP following a disagreement with his protégé Dr. Wickramabahu Karunaratne who now leads the NSSP. However, in 1999 Vasu, who was LSSP member of parliament elected from Ratnapura, was expelled after having publicly criticized the PA Government.

After his expulsion Vasu floated the Democratic Left Front (DLF). At the 2004 elections, LSSP won one parliamentary seat. Its lone MP, Tissa Vitarana, was named Minister of Science and Technology. The LSSP has gradually decreased in strength. The Congress of Samasamaja Youth Leagues has been disbanded. At the 2010 elections both LSSP and DLF contested under the United People's Freedom Alliance. LSSP members did not win any seats but its current leader, Dr. Tissa Vitarana (the one who impressed Vasu as a school boy at Richmond in the fifties to be interested in socialism), was named as a national list member and appointed as Minister of Scientific Affairs. Once again, Vasu won elections as an MP from the Ratnapura District and was appointed as Minister of National Languages and Social Integration.

Vasu had always been the maverick in the LSSP and ready to criticize the government and even the party, whenever he felt either was deviating from its stated mission. That resulted in his shuttling in and out of the party, but he never joined any other party. He of course formed his own breakingaway party, whenever he was out of the LSSP.

After half a century of political life, he still remains possibly the only politician who is considered sincere to his cause and untainted with any allegation of corruption or wrong-doing. That in itself is quite an achievement for a politician who has been in the forefront of politics over such a long span of time. That may also be his ultimate legacy.

* * *

While I was on the field captaining the Richmond College Cricket team, I am told that Vasu used to come to watch the matches and engage in political debates distracting the rest of the spectators from watching the game. At Richmond, Vasu took part in sports but he left behind an ignominious record of having allowed the leading soccer team in the South, St. Aloysius College, to score seventeen goals!

Growing up I was close to Vasu's family and was a frequent guest at his ancestral home in Mihiripanne in the south of Galle. His mother has always been kind to me and in spite of our age gaps his younger siblings have also been like family to me.

One of Vasu's brothers, Hemakumara Nanayakkara, took up politics, but as a UNP member. He represented the Galle District in parliament. Vasu represented Ratnapura District, where he had no roots, but it was an area where leftist politics were more rampant. Hemakumara later crossed over to the SLFP and was Minister of Agriculture before he retired recently for health reasons.

Another of Vasu's brothers, Yasapalitha Nanayakkara, became one of the most popular movie producers in the country at a very young age. Unfortunately, he passed away at the peak of his career. The two youngest brothers of Vasu, Asanga and Nilmin, became successful businessmen managing the family- owned plantation and business in the mercantile sector. All his brothers were educated at Richmond College at the same time as I did. His four sisters, Swarna, Ranjini, Lanka, and Dharma, were educated at Sacred Heart Convent in Galle. Some of them became lawyers and married lawyers, and they are all well settled in life.

Vasu married his Law College girlfriend Wasanthi Gunasekare, who came from a family with a political background. She joined the

Inland Revenue Department and became the Deputy Head of the Department (Commissioner). Later, she served as a legal adviser in the Ministry of Foreign Affairs and as the Director of the government agency overseeing the operations of the Non-governmental Organizations (NGOs). They have two sons, Chiranjaya, a lawyer based in Texas; Shankajaya earned an Anthropology degree in the United States; and a daughter, Tharushi, also educated in the United States is on the staff of the Overseas School in Colombo, and married to a lawyer serving the Attorney General's Department.

I have been fortunate to have many friends around the world; several of them are very close to me, and others have been friends for a very long time. But if I were to single out one, who has been the closest friend for the longest time, it would have to be Vasu.

Chapter 13

Best of Times-
Best of Friends

Life at Richmond, especially in the hostel, was enriched by the pranks we enjoyed and the friendships we formed; friendships which have weathered the ravages of time and still stand as firm as the rocks that form the Galle fort.

While each dormitory had an academic teacher in charge, the punishments, particularly the severe ones including corporal punishment, were meted out by the Boarding Master, Mr. G.W.S. De Silva. An old boy of Richmond, he was also the head of the administrative staff. He was also the soccer coach for both senior and junior teams. He was warm and kind as long as you did not break any rules. Once you did, you were in trouble.

When Mr. Silva married late in his life, he went into residence in a college bungalow. Mr. J. Jesudason, a math teacher who acted for Mr. Silva, took over as Boarding Master. At the time Richmond, like many private schools in the country, had Indian teachers because there was a dearth of science and math teachers in the country. Mr. Jesudason was one of them. During our time Jesudasan was a very serious and stern teacher, of whom the students were mortally afraid of. Later on I believe he joined the staff of St. Thomas' College, Mount Lavinia to the relief of many students who had been caned by him.

We had two other Indian teachers; Mr. K.K. Cherian who sported a bushy beard and taught us chemistry; and Mr. J.T. Ariyaratnam who was our biology teacher. They were also rather stern though friendly. They all resided in the hostel and were dorm masters.

The only other dorm master was Walter May, a Sri Lankan Burgher. He was also an alumnus of Richmond before he proceeded to St. Thomas'College, Mt. Lavania. He had a distinguished career at the University of Ceylon, Peradeniya. He was a versatile sportsman playing cricket and an athlete representing his schools and the university. He also represented the country as a member of the national athletic team and he won the Hurdles event at the annual Indo-Ceylon Athletic Meet. He was our English, history and civics teacher in different years, and was the coach of both senior athletic and cricket teams.

Walter May was a very friendly person and generally did not take too seriously his functions as a dorm master although he was a first-rate academic teacher and sports coach. After his coaching functions, at about six in the evening, he would disappear to the Galle town and return very late in the night, long after the entire hostel had gone to sleep. The general story was that in town he would visit his favorite bar at the Sydney hotel and imbibe in the heady stuff.

On one such night he suddenly appeared in the dorm quite late when we were all in our dream world, and got hold of G.P.T. Karunaratne (Gippa) by his throat and threw him to the compound outside. He then locked the dorm door. It was only the next day we learned the reason for the commotion. Apparently, after returning from his usual sojourn in town, he was correcting an assignment given to us in the civics class to write an essay on the various communities in the country. Gippa was never a good student and cared less to be one. In his essay, quite innocently he had written derogative stuff about the Burgher community. He had picked up the information by listening to gossip, for he would never have found it in books, which he hardly read. Walter May had taken this as a personal insult, thinking Gippa purposely wanted to annoy him.

The incident was nothing new to Gippa who used to get into trouble quite regularly both in class, for not taking things seriously, and in the hostel, where he was ready to be part of any prank or action that most discerning people would dare not indulge in. His parents passed away when he was fairly young, leaving him and his only sibling, quite a fortune. This may have been partly the reason for his carefree attitude. His younger brother Upali Karunaratne was a Cadet of the British militeray training school Sandhurst, and rose to be a Major General in the Sri Lanka Army.

Gippa was a close friend of mine and continued to be so even after we left Richmond. He used to visit me at the Law College and during the holidays he would spend time at my home. He was the only one among us who owned a car during those early days. He and I, at times with other friends, have travelled to many a place in his *Hillman Minx* automobile. I have also borrowed it from him when needed. It was Gippa who drove me to the airport when I left for graduate studies to Canada.

Not long after I had left, the then Prime Minister Mr. Ranasighe Premadasa visited Gippa's home in Bentota to have breakfast on his way to Kataragama, the holy shrine in the deep south of the country. Gippa was an ardent supporter of Mr. Premadasa and his UNP party. The visit happened to be made during the time of a JVP insurrection in Sri Lanka, to which reference has already being made. That night, the JVP insurgents visited him, and sadly, slaughtered him to pieces. His wife, a graduate teacher, was away at the time. Later, she and their young son and daughter left the country and went to the Seychelles, where she took up a teaching assignment. Many years later, they immigrated to Canada, landing first in New York where I met them at the JFK airport. I drove them to our home to spend a few days with us, before proceeding to Canada to settle down.

The other prankster among us was Nihal Gunawardane, who was known as Kaputa (crow) due to his dark complexion. I am glad he beat me to it as far as nicknames go, as I cannot imagine how anyone can be of a darker complexion than I. He, along with Munidasa

Abeywickrama and DJ, who were referred to earlier, were part of the gang that enjoyed scrapes often, and were found on the bench (made to stand up on their chairs), during study periods in the hostel, for all to see. That punishment was mostly for breaking rules such as not observing silence after the lights-off bell, which required that everyone go to bed. Another prank was plucking 'Kurumba' (young coconuts) from the many trees in the college property. This act was forbidden, mainly for safety reasons.

Though I was part of this gang, and was around when such activities took place, I usually got away, escaping in the nick of time. Nihal took part in sports, but unlike his elder brother J.N.A. Gunawardane, who was an outstanding cricketer with whom I played in the College team; Nihal was never really good at any sport. Later, having become a trained teacher, he joined the College staff. To my surprise, he was also the cricket coach for the senior team. He must have mastered the art of coaching because he was later appointed as the coach to a junior national team which toured Hong Kong and Malaysia.

* * *

All this occurred while we were gradually moving from the junior dorms to the senior dorms: Cambridge (Mr. Cherrian, dorm master), Winchester (Mr. John and Walter May), Hanover (Jesudasan) and Windsor (Mr. Silva), in that order. While at Cambridge, we had as our prefect in charge Walter Fernando. He was an avid reader of news and one of the few who had a private subscription to the Times of Ceylon, a leading national evening newspaper, which was perhaps the most literary of the papers at the time. He allowed me to go to his cubicle and read the previous day's newspaper before he disposed of it. It is to be noted that those days the newspapers were limited to less than ten pages, including all the advertisements. Consequently, it didn't consume too much time to go through them.

Eventually, he convinced me of the value of reading the newspapers and persuaded me to share the cost. Whether it was done in good intentions to help me, or for his budgetary reasons, I do not know.

However, I did get used to reading the editorials and improved my knowledge of political and social issues, and more importantly, considerably improved my understanding of the English language. Up to now I am addicted to reading newspapers first thing every morning. While living in Canada 'The Montreal Star', in New York 'The New York Times', in Austria or when travelling abroad 'The Herald Tribune', and now in Los Angeles 'The Los Angeles Times'. When in Sri Lanka 'The Daily News' and 'The Island' are my choices.

Being in the hostel offered us the opportunity to forge many friendships and indulge in sports, literary and other activities throughout the day and even during the weekends. Since Richmond was a Christian school, Sunday was supposed to be a day of rest. The Wesleyan Mission was not that strict as to what one did during weekends, as long as there were no organized events. We did get to go to the city center in Galle once a month to see a picture (movie). That was an occasion we looked forward to as the only other time we boarders were allowed off the College premises was for sports or other public events taking place in Galle. Once, a student who, like me, was not that conversant in English at the time was so excited at going to a movie announced with glee that: "We are going to see a movie featuring 'Gini Keli' (fireworks in Sinhala)". But on arriving at the theater we realized he was referring to Gene Kelly, the famous movie star.

As I moved from Cambridge to the more senior dorms I associated mostly with a trio of friends whose friendship has endured through our adult life.

Two were my seniors, Dayananda Abeywickrama from an illustrious family in Morawaka, and G.H.H. Perera (Hema), nephew of a wealthy merchant from Wadduwa, who also had been at Richmond. He had donated lavishly to the College building fund and had our carpentry building named after him. The third was in my class, Senarath Mendis, son of a Mudalier in the Balapitiya courts.

Several times a week, we used to go together to the Tuck Shop, where savories like cutlets and patties and sweet goodies like musket and 'kalu dodol' were available to go with a good cup of tea. We used to chat and joke around while enjoying the fare. The four of us took turns to stand (to pick-up the tab). Dayananda and Hema, for obvious reasons, and Mendis, with an ample allowance he received, were flush with cash and had no problems standing the frequent treats. I had much less of a monthly allowance for my pocket money, and was a delinquent in paying, but it did not bother my pals. It must have bothered me though, because I still have a letter written by me to my father pleading for an increase in my allowance by telling him that I was often embarrassed in the company of friends when I constantly ran out of cash. This was in spite of the fact that, as noted earlier, I used to supplement my allowance by frequent visits to Muriel Akka, who never failed to dole out a few rupees each time I visited her. Of course my father, who tried to instill in me frugal habits, was not swayed by my pleadings, though the next year he increased my allowance by a few cents. Though we did not have much money, we had enough. But my father would not do anything ostentatious to demonstrate it. I sure learned a lesson, because throughout my life, I was instinctively conscious of the possibility of being in want someday.

The foursome continued till one by one, we left Richmond. Dayananda was an outstanding scout and the College Troop leader. After leaving Richmond, he had a successful career as a business person and ended up as the General Manager of the Island Group of Publishers. The Group published several daily and weekly national newspapers, journals and magazines. Senarath Mendis was the quietest and calmest among us. He became a lawyer with a successful practice at the Balapitiya courts. He lived at his ancestral house near Balapitiya, where I used to make brief visits to him on my way to and from my hometown and Colombo, whenever I was in the country.

First to leave Richmond was the most brilliant among us. He did not have a dignified exit. While he was brilliant, and did well in his scholastics, Hema was a prankster par excellence and remains so today, as this is a trait inborn in him. He was expelled from Richmond for just one such prank. Being expelled meant it was not easy for him to enter another school of similar repute, and he was only a few terms away from his the university entrance exam. With the influence that his uncle wielded in the area, he was able to register at Sri Pali College, Horana, not far from his hometown. His sister, Chandra, was a teacher there and accepted his entry to the school on the strict understanding that he agree not play the fool and to behave properly. Otherwise, she too would have to leave the place, she explained. It was on that clear understanding that she consented to his enrolling in the new school. Though it was an institution started with the help of Rabindranath Tagore by a local icon, Wilmot Perera, it was hardly a school anyone serious about a university education would attend. It catered mostly to rural folk in the area.

I doubt Hema actually attended any classes there. The feeling among friends to date is that he may have been registered there by the principal as a courtesy to his uncle, on condition he would not attend classes and corrupt the students. In any event, what mattered was that when the time came for the university entrance examaniation he was able to sit for the exam as a student of Sri Pali College. Even at the entrance exam, his attention was less on the question paper in front of him than the student seated next to him who distracted his attention by visiting the toilet quite often. But when the results were announced in the *Ceylon Daily News* Paper, as was the custom in those days when the numbers of successful candidates were small enough to be printed in the leading daily paper, it was no surprise that Hema passed with flying colors.

The person who was at the same examination center that attracted Hema's attention by distracting him from the serious business of the day by making constant visits to the toilet was Namel Weeramuni. He too entered the University of Ceylon, Peradeniya, and they became close friends. Naturally, Namel became a dear friend of mine and the friendship between the trio has thrived for more than half a century.

Up to date, Hema claims that he is not aware why he was expelled from Richmond. Though a most implausible explanation, he feels that it must be because his Sinhala teacher, at whom he had directed jokes during his class, would have reported him to the principal. Having done brilliantly well at the university entrance exam compared to the colleagues he left behind at Richmond, he made a visit to Richmond on the occasion of the annual sports meet. The principal who sacked Hema welcomed and congratulated him and commented that it was the bad company he kept that spoilt him. This was ironic because when his uncle, an important benefactor of the school, took Hema to the principal to make an appeal, principal for some reason was not moved and informed the uncle that Hema was a bad influence on others and therefore the decision could not be reversed.

Hema became a scholar in oriental languages and economics at the Peradeniya campus. He was always in the midst of pranksters and constantly getting into scrapes, but this time around he survived the full academic course. He also became a leading advocate of socialism and was the President of the Communist Party on the campus. Many years after his graduation he became an ardent UNP supporter, confiding that he saw the Communist Party as a good vehicle to roam the world, at least the socialist world. At the time, the Communist Party used to finance sojourns to visit socialist countries from funds doled out by the embassies of those countries. The Soviet Union and its satellites in Eastern Europe used to sponsor such trips for university students and politicians, with the obvious aim of convincing them of the superiority and philosophy of socialism by exposing them to the best that they could offer in those nations. It often worked. Hema did tour the Soviet Union and some Eastern European states, thanks to the generosity of such study tours. But shortly after he left the university he quickly shed his socialist philosophy and activities. Although he never took any active part in politics thereafter, he remained a keen observer of the political scene with an unmistakable bias toward capitalism!

Hema's conversion was delayed a bit longer because, after graduating his pal Namel invited him to teach night school with him at an institution run by a well known Buddhist priest, a stalwart of the socialist political parties. First, as part time teacher in Colombo, and then he followed Namel to a school in Ratnapura, as full time teachers. There they rented and shared an apartment. By this time, Namel was beginning his career as a dramatist and he held rehearsals in their apartment. This included the use of local 'Beres' (drums). After a while, their landlord began to get complaints from the neighbors, and warned them not to make too much noise. Those requests fell on deaf ears, and the landlord cut off their electricity, expecting them to move out. Undaunted they carried on their rehearsals, and one day when both of them returned from their teaching assignments, they found their bag and baggage on the street and the apartment locked up. They had no option but to move. They did not last too long in Ratnapura before they both decided to study law. In Law College they also were notorious for their pranks and what can elegantly be described as naughty behavior, but eventually both graduated as advocates (attorneys-at-law).

No sooner than Hema donned his lawyer's garb he decided to marry his Law College sweetheart Mallika Hunukumbara, a pretty damsel and fellow lawyer hailing from the Manikdiwala Walauwa, near Kandy. They took wings to the island of Jamaica in the West Indies. There, he had secured an appointment with the Ministry of Finance as a senior adviser. More about him is elsewhere in this narrative.

*　*　*

Among my other friends at Richmond was classmate Punya Illeperuma, who was at the top of our pack. Punya graduated from the University of Ceylon, Peradeniya, with an arts degree and later became a lawyer. He married Vijiyani who was one of two girls in our HSC class of about ten. Punya became a very successful criminal lawyer in Colombo very early in his career. I used to see him often when I visited Colombo. His wife Vijiyani was also a close friend of mine. Vijiyani was employed at the Central Bank of Ceylon and from time to time she used to assist me whenever I visited the bank, mainly for foreign currency issues, which at the time had stringent regulations. Unfortunately, they were separated when Punya met an early death. Vijayani immigrated to Australia with her daughter. Many years later, she used to make extended annual visits to the United States to be with the family of her son in Dallas, Texas. She never failed to call me to chat about the old days.

Among the others in my HSC class were Vasu, Ifam Azeez, who became a lawyer and later a judge, Lalith Edirisinghe, who became an editor of the well-known newspaper 'The Sunday Observer,' K.H Samarawardane, a graduate in Arts from the University of Ceylon, Peradeniya, who became a teacher, Ananda Manawadu, who joined the Air Force, and Premalatha Thenuwara with whom I have lost contact since leaving school. There were a dozen science students in the parallel class, including three with whom I have kept contact. Lalith Fernando became a medical doctor and migrated to the United States. He lives in Kansas. A. Abeysirigunawardane and Raja Wannakkukorale, who became medical doctors and migrated to the UK. Raja's father was a scholar in Sinhala, who was responsible for the credit pass in Sinhala I obtained in the SSC exam. The only other friend from the Science Class with whom I had continuing contacts after leaving school, was D. Bandusena, who graduated from the University of Ceylon, Colombo, with a science degree and became a science teacher and later a school principal.

There were about another dozen among those who had progressed from primary school with me in the same class, but they left school without proceeding to further their education beyond their Senior School Certificate (SSC). This certificate required passing a countrywide public examination held by the government department of education. They took up various professions such as business, planting, mercantile and government jobs, and as teachers. Among them, I continued to have contact with Nihal De Silva who joined the police and retired as a senior superintendant. He visited me in Vienna when he was on assignment there. I also had sporadic contact with W.G.N Yapa and P.V.D Gunawardane, who joined the postal department and retired as postmasters; and B. Jayaratne who joined the Bank of Ceylon.

The only other classmate I have kept lifelong contact with is Lakshman Wickramasinghe. He lived just outside the premises of Richmond College. His father was the head of the primary school and his elder brother, Raja, was a sportsman who later held national records in put shot and discus events. After graduation, Raja joined the Air Force and retired as a high ranking officer. He became a national sports administrator. When we were about twelve, Lakshman, for some reason or other, annoyed me, and I challenged him for a fight. This was an accepted thing at the time. When the fight took place on the appointed date and time, with other friends watching and cheering us, I knocked him to the ground with a blow to the jaw. In the process, he lost a tooth and to my consternation he carried the scar for life.

Of course, my fame was short-lived, as another friend, Wilfrey Rodrigo, challenged me for a fight not long after, because I had somehow managed to upset a friend of his, Ranjith Fernando. Wilfrey was a strongly-built chap. This time it was a more publicized affair and a fair number of friends gathered to witness the event, expecting a full-blooded fight. I was still new to Richmond and was not entirely familiar with the rules by which the challenge fights were fought out. The referee, another friend, summoned both of us and asked us to shake hands. I expected thereafter we would break and the referee would signal to start the fight. But as the hand shake was being released, quite unexpectedly I caught an upper cut from Wilfrey that sent me to the ground. Before I knew what was happening, he was on top of me well and truly boxing me around to the cheering from his many pals, until the referee mercifully said time was up. I was lucky to escape with a few bruises and all my teeth intact! This was the last time that I was involved in any kind of physical fight to this day.

Wilfrey went on to become a surveyor and Lakshman joined the Central Bank. I have seen Wilfrey on very rare occasions, and I shared a long lasting friendship to date with Lakshman. Lakshman also became an important official in the Scout movement. He worked at the Scout Headquarters after he retired from the Bank. I visit him regularly at Melder Place in Nugegoda, a suburb of Colombo, where he resides. His brother Raja lives next door.

Looking back at my life at Richmond, I realize a good part of it was filled with sports and other extracurricular activities, in which I lavishly indulged. I also had great teachers, who showered their love and guidance on me and the wonderful circle of friends I knew. Some of those friends have sadly fallen off the radar. I wish there was time enough to reconnect with these souls. We had great times together as school kids. Sadly, several have passed away but, thankfully, quite a few are still in touch through alumni associations and other personal contacts that have survived the passage of time. From Vasu to Hema, Gippa to Lakshman, my school friends were the brightest stars that illuminated my sky.

— ❖ —

Chapter 14

Scorching sun, benign breeze

I walked as softly as I could across the front garden and reached the side door. Click. Click. My heart stopped momentarily. Would my father or stepmother hear the sound of my key turning in the lock? I counted to three. All was quiet within. I tiptoed to my bedroom, breathing once more. I had just returned from watching Gene Kelley, "Singing in the Rain", at the cinema. It was a Saturday night on Wakwalla Road, Galle.

It was natural that I should leave the hostel and move in with my father and stepmother, when they rented a house in the picturesque seaside city of Galle in the late 1950s.

Galle, the main city in the most southerly part of the island, is the administrative center of the Southern Province of Sri Lanka. Galle is located 20 miles south of Ambalangoda (72 miles from the capital of Colombo). Galle got its name from the word 'Gaalla' which, in the native tongue, was used to identify a large number of bullock carts that were stalled in one place. The locality where there were more numbers of carts and bulls stationed was called 'Maagalla' or Magalle, which now forms the southern part of the city. Galle was the main port on the island before the arrival of the Portuguese in the 16th century. It is recorded that Romans, Greeks Persians and Arabs were trading through the Galle port. The Dutch constructed huge ramparts and an enchanting fort, which forms a landmark in

Galle that gives splendor to the town. The fort is considered the best example of a fortified city built by Europeans in South and Southeast Asia, showing the interaction between European architectural styles and South- Asian traditions. The atmosphere of the Dutch days is still preserved with many old Dutch buildings intact. The fort is a world heritage site and the largest remaining fortress in Asia built by European occupiers.

The Boxing Day tsunami caused by the 2004, which occurred Indian Ocean off the coast of Indonesia a thousand miles away, created havoc in Galle. Thousands were killed in the city alone and the population incurred much property damage, including the famous cricket ground (the Galle International Stadium). It was rebuilt after the tsunami and test matches resumed there on December 18, 2007.

Galle is the second largest city in Sri Lanka with a population of about hundered thosand, the majority of who are of Sinhalese ethnicity. There is also a large Sri Lankan Moor minority (about 25%), particularly in the fort area. The Moors are descendents from Arab merchants who settled in the ancient port of Galle, along with a sizable number of Burgher families. More recently, there is a notable foreign population, both residents and owners of holiday homes. Galle is fast becoming a highly sought-out location by tourists.

The Galle Municipal Council governs the city of Galle. The municipality was established the year I was born. Mr. Wijayananda Dahanayake, a distinguished student of Richmond College, became the first mayor of Galle in 1938. He later became the Prime Minister of Ceylon.

Galle is home to some of the oldest leading schools in Sri Lanka. Ten schools with a long history behind them (five boys' and five girls' schools) are located in Galle. Among them, Richmond (Methodist), Mahinda (Buddhist) and St Aloysius (Catholic) are the leading boys' schools. Sanghamitta Balika Vidyalaya was the first Buddhist girls' school to be established in the country in 1919. Along with Sacred Heart Convent (Catholic) and Southland (Methodist), these are the leading girls' schools. There are also several vernacular schools in the city, including the one I attended at the kindergarten level.

Today, twenty-nine government schools providing free education and five fee-levying international schools are situated in Galle, and several are now co-educational. In recent times, more than two decades after I left Galle, it has also become a center of university education. Two main faculties of the University of Ruhuna, established in late seventies, are located in Galle. The Faculty of Engineering is located at Hapugalle, about 5 km from the city center. The faculty of medicine is located at Karapitiya, near the Karapitiya Teaching Hospital, also located about 5 km from the city center. A study centre of the Open University of Sri Lanka is also located in Galle at Labuduwa junction.

Labuduwa, about 6-km from the city center, was the location of an excellent farm during my time in Galle. The Agricultural Technology Institute established there was a pioneer in technological education. More recently it has been expanded to include the Galle Advanced Technological Institute, offering Diplomas in Agriculture, as well as in the field of Information Technology (IT).

* * *

Our home on Wakkwella Road was spacious with a modern bathroom and toilet facilities, which the railway bungalows lacked. It had a covered porch with a verandah. In addition to the main door to the house, the verandah had a side door leading to the front bedroom, which was mine. The side door, a facility that I immensely enjoyed, provided me access to the house on late nights. There were three additional rooms; a spacious living and dining area, with a long back verandah that led on one side to the storeroom and the kitchen and on the other to the bathroom and toilets. The back verandah faced a yard that was walled off as were the two side and front yards. The front parapet wall of the house was set about 15 yards from the road allowing sufficient privacy from the hustle and bustle of the road.

Next door was a mansion owned by a well known businessman in Galle, L.O.E. De Silva, whose two sons attended Richmond with me. On the other side were the premises of a saw mill owned by another successful merchant in town, whose house faced ours. Next to that, was the well known Thasim Chest Clinic, the only facility in the south of the country at the time for treatment of tuberculosis. and other chest ailments. The medical specialist in charge, Dr. Cooray, had a house behind our house facing a side street.

My home was also walking distance from the 'pacha gaha' (the tree of fibs). It was so named because there were several palm and horoscope readers and other soothsayers who practiced their craft underneath this tree. People came to consult these clairvoyants and were entertained by snake charmers, and others who performed all manner of tricks, including 'kavi kola karayo' (who recited poetry mostly composed on the spot). They all gathered under this gigantic tree.

About two houses from the 'pacha gaha' was the house to which our family friend, Muriel Akka, had moved several years before us, after marrying Uncle Gulavita, who was an executive of the Bank of Ceylon, Galle Branch. This was the only bank in Galle at the time. It was they who found the house for us when my father was transferred to Galle. They had a son of about ten who attended Richmond during my time but who was much junior to me. They also had two younger daughters.

Son Sunil Kumar Gulavita graduated as a medical doctor and migrated to the U.K., where he specialized in oncology at the Royal Marsden Hospital, the best known cancer hospital in the U.K. Having served there as a specialist for ten years, he moved to the United States where he was attached to the Mayo Clinic, one of the leading medical facilities in the U.S. After serving five years at the Mayo Clinic, he moved to the remote Canadian town of Thunder Bay in the Midwest. There, he established a private clinic and became a well-known oncologist in that part of Canada. He was also the head of the Radiology Oncology at the Thunder Bay Regional Health Science Center. When I consulted him regarding a close friend, Norman

Weerasooria, who was unsure whether to receive treatment in the UK or the U.S., Kumar told me, after having served in both countries, he believed that the cancer treatment in the UK was decades behind the U.S. He mentioned that the specialists who had seen my friend's reports in the UK were his professors and were very competent, but they suffered from the lack of funding to acquire cutting-edge technology for treatment. Research in the UK did not compare to what was available in the US. I have kept in touch with him and he has been most willing to offer advice whenever I had the occasion to consult him.

Sunil's younger sister Shanthi also became a medical doctor and migrated to the UK. I have seen her on my visits to London. She sought my advice regarding the educational facilities in the US for her daughter. The youngest sister, Sandamali Guruge, was inflicted with polio but was given a good education and married a caring person. She had a daughter and they lived off the canal road in Wellawatte in Colombo, where Muriel Akka spent the last few decades of her life well cared for. I always went to see her during my visits home to Sri Lanka, and she always had tears of joy on those occasions to see the little fellow she carried in her arms now a grown man.

Not far from our home lived Muriel Akka's younger sister Norah, who was married and had a family of her own. Living within walking distance of both houses, I visited them often during the days I was with my father and stepmother in Galle. I always had a suspicion that my father and Murielle Akka had a soft spot for each other, which was possibly reflected in her close attachment to me. Suspicions began when at some stage I saw my father's photograph in her living room. But this was at a time when my father was not ready to remarry, and long before Muriel Akka was married. Regrettably, Uncle Gulavita, a vivacious man, who was game to enjoy the good life that Muriel Akka and indeed her whole family fancied, passed away early in mid-life of a sudden heart attack.

Our new residence was a stone's throw away from the junction of four cross roads. The intersection faced the Vidayaloka Vidyalaya, a boys' vernacular school, which was originally a 'Pirivena', a monastic college (similar to a seminary) for the education of Buddhist priests. Such Pirivenas were centers of secondary and higher education in ancient times for lay people as well. I used to take the local bus from that junction to Richmond, about a twenty-minute ride. On some days I rode my bike back and forth to school, but not all that often. A bus full of girls on their way to Sangamitta Girl's School, which was half-way from my house to Richmond, was far more tempting to me than a bike ride.

Our house was also within walking distance to the Galle Cricket Grounds and Esplanade and the two cinemas in Galle. By then, I was a cinema fan and found the time to see most of the good movies shown at the Queen's Theater. I was first introduced to cinema when we were originally resident in Galle at Kandewatte and Kalegana. As a very young child my father took me to the cinema in a rickshaw, and I sat on his lap in the first Class section of the movie house. I guess it was too expensive for him to buy two tickets. Most of the movies were war films, and quite old by the time they reached Galle. I remember well two movies that I saw with him; *Casablanca* with Humphrey Bogart, as a heroic tank driver in the desert, and the silent classic *Mark of Zorro* with Douglas Fairbanks Jr. There were others with such stars as Clark Gable, James Stewart, William Wyler and Rita Hayworth, but my memory fails when I try to recall the movies they acted in.

During my time at the Richmond hostel, we were permitted to go to the theater one Sunday a month. I would not miss the occasion, even if I had to beg or borrow to buy the movie tickets. Mostly we watched from the gallery, often seated on the front row, looking right up at the screen. We were allowed to watch mostly educational movies such as *Pride and Prejudice* with Maureen O'Sullivan, The *Grapes of Wrath* with Henry Fonda, *Citizen Kane* with Orson Welles; and cowboy movies featuring Roy Rogers and Allan Ladd, as well as the musicals such as *Singing in the Rain* starring Gene Kelly.

* * *

This was also a time when I ventured out on bicycle trips that took me to far-flung places in the south of the country. We loved cycling to the pulsing rhythm of spinning wheels through the scenic southern coast and the undulating hills of Morawaka. I was part of a group of Richmond students who were keen on taking such trips. Our leader was Elmo Perera. Both hostellers and day scholars were in the group. The range of our trips was about 50 to 75 miles each way. We went on these trips mostly during long weekends and occasionally during holidays.

We loved cycling along the scenic southern coast. We especially enjoyed the ride through the road that hugs the sandy beach along the bay in Weligama (the village of sand), with the sea breeze cooling our sweat-drenched faces. As we rode by the Weligama bay we gazed with awe at the unique site of fishermen perched on stilts in the deep ocean. We also visited the famous Kustarajagala rock carving, which dates back many centuries. The picture depicts a *Bodhisatva* (potential Buddha), about which many legends have been told. My memories of the visit are rather dim as I have not visited it recently.

Another point of attraction was the offshore islet, *Ganduwa* (rock Island), also known as Taprobane, where French Count de Mauny built his dream house. Count de Mauny was an exiled French aristocrat, who became a British national and lived in Ceylon for over twenty years. He built his impressive home in French style with a mixture of Dutch architecture. His residence today serves as a tourist attraction. I visited it much later in life with nostalgic memories of the time we whizzed past it on our bikes.

A stop generally never missed was at the *Devundara* (Dondra) temple. Perhaps because we had to pass by the temple, with statues of many gods, Dondra is known as *Devinuwara*, (Gods' town). As is the custom with most passersby, someone in our group would make an offering of a coin or two to the Gods. Located in the southern most tip of the country, the Devundara temple is one of the few surviving buildings from the ancient classical Dravidian architectural era. It was destroyed during the Portuguese rule. In the vicinity of the temple is the Dondra fair, the market which sells the local pottery. This pottery is painted in vibrant colors, which we always admired. Not far from the temple is the Dondra Head Lighthouse. This is the tallest lighthouse in the country, which we visited during these trips. Dondra Head was once briefly the Capital of the country.

Before we reached Dondra, we would pass through the picturesque town of Matara, with its Dutch Fort and the Nilawali River, which winds its way through the town. Invariably, we would visit our school friend S.K. Piyadasa's family home. He and his brother Munidasa, along with their cousin S.K. Munasinghe, were our hostel mates who often joined us on our trips. Their family-owned business, S.K. Peter Appu & Sons, named after their father, was considered one of the most successful business enterprises in the Southern Province. After we were treated to a sumptuous meal at their home, we would continue our journey along the road that hugs the scenic southern coast dotted with quaint towns and villages of Dickwella, Tangalle, Ambalantota and Tissa.

We usually made a stop at the attractive little fishing town of Hambantota. On a recent visit I marveled at the transformation of the town, which now sports an international airport and harbor, along with a modern cricket stadium, which is venue for world cricket championships.

Kataragame was a popular destination for our trips. On the way we made stops, for meals and overnight rest at friends' homes. Once we reached Kataragama, we slept on the banks of the *Manik Ganga* (river of gems), and performed our morning ablutions in the river.

This is a multi-religious sacred town, popular with Buddhist, Hindu, and Muslim pilgrims of Sri Lanka and South India. The Kataragama temple complex contains the Hindu *Devalaya* (temple), the Buddhist stupa (ancient Kiri Vehera), and an Islamic Mosque. Legend has it that Lord Buddha, on his third and last visit to Sri Lanka, met King Mahasena, who ruled over the Kataragama area in 580 BC. It is said that King Mahasena listened to the Buddha's discourse and as a token of gratitude, built the stupa. Thus the local Sinhalese Buddhists believe that Kataragama was sanctified by Lord Buddha. In spite of the differences of caste, creed and ethnicity, many Sri Lankans show great reverence to God Kataragama. They honor him as a very powerful deity and beg divine help to overcome their personal problems or for success in business enterprises etc., with the fervent hope that their requests would be granted. They believe that God Kataragama is vested with extraordinary power to assist those who appeal to him with faith and devotion in times of distress.

The town has a venerable history dating back to the last centuries before the Christian era. It was the seat of government of a number of Sinhala kings during the days of the kingdom of Ruhuna. It provided refuge to many kings from the north of the Island when the north was invaded by South Indian rulers. It is believed that the area was abandoned about the 13th century. Although Kataragama was a small village in medieval times, today it is a fast-developing township surrounded by jungle in the South Eastern region of Sri Lanka, which adjoins the popular Yala wildlife park. The local river *Manik Ganga* functions as a place of ablution where a sacred bath is taken to purify oneself before entering the sacred area. Local residents declare that one can be healed of ailments by bathing in it, because of the high content of gems in the water, and the medicinal properties of the roots of various trees that line the banks of the river that glides its way through the surrounding jungle.

Another popular destination on our cycling trips was Morawaka, in the southern hills. The journey was challenging and rather tiresome to say the least, because of the hilly terrain, but the stunning views of hills dotted with tea estates were compensation for the grueling climbs uphill. We used to spend a night at our fellow student, Kirthisena Abeywickrama's home. Kirthisena later became a member of the parliament from the area, but regrettably, succumbed to wounds caused by a terrorist bomb blast at the parliament building. He had a brother, Wijepala Abeywickrama, who was my dormitory prefect in the Upper Lincoln dorm. He later became a prominent lawyer in the town of Matara. In Morawaka his relative and my friend and schoolmate Dayananda Abeywickrama and his family were our hosts.

On the way to Morawaka and back, we used to have tea breaks at our friends' homes in Kalahe, an interior village in Galle. At times it was at Nihal De Alwis' place. Nihal was my classmate and has remained a close friend over the years. He had two elder brothers who, like him, were in the police department. After Nihal left the police he worked for KLM Airlines, which gave him the opportunity to frequently travel abroad. He and his wife, their son and daughter have visited me both in New York and Vienna. He later established a private security service. Whenever I returned to Colombo we would see each other. He and his wife never failed to host a lunch or dinner for my wife Shanthi and me. This offered us a chance to meet other friends from school days. Among them were the lawyers Elmo Perera and Tudor Jayasuriya, along with Rajawasam a building contractor, Nihal Rajapaksa, a businessman, and Neil Dias, a successful attorney and left wing politician.

Nihal's two senior brothers, Veer and Elmo, were also at Richmond during my time. The elder of the three, Veer, left the police and migrated to Australia. Elmo migrated to Germany. I have seen them from time to time when all of us traveled back home to Colombo during Christmas vacations. I have visited Elmo in Bonn, Germany, on two occasions. It is with a heavy heart that I record the news of his demise, which reached me as I was writing these notes.

In later years, Nihal's eldest brother, who had left Richmond by the time we were in school, used to host the sixty plus club of Richmond alumni. Nihal used to invite me to this event whenever I was in Colombo. These were occasions to meet others who were in school with me. Those whom I met included the trio of brothers Wilmot, Chandra, and Wickramapala Samarasinghe, who were all great sportsmen at Richmond. Wilmot was a planter, Chandra an engineer who migrated to the UK, and Wickramapala was a physician who migrated to Australia. They were all my close friends in school, and the annual Christmas gatherings of the 60 plus club offered us a convenient opportunity to meet.

There were also three sportsmen who were senior to me but who remained my friends; Winton Pieris, G.W. Dissanayake and Nissanka Perera. Nissanka, a senior civil servant, married his Cousin Chitrani who was also at Richmond during my days. Chitrani was the daughter of our school principal E.R. De Silva. Nissanka and Chitrani hosted a party once for my wife and me at their residence in Moratuwa, where we met many friends from school days. Partiers included Dr. Buddadasa De Silva and his wife, who were visiting from the U.K. I continue to be in contact with the Budde, particularly after his retirement and returned to Sri Lanka to become a member of the Board of Directors of the Bank of Ceylon.

On our bicycle trips, the other tea stop used to be at Nihal's neighbor Lalith Edirisinghe's home. He was my classmate and a good student, who later became an editor of the national paper "The Sunday Observer." I kept in touch with him intermittently and visited his home in Maharagama, Colombo. I met him for the last time a few months before he passed away.

Thus, we rode to the mechanical melody of chains running over cogs while the beautiful landscape and historic places of the South passed by. Thankfully the air was still pristine. Today the crammed roads are clogged with vehicles belching diesel fumes.

* * *

During my years in the hostel Sundays were mostly spent on informal games of cricket, soccer or paddle tennis. The Christians, of course, attended church first. The Richmond Hill Methodist Church was part and parcel of Richmond, located at the entrance to the College. It was founded by the first British missionary principal of Richmond, Rev. Samuel Langdon in 1878. The church celebrated its 125th anniversary in 2003.

When living at home with my family, I could spend weekends visiting friends and relations in and around Galle. I would often go for a sea bath with friends on Sunday mornings, mostly to Clossenberg, an area of high ground projecting into the sea at Magalle. A British seafaring officer named Captain Bailey took a fancy to this delightful small peninsula. He bought it from the government in 1859 and built a beautiful house there. The house had spacious rooms with large doors and windows, and a low roof covered with local tiles. In front of this house were a large garden lined with coconut and Palmyra trees and elegantly laid out seats and resting places. Clossenberg faces the open sea and Buena Vista on the East. From here one could see the Galle Fort with the towering Light House and Clock Tower, and the spire of the Anglican Church. The sea here offers a safe spot for bathing. After Captain Bailey relinquished this house, a local businessman and planter, Simon Perera Abeywardena, son-in-law of the Moratuwa philanthropist C. H. de Soysa, bought the residence. He lived there until his demise. The owner during my time was his grandson, who ran the place as a popular Guest House.

In 1915, when Rev Small was principal of Richmond a sad drowning fatality occurred at Closenberg. The principal had for some time been taking a party of masters and boys with him on Saturday mornings for a bath at Closenberg. It was considered a safe place for bathing. That particular day there was an abnormal current, which carried some of those who could not swim out of their depth. One master and two boys were drowned. This put an end to sea-bathing trips of Richmond staff and students for a considerable time.

Although such accidents have occurred from time to time, this did not prevent us from going for a swim in the sea near Closenberg. We thoroughly enjoyed the endless hours we spent there, under a scorching sun and a benign breeze that created soft music among the palm trees.

The other popular place for Sunday sea baths was the Unawatuna bay, which, protected by a reef, provided a place for safe swimming. Whenever I visited my stepmother's family home in Unawatuna, I almost always ended up on the beach, either to wade into the cool waters for a swim, or to play soft ball cricket matches under the coconut palms. This area adjoined the compound of the famous cricketing family of De Silvas. Brothers Hemachandra, Premachamdra and Somachandra, later played for the national team, and the youngest, Gunachandra was also an accomplished cricketer. Though they all played for our rival school Mahinda College, they were my good friends, particularly the elder two. Often the Amendra brothers, who also played for Mahinda, joined us. I was the only Richmondite although there were other local boys who played with us.

On most Sunday evenings I would attend the weekly Buddhist Sermon (Bana) at the Galle Young Men's Buddhist Association (YMBA). The Galle YMBA was in an impressive walauwwa, a gift of Mr. Henry Amarasuriya Sr. and his wife Carolina, whose portrait hung at the entrance. He was a great philanthropist. I was among the few young men to attend these sermons, which were mostly attended by grownups.

The head of the organization was Mrs. Kularatne, then benefactor of the YMBA, the mother of the well known physician in Galle Dr. Damon Kularatane, a nephew of Minister P. de.S Kularatne. They both occupied mansions near the YMBA. Dr. Kularatne was a very successful physician and a sports fan. He was the sponsor and presenter of the cricketing bats to the highest scorers on each side at the Mahinda-Richmond Big match. I had the honor to be presented with one during my school days. I still have that bat in my office. Dr. Kularatne later became widely known in the country when he had to stand trial with his mother, accused of murdering his wife. He was acquitted after a lengthy legal process. He remarried and died shortly thereafter. His second wife (sister of a primary schoolmate of mine from Dodanduwa) and a daughter who was born after his death lives in New York, U.S.A.

Before I went to the YMBA, I would walk to the ramparts of the Galle Fort where I was certain to meet a few friends. I would often raise my head to check the time on the Galle Clock Tower, built by an appreciative patient in memory of the most prominent surgeon of the day Dr. P.D. Anthonisz. He had saved the patient' life. Dr. Anthonisz place was taken by Dr. P.R. Anthonis as the leading surgeon during our days.

Two of the regulars I met on the ramparts were Vernon Wambeck, a sportsman from Richmond, who later migrated to Australia; and Nalin Samarasinghe from Mahinda, who later was a Director at the Asian Development Bank in Manila, Philippines.

I would watch from the edge of the ramparts, the tennis games and competitions that took place at the Galle Gymkhana Club. I did so with envy, because I did not have the opportunity to play tennis. The Richmond courts were reserved for the staff and a few excellent players like Nissanka Perera and Elmore Perera, who were called upon to join them to play, when the staff needed partners.

The Galle Gymkhana Club also conducted the annual horse racing competition that lasted a few weeks at the Boossa Race Course, where we used to go for scout camps and for the southern province intercollegiate athletic meets. During those few weeks of horse-racing, the elite of Galle were joined by the elite of the capital, Colombo, who congregated dressed in their best clothes. As a child, I went with my father and later with my friends to see the races. The well-known horse at the time was named Cotton Hall and the famous jockey was Fordyce. This combination became a legend in the country. They won most of the races they took part in. Racing attracted me a lot, though not as a gambler, but as a spectator. Many years later I visited racing venues in a few countries, and went to the Aqueduct Race Course, not far from where I lived in New York, particularly to witness the final leg of the U.S. Triple Crown race: The Belmont Stakes. I was privileged to see the record breaking run by Secretariat, the super horse whose record still stands. Whenever I could, I have not missed watching the annual Triple Crown race in the United States on television: The Kentucky Derby, the Preakness Stakes, and the Belmont Stakes.

During the days in Galle, on many evenings I would stand on the ramparts, watching the sun dip slowly into the sea. As darkness began to shroud the houses inside the fort, and the beam of the lighthouse swept across the dark water, I returned home realizing my school days were coming to an end. But, I did not think too much about my future. I already knew what I planned to do in the years immediately ahead. Cocky? Perhaps, as any eighteen-year-old is bound to be.

— ❖ —

Chapter 15

Farewell Gift

The life at Richmond was a life of sports and literary activities. The development of sports and the attitude associated with it had to do with the establishment of British colonial rulers based on the British public school system. In such schools, both in the UK and in British Ceylon, sports occupied a vital place in the curriculum as an essential element creating a young gentleman endowed with a rounded education. It would seem that it is this same competitive streak, inculcated through sports, that has further evolved to drive people like me to seek ways and means to overcome the hurdles that are part and parcel of one's life. Literary activities added to a rounded education. They endowed one with an interest in worldly affairs. It is certainly the experiences in such activities in school that established in me an abiding interest in politics, art, drama and music.

All of this of course meant that academics were of secondary importance to me in school. I was able to follow the subjects taught by the teachers in class, and with a minimum of homework get through the exams. Usually, I was able to be somewhere in the top third of my class, which averaged close to thirty students, except for the last two years of our university preparation class, where the number was less than ten. This was not too bad a position to be in, among some who were nerds, devoting their entire time to academics, and others who were attending school for the formality, of it with no interest in higher education. Either their families were well to do, or therefore they did not feel the drudgery of studying was worth the while, or because by nature they were mischievous. The teachers did not show any concern about where our interests lay, and sports being my priority, I was satisfied with my academic achievements.

Not so with my father. He had always placed a premium on getting a good education as an absolute necessity for a successful life. When I was young his priority was to give me a solid background in the vernacular and Buddhism including Pali, the language of Buddhism. He also wanted to instill in me solid study habits.

Once he thought I had a foundation in what he considered to be the essential basics, he enrolled me at Richmond. He had single-minded desire that I become a medical doctor. He used to compare me with my sister, who at the time was doing well in her school work and was at the top of her class. By praising her, my father tried to make me feel ashamed of myself. He hoped that this would make me realize I was squandering my opportunities by not achieving the same stature my sister reached. Such repeated comparisons, especially with other members of my extended family, not to mention friends of the family as well, only resulted in my being even more stubborn and doing my own thing. On the surface though, I was careful to show my father that I was taking his advice seriously.

It was his disappointment in me for not doing as well as he wanted in my school work that made him, not only openly discourage, but also show outright contempt for my achievements in the sports arena. He would stubbornly stay away from a cricket match if I was playing in it, even the "big match", which practically the whole of Galle town turned up to watch.

Eventually, when I revealed to him that I would like to be a lawyer, he dismissed me admonishing me that he had no respect for the legal profession and that he would rather see me unemployed. His scant respect for the legal profession was a result of a couple of land cases in which he had been involved, where lawyers, including his own, requested postponement of cases for flimsy reasons and dragged on the cases, while collecting fees from their clients. Through all this, of course, I was distinctly aware that he was doing what he did because of his great concern and love for me.

It was a trial for me to be living under the same roof with him in Galle because before then, I was in the hostel and visited him only during the school vacations. Naturally, the situation led me to adopt the book cricket method that led him to believe I was hard at work. This was also a time when I was reading anything but school books that I ought to have been reading.

I read several books on astrology, palmistry, and on belief systems like *The Golden Bough*, a wide-ranging, comparative study of mythology and religion written by Scottish anthropologist Sir James George Frazer; and books like *How to Win Friends and Influence People by Dale Carnegie*. Some of them are still in my possession, such as *The Revolt in the Temple* by Wijewardane, a societal interpretation of religion from a Buddhist perspective, reprinted in 1953, priced at rupees five, with a notation that indicates I had bought it in early 1958. How times have changed, today one might be lucky to get a pencil for five rupees!

I take solace from the words of Stephen Hawking, the famous theoretical physicist who held the same chair of mathematics as Isaac Newton at Cambridge University for thirty years. Hawking studied black holes, expounding the theory that the way the universe began was completely determined by the laws of science. Hawking spoke about his life at Caltech in Los Angeles in 2011, and talking of his childhood and his parents, he recalled his upbringing in London. Being not the greatest student as a young child, although smart, he didn't learn to read until he was 8. His father, a medical researcher, had wanted young Stephen to go into medicine as well, but the boy did not love the field of medicine. "The smartest people did math and physics," he said, to laughs from the audience. "It doesn't matter what school you went to or to whom you are related. It matters what you do." Hawking added that he was very lazy while an undergraduate at Oxford and admitted "I'm not proud of it."

I often wonder where some of my fellow students who were at the top of the class are today. No doubt many of them made their own mark in chosen fields, although not as doctors, lawyers and the like, because I am familiar with almost all who became either one or the other.

As I progressed to the senior levels I began to acquire an interest in subjects such as history and government, primarily because of the excellent teachers who taught those subjects in an exciting and meaningful way. Ana Wijesekara, who later became a lawyer and president's Counsel and he taught us the subject of government. Walter May in history and Iranganie Haththtotuwegama (GK's sister) and D. Alahaperuma in history and government were prominent among those who inspired me. This was the reason that the four subjects I had chosen for advance level exam were Government, Ceylon History, Western History and Geography.

Just prior to the Advanced Level class I had won the prize for civics (the subject that is known as 'government' at the Advanced Level) in 1956. At the College Prize Giving in 1957 the Chief Guest was Sir Cecil Syers, the British High Commissioner (Ambassador). I received the prize from Lady Syers. I still have the book with the college crest entitled *Modern Political Constitutions: Comparative Study of their History and Form* by C.F. Strong O.B.E., Ph.D; a colleague of renowned constitutional scholar Harold Laski. The book introduced me to the interplay between politics and constitutions, including political organizations such as the United Nations, and advocated application of the Federal Idea to international affairs.

I was quite satisfied when I received the credit passes in English and Sinhala at the S.S.C. level, which was a requirement for admission to the Law College. By the time the S.S.C. results are known, one has already spent part of the following year in the Advanced Level (H.S.C.) class. Still not having made a final decision I continued to enjoy the Advanced Level studies which allowed me to continue my final two years of sports and literary activities. However, in the middle second year, I left Richmond at the end of the cricket and soccer seasons to join the Law College.

* * *

A while before I left Richmond, I was also made a prefect of the school and enjoyed the additional responsibilities of helping to keep order in school. Punya Illeperuma was the Senior Prefect. An incident that is etched in my mind during my final days of school in 1958 relates to being a prefect (later I too was Senior Prefect). When the entire school gathered for the morning assembly it was rather noisy. When the bell rang the prefect on duty for the day walked up to the podium and called for silence. The prefect was in charge of the assembly until the principal and the staff took the podium, after the Christians had finished their prayers next door and joined the assembly. When my turn came I would enter the Hall and before I could go up to the podium the assembly would fall silent. This was simply because of the respect for a colleague who was the captain of all three major sports teams of the College.

At Richmond I came under the tutelage of two of the most outstanding Principals anyone could hope for. They were both very firm disciplinarians who ran a tight ship, but they were very warm and friendly at the same time. They were excellent academics as well as sportsmen with a wide variety of interests.

The first native principal of the school, after a string of British principals, was E.R. De Silva OBE, MA. He had taken over a few a years before I entered Richmond. My first experience with this stern-looking gentleman was recounted in an earlier chapter, when following the entrance exam to Richmond, my father had to agree to the principal's suggestion that I should be entered to grade four rather than grade six due to lack of knowledge in English, although I had already completed grade five at the vernacular school from where I was transfering to Richmond.

E.R. De Silva hailed from Ambalangoda, my hometown, where he was born and had his early education in the Wesleyan School there.

He continued his education at Richmond where some of its most distinguished alumni also had hailed from Ambalangoda. Among them was Thomas de. Silva, the mathematician, in the very early years; C.W.W. Kanangara, who is considered the father of free education which he introduced as minister of education; P. De S. Kularatne, another minister of education and former principal of Ananda College; L.H. Methananda, another principal of Ananda College; M.W.H. De Silva, King's Counsel, Solicitor General and Minister of Justice.

An all-rounder in the best sense of the word, E. R De Silva was a scholar of Latin, mathematics and English and taught all three subjects in a lucid manner. He played in the school cricket and soccer teams and was a member of the athletic team. Later, as member of the Richmond staff, he coached all three teams at one time or the other. As principal, he would have an eye on each of the teams and even particular players and often have a wise word for those lagging behind. He would follow school plays and would watch them a few days prior to the performance in public and offer very incisive comments that would bring life to those plays. He demanded excellence in every pursuit. He had a commanding manner about him that engendered respect among the staff and students. He was a great student of the psyche of his pupils and had a way of dealing with them in a manner that would bring about positive results.

He was a great educationist highly regarded by national leaders who appointed him to several important educational commissions. He was a fine orator who spoke with sense and vision. As the chief guest at the Jaffna College Prize Giving in 1953 he had warned that nothing could compensate for the tragedy of a disintegrated nation and pleaded for communal harmony in bringing about change in educational affairs of the country. He said that, even though Western culture throve in the past at the expense of our own culture that in itself was no reason for us to jettison the advantages which we could derive from English as a uniting language among communities and for our cultural renaissance. These words were spoken more than three decades before the country was engulfed in a thirty-year terrorist war.

Such was the man who was my principal for a decade. It was impossible to come away without being influenced by the traits of such a great personality.

Just as he did at the beginning, placing me two classes below the level I should have entered, he made a mid-course correction in my school career that no doubt helped me in the long run.

It was usual for students in outstation schools to go to more prestigious Colombo Schools to advance their studies. So it was natural for me too to look in that direction at a time I felt I was doing well enough in school to look for greener pastures, particularly with regard to my sports career. I was blossoming into a reasonably talented sportsman at the time. After considering some options and influenced by my Cousin Sarath, who was already there, I sat and passed the entrance examination to Ananda College. In order to finalize the formalities, I had to obtain a character certificate from my principal. I placed a request with his office. The next thing I knew the principal had summoned not only me but also my father, to his office. He was stern as usual, but took the time to explain to us the pros and cons of my proposed move. He was certain that I would fall through the cracks at Ananda, where I would face stern competition. I could nurture myself at my own pace at Richmond, where he saw me on the verge of a career that would bring me glory. He was very persuasive in his arguments, but said he would not stand in my way if my choice were to leave.

My father was somewhat surprised at this lengthy explanation, because I had not revealed the full extent of what I was planning, although he knew my general interest in a possible move to Colombo. Once the principal had spoken, my father immediately agreed with the principal leaving me no choice. I was disappointed at first, but I began to see the light after the principal's lucid exposé, particularly because he was not in the habit of discouraging those who wanted to move. In retrospect, I realize the wisdom of his thinking. I had a satisfying career at Richmond. Not everyone who moved to Colombo schools was as fortunate as I was by staying put.

The principal's wife was a very pleasant and caring person who made all of us at Richmond feel she was our surrogate mother. His son Ranjan, an all-round sportsman, was in school during my time but was a few years senior. His elder daughter Chitrani was also at Richmond, although senior to me in the Advanced Level (HSC) level classes. She won the Darrell Medal for the Outstanding Student of the Year. She entered the Colombo campus of the university and graduated with a science degree. She later joined the Bank of Ceylon and retired as a Manager. She married Nissanka Perera, a distant cousin, who was also my senior at Richmond.

Nissanka was an outstanding sportsman at the Public Schools Meet and at the University of Ceylon. He won the All Round Student of the Year Award at Richmond. He graduated with an Arts degree and joined the Administrative Service of the country and retired as the deputy head of the National Treasury. The Youngest daughter of the principal, Nayeni, schooled in Colombo and after graduation joined the Central Bank of Ceylon. I was close to the entire family and used to visit my principal in later years whenever I was in Colombo. I have been in contact with the rest of the family until recently. Nissanka and Chitrani have been kind enough on occasion to arrange a dinner party for Shanthi and me when we were visiting Colombo, so we could meet old friends from College days. Shortly after I began recording these notes I received the sad news of his demise. I was happy to have spoken to him by phone not long before his death while he was terminally ill.

During my last couple of years at Richmond, upon the retirement of E.R. De Silva, another alumni, Shelton Wirasinghe, the then vice-principal, took over as the new principal. Shelton Wirasinghe who had mastered classics and mathematics, was a great exponent of music and drama, and was a great sportsman. He was a burly man with a booming voice, and a disciplinarian, yet with a great sense of humor. If ever there was a definition of a gentleman he would easily fill the bill. All of his wonderful traits naturally rubbed off on those of us who came in close contact with him. I had the privilege of having him as my English teacher, cricket coach and scout master. On most occasions he kept an eye on drama and debating activities, where I also happened to be a participant. He said education does not end by getting a job; what matters is the training and discipline of the individual. I feel a sense of gratitude to this day for the values he inculcated in us, and I carry vivid memories of the poise and dignity which pervaded his presence.

Shortly after I left school he was transferred as principal of Wesley College, Colombo. He married Manel Dunuwila, a Kandyan beauty. Manel was the sister of Damayanthi Duunuwila, based on whose escapades at the university, a musician composed the famous baila *"Running Shoes Daala Thamai Manike Duwanne...100 Meters 200 Menike Dinnanne" and "Dawasak Daa Mama Yanakota Lover's Lane Eke, Manike Hitiya Lecturayage Benze Car Eke."* I used to visit Shelton at the principal's bungalow at Wesley, and after his retirement at his Nawala home.

* * *

There was another important group of individuals who, one way or the other had an influence on those growing up at Richmond. They were the staff who provided our every need. The minor staff was a part of the family and made their own mark on all of us. There was Danny, short and strong, the doyen of the hostel staff, along with Sirisena, Henry and David who took care of our dining room, laying out the meals and cleaning up. They often obliged us by reserving an extra portion when requested.

Breakfast in the hostel was mostly stringhoppers with 'dhal' (lentil) curry and 'pol sambal' (coconut and chilly mixture), or bread with dhal along with butter and jam followed by tea with milk. Eggs were provided to those who pay extra and have a standing order as was the case for milk. Lunch and dinner were rice and curry, quite regularly featuring dhal curry which was a staple those days.

There was also Henry, who mostly attended to the teaching staff. However, he was ready to reserve to the sportsmen, when requested, the left-over courses (western dishes) served to the faculty members. They were supported by Simone, the cook and his ever-changing assistants. The strength of short Danny and that of heavy Henry were most useful in carrying huge buckets full of *kiri thae* (tea with milk) from the kitchen to the dinning room, some distance away. The tea was dished out twice daily into cups laid on the long tables of the dining room.

Then there were the school peons, Handy, who rang the bell in the historic belfry signaling the beginning and end of each class period, and Sirisena, the laboratory assistant. The sports assistant who took care of the grounds and equipment was Simon. He was tall and muscular and was a great sportsman himself. He played soccer for the Galle Club as goalie. He was also a good batsman and bowler who often played with the teaching staff or alumni when they played friendly cricket matches. He was succeeded by Sirisena, who was on the hostel staff.

These legendary characters served decades at Richmond, and had a daily influence on our lives as we grew up. Many years after I left Richmond I used to visit them whenever I visited the school. They took delight in seeing me and other fellow students as grown-ups. The admiration was mutual for they were a vital part of carrying on the traditions of the school.

* * *

Finally, the Old Boys Association (OBA) was another element of encouragement at Richmond and there periodic meetings brought to the school distinguished or accomplished alumni whom one aspired to emulate. They came from the high levels of the government service, private sector, academic circles and the field of sports. As students we admired their achievements and looked up to them for inspiration. Later on in life I used to attend the gatherings, mostly of the Colombo Branch, whenever I was in Colombo. The association assisted the school in various projects. The latest was to renovate the old College Hall that was built, like the library, in Tudor style. They are presently engaged in building a Museum to document the history and to house the historical records of the school. On being informed of the project, I was more than delighted to have sent a contribution to the Museum fund.

In due course, I was qualified to join the over sixty club. Often I happened to be in Colombo during their gatherings, which were mostly social. These were occasions to meet with friends with whom I had been in school several decades ago. I enjoyed the camaraderie of these occasions especially because there were no other opportunities to meet colleagues you had known many years ago. Sadly, these occasions remind one of the mortality of human life. The number of people from our time at Richmond slowly but surely dwindled.

* * *

To write about the old school is always a very joyful thing. One's mind goes back to the days at Richmond, experiences within the classroom, the hostel, and on the sports field; teachers who were admired and loved and some who were not! I recall prizes won, classes repeated, and punishments endured, as a whole mixture of memories. Writing is a way to relive the past that one still holds very dear. These pages were written to rekindle the nostalgic memories of Richmond.

As August 1958 approached, having obtained admission to the Law College, I was looking forward to the next chapter in my life. In mid-year, at the school annual Prize Giving, I had reached the zenith of my school career when I was awarded the coveted Colombo Old Boys Prize. The final prizes to be awarded at the end of the Prize Giving are the Darrell Medal, awarded to the student with the most outstanding academic achievement of the year, which was awarded to my classmate H.G. Sirinivasa (GK's younger brother who later became an engineer); and the other is the Colombo Old Boys Prize given to the all-round student of the year. Winners of the two awards are the only ones entitled to have their names etched on the award boards that hang permanently on the walls of the college hall; along with the list of principals, and those who had outstanding achievements at the national level examinations. It was a great honor and privilege when I won the award. I could not have asked for a more fitting farewell gift knowing that my name, J.L.N. De Silva, by which I was known at Richmond, is up on the wall of the College Assembly Hall for eternity.

The only regret was that my father was not there in the audience the day I was awarded the prize. He would have sat in the front row if I had been the recipient of the Darrell Medal, or if I had entered the Medical College. He stayed away because his choice clashed with mine. I was adamant in my decision to enter the Law College.

Dodanduwa Oya & Poya Seemawa

Sporting Days

▲ *Richmond Cricket Team, 1957 (self seated as captain, 3rd from right)*

▶ *Combined Schools' Team with the first visiting Australian Schools Team (seated center in blazer as Captain)*

*Going in to
Bat in the
Big Match:
Richmond
v. Mahinda
Galle
Esplanade
(right)*

*College
Athletics
Team, 1957.
Seated 2nd
from left as
Captain*

Part 3

Halfway Through

"Future Depends on what you do today"

– Mahatma Gandhi

Chapter 16

No. 244, Hulftsdorp Street

Sir Sydney Abrahams, who had served in many Commonwealth Countries, on taking up his duties as Chief justice in 1936, is quoted to have said; "Every entrant to the colonial legal service dreams that one day he may have the joy of occupying this seat, which has been called the pride of the Colonial Service and head the judiciary which has been said by learned predecessors to be the finest in the whole British Empire".

I caught my first glimpse of the grandeur he described, on the first day that I stepped on Hulftsdorp Street to enter the Ceylon Law College. Established in 1874 to impart a formal legal education to those who wished to be lawyers, it is housed in an impressive building typical of colonial architecture. The Law College operates under the Council of Legal Education, which includes the Chief Justice, the Attorney General, and the Secretary to the Ministry of Justice. It is one of the oldest, if not the oldest, institution for training of professionals in the country.

In order to practice law in Sri Lanka, a lawyer must be admitted and enrolled as a member of the Bar of the Supreme Court of the country. To receive admission to the bar (the legal profession), a law student must complete a three-year course and law examinations held by the Sri Lanka Law College, followed by an apprenticeship period of one year under an experienced lawyer. The faculty is composed of leading practicing lawyers, who are more academically inclined.

From its inception, members of the Bar belonged to two branches – Advocates and Proctors. Since 1974, a century after the Law College was established, and more than a decade after I had completed my education, the two branches of the profession were merged and its members were called Attorneys-at-Law. Admission to the college is based on a very competitive entrance examination, required by the high number of applicants. Once the training is completed at the Law College, graduates enter the Legal profession, becoming members of the Bar (professional practitioners) or the Bench (the judiciary).

Since my time at the Law College, some of the luster of the Bar and the Bench has been tarnished by politicizing of the two institutions. During the early-to-mid 20th-century they were held in the highest esteem. Many members of the profession were leaders in the independence movement and other important reforms in the country. The Bench in the country has been considered among the best and lauded by leading jurists around the world, as illustrated by the above observation of Sir Sydney Abrahams [1].

*   *   *

Such was the reputation of the field on which I embarked on at the age of twenty, coming from my Aunt Doty's home on Lauries Road, Bambalapitiya, where she was living with her family at the time. By then, her husband (Sirisena mama) had become a member of parliament representing the Bingiriya electorate. His district included the Dummalasuriya area, the location of the Himmaliyagara Group coconut estate, where he functioned as the Managing Superintendent. He had also by then founded a thriving commercial establishment in the nearby town of Madampe. Thus, he commuted to Colombo whenever he had free time, where the family was based, so that the children could acquire an education at good schools, most of which were located in the capital city.

When I went to live with Aunt Dotty, the two daughters, Pushpa and Saroja were attending Visakha Vidyalaya, and the three boys were attending the Royal College Primary. Both schools were almost within walking distance from the Lauries Road residence.

Aunt Dotty was very keen that I live with her. My father was happy at the prospect of having someone to keep an eye on me. I enjoyed the security of her nest and the delicious food and service of the domestic staff. I also enjoyed being around my young cousins. But soon I found that, in spite of it being a large, two-storey house in a very desirable neighborhood, it was not the best place for serious studies. I had decided by that time to immerse myself in some serious study! Having had more than my fill of fun and games at Richmond, I realized that it was time to turn, however reluctantly, to academics in a more methodical manner, if I were to achieve any success in life. It was with mixed feelings that I decided to leave the comforts of the family environment and step into what was still to me, somewhat of a strange city.

Happily for me my, Cousin Sarath, who was at Ananda College, was studying for his medical entrance examination and residing at a boarding house at Katewelamulla Road, Maligakanda. These lodgings were near Ananda College and in closer proximity to the Law College than Lauries Road. The place also provided an atmosphere that was conducive for studying as the other lodgers also were students.

The house belonged to a very friendly couple, Mr. and Mrs. Wickramasinghe. There were two rooms on either side of the front verandah. One was shared by Cousin Sarath and me, and the other, by a distant relative of ours and his brother who were at the Technical College. There was a cook who prepared breakfast and dinner for us. We were all busy with our studies, but during meals and whenever we had some free time, we enjoyed each other's company.

Mrs. Wickramasinghe was a retired teacher, and her husband, Mr. Wickramasinghe, a retired officer who had worked for the Colombo Municipal Council. He spent most of the day seated on his arm chair on the front verandah watching the activities of the people in the house and on the road. The house was undoubtedly a safe place to live in, with him always on duty on the front poach. The boarding fee paid was Rs. 75.00 per month including meals. Today one meal would cost about that much in a wayside restaurant.

For the first time in my life I buckled down to serious studies and began burning the midnight oil as my cousin, Sarath, had been doing for some time. Unfortunately, he was unable to get admission to the Medical College after three tries and left to join the German Technical Training College in Amparai, where he successfully qualified in civil engineering.

His place in my lodgings was taken by Nihal De Silva, a friend from Richmond College days, who came to Colombo to study accountancy at the Technical Training College. He later joined the police, and retired as a senior superintendent of police. Many years later, he visited me while I was living in Vienna, and was taken seriously ill at my home. Though he recovered after being hospitalized and cared for in Vienna, he developed multiple health issues, and not long after the visit to Vienna, he passed away at a relatively young age.

During the course of my first year at the law school, I worked as a substitute teacher at the afternoon sessions of the premier Muslim School in the nation, Zahira College. Zahira was only a long walk from our boarding house. This was possible because the lectures at Law College ended by lunch time. I was paid by the hour to substitute for absent teachers. Being young, I enjoyed the importance of the post. My duties were mostly a matter of keeping the students relatively quiet by getting them to read or write a note on the subject that they were supposed to have learned that day. I made enough pocket money by working a couple of hours almost daily at Zahira.

During the days of the boarding house, I used to visit the nearby Kuppiyawatte temple from time to time, a continuation of the habit I had acquired during my YMBA days in Galle. Ever since then, on important occasions (such as examinations, interviews for jobs and scholarships, and travel abroad), I used to visit the temple and for many years, I considered it to have a salutary effect on my endeavors. But, for multiple reasons, this is a practice that I have now long forgotten.

From the boarding house I used to walk up to Ananda College bus stop, pass the Vidyodaya Pirivena, where monks were trained, take the trolley to the Technical College stop and walk up the hill to the Law College.

* * *

It is somewhat of a surprise that while the environs of the Law College have completely changed with the new Court Complex and Law Offices, the Law College is still housed in the same majestic building at number 244, Hulftsdorp Street, which is no larger than a big mansion. Basically it had three large lecture-rooms accomodating the students of three classes taught each year; a library of two very large rooms and one small study; the principal's office and an administrative office. All of this was on the first floor, reached by the majestic looking staircase. On the ground floor were the common room with a table tennis table, the ladies common room and the large canteen that housed the 'Cut table'. The lecture halls had very high ceilings, making them airy, with walls full of windows which provided natural airconditioning. Each student had a desk and a chair. There was a tradition that while attendance was being checked, if the desk next to you was vacant, you would automatically answer "present" for the absent occupant. The lecturers were attuned to the practice. With rare exceptions, they rapidly marked the register without raising their heads to see who was present or not. The reason for this practice was that living in the capital city and tuition at the law college were expensive undertakings. Several law students at the time were employed in part-time or even full- time jobs, where their employers permitted them time off to attend the lectures.

In my first year at the Law College, there were about seventy students in my batch that included five girls. Each year there were two examination periods in August and December. At the time, about fifty would eventually complete their courses in the normal number of years while most others would do it in subsequent years. In my batch, about two-thirds were following the Proctors course, as I did, while the rest, were following the Advocates course. Lectures, however, were held for both groups in unison for subjects that were common to both courses, while they were held separately, for a few of the special courses that were required to be followed by each of the two groups. Lectures were given by leading lawyers at the Bar, most of who went on to receive the highest honor of being a Queen's Counsel (later renamed as Presidents Counsel).

One interesting subject we learned was Constitutional Law and Legal Systems, which was taught by a foremost exponent on the subject J.A.L Coorey. He was a prominent author when the constitution of the country was revised. We also had to study arcane subjects, such as Roman Law with texts in Latin, taught by a scholar on the subject M.L.S. Jayasekare, whose sleepy manner of teaching made the long hours in class very tedious. Roman Law, which was the basis for Roman Dutch Law that governed our legal system, was considered an important basis for the legal education in our time.

There were also somewhat difficult subjects like Jurisprudence (theory of law), the full import of which we did not begin to comprehend until we were in the final year.

Jurisprudence was taught by Naina Marrikar. He was an elegant person who went on to become the minister of finance in the cabinet, and later speaker of the parliament. The acquaintance I made with him as a lecturer blossomed to a friendship in ensuing years, as his electorate, Puttlam, was next to my Uncle Sirisena's electorate in Bingiriya, and they were ministers in the same cabinet (my uncle being minister of social affairs). Naina Marrikar has visited my home in New York on several occasions when he was part of the national delegation to the annual sessions of the General Assembly of the United Nations.

Local Government Law, a subject that dealt with the rules, regulations, and functioning of local bodies such as the Municipalities, Urban, and Village Councils, was taught by a practicing lawyer specializing in the area, S. Thangarajah. Those like me who were following the Proctors' course were required to learn the subject on Accounts and Bookkeeping, because proctors were expected to keep the clients' funds in trust during legal proceedings. This was taught by B.R. De. Silva, senior partner of a leading accountancy firm: De Silva & Mendis. He happened to hail from Ambalangoda and had a particular affinity towards me. Even though I didn't think much of the subject, I did take extra care in my work to please him.

Thankfully, since 1980s, long after my days at Law College, subjects like Jurisprudence are now taught in the final year, and others such as Roman law have disappeared from the curriculum. They have been replaced by more practical subjects such as Family Law and Property Law, which are essential for lawyers in their day-to-day legal practice. These subjects were taught us in later years. In the university courses, which by nature were more academically oriented, subjects such as Roman Law were considered an essential part of the curriculum, because the university provided an academically rounded education. In contrast, the Law College prepared students to deal with the more practical tasks that their clients demanded.

Law lecturers had an aura about them. They were not only well known names in the country, but dressed the part as they came in their full legal attire in black, carrying in hand the black cloak they donned when they entered the court premises. They were all enthusiastic lecturers and took their tasks seriously. We students listened to them carefully, taking in what they had to say, but how much was appreciated and absorbed was another matter.

In addition to the lecturers we were also supervised and guided by the principal of the Law College. We were very fortunate to have as principal of the Law College some outstanding personalities who gave effective leadership to the Institution. When I joined the principal was G.M. De Silva, who hailed from my hometown, Ambalangoda. A revered principal, the friend and philosopher of the students, with his quiet manners and sober ways; with a firm belief in 'Uppekkha' (equanimity) he always took a highly detached view of the mundane things that surrounded him and his students.

On his sudden demise, S.R. Wijayatilake assumed duties in 1960, as the acting principal. One good man was followed by another. A staunchly religious person, he tended to the welfare of the students in a very calm and quiet demeanor. He was a District Judge and Secretary to the Judicial Service Commission when he assumed duties. Later he went on to become a judge of the Supreme Court.

During my final year, Justice M. F. S. Pulle Q.C., retired as a judge of the Supreme Court and assumed duties as principal of the Law College. He too was dedicated to ensuring that the Law College imparted good legal education, and he commanded the respect of the student body.

They were exceptional leaders and respected lawyers who ensured that the Law College maintained the highest possible standards in training future lawyers. Among the staff of the Law College I fondly recollect the services rendered by the long-serving, amiable librarian S. Shanmugalingan (Shan). He was a fountain of knowledge as far as the resources of the library were concerned and spared no effort to assist the students; even to the extent of advising them on good study habits. I often sought his advice, particularly in the first year, where I needed the type of guidance he was able to provide. Then there were some helpful members of the minor staff whose preoccupation was to cyclostyle lecture notes and sell them to students, particularly to those who were employed, and therefore often had to miss their lectures.

*   *   *

Though committed to academics, I couldn't completely shed my interest in sports and I found a limited amount of time to play cricket. I was living in Maligakanda, so I joined the nearby Bloomfield Club (then located at Campbell Park off Baseline Road, Borella), and played a few matches on the club team in the inter-club Daily News

Trophy tournament. The club produced many who played in the national team such as Dhanasiri Weerasinghe, one time captain of Ananda College, cricket team who played during my days, and much later, the legendary Sanath Jayasuriya.

I was also on the Law College team, which played against some minor clubs and mercantile firms. The big match of course was the Law-Medical match, which was an occasion for greater revelry in the city of Colombo than rivalry on the field. Nevertheless, the setting was the Oval, the Mecca of cricket during those days, where visiting teams from England and Australia played the local national team. The Law College team was captained by Ranjith Malawana, formerly of St. Joseph's College. The star of the team was T. Jothilingam, formerly of Royal College. The Law College team was always considered the weaker side as the Medical College sported several club players including H.I.K. Fernando, formerly of St. Peter's College, who was at the time the wicket keeper-batsman in the national team; Raja De Silva, formerly of Royal College; and Mahinda Silva of St. Joseph's College. The following day the national paper, Daily News carried the headline "Medicos Win Easily", but the text noted that "Of the Law College batsmen only J.L.N. De Silva impressed, and he defied the Medical bowling to remain unbeaten". In the field of sports I was still using the De Silva name by which I was known at Richmond, not for long though as my sporting career ended soon thereafter.

Of the friends I made from my cricketing days at Law College, Mahinda Silva remained a close friend. He was practicing medicine as a Dermatologist in New York during the time I was living there. Much later, he moved back to Sri Lanka and established a clinic on Cotta Road, Borella. He married Rohini, who inherited the Savoy Theater at Wellawatte. While in New York she attended Columbia University Law School and became a lawyer. She later married Mark Conley, also a lawyer, and relocated to Los Angeles, where I renewed my acquaintance with her when I moved there on my retirement.

Following the Law-Medical match I was on my way home, when my friend Vasu beckoned me to help his pal who was stuck in his car.

On arrival, I was impressed by his friend who was in an impressive *British Jaguar Mark IV*, which at the time we used to see only in the movies. Though the car was impressive, it needed a 'thalluwa' (push) to get it going, at least on that occasion. Vasu's friend happened to be Walter Jayasinghe, another medical student. He had interrupted his medical school education to visit the United States. He had back-packed and travelled around the country along with an engineering student Don Dharmalingam (Drachand), who stayed behind in the United States. Since, Shanthi and I moved to Los Angeles, we have been close friends with Don and his wife DiAnne. It was on that trip that Walter had arranged to bring the car that I joined Vasu to help get started. I was glad I made his acquaintance on that occasion, as I would later meet and get to know him and his wife Aeshea in Los Angeles, where he practiced medicine and established a lucrative medical establishment.

Walter also established the Sri Lanka Foundation, USA, to assist the Sri Lankan community in the United States and popularize Sri Lanka among the American public. Many public programs and annual events are organized under the Foundation's sponsorship, and I was happy to be a part of those activities. The Foundation holds an annual Awards Ceremony to recognize the work of expatriate Sri Lankans, and I was honored to be the first recipient of a Lifetime Achievement Award, the highest award given by the Foundation. The Foundation has established a scholarship program for Sri Lankan children in the United States. There is also a website to promote Sri Lankan culture and to notify major developments back home and among the Sri Lankans abroad. One highlight is the annual Sri Lanka Day, showcasing every aspect of Sri Lankan life from music, dance, drama to cuisine, held at the Santa Monica Promenade, one of the most popular locations for such events in the center of the city of Los Angeles. Large numbers of Americans congregate there during week-ends. This exposes to the American public what Sri Lanka offers. Proceedings are carried in the local TV channels and reported in other media outlets. Among his medical establishments, the primary center, along with the offices of the Sri Lanka Foundation, are located in twin towers with twenty floors each with a connecting roof garden,

Walter is such a patriot that he displays the Sri Lanka national flag on top of the roof garden, located at the city center of Los Angeles on its main thoroughfare, Wilshire Boulevard. Thus, among the many American flags, the Sri Lankan flag is proudly fluttering over the sky of sunny southern California. I wish there were more Sri Lankans like Walter to honor and promote the culture of their motherland.

Cricket was at best a minor distraction from my commitment to studies. I did decide that I will play no more club cricket and ended my membership at the Bloomfield Cricket Club after the first year of membership. I felt that all the sacrifice and commitment to academics was worth it, when, at the end of the first year, the results were posted and published in the daily newspaper. I had secured a first class, and won the scholarship awarded to the person standing first in the order of merit.

This meant a great deal because, for the first time, my father seemed to be pleased that I was not wasting my time enjoying sports. Equally important was the confidence it gave me in terms of my academic abilities. This was the first occasion on which I had truly tested them. I knew then that I could compete with the brighter colleagues, although I would have to work harder than some of them.

At the end of the first college year it was with a sense of satisfaction that I went home for the holidays, knowing I would have a friendly welcome at home. I had proven my academic worth to my father for the first time, even though it was not in his preferred field. I knew, at least, I would not be compared to my sister any more.

* * *

During these holidays we also moved from Galle to Ambalangoda. By then my father was thoroughly engrossed in managing the agricultural land that he had mostly inherited from my mother. He had already expanded the acreage by acquiring adjoining lands whenever they were for sale. He had small acreages of rubber, cinnamon and paddy cultivations. He also had intentions of expanding further and replanting the older plantations. He hardly spent time at home. He was either at work in the railway office or managing the agricultural lands. He arranged a transfer to Ambalangoda precisely because of the proximity to the agricultural lands. For the same reason he decided to build a retirement home in Ambalangoda and take early retirement in order to manage the properties on a full-time basis. This was a task he immensely relished.

By the time we moved from Galle he had already acquired the land and finalized the plans for a house with four bedrooms, two bathrooms, living area and covered verandah along with kitchen and servants' quarters, and a garage that was set at the back of the twenty perches of land. His plan allowed space for a garden that provided enough privacy from the activity on the Main Street that abutted the property. The location of the land was at the northern end of the town center. My mother's ancestral home at Hirewatte was at the opposite end. The land already had a small house abutting the road, which in his retirement, my father converted to a grocery store. He was very fond of overseeing the store mainly as this provided an opportunity to meet and speak with the towns' folk who came by to purchase groceries. As there was no buildings right across the land, one had a clear glimpse of the beach and the ocean from the house.

The Post Office was situated almost opposite our house. Next to the Post Office was the impressive house of a leading merchant Rohana Mudalali, whose two lawyer sons, Patrick and K.D. Fernando, were close friends of mine. Much later, my friend from Richmond days, Sumanatilake De Silva (Sumane), the vice captain of the Mahinda College cricket team, built a spacious house neighboring our home. He managed the family jewelry business with his wife Nirmalee. He also did much social service and was the Mayor of the town for some time. Our friendship from school days continued; Sumane and Nirmalee have visited us in New York, Vienna and Los Angeles where Shanthi and I have been residing over the years.

Further north on the same street was the mansion-like ancestral home of my close friend A.M. Bandularatne (Bandu), who was a hostelmate of mine during our days at the Law College Hostel. He was a leading lawyer, practicing at the Balapitiya courts, just as my neighbors, the Fernando brothers. Bandu married my sister's classmate from Visakha Viddyalaya, Sujatha Perera, a pretty damsel whom my friend had courted while we were in Law College. They had two daughters, Yenuka (Tikiri) and Lumbini (Nangi), who also became lawyers and married two lawyers. Tikiri married Anuja who was the son of a Law College hostelmate of mine W.K. Premaratne. Nangi married Dushantha, son of Chandananda De Silva, a senior government official who retired as Defense Secretary, and later served as Ambassador in a Gulf State. His wife Dayani, who retired as head of the Bank of Ceylon, was a close relative of my Aunt Kusuma and Dayani's parents, lived opposite Bandu's house in Ambalangoda. Quite by accident, Dayani happened to be my partner at the graduation ball at Peradeniya campus many moons ago.

Bandu and his family were like my own. Many times when I visited my home country, I stayed with Bandu and his family both at Ambalangoda and at his Colombo residence. He had purchased the residence in Colombo so that his daughters could attend Ladies College and later, Law College. Bandu and his family were there for me, my siater, and my parents whenever the need arose. Bandu was also the bestman at my wedding. In later years, after the demise of my father, it was Bandu's wife Sujatha who attended to our agricultural lands until they were sold by my sister.

Thus, our home was set in the neighborhood of close friends. They were not only my friends; they were also friends of my parents. Of course, Ambalangoda is a town where almost everyone is related by blood or marriage, and most were known to one aother. This turned out to be extremely fortunate, because my sister and I were mostly living abroad. We were able to rest assured that our parents were happy and well attended to, particularly by Bandu and his family, during my father's years in retirement and even during his years of bad health, prior to his demise.

* * *

During the holidays I was not too happy puttering around at home in my hometown. On hearing that one of my friends from Richmond days was going on his circuit to upcountry, the green hills of the tea land, I asked him whether I could join him. He readily welcomed me as a traveling companion.

My friend Upali De Silva also had roots in Ambalangoda although his hometown was a few miles to the south in Dodanduwa, where I had spent my primary school days. On leaving Richmond, he had joined a leading international commercial establishment "Levers' Brothers", as a traveling salesman. His task was to ensure that the company products (mainly oil-based items such as soaps) were well stocked in the local grocery stores in the towns and villages in the circuit area under his supervision.

The trip turned out to be a week's sojourn for me at minimal cost. Traveling and accommodations for Upali were paid by the company and I was a guest sharing his hotel rooms. Except for driving around in gorgeous tea country, we did not do much on the tour other than the work required of Upali.

We spent a day of rest in Diyatalawa, the town where a British garrison was established to house the Boer prisoners of war. Today, a military camp and the Military Academy are established there, along with the training center for the survey department, where young surveyors are trained. We had friends in training in both camps and we took the opportunity to visit them. In the process, I had a firsthand glimpse of the facilities of the two establishments from where several of my friends had graduated over the years. During this break from work, Upali had also made arrangements to purchase a *Peugeot 203* to replace the old *Morris Station Wagon* that he had been using for sometime.

Once Upali's duties were completed, we headed back to Colombo with two other friends. They were Ernest Kulasuriya, who was at the Richmond hostel along with Upali and me, and my friend Bandu. After an early dinner, from Diyatalawa at four thousand feet, we climbed to Haputale, which is over five thousand feet, and headed towards Ratnapura. As usual in the hill country towns, it was drizzling and cold. It was also dark and I was falling asleep, while Bandu and Ernest were singing popular tunes to keep company with Upali, who was driving. Suddenly, I felt we were tumbling down a hill, and equally suddenly, the car stopped with the roof facing down. We got out with difficulty and were relieved to find no one was hurt.

Only after we had got out of the car, we realized we had skidded and fallen down a precipitous slope several thousand feet. A single mango sampling had prevented further descent and saved us. Even today I shudder to think what fate would have awaited us down below! We had hardly any time to catch our breaths before fast-thinking Bandu waved down a lorry, and he was on his way to fetch a crane from Ratnapura, which was the nearest town where it would be possible to hire one. He was of course aware that our friend Palitha was based in Ratnapura, and any necessary assistance could be easily obtained. Ratnapura was a distance of about 170 km from the vicinity of the village Haldumulla, where we had skidded off, and therefore we knew that it would be sometime in the morning before we would have any help to hoist the vehicle.

The rest of us trudged downhill with great difficulty, and walked up to a little building, which we found to be the home of the local school teacher. He gave us shelter that night. In the morning we were treated to an excellent village breakfast. Knowing we had to while away our time, we decided to take a bath in the local well and then found our way back to the top of the main road. This time we walked up the path used by the villagers, which was so much easier than climbing down the steep hill, the way we had come in the dark the previous night. We were seated by the road when a passing vehicle screeched to a halt and reversed to where we were. It was an impressive Mercedes car and the person in the back seat was none other than the ex-Prime Minister Mr. Dudley Senanayake. Having seen the toppled car he had stopped to inquire from us what assistance he could render. We thanked him and explained that we were waiting for a crane to pull the car back onto the road.

He advised us to get back home promptly, but safely, and continued his journey to a political meeting that he was scheduled to address.

We were elated that someone noticed and offered us help, and that too, a prominent person who, as students we looked up to. That was my first fleeting encounter with the man with whom, many years later I had the high honor of discussing national affairs as they impacted the international scene. Shortly after this encounter, Bandu arrived with Palitha and the crane. Having hauled the car back on the road, which luckily had only a few dents, we continued our journey to Colombo.

The holidays were over. It was time to get back to the Law College with its lectures and textbooks.

FOOTNOTE:

[1] The historical high standards of the legal profession, the judiciary, and the legal system that was in place during the time I had the privilege of entering the profession, have been eroding gradually over the years. Regrettably, the entire justice system now suffers from many a malady. Even the personal integrity of the members of the Bar, including the members of the once respected Attorney General's Department, and once revered members of the the Bench, is now being questioned. Thus, the entire legal process and the justice system seem under challenge on many fronts. The current state of affairs, and the reasons behind the radical decline, are well documented in the courageous and frank expose, *Lore of the Law*, published in 2012, by S.L. Gunasekara, a leading member of the Bar, and son of a Supreme Court judge who was on the Bench during the glory days of the legal system of Sri Lanka.

Chapter 17

Voet Inn

Emboldened by the positive results of the first year exam, with a certain amount of confidence and renewed vigor I began the second year at the Law College. This year I studied not only complex subjects that exposed me to the practical aspects of law such as Criminal Law, Torts (civil wrongdoings), Law of Contracts, Law of Persons (family law pertaining to marriage, divorce and adoption), and Law of Property (sale, lease, inheritance and partition), but also I learned the intricacies of ballroom dancing; the foxtrot, the Latin dances and the waltz.

In the second year at the Law College, just as in the first, we were blessed to have excellent teachers, who were experts in their fields and considered to be the most prominent practitioners in the country.

Criminal Law was taught by W.D. Gunesekera, alumni of my Alma Mater, Richmond College, where he excelled not only in academics, winning all the coveted prizes, but in sports as well. He won the Best All-Round Student's award. Later he became a judge of the Supreme Court. The lecturer in Torts (non-criminal wrongful acts for which damages can be sought by the injured party), was G.F. Sethukavalar, who at the time was one of the leading civil lawyers in the country. He practiced in the District Court of Colombo as well as in the outstation courts. He later became a Queen's Counsel, the highest honor bestowed in the legal profession. Sethukavalar, the smiling lecturer, gave interesting lectures interspersed with witty comments. Not surprisingly, Sethu's lectures always attracted a full house.

Contracts law was taught by Neville Samarakoon, who had established himself as one of the leaders of the civil side in both Colombo and provincial courts. Only a few years after he taught us he too was appointed a Queen's Counsel, and later, was appointed the Chief Justice of the Supreme Court. This was the very first time a member of the Unofficial Bar (those representing clients rather than members of the judiciary or the Attorney General's Department) became the Chief Justice.

Law of Property was taught by M.L. De Silva, a leading lawyer in Colombo, who later became a Presidents Counsel. Law of Persons (Family Law) was taught by C.G. Weeramantry, a prominent civil lawyer in Colombo. He later became a judge of the Supreme Court, and went on to become a Judge of the International Court of Justice (ICJ), a distinguished professor at Monash University, and prolific author. He is considered not only the greatest international lawyer produced by Sri Lanka, but one of leading international lawyers in the world. I came to know him quite well during the time we both spent abroad. You will read more about that later.

Learning the subjects of Family Law and Law of Property was particularly complex in Ceylon (Sri Lanka), because of the multiple legal systems that apply to these areas of the law. In some countries, such as the United Kingdom and the United States, the law is based on the English Common Law. In Europe and Latin America, the law is mostly in written civil codes. Sri Lanka has a mixture of legal systems on which our laws are based. The general Law of the land is mainly based on Roman Dutch Law (now prevalent only in South Africa) and English Common Law. That alone is sufficient challenge for a law student and even for practicing lawyers. But, when it comes to family law and property law, most are governed by Roman Dutch Law, while Kandyan Law is applied to those from the Kandyan areas or the hill country, Tesawalamai to the Tamils, and Muslim Law to the Muslims. One can imagine the complexity of the situation when

SAME SKY, DIFFERENT NIGHTS

there are intermarriages which are not infrequent. Tesawalamai and Muslim law were not taught as parts of the subjects of family law and the law of property. These subject areas are governed by sectarian laws which are taught as separate subjects.

Tesawalamai was taught by one of the leading practitioners, S. Sabapathipillai, who during the time he was our lecturer, published a book on the subject. His work is considered a classic. Muslim law was taught by Naina Marikkar, who taught us Jurisprudence in the previous year.

It was indeed a great privilege to have learned the law under the expert guidance of such a distinguished array of lecturers.

* * *

Studies occupied most of our evenings and nights. There were occasional breaks when friends got together and planned youthful expeditions, either to the dance floor of a hotel, or to the movies. By then, thanks to a vacancy at the Law College hostel, I had moved into the Voet Inn, the name by which the Law Hostel was known. [1] It was established in a colonial mansion in the most desirable residential location of Cinnamon Gardens in Colombo. Located in the vicinity of the Colombo Municipal Building (City Hall) and the most prominent city park, the Victoria Park, during its proud history the Law Hostel accommodated some of the finest men of the legal profession. The hostel was a place most conducive to studies as almost everyone was committed to succeeding when the exams came around. It was also a place for great fun and animated discussions on topics of the day.

Just a short time after I joined the Law College hostel at No. 19, Barnes place, a dramatic event took place nearby. It was in a mansion, just a stone's throw away from the hostel, located behind the Law Hostel, on Rosemead place. It was on 25the September 1959, when the then popular Prime Minister, Solomon Dias Bandaranayike, was shot by Rev. Talduwe Somarama, a Buddhist

257

monk in suffron robes. The Prime Minister succumbed to the injuries the next day, in his third year in office, at the age of 60. He died despite the best efforts of the most skilled surgeons in the country. The previous day, 25 September, Somarama visited Bandaranaike at his private residence, Tintagel, in Rosemead Place, Colombo. Since Somarama was a member of the Buddhist clergy, he was not searched for weapons and was given free access to the Prime Minister as he began his routine meetings with the public. When the monk's presence was intimated to him, Bandaranaike rose to greet him in the traditional Buddhist manner. The assassin then raised the revolver, which had been hidden in his robes, and fired at the prostrate prime minister.

Earlier in his career, when Bandaranaike visited Galle on his campaign tour, I was at one of the two public meetings held on the grounds facing my home. Wijayananda Dhanayake, the candidate from his party for the Galle electorate, who later assumed the Premiership following Bandaranaike's demise, was the speaker before the address of Bandaranaike. Dahanayake, a great public speaker, on that occasion uttered the famous words in Sinhala "I will shake the 'money tree'. Collect as much as you wish, and then vote for me". The reference was to the fact that his rival, Henry Amarasuriya, one of the wealthiest in the country was spending millions on the campaign. At the time, vote-buying was quite rampant in the electoral process. Dhanayake did not have any money to spend on the campaign, except for the very bare necessities. Indeed he used to attend parliament by public transport until; his supporters collected funds and eventually bought him a car.

If the appetizer was a treat, the main course, the speech of Bandaranaike was eloquent, enthralling, and persuasive. It was a brilliant speech, of the type to which Galle had never been treated. Along with most others in the vicinity, I was simply mesmerized by his fiery oratory. As an eighteen- year-old and a member of the Richmond College debating team, I was left wondering about the brilliance he must have displayed in abundance in his student days as Secretary of the famed Oxford Union.

On September 25, 1959 the very forces that brought him to power, the coalition of Buddhist priests (Eksath Bikku Peramuna) and Ayurvedic Physicians succeeded in terminating not only his political career, but also his life. Leaders of these two forces were accused in a court case, which turned out to be the most sensational trial in the judicial history of the country. It must be noted here that it was Prime Minister Bandaranaike who suspended capital punishment. Ironically, his wife, Sirima Bandaranaike, who later became prime minister, reintroduced capital punishment in order to punish the culprits who assassinated her husband. At the trial, Somarama was defended by his counsel, Lucian Weeramantry, who later joined the United Nations as a Human Rights Lawyer. We became close friends. In spite of his best efforts it was a case where the evidence was well and truly stacked against the accused. Lucian (brother of Christie), later published a captivating book on the entire episode entitled: *Assassination of a Prime Minister*. We were riveted by the shock of the assassination and its aftermath, including the historic trial and the political turmoil that ensued.

* * *

A few days after the turmoil, life began to return to normal in the country, and I settled down to my routine at the Voet Inn. I also began forging lifelong friendships with some of my hostelmates. I started by sharing one of the two massive rooms in the old mansion with Palitha Wanasundara (Palitha), and A.M. Bandularatne (Bandu). Palitha was a fellow hurdler at the All-Island Public Schools Athletic Meet; he was a member of the Ananda College team while I was competing for Richmond. Palitha was a serious student, but he always found time to have fun. Over the years at Law College we became close friends. Later he became a leading lawyer at the Ratnapura Bar, and was elected as the mayor of the city of Ratnapura (city of gems). He married Indramala, an accomplished teacher at Devi Balika College, Colombo.

Whenever I was in the country on vacation, we never failed to meet, particularly on New Year's eve, when a group of friends always came together for a party in one or the other Colombo hotels. Palitha also has visited us in Los Angeles. As he desired I stopped for a meal, often at his home at Ratnapura, when taking trips to the interior of the country.

Bandu was from my hometown, Ambalangoda, so it was natural for us to be close friends. By the time he entered Law College he was responsible for managing his ancestral property. His parents had passed away and he was the only child. Partly for that reason, he had limited interest in legal studies. He had only turned to the law because his great ambition of being a medical doctor had not materialized. But he did still aspire to have a professional practice serving the community in his hometown.

Bandu was one year ahead of me. In his final exam he focused on one subject: Law of Evidence. Having not prepared ahead of time, I remember he came to me and sat through one whole night with me going over the entire syllabus for the subject. Next morning he sat for the exam. It is not easy to bet on a one night commitment, but Bandu had a perfect memory. He displayed it convincingly on that occasion. When the results came he was jubilant that at last his student days were over, particularly as he was a few years senior in age to some of us, because of the years he spent in premedical studies.

Though generally a serious person, Bandu was ready to play pranks on others. Unlike most Law Students, he was a teetotaler. Few realized this because he was good at sporting a glass of water, pretending it was a glass of gin and tonic. Eventually, he settled down to practice as a proctor and was one of the leading lawyers at the Balapitiya Bar. Without doubt he executed more Deeds, recording property transactions, and Wills, and inheritances, than anyone else in the Balapitiya Bar. This came as no surprise to anyone. He had a reputation as forthright with unquestionable integrity and honesty in his work. You will read more about our friendship, elsewhere in this narrative.

By the end of the term, a vacancy had come up in the smaller room next to the room to which I was first assigned, and I opted to move in there. I spent most of the next three years in that room, until I completed my law studies. It was one of the two front rooms next to the upstairs balcony facing the front lawn and the main road. It was one of the more desirable rooms in the hostel.

My roommate was Aelian Perera. He was dedicated to doing well in his law studies and this suited us both as we regularly used to study very late into the night. Aelian was a paradox. Even though he studied hard, he was a fun-loving person who did not take things seriously. Nothing bothered him, but he was very ambitious and wanted to succeed in life. The lightheartedness he displayed going about daily affairs influenced those around him. It was fun being around him and invariably he was the center of attention whenever we congregated. He worked hard and at the same time enjoyed life to the hilt.

Early that year, at the behest of Aelian, a group of close friends decided to take ballroom dance classes. We decided to register at the dancing school of Vevil de Kaw near the beach in Bambalapitiya. The classes were run by him with his sister Erine, and were the most popular and possibly the best school of dancing at the time. We started with the foxtrot and gradually mastered the Latin dances and even the waltz. It was to the credit of our teachers, the brother sister combination, that eventually most of us became good ballroom dancers. We enjoyed hitting the dance scene whenever the opportunity presented itself. This too was mainly due to the persuasion of Aelian, who generally took the lead and organized the outings.

First, it was the Law-Medical dance that was the target. The annual dance brought together the law and medical students at one of the leading hotels in Colombo, with popular cabaret artistes and bands performing. Thereafter we used to attend the more popular public dances of the day. As time went on, Aelian and I became good *Baila* dancers (a form of Portuguese kaffrinya), and we participated in the *Baila* competitions. Often, Aelian and I would find ourselves competing with each other in the final rounds. Aelian's partner was a distant cousin. I was partnered by the sister of a good friend, Upali Samararatne, who was the wicketkeeper of Wesley College when I was captaining the Richmond College cricket team that beat Wesley the first time after many years. She was a dynamic dancer and in a span of one year we had together won the *Baila* competition at the Law-Medical dance as well as two premier public dances of leading commercial establishments, Shell and Car Mart. We also won the Kurunduwatte christmas dance. In the latter dance our final competitor was film icon Rukmani Devi and her partner.

Of course, *Baila* was a side show to the popular music and dances of the fifties and sixties. Popular bands such as Harold Senaviratne Combo and Jetliners, and soloists like Mignon Rutnam, Sam the Man, Peter Prins and Desmond Fernando presenting the tunes of Doris Day, Frank Sinatra, Dean Martin and Elvis Presley. They all entertained at the popular locations of the time: Galle Face Hotel, New Oriental Hotel (NOH), later known as the Taprobane, and popular dance halls such as Girl's Friendly Society next to the Lionel Wendt Theater. Our dancing group included Aelian, Bandu, Palitha Wanasundra, Lankatilake (Lanke), Ananda Wickramasekara (Ana), Nawaz Dawood (Nawaz), Herath Guneratne (Gune), Rohan Happugalle (Rohan) and me.

This eventually led us to form an inner circle of friends, and we kept close contact with each other all our lives. As of this writing, regretfully, five of the eight of my closest friends have departed us through one ailment or the other.

* * *

As noted earlier, Aelian was perhaps the most enterprising and vibrant of all and sported a happy-go-lucky attitude to life. He hailed from Negambo, and was the son of a prominent Surveyor. He did well in his studies at Law College, graduating with first class honors. He married Swarna Perera, daughter of a leading medical practitioner in Negambo Dr. Frank Perera. She was a contemporary at Law College though junior to us. They both set up a legal practice in Negambo.

Shortly after, Aelian joined the Ceylon Insurance Corporation as a legal assistant and worked his way up to be a senior attorney for the Corporation. After a few years, he contacted me when I was in New York to say his marriage had ended and he asked for my help in leaving the country for a while. I suggested that, I might be able to arrange a scholarship for him to study for a Masters degree in Canada. He was delighted with the suggestion and I went ahead making arrangements for him to come to Canada.

By then Swarna had remarried an army officer and Aelian was engaged to a leading film star, Nita Fernando. Sometime in the late sixties he arrived in Montreal and settled down to study for his Masters degree. Shortly thereafter, true to his character, he befriended a Canadian lady influential enough to find him employment as a legal officer in a leading insurance establishment in Montreal. In due course, he gave up his studies and settled down in Montreal. His wife Nita joined him shortly thereafter and was able to secure employment as a receptionist at the Montreal General Hospital.

It was a serendipitous story in that these two people deeply in love were able to settle down rather easily in a city where, at the time, French was essential for employment and neither was conversant in French. They bought a spacious home near the Montreal Dorval airport and settled down. I used to visit them in Montreal and they used to visit me in New York. Our friendship kept up through the decades they lived in Canada. After nearly three decades in Canada, in the late nineties, they decided take retirement and return home to Sri Lanka. One motivating factor was the promise Aelian had made to himself that he would someday find a way to resurrect Nita's acting career. That career had been sacrificed because of their marriage and immigration to Canada. By the time they left their native land Nita was at the peak of her career, with more than fifty films to her credit. She had the lead role in most of her movies where the male leads were the most popular actors of all time.

Among them are well-known seventies films *Lasanda* with Gamini Fonseka, *Mangala* with Tony Ranasinghe, and *Shanthi* with

Ravindra Randeniya. She was also a popular actress on stage. Among her credits are dramas of well-known producers such as Gunasena Gallappatti's *Sandakindura*, Ranjith Bogoda's *Hadawatanatto*, and Namel Weeramuni's English play *Right Hand of God* with Kamal Addelaratchi. It was my fortune to see Namel's production where Nita gave an outstanding performance.

On returning to Sri Lanka, as promised, Aelian produced a movie *Pauru Walalla (Fortress)* with Nita in the lead role with the iconic Sri Lankan film star Gamini Fonseka. It was a demanding role in a movie set entirely within the Dutch Fort in Galle, based on a love story during the colonial times. The two were the only actors in the movie and it not only won high accolades in the country but also won awards at the Singapore film festival. Nita carried away the best actress award and that was the first such award won by a Sri Lankan at an international festival. It was such an honor that the President of the country, Ranasingh Premadasa, a patron of the arts, saw fit to gift Nita a house in recognition of the honor brought to the country.

There began a second phase in Nita's acting career that continues to flourish to date. She has many films, produced and directed by her in addition to being a star herself in the movies. Several of them have won awards.

Once they moved back to Sri Lanka I visited them whenever I returned to the Island. Shortly after I had retired, we were in Sri Lanka on an extended vacation. We had rented a house in Nugegoda, a suburb of Colombo. There we used to have friends over in the evenings if we were not going out ourselves. On one such occasion, just a few weeks prior to New Year's Eve, we had some friends to dinner and Aelian and Nita were among the guests. A few days later, Nita called to invite us to their home and mentioned that Aelian wanted her to invite us before that Friday. As she was busy the only day available was that particular Thursday. If we were available to come, she was going to invite a few other friends who normally met together with us.

On the appointed day we went to his place to dinner along with Hema and Mallika Perera, Nihal and Kusum Pieris and a few others. Most of those present including Aelian and Nita were planning to go together for the New Year's eve party at a Colombo hotel, as we usually did. By then, Aelian had slowed down a bit due to a few nagging health issues. He had a chronic back pain he had developed over the years, and recurring discomfort from a surgery he had had several years earlier to correct a problem in his nasal passage.

That evening we had a very enjoyable dinner party hosted by Aelian and Nita reminiscing about the happenings during our younger days and exchanging views on the political scene of the day. It was well past midnight when we broke up. Aelian had bought a new pair of shoes for the New Year's eve party, but he said, they did not fit him well, and was going to exchange them early next day. He came to the door to say good night, and we headed home after a most agreeable evening of food, drink and friendly banter.

It was about half past one when we went to bed. The strangest thing happened early next morning when we heard a banging on our bedroom door. It was so loud, it sounded like a bolt of thunder. My wife and I both got up, startled at the noise. Finding nothing unusual on inspecting the surroundings we went back to bed. Within an hour or so we got a telephone message from Nita, crying uncontrollably, hardly able to tell us that Aelian had passed away.

It was unimaginable that a person who had had such a great time that night, though suffering from a few minor ailments, had passed away without any warning. We said we would be on the way soon to her place and asked Nita to be calm. But knowing that she would not have the presence of mind in the wake of the unexpected event, I called the funeral undertakers (Jayaratnes) directing them to Aelian's residence before leaving home. On arrival, we found that Nita was uncontrollable in her grief and was crying hugging Aelian to her. It was a difficult task for my wife to drag her away. By then the neighbors who knew them had arrived, along with a couple of other friends who were informed of the tragedy.

Later we learned that soon after we left Aelian and Nita had gone to sleep. After sometime Nita had heard Aelian in the bathroom coughing and trying to clear his throat of mucus, a situation not unfamiliar to him since he had surgery while they were in Montreal. As she was tired from the day's events, she had fallen into a deep sleep and had not paid much attention to the coughing as she normally did. Early in the morning, when the maid brought Aelian his bed tea, he had not got up as he usually did. After a while she had alerted Nita and only then they realized what had occurred.

Thus ended, in an untimely manner, the life of a good man; my roommate and lifelong friend, who enjoyed life to the fullest and left with no regrets.

But, the friendship with Nita did not end. We continue as close family friends. Even during my last visit home, she made it a point to invite me to a special screening to preview her latest production *Swara* (seven notes), to be released soon. It is a masterpiece on the theme of HIV/Aids which she produced, directed, and played the main role in, and is certain to bag national and international awards.

* * *

Among my other friends at Law College was Lanke (Lankatilake), tall, fair handsome Kandyan from Narammala, near the town of Kurunegala. Lanke was a cricketer from Maliyadewa College, Kurunegala and played in the Law College team with me. He was as Aelian and Bandu were a bit more advanced in age than me. He was also someone who liked to live the good life and saw academics as merely a ticket to good employment. His parents had died when he was young. His stepmother, who had brought him up, was living in the ancestral home. As the only child, he was by then already responsible for managing the family property, which was rather considerable. It also meant that he had deeper pockets than most of us.

Lanke graduated and joined the army as an assistant Judge-Advocate and after a few years began a private law practice in Kurunegala, becoming one of the leading lawyers in town. He went back to live in his ancestral home. He married his dancing partner, Blossom, who was full of life and often the center of any gathering among friends. They had two daughters (Kokila and Udeni), who later studied in the United States. Both of them settled down in Toronto, Canada. Lanke and Blossom were active members of the Lions International and used to visit the United States when they held Lions conferences. We kept up our friendship, visiting each other whenever I was back home. We always attended the New Year's eve Dinner Dances in each other's company. Lanke always insisted we visit him whenever we happened to pass Kurunegala.

Once, when a dozen of us were on the way to Dambulla to watch a cricket match between Sri Lanka and Australia, he made arrangements for us to visit him for breakfast. It was the most lavish breakfast one could imagine with all the village breakfast favorites laid out for us by Blossom, a culinary expert. On another occasion, more recently, about ten of us were on the way to the east coast of the country to observe the developments after a protracted regional war, when Lanke graciously agreed to have us for a lunch break at his home. On this occasion, as on previous occasions, it was a hearty meal that was offered to the guests. This meal proved to be extra special to all of us. Blossom, his wife of over four decades, was in bad health at the time and we were all shocked when, within two months of our visit, she passed away. Lanke is now retired and spends his time between his Narammala home and that of his daughter in Toronto. I was delighted to have him and his daughters and son-in-law visit us in LosAngeles recently.

* * *

Ana (Ananda Wickramasekara) was Lanke's roommate at the Law Hostel. He hailed from Mihiripanne, Galle the same as Vasu. They were classmates at Law College and were one year junior to the rest of us in our close knit group. Ana was a good student but acted often on impulse. He was known as 'Flash' among friends. During the vacations Ana, Vasu and I travelled around the country in Vasu's *Mini Austin*.

On graduation, Ana established a lucrative legal practice in Galle. Indeed he is an advocate who is in high demand in courthouses throughout the southern part of the country. He spent a few years in London practicing law. His then wife, Indu, was based there. They too joined our group on New Year's eve dances whenever they were available. He has also established a tourist hotel named *Pointe de Galle* by the side of a scenic bay well regarded by sea bathers near Unawatuna beach. I have had occasion to be his guest there, to spend the day swimming and enjoying the local fare with friends, both local and foreign.

*   *   *

Nawaz (Nawaz Dawood) was perhaps the brightest of us all. He hailed from Gampola, and was the grandson of a prominent Muslim figure in the country, a judge of the Supreme Court M.T. Akbar. A chain-smoker and a lover of flashy cars, Nawaz had a Sunbeam convertible sports car when he was at Law College. He won the coveted Law College Gold Medal for oratory, the previous recipients of which had gone on to become leading lawyers of the country.

Nawaz graduated with first class honors. He married his classmate, Marie Wickramanayake, a member of the leading Wickramanayake legal family. For a while he worked as the attorney for the World Council of Churches in Geneva, Switzerland. For some years, I used to visit him there when I was attending conferences at the United Nations in Geneva. His wife used to serve us great meals and we enjoyed our banter late into the night, fueled by good cognac, which he loved. Most regretfully, early in his thirties, he suffered a heart attack and passed away quite unexpectedly while he was visiting India.

*   *   *

There were two in our group Gilbert (Gilba) and Rohan, who were not resident in the Law Hostel but spent most of their spare time visiting us in the hostel. Gilbert Herath Guneratne hailed from a distinguished family from the Galmuruwa Walauwa (mansion) in

Madampe, my uncle Sirisena's electorate. Before my uncle, one of his uncles, T.B. Subasinghe, had represented the same Bingiriya electorate. Several of his uncles were physicians and one became a Director at the World Health Organization (WHO). I came to know him later during my visits to Geneva. He later served as WHO Regional Director for Asia, based in New Delhi. Gilba loved his bicycle and used to cycle to the hostel from his home at Punchi Borella junction. He was always game for a prank and was in great spirits, constantly sporting an unending smile. He always joined our group attending dinner dances, as well as our other pursuits. In later years, he and his unassuming wife Ann joined us at the New Year's eve dances. I used to visit him whenever I was in Colombo. Once he graduated as a lawyer he joined the oldest legal firm in the country, F.J. & G. De Sarams, and rose to become a partner in short order. He ended up as its senior partner. He took over the position from another close friend of mine at Law College, Elmore Perera, who played in the cricket team with me and graduated as the first in his batch the year preceding mine.

Gilba was succeeded by U. Kadurugamuwa, who was in the batch following mine. Thus the 175 year old hallowed law firm was headed during its last thirty years by my contemporaries at Law College. It was also the law firm where I apprenticed for a year in 1961, in order to fulfill the requirements of being called to the Bar as a proctor (solicitor) and notary public. That year the firm selected two apprentices. The other was M.I.M. Jaffer, whose uncle was a partner in the firm at the time. The firm was headed by the legendary lawyer A.R. Tampoe. We learned mostly conveyancing, which entailed the drafting of deeds, wills and other contractual legal documentation related to property transactions. It was a chore that I did not particularly enjoy, but the privilege of working in such respected environs made up for the drudgery. Many years later, upon the retirement of the then senior partner Tampoe, my friend Elmore Perera took over the reins of the firm.

My apprenticing partner Jauffer was also a regular visitor to the hostel and became a member of our inner circle. He also joined the law firm of FJ & G De Sarams and became a partner. The firm handled the work of a large number of leading commercial establishments as well as prominent people. Clients included the leaders of the two major political parties who trusted their work to the famous law firm, including the Prime Ministers elected from the two opposing parties D.S. Senanayake (U.N.P.) and S.W.R.D. Bandaranayaike (S.L.F.P.).

During his tenure in the firm, Gilba handled the personal legal work of the Prime Minister, Mrs. Sirimavo Bandaranayaike, and her family. They confidently entrusted their legal affairs to his skilled and discreet hands. After a distinguished career, Gilba passed away shortly after his retirement.

* * *

The other member of our group, Rohan Hapugalle, was also an enthusiastic cyclist. He too cycled to the law hostel frequently from his residence at Vidyalaya Place, not far from Gilba's house. He too hailed from a distinguished family down south. Rohan was a very enthusiastic dancer and never missed a single opportunity to attend a dance. In later years he joined us in our annual New Year's Eve dances. By the time he joined us he had already earned a degree from the Peradeniya campus of the University of Ceylon. After taking oaths as a lawyer, he practiced law at the Colombo Bar. He soon moved on to the commercial sector and became a successful business person. His mother was one of the early presidents of the United National Party (UNP) Women's Federation.

Rohan married Neelakanthi, daughter of M.D.H. Jayawardane, Minister of Finance in the UNP cabinet. It was natural that with such political connections he should gravitate towards politics, but he never was interested in being an active politician. Nevertheless, for some period, he functioned as the executive secretary to Mr. Dudley Senanayake during his tenure as leader of the opposition in the parliament. After a while Rohan reverted to his commercial activities and functioned for many years as Chairman of Ceylon

Bulbs, a very successful family enterprise. Much later, during the tenure of his classmate at Royal College, Lalith Athulathmudali, as the Minister of Trade and Commerce, Rohan was appointed as Chairman of the State Trading Corporation, the premier government commercial enterprise involved in imports and exports.

Throughout the years Rohan and I were in close contact, visiting each other on every possible occasion. Whenever I was on vacation back home in Colombo he would invite friends and entertain us lavishly at his residence. His charming wife continued this practice long after the demise of her husband.

On one occasion when I had returned home to Colombo from New York, where I had just remarried, Rohan and Neelakanthi held a welcome party for Shanthi my wife and me to which he invited all our close friends. It was held on the lawn with its checker board of white and black tiles of the historic Galle Face Hotel facing the beautiful Indian Ocean. The hotel is a luxury heritage masterpiece of Victorian architecture built by the British in 1864 (nearly 120 years prior to the event). This hotel has hosted Royalty, world leaders and celebrities from colonial Ceylon to modern Sri Lanka. It continues to be one of the most exquisite hotels east of the Suez, along with the Raffles of Singapore. This caring gesture epitomizes Rohan, the ever thoughtful gentleman of culture and class, who indulged in the best that life had to offer, but never forgot those in need.

It was his concern for the needy that made him work tirelessly in the Lions movement, which sponsored many charity projects. As usual he excelled in whatever he did. Naturally, he ended up the President of the Rotary Club of Colombo, where he spearheaded several projects to help those in need. In addition to his business affairs it was his interest in the Lions movement that often took him abroad.

This was serendipitous because it allowed Rohan to visit me whereever I happened to be, whether in New York, Vienna or elsewhere. Whenever he visited me, we had a great time and he enjoyed meeting the Ambassadors from various countries whom I would invite home. I carefully selected the friendlier and informal Ambassadors that I knew Rohan would be interested in meeting. One of the last of theses occasions was in Vienna when he visited me with one of his daughters. I remember him being unbelievably happy on that occasion.

Not too long after the visit he was scheduled to go to a Rotary conference in Peru. His wife Neelakanthi was planning to visit us in Vienna while he was in Peru. In a last minute change of plans, his wife decided to join him. After the conference in Lima, Peru, he had arranged to visit Machu Picchu with his wife. I had warned Rohan that it is somewhat of an arduous trip. I had taken that trip when I was very much younger and it was not the best of experiences. Of course no one who visits Peru can be dissuaded from a trip to Machu Picchu, no matter what the warnings are.

Fifty miles from the mountain city of Cusco, 7,000 feet above sea level and nestled on a mountaintop among the Andean Mountains, a majestic city soars above the Urubamba Valley below. The Inca built this Pre-Columbian, 15th century structure. It has been deemed the "Lost City", unknown until its relatively recent discovery in 1911. Archaeologists estimate that approximately 1200 people could have lived in the area, though many theorize that it was most likely built as a retreat for Incan rulers. Because of its isolation from the rest of Peru, living in the area full time would require traveling great distances just to reach the nearest village.

In order to reach Machu Picchu I had taken the flight from Lima to Cusco, which is at a height of 11,500 feet, where I was told to move slowly, as the thin air at that height would make one feel sick. Getting off the plane I walked extremely slowly. When we registered at the hotel, all the visitors were served a cup of cocoa leaves (the same leaves through a complex process convert to cocaine). We were told that it would help prevent mountain sickness caused by the lack of oxygen at that height.

By the time we had checked in I felt fine and more confident. I decided to take a stroll through the interesting town. Along the way

I purchased a llama carpet, which I still possess, and returned to the hotel for the evening. Feeling fine, I went to the restaurant and ordered a good local dinner and a glass of wine. Just as the meal was arriving I felt the world go around and my head started to ache. With great difficulty I found my room and spent a good part of the night throwing up.

In the morning, at eight sharp, the mountain train was scheduled to leave for Machu Picchu and I was not in a state to move from my bed. Somehow I dragged myself to the station, not knowing whether I will be in a state to take the trip. It was a gutsy and perhaps foolhardy move on my part to get on the train. As the train trudged along I felt better. Eventually, when we reached the terminal station, I was in fine shape, although quite worried the sickness might return when I got to the ancient city.

It is certainly a marvel that so many centuries back, without modern techniques or machinery, a city was built on such a remote peak. But what I saw, in some measure disappointed me, compared to the ruined cities of Anuradhapura and Polonnaruwa in Sri Lanka, built more than 20 centuries before Machu Picchu. Even compared to the remains of the fortress built on top of a massive rock at Sigiriya in Sri Lanka, about the same time as Machu Picchu, what remained there is more akin to a load of bricks rather than the remains of identifiable structures. Of course, everyone's experience is different, and mine may be one of those exceptions, as Machu Picchu remains a leading tourist attractio and is even listed as one of the wonders of the world.

Following his conference, Rohan and his wife undertook the trip to Machu Picchu. They made it to Cusco, but from there Rohan was unable to venture further due to an incapacitating headache. They returned to Lima after some medical help. Regretfully, on his return to Lima he suffered a massive stroke. Even with all the medical attention he received he did not recover. He fell into a coma following the stroke. He had to be treated for three months in Lima where his wife cared for him most attentively. She was in a faraway place, where the language was foreign to her, and she had very few known contacts other than the medical personnel attending Rohan. Once he was stabilized the health insurance company arranged an air ambulance to fly him home via London. On the way he suffered a relapse and had to be hospitalized in the UK. After a while he returned home and spent over a year in the loving care of his committed wife, who along with his family provided the best of care, despite the fact that he was completely unconscious.

I visited him at his home in Colombo and it was a most heart-wrenching experience for me to see my dear friend, who loved life and knew how to enjoy it to the hilt, lying in bed unable to communicate with me and possibly even with no mental consciousness. I tried my best to speak to him and I hope he heard me. Soon thereafter he passed away and it was providential that I was back in Colombo on the occasion of the alms-giving commomorating his first death anniversary.

* * *

Another lifelong friend whom I met at Voet Inn is Bertram Tittawella. He was the philosopher in our group, always speaking like a sage, and making wise cracks. It is a trait that he honed to the highest level in his later life. He sported a pipe that added as a prop to enhance the aura he projected as a thoughtful person. He visited me in New York while he was at Harvard long after our Voet Inn days.

Bertram went on to become the Secretary-General of the Parliament in Sri Lanka. He was highly respected for his integrity and impartiality. I have visited him in the parliament where he entertained me to lunch along with mutual friends, who were by then members of parliament. On his retirement, he resided in his ancestral *Walauwa* (mansion) on top of a scenic hill in Kandy. Whenever I was passing by he would always arrange a lunch or dinner party enabling me to meet our mutual friends in the Kandy area. Often, I have spent nights at his residence. Once I was visiting him with our Austrian friends Dr. Ernst and Gerti Fasan. My friends and I had an eventful night that day. I will let my friend Ernst relate the experience, the way he wrote in a travelogue, that he sent me after his visit to my country. He wrote:

> *"In Kandy – higher up and with far better air – we have a private invitation by a friend of Jasentuliyana's, Mr. Bertram Tittawella. He is a former Secretary General of the Sri Lankan Parliament. Now, at about 60 years old, he is retired. His house, where we are welcomed with greatest cordiality, is most beautifully situated above Kandy, and has a spectacular view over the city and the lake. Dinner is preceded by drinks, and I fear that we have been spoiled for the rest of our lives: repeatedly we are served Arrack with Ginger beer. Of course, all of them maintain that ice cubes have to be added to this drink. But I refuse, and they all (including my loving wife) ridicule me about this.*
>
> *Bertram is a bachelor. He says that this is only because Kusum had chosen Nihal, our traveling companion couple. But we have the feeling that he flirtingly says this to all ladies who are as charming as Kusum and Nandi's wife Shanthi (I overheard a lady, who is present at dinner with her husband, also receives this compliment). Nandi and we are shown to our rooms, and then we hand over our little present (a book about Austria) to our host.*
>
> *We have our own bathroom, and can sleep quite well with open windows. Some mosquitoes, but bites do not disturb us too much. During the night Gerti and I hear the noise of clattering of metal on stone. We look at each other and go back to sleep. Next morning at breakfast, Nandi tells us a strange story of some coins which he had put on the window sill. They had fallen down during night, without being touched and without a breeze. Is there a (friendly) ghost in Bertram's house?"*

As we retired to bed, Bertram, in saying "Good Night", added that we should not be disturbed by any noises around the house. We took his comment to mean outside noise in the forest like surroundings of the house. Only on return to Colombo, we learnt from a friend, that in fact, such occurrences were common in Bertram's residence! Bertram remains a close and respected friend of Shanthi and me. We are grateful for his friendship. You will meet him again later in this narrative.

* * *

Voet Inn was thus a place for serious academic work, but the years spent there were also a time of great fun and frolic. Most of all it was a time when the bonding among friends were so intense to have lasted the test of time. No matter how enticing the distractions arising from good friendships, with a demanding course load and exam schedule at hand, I made sure not to waste a single moment of my days at Voet Inn. Those were grueling but fun-filled days at the Mansion named after the great jurist which one recollects with great nostalgia.

FOOTNOTE:

[1] The popular belief is that the name is "The Voet Inn" named after the great Dutch Jurist Johannes Voet ('Voet' being pronounced 'foot'). But others believe that the hostel being named after Mr. Voet should mean "the Inn of Mr. Voet" or "The Voet's Inn".

— ❖ —

Chapter 18

Azdak's Lore

We asked once, we asked again, all to no avail. Our requests for a refrigerator, radio, and telephone at Voet Inn, fell on deaf ears.

The radio in particular was important to us. Radio music and films were our main forms of entertainment, except for the occasional dinner dances and sports events. These were the late 50s and no one knew much about TV in Ceylon.

We listened to the broadcasts on Radio Ceylon, whenever we could. Considered the oldest radio station in Asia, Radio Ceylon started broadcasting on an experimental basis, (conducted by the Telegraph Department) in 1923. This was just three years after the inauguration of broadcasting in Europe. In the golden age of radio, spanning the 50s and the 60s, the Ceylon Commercial Service was a popular spot on the dial. It played mostly film music and more often than not, Hindi music. For this reason the service was very popular, not only in Sri Lanka, but in some parts of South East Asia as well, particularly in India and Pakistan. Radio Ceylon had a very lucrative Commercial Hindi Service launched in the early 1950s. Millions of rupees in advertising revenue came from India, playing a vital role in establishing Radio Ceylon as the 'King of the Airwaves' in South Asia. Over the years Radio Ceylon has produced some of the finest announcers of South Asia, among them: Livy Wijemanne and Vernon Corea, who have been considered among the best in the world.

We were particularly attracted to the broadcasts as one of our fellow law students, Ranjith Heendeniya, was an announcer in the English Service. He read the evening news and also acted as DJ for the weekend popular music program 'Your Request'.

We had little time on our hands for outside entertainment. Even going out to the cinema was not that frequent, and only when a well publicized movie reached our cinemas. Among the memorable films we watched were the classics: *The Ten Commandments,* with a galaxy of stars led by Charlton Hesston, Yul Bryner and Yvonne De Carlo; *Ben Hur*, an equally mega production with Charlton Hesston and Jack Hawkins; and Alfred Hitchcock's thrillers, *North By North West* and *Vertigo.*

Among the Musicals *The King and I* with Yul Bryner and Deborah Kerr; and *South Pacific* with Mitzy Gaynor, were the most popular. Much later, I was fortunate to see these two musical classics on stage, at West End in London and on Broadway in New York, with some of the same actors. I have been fortunate to see these stage productions of the musicals not once but many times in different cities or with different casts.

Many war films fascinated me. One I remember most from my Voet Inn days was *Bridge on the River Kwai,* which had a fabulous cast and was filmed partly in Ceylon. The story revolved around the building of a bridge by British war prisoners in Burma. There were also the Laurel and Hardy comedies that kept us entertained. Over a five-year period in late 50s and 60s we were lucky to see such a galaxy of fine films among many that were screened at that time.

I was an avid fan of Sinhala movies from my Richmond days. I have seen some of the films that initiated the movie industry in Ceylon, such as *Asokamala*, a historical love story produced in 1947 by the famed producer Shanthi Kumar. Much later, I saw the screening of perhaps the first Sinhala movie *Rajakiya Vikramaya*, produced in 1925. This movie starred N.M. Perera as a young artist. He later became the pioneering socialist leader and a cabinet minister. Among the other pioneering movies I saw was *Kadawunu Poronduwa (Broken Promise)*, produced also in 1947 by the equally famed B.A.W. Jayamanne. He was the brother of Eddie Jayamaana, the veteran comedian and singer, who was a star in the movie. *Kala Handa (Wild Moon)* and *Seda Sulang (Storm)* were also produced by him. Then there were the movies produced in the fifties, which I went to see as soon as they were released. Among them were *Prema Tharange (Lover's Quarrel)*; and films named after their characters - *Sujatha; Mathalang; and Dingiri Manike*. In those films I saw the leading stars of the day give some memorable performances. Among them was arguably the queen of the Sinhala silver screen, Rukmani Devi, actress and singer. She is first among equals because she is the only actress who needed no dubbing, whether speaking or singing. Among the others were the pioneering actresses Mable Blyth, Ruby De Mel, Kanthi Gunatunge and Irangani Serasinghe. They were followed by one of the more versatile and perhaps the most popular of them all, Malini Fonseka. I have met her during her multiple visits to Los Angeles. I have also had the pleasure of meeting another star from the early ears, Punya Heendeniya. I met her during a visit to Australia, where she now lives with her physician husband. He happens to be a brother of my close friend, Ajantha Wijesena. I have referred elsewhere to our personal friend, actress, producer and director, Nita Fernando.

Among the pioneering actors I was lucky to have seen was Gamini Fonseka, arguably the King of the Silver Screen. Others of the early vintage who left an indelible mark on Sinhala movie history were Dommie Jayawardana, from my hometown, Ambalangoda, Joe Abeywickrama, Tony Ranasinhe, and my friends Henry Jayasena and Namel Weeramuni. I saw most if not all, of thier masterful performances.

Most of those movies were filmed in studios in India and were unabashed copies of Indian Hindi films. Later in my youth, the industry changed and became more domestically oriented. Two of the classics of that early era I saw were *Rekhawa'(Fortune Sign)*, and *Gamperaliya (Village Transformation)*. The latter was based on one of the most reputed Sinhala novels, of that time, written by the venerated Martin Wickramasinghe. By the sixties, films were being produced and filmed locally in Colombo, and they began to take on genuinely local flavor. They were first produced by the doyen of Sinhala movies, Lester James Pieris, whom I had the privilege of meeting many years later, in Paris, when he was there with his wife as Ambassador of Sri Lanka to France.

I also saw a few Indian Hindi and Tamil films, but I didn't much enjoy them. Among them were *Awara* and *Sri 420* with the most well-known film stars of India, such as Raj Kapoor, Dev Annand, and Nimmi, with background singers Latha Manjeskher, Mukesh and Nawshad.

* * *

If my studies at Law College kept me away from the world of arts, I easily made up for it through my acquaintance with Namel Weeramuni. My friendship with Namel is another association that turned out to be enduring, and one of personal importance to me.

After graduating from the University of Ceylon, Peradeniya, Namel joined the Law College and graduated as a lawyer. He married his cousin and childhood sweetheart, and now famous actress par excellence, Malini Weeramuni. Malini has become part of our close-knit group of friends. They were cousins, hailing from Balapitiya, the next town to my own hometown. They fell in love and formed a lifelong partnership.

After becoming a lawyer, Namel worked as a specialist in preparing parliamentary legislation at the department of the Legal Draftsman. During this time he also became a playwright, actor, director and producer of Sinhala drama. His interest and involvement with theater originated while he was at the Peradeniya campus. He was a protégé of the famous playwright, producer and director who resurrected Sinhala dance drama, Prof. Ediriweera Sarathchandra. In Prof. Sarathchandra's production of *Rattharang (Gold)*, Namel played the lead role alongside Somalatha Subasinghe, who later became a legendary actress. After graduation Namel presented several acclaimed productions while continuing his professional work.

On one occasion, in mid-1970, I had just landed at the airport in Katunayake, Colombo, when I learned of the staging of his major production *Nattukkari (Actress)*, a translation of Jean Anouilh's *Colombe*. It was being presented at the Y.M.B.A. Hall in Borella. I went there that evening and found the house full with no available tickets. I sent word backstage to Namel. He promptly got someone to place a chair just in front of the stage. I enjoyed his production which took my breath away, and up to date, *Nattukkari* remains as an important production in the repertoire of Sinhala drama.

On another occassion, Shanthi and I went to see Prof. Sarathchandra's dance drama *Pemathi Jayathi Soko*. The house was sold out! We enjoyed a similar accommodation when Prof. Sarathchandra arranged for two added chairs for Shanthi and me in front of the stage.

Namel's production of *Nattukkari* received rave reviews. "Theatre at its best ... the best theatre event in a long time ... translation is excellent ... the language is earthy and racy and totally Sinhala in idiom ...... clever and amusing in the original ... moving theatrical experience ... the capacity audience filled the theatre with rocking laughter", wrote a leading literary critic of the time, Nihal Ratnayaka. Namel was also able to marshal an outstanding cast that included a group of the most acclaimed artistes of our time: Somalatha Subasinghe, Upali Atthanayake, Dhamma Jagoda, Namel and Malini Weeramuni, Wickrema Bogoda, Prema Ganegoda, Wimal Kumar de Costa, Cyril Wickremage, Lionel Fernando, W. Jayasiri and Daya Tennekoon. Later, in 1986, it was staged at the Commonwealth Institute Theater in London, and at the Bernard Shaw Theatre in that city's famed West End. Well known film stars of Sri Lanka Tony Ranasinghe, Douglas Ranasinghe and a close friend, Edmund Jayasinghe, were included in the cast.

Another of Namel's acclaimed productions from that era, which I was privileged to watch, was *Golu Birinde*, an adaptation of Anatole France's *The Man Who Married the Dumb Wife*. This production introduced Malini to the stage. Since then Malini has had a series of dramatic roles on stage and in film. Today she is a preeminant actress of the Sinhala teledrama; seen daily on the Sri Lankan television. There followed a number of plays by Namel who wrote, acted in, and produced them, featuring Malini as a lead actress.

Shortly after these theatrical successes Namel went to the U.K. and the U.S. on some sort of official assignment and visited me in New York. While abroad, he felt that with a young family of three children he had to seek employment that would guarantee a good education for the children. When he came to New York, there was a vacancy for a broadcaster of news to Sri Lanka in the Radio Division of the U.N. One of the conditions for the post was that the Radio Ceylon, as it was known at the time, would guarantee that it would broadcast the reports sent from New York. I had known the then Director-General of the Ceylon Broadcasting Authority, Ridgeway Thillakaratne, a high-level civil servant. He happened to know Namel and his work. I called him and he promptly agreed to the proposition. However, it took an inordinate amount of time for the bureaucratic procedure to release the letter. In the meantime, the leave of absence Namel obtained to go abroad from the Legal Draftsman's Department had expired, and there was pressure on him to return home.

While waiting for the letter to arrive, I took Namel to see a number of Broadway and Off-Broadway productions. As an aficionado of theater he savored every moment. Over the years he has continued to return to New York and Broadway. It was a great pleasure to see plays by Neil Simon, Arthur Miller, Eugene O'Neille, and Rogers and Hammerstein; and productions such as *Les Miserables, Man of Lamancha, Night Must Fall*, with actors like Glen Close, Barry McGovern, Jack Lemmon and Walter Mathieu. We would discuss the evening's production on our way back home, and always paying close attention to Namel's perceptive comments, which broadened my appreciation of the theatrical world.

By the time the letter of agreement eventually arrived from the Broadcasting Authority, frustrated Namel had already left to return home via London. Once in London he had a change of heart. By then, the Permanent Secretary of the Ministry of Justice had notified him that unless he returned within a week his post will be considered vacated. He had little option but to try his luck in the U.K. The permanent secretary issuing the order was our mutual friend and his university-mate Nihal Jayawickrama. When we met in later years, we used to make fun of Nihal for the great favor he did, because as it turned out Namel became a very successful lawyer in the UK.

But at first, he had to struggle to find a base in London. In order to practice law, like all other lawyers from the Commonwealth countries, he had to do an internship in a British law firm. Internships do not pay more than a small allowance. He had to find temporary or part-time work to survive. This was so because, at the time, no foreign exchange was released from Colombo for the use of individuals abroad. On his way back from attending an interview for a position in a law firm in London, dressed in complete attire fit for a lawyer, he stopped at a gas station to inquire if there were any vacancies there. "If you can pump gas, you can start now", was the answer from the manager. Without any hesitation, Namel removed his coat and tie, rolled up his sleeves, and began pumping gas.

Once he had an internship, he continued to do odd jobs to keep him going. Shortly after, Malini too arrived with the children. About the same time, I happened to spend a sabbatical year in 1970-71 at the London University Institute of Advanced Legal Studies, sharing seminars and research work with famed aerospace professor Dr. Bin Cheng. During the course of that time I visited Namel's family in a basement apartment that he was renting from a friend. Even though they were both far away from the theater scene in the motherland, they always envisioned returning home one day to establish a theater of their own. Namel is fond of telling the story of how Malini put the small year-end bonus that Namel got from the gas station into a kitty, and told him it was for their Punchi Theater (Small Theater).

Even though times were hard for them, the intentions were very clear.

Malini also started working at 'Waitrose', the reputed super market chain. Slowly things started to fall into place. Namel finished his internship and other requirements to practice law in the U.K., and established a law firm of his own, specializing in immigration and property matters. The business flourished and soon he had a large staff working under him. Being the man he was, it was almost a twenty-four-hour a day job, for he would never ignore a client's need, no matter how tired he was or what time it was on the clock. He used to bring his family to visit us in New York. Once we took a long drive from New York to Florida to take our children to Disney World, Sea World and the Kennedy Space Center. We had a wonderful time together.

On one such visit, when Namel was lounging in my garden reading a book, his phone rang. The person calling informed him that his trusted assistant, a national of South Africa, who used to call Namel *Mama* (Uncle Namel in Sinhala), and to whom he had entrusted the office had vanished, with a substantial amount of client's money that was in the custody of the law firm. Namel returned immediately to sort out the situation, and though he managed to take care of the crisis in due course, it nevertheless was a great strain on him.

Being the man he is, he bounced back and while in London produced a wonderful movie *Ratagiya Attho* (those gone abroad), that was a hit back home. During those years Shanthi and I were regular visitors to the spacious house that he had purchased in North London. Whenever we traveled we always made a stop to visit them. They in turn entertained us most generously, and it was usual to invite mutual friends to dinner parties that Malini graciously hosted. Whenever we were on holiday in, Rajagiriya, Colombo, they insisted we stay with them in their home. They had a wonderful two-leveled house, with a nice roof-top garden, designed by a mutual friend Valentine Gunesekare. The house beautifully incorporated local architectural elements. It was built in 1962, on seven perches of land. Such an arrangement was unheard of in the days when double that ammount of land was considered the minimum for a residential house.

*   *   *

I was introduced to Valentine Guesekara at the airport in Colombo, when I was returning to New York after my first visit home, since joining the United Nations. He was my travelling companion to New York, and shortly after we arrived, he made my introduction to western opera a memorable one. He was a partner with the famed Sri Lankan architect of modern times Geoffrey Bawa, at Edward Reid and Begg. It was the premier architectural firm in Colombo, originally established by the British. Valentine had been awarded a Rockefeller grant to work for a year in the United States. He was assigned to work with the doyens of modern American architecture Kevin Roche, Louis Kahn and Richard Neutra. On the flight to New York we became friends fast, partly because, he was the youngest of the celebrated cricketing family of Gunasekaras. Three brothers including Valentine, played for the national team, and I was delighted to reminisce about his cricketing days.

We also had several common friends including Lal Jayawardane, who was a colleague of mine at the U.N. The day after we arrived in New York, Lal invited us both to dinner. Valentine and Lal were opera buffs. They were introduced to western classical music in their westernized Colombo homes, and during their student days at Cambridge. No sooner had we arrived than they began listening to opera on Lal's stereo on Pizza sized records. Little did I know they were going to listen to the entire recording of Mozart's opera *Don Giovanni*. As the night dragged along, they were nice enough to ask me, from time to time, whether I was enjoying the music or bored by it. I was equally polite in indicating that I was enjoying it all, although it was all Greek to me and I was suffering from jet lag as well. I somehow survived the experience.

As time went on, I did cultivate an interest in opera; perhaps, thanks to the penance I paid at the altar of my two friends Valentine and Lal.

It was the interest in opera, which led me to move to an apartment at Lincoln Towers, a newly built apartment complex next to the Lincoln Center. The Lincoln Center for Performing Arts is a beautiful complex of buildings housing the Metropolitan Opera (Met), along with the New York Philharmonic and the New York State Theater. The Met is considered the premier opera company in America. Later, when Shanthi and I moved to Vienna, we happened to live very near the Vienna Opera in Austria, one of Europe's premier opera houses, along with *Las Scala* in Milan and the Paris Opera. I frequented them whenever the opportunity was presented. I have a book entitled *One Hundred Great Operas*. I always read about each opera before attending one, and marked when and where I saw it and with whom. A good number of them are marked now. As time went on, I am not sure either Valentine or Lal, had that opportunity to see as many operas as I did, because neither lived long enough in New York, and they spent their careers in cities that offered less opportunity to enjoy their love of opera. They both remained as lifelong friends of mine. I have written about Lal elsewhere in this narrative.

After Valentine's stint in the U.S. he worked for a year in Nigeria and designed a few notable buildings there. Thereafter, he returned to the United States and spent a year at Yale University. I used to visit him there and his most amiable wife Ranee who is a gourmet cook, provided delicious meals to me and my travelling companions. Following that, he worked in a leading architectural firm, and eventually, was a professor of architecture at the Wentworth College, in Boston. In between, he returned to Sri Lanka for some years and designed several landmark architectural gems. He also taught at the University of Moratuwa, the premier engineering and architectural institutions in Sri Lanka.

I had continued contacts and visited them whenever they were in the United States, and often they have visited us. Those occasions were most pleasant, with good banter accompanied by wine and Ranee's gourmet food. Eventually, on retirement, they moved to Sacramento, California, where my wife Shanthi and I have visited them. The Sri Lanka Foundation in the United States recently honored him with a Lifetime Achievement Award. An Australia-based professor of architecture, Anoma Peiris, published a book on his work recently titled, *Imagining Modernity: the Architecture of Valentine Gunasekara*. I feel most blessed to have had the friendship of Valentine, who is not only a wonderful architect, but also more importantly, a great human being, and not forgetting of course, the friendship of his loving wife Ranee. On my 70th birthday, it was a great gift for me to have received a touching note from him. In part it read, "It is a signal honor to have become friends (over forty years ago, in space!!), with an illustrious intellect of your caliber on our flight to New York.

We lovingly salute you and stand grateful that our destinies were that our paths in life crossed at that point. We wish you many years of peace and contentment, as in my religious belief we go on contributing as best we can in the evening of our lives until we are called to eternal life. It is so good to have the computer giving us the technology to communicate so easily and keep in touch." The sentiments are naturally mutual.

* * *

Let me return to Namel and Malini. Even after their return home, for sometime, we were their houseguests whenever we were in Colombo. On the latter occasions, they would host dinner parties that would allow us to listen to classical Sinhala music and meet mutual friends. Guests included legends of the Sinhala Theater: Prof. Ediriweera Sarathchandra and his wife Lalitha, Henry Jayasena and his wife Manel, as well as some notables of the younger generation.

Perhaps, thanks to the move he made to seek a career abroad, Namel's children benefited as much as Namel and Malini had hoped. Slashna, their daughter, the eldest in the family, became a physician. She married Simon and moved to Auckland, New Zealand, where she runs a successful medical clinic. Shanthi and I were happy to have been guests at their wedding in London, and we later visited them in

New Zealand. The elder son, Heshan, had his university education in the United States. He obtained a Ph.D. in sociology and is settled down with his wife and family in Boston, U.S.A. I remember driving Namel and Malini to his graduation from New York and speeding all the way to make it in time. Police stopped me multiple times and I had to pay a hefty fine, which was not revealed to my wife till many years later. Both Heshan and his younger brother Tharindu used to spend holidays at my home in New York, while they studied in the United States. Tharindu graduated from Ohio University in the United States, and joined the New Zealand Navy. He settled down with his family in Auckland. Now Auckland is a regular destination for Namel and Malini during their vacations, in order to visit the family including four grandchildren.

* * *

While living in the U.K., and dreaming of returning to his home country to establish a theater, Namel continued to produce plays for the local audience made up of his expatriate compatriots. Once the children were well settled, and they were fortunate enough to collect enough funds to put into effect their theater project, it was time to return home. After three decades Namel and Malini returned to Colombo and began their dream project. I happened to be there at the time and had reservations about the undertaking. The reason was that it was begun during the height of the ethnic war that discouraged the theater public, who were uninterested undertaking evening travel. They preferred to watch teledramas on television, which had blanketed the prime time and morning hours.

Yet for all this, they pursued their dream. A wonderful small theater, entirely in local style, was completed in rapid time and opened in 2003. Three floors of the building are allocated to the theater, including rehearsal halls. On the next two floors, they built living quarters for themsleves, so they will be on location at all times. *Namel and Malini Punchi Theater* (small theater), now serves as a venue for productions of the theater lovers and producers who hitherto were unable to meet the heavy cost of the elite theaters that operated in Colombo. It is not run for profit. Indeed, Namel is even providing for the ongoing running costs of the place, so that a place is available to showcase all forms of theater, film, drama, workshops, seminars, religious events and other cultural events, at an affordable cost to their producers.

Undoubtedly the *Punchi Theater* has filled a longstanding need as young artistes and others on limited budgets now have a place to work in. Hitherto, the places available had seen better days and were not suitable. In this category was the 'Lumbini Theater', a school hall where I had seen the classics of the Sinhala drama produced by Prof. Ediriweera Sarathchandra, Henry Jayasena, Gunasena Galappaththi, Dhamma Jagoda, Parakrama Niriella, Dayananda Gunawardene, and Namel himself. There was also the Y.M.B.A hall, where similar productions were staged. But, by the time Namel began building the Punchi Theater, both locations were in a dilapidated condition. Actually, they were never in a good state for theater productions. There was also the John De Silva Memorial Hall that was of a later vintage, where I had witnessed a wonderfully entertaining satire *Kelani Palama* by R.R Samarakoon. But, its construction with half-walls was never suitable for serious theater. Then there was the 'Elephinstone Theater', built in 1925, which for many years had served as a movie house. I saw Sinhala and Hindi movies there in the 1960s. It was only recently converted to a theater.

Foremost among available theaters is the refurbished legendary 'Tower Hall', originally built in 1911. It served as the cradle of Sinhala theater, beginning with the incomparable dance dramas such as *Padmavati*, and staged the pioneer theater productions of classical masters John De Silva and Charles Dias. It is a venue where I had enjoyed numerous classics of Sinhala theater, as well as musical and dance performances by leading artistes of the times. These locations while desirable were relatively large and were costly for producers, at a time when the theater-going public had dwindled, because of the ongoing social unrest at the time. Theater-goers turned to watch teledramas in the comfort of their living rooms.

The same was true of even larger and costlier, more modern facilities as the 'Lionel Wendt Hall' and the 'Bandaranaike Memorial Hall' (BMICH). The latter, built in the 70s, was a gift of China, and is only suitable for mega musical productions. The same is true of the newest addition to the list, the National Theater *Nelum Pokuna*, also built by the Chinese and completed in 2012. 'Lionel Wendt Theater', built in the 50s, has become a national landmark where I had witnessed many performances like Henry Jayasena's *Hunuwatiye Kathawa*, Sarathchandra's classic *Maname*, and *Kapuwa Kapothi*; along with ballet performances of the preeminent dance duet Chitrasena and Vajira in their brilliant performance of *Karadiya*. This is the location where almost all English productions were previously held and continue to be held. I had seen many productions in the sixties like the masterly satire *He Comes from Jaffna*. The charges for hiring the hall were definitely excessive, and could be afforded only if a producer was certain that the particular production would have a full house. It was in this context that Namel moved to fill the void with a low-cost venue for less affluent theater enthusiasts.

I was in Colombo when the first theater workshop was held at the Punchi Theater, conducted by Prof. Dick Fox, Professor in the Theater Department of the University of California, Northridge. This was a great opportunity for the young theater artistes. Later Prof. Fox made several more visits, sponsored by the Fulbright Scholarship Fund, and recently produced a play with leading artistes and actors in the country.

Prof. Fox was Namel's professor when he was in California to read for a Masters degree in theater arts, while plans were being finalized for the construction of the *Punchi Theater*. As his project for the degree, he produced Prof. Sarathchandra's play *Sinhabahu*, which Namel translated into English. The production was done with American Students at the University of California, and it was a resounding success.

It is a stylized dance drama based on village forms of music and dance in the *Naadagam* style. But the play represents both Eastern and

SAME SKY, DIFFERENT NIGHTS
SAME SKY, DIFFERENT NIGHTS

Western classical dramatic traditions that Sarathchandra masterfully brought to bear in creating this historic piece of our culture. The story was based on the *Mahavamsa's* folklore (the chronicled history of Sri Lanka), according to which, Sinhabahu's father was a lion and his mother a princess of Kalinga. When Sinhabahu was sixteen, he escaped with his mother and sister, Sinhasivali, and arrived in the capital of Vanga. He later killed his father for a reward, who was enraged and devastating the land in search of his family. As the reward he was offered the throne of Vanga. He refused the throne, instead founding the city of Sinhapura, in his native country of Lála. He lived there with Sinhasivali, whom he made his consort. They had thirty-two children, of whom Vijaya, the first king of Sinhala nation, was the eldest. In the foreword to Namel's translation Professor Anuradha Seniviratna writes, "Sinhabahu is a play with a universal theme based on a legendary story. Sarathchandra developed the plot into a beautiful play depicting a psychological conflict and confrontation between father, mother and son in the play giving all sorts of dimensions to the working of the human mind in conflicts. The dramatic essence and the literary quality of Sinhabahu have made the play a masterpiece in history of Sinhala drama."

Namel's compatriots in Los Angeles who were lucky enough to see that production are still speaking about it. That was the production that won him the respect of Prof. Fox to accept Namel's invitation to conduct a workshop at the *Punchi Theater*, the entire expenses borne by Namel until later visits when the Fulbright Fund assumed the expenses. Namel won the President's Award in 2002 for his English translation of 'Sinhabahu'.

Since returning to Colombo from the U.K., Namel has written, acted in and produced several outstanding plays, including *Hataraweni Tattuva (Fourth Floor); Virupi Rupa (Distorted Images); Vanasakkarayo; (Destroyers); Kasi Raten (From the Land of Kasi); Kora saha Andhaya (The Lame and the Blind); Golu Birinde (Dumb Wife); and Nattukkari (the Dancer)*, featuring Malini in the lead role. With an island-wide fan base, Malini has become the queen of the Sri Lankan teledrama.

Namel also wrote, produced, directed and acted in a very courageous production *Maadyawediyakage Asipatha, (a Journalist's Sword)*, a politically critical satire that is widely acclaimed, as perhaps, his best work to date. What is most significant is that it was produced in the midst of a civil war in the country. I was privileged to be there when it was staged at the *Punchi Theater*, and felt compelled to write a review driven by the sheer effect it had on me. The review appeared in the 'Sunday Observer' in October 2007. In the review I wrote:

> "Welcome to Greek Tragedy - Sri Lankan style. In a time of war and terrorism both local and abroad, theatre audiences crave escape and entertainment to balance out and emotionally heal from the daily horrors printed in the newspapers and seen on the television. Namel Weeramuni's Maadyawediyakuge Asipatha" (The Journalist's Sword), is not that kind of production, and in fact, unflinchingly presents subjects that many would choose to avoid in the best of times: the use of torture against detainees and the importance of preserving human rights in times of political chaos, terrorism and war. It is a courageous production by a veteran playwright and producer, and it is arguably his best. "Maadyawediyakuge Asipatha" works despite its emotionally draining and sometimes harrowing subject because of the beauty in its production: the scenes of abuse and torture at its worst are presented via balletic dance choreography performed without dialog, to music. "The director's choice to do so allows him to present otherwise unwatchable horror in an emotionally tolerable way. There is still enough realism to shine a harsh light on torture. This is top shelf drama of the type written by Eugene O'Neill and Arthur Miller - the kind of rare production that every theatre lover must dare to experience.

In 2012, I was once again privileged to see his equally daring and hilarious political satire in a two-act play *Kandoskiriyawa saha Hediyan Maruwa (Agitation and Transfer of Nurses)*.

Our close friendship continues, and we have often travelled the world together. We particularly enjoyed our cruises along the river Nile in Egypt, river Mekong in Cambodia, and the Alaskan cruise in the Pacific. We have travelled many a mile on the road in the United States, Europe and Asia visiting historical sites, national parks and monuments, and great cities.

Hema and Mallika, along with our friends Nihal and Kusum Pieris and Shanthi Fernando have joined us on several of these sojourns. Most recently, in 2012, we took a memorable trip to the North and East of Sri Lanka to witness the ravages of three decades of civil war and its aftermath. We also saw the hopeful signs of reconciliation among the warring parties, and the recovery from the unimaginable destruction that a savage conflict had inflicted on all concerned.

*　*　*

There was one other leading figure from the cultural world that I came to know very well, particularly through my association with Namel. It was none other than Henry Jayasena, acclaimed as an outstanding stage actor, film star, writer, producer, director and translator, all rolled in to one. He is a legendary artiste of our times. I first met Henry in the early sixties when on a visit to Colombo, and had the good fortune to see his production, *Kuveni (Demon Queen)* in which he sang the mesmerizing song *Andakaren (From Darkness)* displaying his prowess as a singer. When the play was over I went backstage to congratulate him for the excellent production of the play. When he learned that I had just come from Canada and made the effort not to miss his play, he joined into a cordial conversation with me. Ever since then we have been friends. Almost on every visit I made to Colombo I have seen him, and he was a guest in my home in New York.

Henry's initial foray into the cultural milieu was as a stage actor in the 1950s, and he blossemed in Prof. Ediriweera Saratchchandra's famed production *Maname* in 1956. It was originally staged at the Peradeniya campus of the University of Ceylon on the occasion of the inauguration of the now famous open air theater in the campus. Henry took the lead role as Prince Maname in this stylized dance drama. The drama woven around a love story, is well known for its music highlighted by the song *Premayen Mana Ranjitave* (mind is full of joy with love), that has been timeless and appreciated by the populace at large. On its 50th anniversary, *Maname* was staged in Los Angeles by Prof. Sarathchandra's wife Lalitha, in 2006. In a program note for the occasion, I wrote:

> *"All the critics hailed Maname as a new genre of theater in Sri Lanka that laid the foundation for a nationalistic identity creating a cultural uniqueness. The style of the play was Nadagam and it created eastern resonance. It was appreciable by everybody, the rural or educated folks of the city, and indeed anywhere in the world. Sarathchandra created a universal language of theater through the vehicle of Nadagam musicality. While the genre of Nadagam was prevalent in the country for centuries in the form of loose theater, which the rural folks employed for their mundane entertainment. Sarathchandra extracted the essence of the Nadagam Story after years of research and being with the rural folks for years travelling from village to village collecting data and making comparisons of styles and different modes of presentation. After such a period of toil he created a great drama in Maname out of the raw material which not only moved the audiences to tears, but forced them to be gripped in the situations that he created in the play. He harnessed in it the essence of humanity, instilled depth into its characters, and impressed as to what meaningful and serious theater is. By this means he demonstrated the possibility of creating a national cultural identity in spirit of theater in Sri Lanka. Its approach was novel and appreciable by everyone, its theme and quality of humaneness impregnated the minds of the audiences with emotive feelings penetrating into the roots of cultural milieu of our country. Thus Sarathchandra ushered in a new era in the theater scene with the production of Maname, which after 50 years, still runs to capacity anywhere it is staged in the country."*

A year or so after Henry acted in *Maname*, he acted in the jewel of an operetta *Hasthi Kantha Manthare (Elephant Charm)*, set to the haunting music of Maestro Amaradeva. It was also produced by Prof. Sarathchandra.

Shortly after, in the sixties, Henry began a stellar career as a producer and director of stage plays. Of the dozen or so of his well-known productions I was fortunate to see six of the best: *Janelaya (Window)*; *Manaranjana Vada Warjana (Glorious Strikes)*; *Ahas Maliga (Palaces in the Sky)*; *Apata Puthe Magak Nathe (Son, We Have No Solace)*; and his crown jewel *Hunuwataye Kathawa (Berthold Brecht's Caucasian Chalk Circle)*, produced in 1967, in which he gave a brilliant performance as Judge Azdek.

At the time he visited me in New York, the *Chalk Circle* was staged at the famous Lincoln Center Play House. I thoroughly enjoyed the play in his company because I had many insights into the production, which otherwise I would never have appreciated. The next night, after dinner, when he was lounging on an arm chair I asked him to sing the melodies from his version of the play. I still have a tape that I recorded with him strumming the tunes, tapping on the chair. Long after Henry had returned to Colombo there was a subsequent production of the *Caucasian Chalk Circle* in New York. The critic who reviewed the production in the New York popular newspaper *Village Voice* happened to have seen Henry's production in Colombo. In his review, he referred to Henry's production and concluded the "producers such as Henry Jayasena should be invited to the United States to show how an engrossing play should be produced".

Henry had come to the United States on a travel grant offered by the U.S. Government to visit playhouses and meet dramatists, mainly in university campuses and small towns. I took the opportunity to see a couple of Broadway plays in his company. All the time he was absorbing anything worth noting, while he was critical of the superficial or added embellishments that made Broadway productions attractive to a larger audience. I was lucky to have watched in his company, Samuel Becket's existential classic

Waiting for Godot. The incisive comments he later made, helped me understand and appreciate the wonderful production and the great play.

One play he admired and enjoyed was Neil Simon's production of *Sunshine Boys*, a hilarious comedy focusing on a pair of cantankerous vaudevillian actors who did not get along with each other offstage, while being a perfect pair on stage. It had just opened in the early seventies when Henry and I went to see it. Later, it had a run of more than five hundred consecutive shows and a similar run when it was revived in the nineties. It was also made into a film and television hit.

In the midst of his writing, producing and acting in stage productions, Henry also became a leading film star. Among the many films he acted in *Gam Peraliya (Revolt in the Village)*, takes pride of place. Henry played the leading role a Piyal an English teacher who falls in love with his student Nanda. The role won him an award for acting, and the movie won the best film award at the national awards ceremony.

Henry started his career as an Assistant Teacher in English in a primary school in a far off village near Nuwara Eliya. That is where he began writing his first play. Then he served in the clerical service in the Public Works Department in Colombo for many years, where he wrote most of his well-known plays. I once visited him at his office to collect an invitation to one of his plays which he had insisted I should see, although I was due to leave the Island later that same night. He later served as Deputy Director of the National Youth Services Council in charge of the Arts Division. During that period he was a star on the silver screen. Finally, before retirement from the government service, he served as Deputy Director General of the National Television Corporation (Rupavahini), overseeing the Programming Division.

Henry was equally conversant in Sinhala and English, writing in both with the greatest of ease. His wife, Manel, was an equally talented actress and singer with a pleasing voice. She acted in most of Henry's plays, giving particularly memorable performances in *Kuveni* and

Hunuvataye Kathawa. She went on to become a popular teledrama actress.

In more recent years I have been in touch with Henry by email. I have received perceptive comments of the cultural scene of the day. Sometime after 2008, I had mentioned to him the recently published trilogy of Sri Lankan historical fiction, (*Freedom at Last in Paradise, Serendipity of Andrew George and Peace at Last in Paradise,* written by Dr. Ananda Guruge. Henry had seen the review of the publications I had written in the Sunday Observer newspaper in Sri Lanka. In the review, that I titled 'Gems of Historical Novels," I noted that: "Only a person of the caliber of Dr. Ananda Guruge, diplomat, national and international civil servant, academician, scholar and renowned author could have given life so vividly to the social and cultural milieu of Sri Lankan society in the last century and a half, blending all his experiences in bringing forth a captivating trilogy which will rank among the best of literary classics produced by a Sri Lankan author." Detecting his interest in reading them, I sent him copies which I received from Dr. Guruge in Los Angeles through my sister-in-law Sujatha. He was most appreciative when she went to deliver them to him at his home. He sent me a note of thanks and after several weeks followed up with a note to say that he had started reading them, and once he finished, he would send me his impressions.

* * *

It was not long after that I received the sad news of his demise. He was a man who had contributed to resurrecting the Sinhala theater along with Prof. Sarathchandra and a handful of others, at a time when it was a vanishing art. Henry was a fine human being whom I was privileged to know. Just about two years before his death in 2010, he treated us to his memoirs 'Play is the Thing' which gives the reader insights to the man and his work.

I have been interested in the theater since my young days. My fortunate association with Henry and his wife Manel, Namel Weeramuni and his wife Malini, Prof. Ediriweera Saratchchandra and, of course, Gamini Hattatuwagama has honed my appreciation of the Sinhala theater, dance, drama, and music of all forms. Others who helped sustain my interest in the theater included the prominent film and stage actress Nita Fernando, writer and critic A.J. Gunawardane, who for a short while was my roommate in New York while he was on a fellowship in the United States, and my fleeting association with the likes of actor producer Dhamma Jagoda. In later years, while in the United States, my close association with Karen Breckenridge, who was serving in the diplomatic service of Sri Lanka in New York, was important in continuing my interest. He was a versatile actor and connoisseur of Sinhala and western theater.

There are others, who now reside in Los Angeles, like Karu Karunaratne, who acted as the 'Vaddha' in the original cast of *Maname* (was an official at the Sri Lanka Mission to the U.N.), and his wife Nimala who was the lead actress in the *Hasthikantha Manthare*; playwright producer Somarathna Dissanayake of *Muvan Palessa* fame; Badrajee Jayatilake; Ananda Makalanda and the committed work of a host of talented young artistes in the United States, who continue to help me sustain my interest in the Sinhala theater in spite of all the years I have been away from the Island.

I continue to enjoy, learn and savor my close association with the arts that my friends inculcated in me. Especially the remarkable quotes of emminent fictional characters like Judge Azdak played superbly by Henry Jayasena in the Chalk Circle. Through everything he does or says Azdak satirizes the court system. He asks Grusha, "You want justice, but do you want to pay for it? When you go to the butcher, you know you have to pay."

— ❖ —

Chapter 19

New Terrain

Encouraged by the excellent results I was fortunate enough to obtain during the first year at Law College, I was ready to be adventurous and undertake a bigger load of academics. I registered for the law degree of the University of London.

In possible anticipation of this venture I had sat and passed the London University G.C.E. Advanced Level, external examination, the previous year, which served as the qualifying exam to register for a degree from the University of London. It was not particularly taxing as I had already completed my G.C.E Advanced Levl at Richmoind College. I was now scheduled to take the Intermediate in Laws (Inter-laws) examination. It was somewhat helpful that I was familiar with the subjects I registered for in the Inter-laws except one, because I had read them in my first year or was reading in the second year at the Ceylon Law College.

However, while the subject titles and concepts were similar the content was quite different. At the Ceylon Law College I was reading Ceylon Law based on Roman Dutch Law, English Common Law, Customary Law of Ceylon, and local statutes enacted by the Ceylon Legislature whereas, for the London University examinations, I was reading English Common Law and Equity, and British Parliamentary Acts. Additionally, the Case Law that I had to study was quite different.

That year, for the London University examination I read Criminal Law, Law of Contracts, Law of Torts and English Common Law (a comprehensive introduction to the English legal system including the court system). Of course, there was a certain amount of overlap but taken together it was an enormous amount of study time that was required to prepare for two different exams, one in June, and the other, in August, of the same year. From May to August, it was a grueling slog spending hours on end in the Law College library, and late nights at the hostel preparing for the two exams.

Luckily, the dance season was mostly from November to January and as for sports, I played for Law College only in one or two games and the Law-Medical match, and that too was done by the time May came by.

All the toiling was worthwhile when the results were published in the *Ceylon Daily News (see annex)*. I had obtained a first class with a scholarship in the Law College examamination, and was placed second in the batch, to Rukmani Fernando, who had come second to me in the first year exam. As for the London University examination, which was taken by not only Law students, but some practitioners and university graduates in non-legal fields, it was heartening to find that I had passed along with my friend and batchmate Nawaz Dawood, and Alphy Williams who was by then a final year student at the Law College.

October 1, 1960 copy of the Ceylon Daily News coincidentally carried the results of the Law College exams under the banner "12 New Advocates and 15 Proctors", next to a banner "London Varsity Results". Two headlines were separated by a picture of the Prime Minister of Poland addressing the university students at the Arts Theater of the Peradeniya campus. It was a thrilling experiance for a young student to have, most unexpectedly, seen his name thrice on the same page of the national newspaper. Twice, indicating that I had succesfully completed the Intermediate exams of the two institutions, and the third, under the category of scholarships and prizes. A copy of the paper that is still carefully filed away in my office is reproduced in the Annex C.

No sooner had the vacation started than we began to relax and enjoy our days of freedom till the next slog rolled by. With the trip to the hill country during the last vacation, I had begun what turned out to be a series of trips exploring the history and beauty of my homeland. This time I travelled with Vasu and Ana, who had joined the Law College one year after me. We went on a trip to the historic cities and some parts of the hill country.

Vasu was one of the few privileged law students who owned a car. It was a brand new *Austin Mini* Cooper, the smallest car made by the British Motor Corporation, which had just come to the market that year (1959). This model was later considered a British icon and voted in 1999 as the second most influential car of the 20th century.

A few fortunate law students owned cars at the time. My batchmate and hostel colleague, Nawaz Darwood had the best of them all. He loved to fly around with great flare in his British *Triumph Coupe*. Kumar Amarasekare was equally dashing in his *Hillman Minx*. Anil Obeysekara had a Ford Prefect. I was a passenger in all four quite often as they were all my close friends, and on occasion, I used to borrow Vasu's *Mini Austin*, which he loaned to me without hesitation. They all remained lifelong friends although scattered over various continents. There were a handful of others with nondescript cars, which had seen better days before they were passed down to them by their parents. New or old, those who drove them were the envy of the rest of the student body.

Even the few, who owned scooters, which were a novelty at that time, were the envy of the rest of us. At Rs. 3000 apiece they were a real luxury for students. Among them were Bandu Fonseka, who had a *Lambretta*, and P. Herath who had a *Vespa*. These were the only two models available. Both Bandu and Herath were with me at the Law hostel. Upon graduation they both went to their hometowns and established successful legal practices. I was lucky enough to borrow their scooters, and roam the streets of Colombo, with the wind in my hair and sparkles of sheer freedom in my heart.

It was on those long trips in areas that were sparsely populated that I learned to drive. I had driven hundreds of miles in Vasu's *Mini Austin* and in my Richmond College friend Gippa's *Hillman Minx* before I obtained my driving license in 1962. Today, I would attribute this illegal and dangerous act solely to youthful pluck.

* * *

On the trip with Vasu and Ana we covered what was later known as the cultural triangle. After driving along the North Western sea coast of the country, the first stop was in Anuradhapura. As we were in the habit of spending the nights at homes of friends or relatives on these trips, in Anuradhapura, we stayed the night with our hostelmate Bulankulame. He hailed from the aristocratic Bulankulame Disawe family of Anuradhapura (a feudal title associated with a high-ranking official appointed by the British monarch to administer a large area of the kingdom). At the hostel, Bulankulame often fell prey to the pranks of Aelian, Bandu and others. A very kind soul who did very well in his studies, he became a leading lawyer in Anuradhapura.

On a later visit with my wife Shanthi many years after our first visit, I found him to be on the Bench as an acting judge. No sooner did he see me than he introduced me to the members of the Bar and requested me to take a seat with the lawyers, although I was in informal dress. As soon as he had adjourned court we found that he had already made arrangements for a police escort for my vehicle and had prepared lunch for us at his residence. We had a very pleasant visit and the escort guided us through the city until we left the city limits. I was thrilled to step into the same house many years after I had been there as a student.

The city of Anuradhapura attained its highest magnificence about the time of the commencement of the Christian era. Although people may have lived in this area as early as the 10th century BC, Anuradhapura became a great city after the introduction of Buddhism with the arrival from Buddha Gaya (Bodh Gaya), India, of a sapling from the Bodhi Tree (under which more than 2500 years ago the Buddha found enlightenment, in the 3rd century BC). Anuradhapura went on to become the country's political and religious capital in the 4th century BC, when it was made the royal capital by king Pandukabhaya in 380 BC. The city flourished for 1,300 years remaining as the residence and royal capital for 119 successive Sinhalese kings and queens till the year 1000 AD, when it was abandoned and the capital was moved to Polonnaruwa.

In its prime, Anuradhapura ranked alongside Babylon in its colossal proportions, in the number of its inhabitants, and the splendor of its shrines and public buildings. The city also had some of the most complex irrigation systems of the ancient world. As the city was situated in the dry zone of the country, the administration built many tanks to irrigate the land. Most of the great reservoir tanks still survive today, and some may be the oldest surviving reservoirs in the world.

With the dawn of the second century BC, adventurers from across the Palk Strait had begun to settle down on the northern coast. One such intruder called Elara, became supreme in almost the whole of the North and reigned from Anuradhapura. He was later challenged by Gemunu, son of King Kavantissa, who reigned in the south of the country. When Dutugemunu of the South met in combat with Elara the latter was killed. For the first time a single kingdom for the island arose. Dutugemunu's reign (161-137 BC), saw the culmination of Buddhism as he contributed immensely to Buddhism. Despite the intrusions and clashes of South Indian Chola, Pandyan and Pallava, stability prevailed in the continuity of the Anuradhapura civilization.

After an invasion in 993 AD, Anuradhapura was permanently abandoned. For centuries, the site lay hidden in the jungle. Rediscovered by the British in the 19th century, Anuradhapura became a Buddhist pilgrimage site once again. A major center of Sri Lankan civilization, the sacred city of Anuradhapura, now lies in picturesque ruins.

The fascinating ancient ruins consist of three classes of buildings, stupas, monastic buildings, and pokunas (ponds). The stupas (dagabas) are bell-shaped masses of masonry, varying from a few feet to over 1100 ft (340 m) in circumference. Some of them contain enough masonry to build a town for twenty-five thousand inhabitants. Remains of the monastic buildings are to be found in every direction in the shape of raised stone platforms, foundations and stone pillars.

The most famous is the Brazen Palace, erected by King Dutugamunu about 164 BC. The pokunas are bathing-tanks or tanks for the supply of drinking water, which are scattered everywhere throughout the jungle. The city also contains a sacred Bo-Tree (The Sri Maha Bodhiya), which is the oldest living tree in the world today. It has a recorded history said to date back to the year 245 BC. It is one of the most sacred relics in Sri Lanka and is respected by Buddhists all over the world.

The revival of the city of Anuradhapura began in earnest in the 1870s. Today, the splendid sacred city of Anuradhapura, with its palaces, monasteries and monuments, draws many Buddhist pilgrims and visitors.

Among them is the Thuparama Temple, considered to be the oldest dagaba in Sri Lanka. It is believed that the dagaba enshrines the collar bone relic of Lord Buddha. Isurumuniya temple built in the 3rd century B.C. is noted for its rock carvings. The best-known among these is the "Lovers". Many poets and song-writers have taken inspiration from this carving to write their masterpieces. It is believed that the carving may represent Saliya, son of the great king Dutugamunu and the low-caste maiden whom he loved, and thus abandoned the claims to the throne. The finest Buddha sculpture in Sri Lanka, the Samadhi Statue in the Mahamevuna Park (3rd century AD), is also among Anuradhapura's many fine stone-carvings. Ruwanveli Seya is commonly regarded as the greatest, and certainly the most popular among the Buddhists, of the stupas at Anuradhapura. This was the pride of the great king Dutugamunu. Raised in the 2nd century B.C., this dagaba or stupa is supposed to have the perfect shape of a water-bubble. Among the many statues in the courtyard there is one that is of a larger-than-life size man. This is considered to be the king himself watching his work from a respectable distance.

The Abhayagiri stupa encompasses the largest monastery complex in the Anuradhapura kingdom. Founded in the second century BC by king Valagamba (also known as Vattagamini Abhaya) the monastery was an international institution by the first century AD. The monastery includes complete components of a Buddhist temple as well as other buildings. The stupa at Abhayagiri is 108m tall and one of the tallest brick buildings of the ancient world. The Jethawana Stupa and the monastery complex are built on the premises believed to be the cremation grounds of the Mahinda Thera, the Indian priest, who introduced Buddhism to Sri Lanka. Founded by King Mahasena (276-303 AD) the stupa, at 120m high, was the third tallest monument in the world at the time of the fall of Roman Empire.

Close to Anuradhapura are two other important sites. Aukana is a 13-meter high statue carved out of solid granite. It dates back to the 5th century, to the reign of King Dathusena. It is situated about 50km south of Anuradhapura. On a rainy day, it is said that one can see droplets of water falling off the tip of the statue's nose hitting the ground exactly between the toes - a testament to the architectural accuracy of the sculptor. The other site is the temple of Mihintale, where Mahinda Thero, the son of Great Indian Emperor Asoka introduced Buddhism to the king of Sri Lanka, Devanampiyatssa. Mahinda Thera's sister, Theri Sangamitta, the founder of an order of Buddhist nuns, carried the sacred branch of the holy Bo tree that gave shelter to the Buddha (the Sri Maha Bodhi).

In the sacred city of Anuradhapura and in the vicinity are a large number of other ruins. These have not been identified properly and many have been destroyed by Tamil invaders or by vandals. Neither tourists nor pilgrims have paid much attention to these ruins, and information regarding these sites is meager. More recently, there have been extensive excavations and the ruins of this region which have attracted many local and foreign tourists.

* * *

From Anuradhapura we continued to Polonnaruwa, the medieval capital of Sri Lanka from 11ᵗʰ to 12ᵗʰ century AD. The history of early Sri Lanka was very carefully recorded and written down by Buddhist monks. The Mahavamsa (Great Chronicle) records the earlier period of Sri Lankan history, and Chulavamsa (Lesser Chronicle), gives an accurate picture of the Polonnaruwa period. Polonnaruwa became the second capital of Sri Lanka after the destruction of Anuradhapura in 993 AD. It was the center of several civilizations, notably that of the conquering Cholas, disciples of Brahmanism, and later of the Sinhalese sovereigns during the 12ᵗʰ and 13ᵗʰ centuries. This immense capital created by the Sinhala king, Parakramabahu I in the 12ᵗʰ century, is one of history's most astonishing urban creations

From the recorded chronicle we learn that Aggabodhi IV (667 - 685 AD) was the first Sri Lankan King who lived in Polonnaruwa, and the town gradually became the 'Country Residence' of royalty. Anuradhapura, the formal and administrative capital, was already a thousand years old, and kings increasingly favored the new city of Polonnaruwa, and developed it. However it was the Cholas of South India who made Polonnaruwa the capital after looting and burning Anuradhapura in 993 AD. The Sinhala King Vijayabahu I liberated the country in 1070 AD, by defeating the Cholas, and kept Polonnaruwa as his capital. Vijayabahu succeeded in repairing much of the irrigation system in the island, encouraged trade, and brought some prosperity back to the country.

While Vijayabahu's victory and shifting of Kingdoms to the more strategic Polonnaruwa is considered significant, the real hero of the history books is actually his grandson, Parakramabahu I. It was his reign (1183-86 AD) that is considered the Golden Age of Polonnaruwa, when trade and agriculture flourished and became completely self-sufficient under the patronage of the king. He was so adamant that no drop of water falling from the heavens was to be wasted, and insisted that each be used toward the development of the land. Hence he built irrigation systems that are far superior to those of the Anuradhapura era, and which to this day supply the water necessary for paddy cultivation during the scorching dry season in the east of the country. The greatest of these systems is the Parakrama Samudraya or the Sea of Parakrama, a tank so vast that it is often mistaken for an ocean. It is of such a width that it is impossible to stand upon one shore and view the other side, and it encircles the main city like a ribbon, being both a moat against intruders and the lifeline of the people in times of peace.

With the exception of his immediate successor, Nissankamalla I, all other monarchs of Polonnaruwa were slightly weak-willed and rather prone to picking fights within their own court. After Nissankamalla's death, Polonnaruwa went into decline with civil war, lawlessness and constant invasions from the South Indian Chola Empire, and Malay barbarians who ransacked the city several times, virtually destroying the social structure and religious order of the country. A whole century followed, which were the 'Dark Ages' of Sri Lanka, a century from which few historical records survive. The capital was shifted to Dambadeniya and Kurunegala, while Polonnaruwa returned to the jungle with its great reservoirs surviving as a series of swampy lakes, and its large brick buildings lost under thick tropical forest. By the early nineteenth century the site was completely lost.

It was in the early years of the twentieth century that the main monuments of the ancient city were uncovered. Due to excellent efforts of conservation, today, Polonnaruwa is a well-preserved city of ancient dagabas, moonstones, beautiful parks, massive buildings and stunningly beautiful statues. Besides the religious monuments (of Brahmnism), constructed by the conquering Cholas, the city comprises the monumental ruins of the fabulous garden-city created by Parakramabahu I in the 12th century. The majestic King's Council Chamber; the Lotus Bath; the Lankatilleke Viharaya, an enormous brick structure which has preserved a colossal image of the Buddha; the Gal Vihara, with its gigantic rock sculptures of images of Buddha, which may be placed among the cream of Sinhalese art; the Tivanka Pilimage (house of statues), where wall paintings of the 13th century illustrate the jataka (narratives of the previous lives of Buddha); and the stone statue of the great king Parakramabahu, are a few of this capital's memorable monuments and sites that date from the 12th century.

The successor of King Parakramabahu, Nissankamalla, although he claimed to be a great builder, was not. He squandered most of the country's wealth trying to match his predecessor's deeds. Yet, the hastily constructed monuments, although less refined than those of Parakramabahu I, were nonetheless splendid: the Rankot Vihara, an enormous stupa 175 m in diameter and 55 m high, is one of the most impressive; its plan and its dimensions are reminiscent of the dagabas at Anuradhapura.

I have since visited Pollonnaruwa on many occasions. To me it is the single most impressive medieval city anywhere, because of the well preserved monuments, particularly the Gal Vihare (Rock Temple), which depicts the grandeur of a lost civilization.

In Polonnaruwa, we stayed the night at the Rest House, which I have visited on each occasion I have been to Polonnaruwa in later years. It was built in the 1870's as a circuit bungalow for British Government officers. It was refurbished in the style of the early 1950's, whilst retaining its colonial charm, to mark the visit of Queen Elizabeth to Sri Lanka in 1954, six years before our visit. In spite of the renovations it has retained its simple features blending with nature and offers a breath-taking panoramic view of Sri Lanka's largest man-made lake in the country the "Parakrama Samudraya".

* * *

From Polonaruwa we traced our way back to Colombo with stops in Sigiriya and Dambulla. Sigiriya (Lion Rock), the spectacular palace and fortress in the sky built by King Kashyapa, stands majestically overlooking the luscious jungle surroundings. Today, the ancient rock fortress and palace ruins surrounded by the remains of an extensive network of gardens, reservoirs, and other structures are preserved as one of the seven World Heritage Sites of Sri Lanka.

The Mahavamsa, the ancient historical record of Sri Lanka, describes King Kashyapa as the son of King Dhatusena by a palace consort. In 473 AD., Kashyapa murdered his father by walling him alive. He then usurped the throne which rightfully belonged to his brother Mogallana, Dhatusena's son by the true queen. Mogallana fled to India to escape being assassinated by Kashyapa but vowed revenge. In India he raised an army with the intention of returning and retaking the throne of Sri Lanka which he considered was rightfully his. Knowing the inevitable return of Mogallana, Kashyapa is said to have built his home on the summit of Sigiriya as an impregnable fortress and pleasure palace complete with beautifully and elaborately landscaped water gardens, which contain a complex network of underground water distribution systems, providing water to the Royal baths and fountains. When Mogallana arrived and the invasion finally came in 491 AD., Kashyapa rode out to battle on his war elephant. In an attempt to out-flank his half-brother, Kashyapa took a wrong turn, where his elephant got stuck in the mud. His soldiers, thinking Kasyapa was retreating fled, abandoning him. He took his own life by falling on his sword.

After the King's death, Sigiriya was used as a rock-shelter mountain Buddhist monastery from about the 5th century BC to the 14th century AD., with caves prepared and donated by devotees to the Buddhist Sangha (Buddhist Prieststhood).

Sigiriya is also renowned for its ancient paintings (frescoes), which are about halfway up the rock in a sheltered gallery. About 500 frescoes were painted on the rock face, reminiscent of the paintings in the Ajanta Caves of India. Beyond the fresco gallery, the pathway circles the sheer face of the rock, to the Mirror Wall with Graffiti protected by a 3m-high wall. This wall was coated with a mirror-smooth glaze, in which visitors over 1000 years ago noted their impressions of the women (Sigiriya Damsels) in the gallery above.

The graffiti was mostly inscribed between the 7th and 11th century AD. The Sigiri inscriptions were deciphered by the archaeologist Senarath Paranavithana in his renowned two-volume work, published by Cambridge, *Sigiri Graffiti and Story of Sigiriya*. In recent years, a person I befriended in Los Angeles, Dr. Benille Priyanka, who is a scholar at University of California Los Angeles (UCLA), has continued to decipher the remaining records at Sigiriya. Prof. Paranavithana deciphered 685 Sigiriya poems, while Benille covered 800, and published a book titled *Recently Deciphered Records of the Sigiriya Mirror Wall*, which was awarded the Best Academic Publication of the Year 2010 at the Sri Lanka Literary Awards Ceremony in 2011.

It is indeed my great pleasure to meet him from time to time in Los Angeles and discuss the arduous work he is carrying on for future generations to understand and appreciate the history and significance of these historical records.

* * *

From Sigiriya we proceeded to Dambulla before we headed home. A sacred pilgrimage site for 22 centuries, the cave monastery in Dambulla, with its five sanctuaries, is one of the largest, best-preserved cave-temple complexes in Sri Lanka. It is an outstanding example of the religious art and expression of Sri Lanka and South and South-East Asia. The Buddhist mural paintings cover an area of 2,000 square meters. The 157 statues, including the Golden Buddha statue within these shrine rooms take pride of place. This collection is representative of many epochs of Sinhala sculpture and Sinhala art. One cave alone has over 1,500 paintings of the Buddha covering the ceiling with the Buddha statues, as well as various gods and goddesses in varying sizes, the largest being 15 meters long. The temple is composed of five caves, which have been converted into shrine rooms. Access is along the gentle slope of the massive Dambulla Rock, offering a panoramic view of the surrounding flat land, which includes the rock fortress Sigiriya, 19 km away.

The Dambulla cave monastery remains the best-preserved ancient edifice in Sri Lanka. It has been occupied by a Buddhist monastic establishment since the arrival of Buddhism on the island. This complex dates from the 3rd and 2nd centuries BC, when it was already established as one of the largest and most important monasteries. King Valagambahu is traditionally thought to have converted the caves into a temple in the 1st century BC (Anuradhapura period). Exiled from Anuradhapura, he sought refuge here from South Indian ursurpers for 15 years. After reclaiming his capital, the King built a temple in thankful worship.

Many other Kings expanded the temple complex later and by the 11th century (Polonnaruwa period), the caves had become a major religious center and they remain so to date. King Nissankamalla gilded the caves and added about 70 Buddha statues in 1190. During the 18th century, the caves were restored and painted by the Kandyan Kings. In the year of my birth 1938, a major renovation was done including the rebuilding of the veranda and the entrance porch, incorporating a mixture of European and Asian detailing of the 18th century style. The Dambulla monastery also has been designated as a UNESCO World Heritage Site.

Today, there is in the vicinity a modern international cricket ground that was built in recent time. I have been there twice to watch Sri Lanka national side play once against Australia and the other time against India. Each time, I have revisited the rock temple at Dambulla with nostalgia. On one occasion, we saw the renovation work that was being undertaken. At the time we visited, a young artist was patiently restoring the ancient paintings inside the caves. It had taken well over a year, and he was only halfway through the project. On inquiry, we found that this talented artist, probably in his early thirties, happened to be the son of the most famous artist who restored and copied artwork from ancient times going back several centuries. He devoted a lifetime of commitment to preserve historic art. His son was now continuing the legacy of his father and presently restoring the unique frescos of the Dambulla caves. It is extremely arduous work that calls for rare expertise and immeasurable amount of commitment and patience with relatively little compensation. We were most impressed by the young man's work, and on an inquiry from Shanthi, he said, it was extremely difficult and costly to obtain the special type of paint he needs to use to restore the frescoes. They were not readily available in the country at the time. On our return to Vienna, my wife arranged to send him a stock of paint that he had specifically requested. We also told him that we were very pleased that we have a line drawing of a temple painting by his famous father, which I had purchased in the early seventies in appreciation and admiration of his lifetime commitment to the essential task in preserving our culture. The framed piece of rare work is still displayed in our living room signed by its creator – Manjusri.

* * *

Following the invigorating and highly educational trip to the ancient cities of my country, I returned once more to my desk at Voet Inn to resume work at Law College and to prepare for the finals of the University of London Bachelor of Laws degree (LL.B), held in two parts, in June that year. Again some of the subjects I read for the final examamination of the University of London were those I had covered during my Law College lectures. But there were other subjects I had to learn on my own as they were practically new, as I had not covered them, as of that time, in the Law College.

The only subject I had read at the Law College, though not necessarily in the depth that was required for the London University degree, was Jurisprudence and Legal Theory (Jurisprudence deals with the nature of law, its place in society and how a legal system operates as a system of rules and as a social institution engaging with ideals of justice and often conflicting moral codes, in classic and contemporary legal theory). The subjects that were new to me were Public International Law (it concerns legal relations between states but also deals with the role of the United Nations and other international organizations and, covers the laws of war, human rights and international criminal law, Law of the sea and air, as well as the environment); Conflict of laws (also known as private international law, the body of rules applied by the English courts to cases mostly of private individuals or entities covered by English laws but with a foreign element, dealing with issues of jurisdiction and applicability of laws of other countries); and Law of Trusts (a part of English Equity law, dealing with the rules and principles governing the creation and operation of trusts – a particular method of holding property that developed historically to preserve family wealth, by minimizing liability to taxation).

I turned to Nimal Jayawardane for assistance in preparing for the exam. He was only an acquaintance at the time, but was an inseparable pal of my friend Norman Weerasooria. Nimal and Norman were classmates at Royal College and had many common interests particularly in appreciating and enjoying wildlife parks as well as the hunting forays they indulged in. Nimal was the younger son of N.U. Jayawardane, the first Sri Lankan Governor of the Central Bank. He had graduated with honors from Cambridge University in the UK and had returned recently to the Island. It was with trepidation that I approached him for help, but he was immediately forthcoming. After giving me some pointers he went to his room and brought me all his note books covering the subjects that I had offered to sit for the final exam. They not only contained the immaculate notes taken by him at the lectures given by prominent academics at Cambridge but were also written in very clear handwriting with the important issues underlined in red. Needless to say, armed with these notes I was confident that I could cover the subjects in time for the exam. I had of course, planned to sit the exam in the following year, in case I was not ready, because I considered completing my law studies at the law college by passing the proctors final exam that year as my priority.

Later we became good friends. I remember with gratitude how Nimal lavishly entertained on my behalf the Director General of the United Nations, who was an avid fan of wildlife, while we were on one of our official visits to the island. The Director General was most impressed by Nimal's wild-life collection complete with Anacondas from the Amazon which the Director General considered as one of the best private collections anywhere in the world. Nimal also took him fishing off the far cost of Colombo in a somewhat dilapidated fishing boat sailing off at four in the morning and returning with a catch of tuna to the great delight of the Director General. Nimal is a renaissance man just like the Director General and they enjoyed each other's company.

Nimal's elder brother Lal Jayawardane, a Ph.D in Economics from Cambridge, became a close friend of mine, as he joined the United Nations about the same time as I did. He later functioned as Director of the U.N. affiliated World Institute of Development Research (WIDER) based in Norway. I have related earlier, how Lal along with our mutual friend Valentine inadvertently introduced me to Western opera which I came to love in my later life. Lal and Nimal's sister Neiliya married Christopher Pinto, a lawyer and one of my close friends from the time he was an attorney for the World Bank. He later became Legal Adviser to the Ministry of Foreign Affairs in Colombo, and still later, became the Registrar of the Iran- United States Claims Commission in The Hague; where he now resides in his retirement. Nimal took over the management of the family-owned company (Mercantile Credit) established by his father. Nimal developed the business into one of the leading commercial conglomerates with several subsidiary companies under it.

I admire and deeply apperciate Nimal's generosity. He was definitely an opener of doors for those who were waiting to be let in. With the help of Nimal's notes, I was able to maneuver part of the new terrain and eventually obtain the London Bachelor of Laws degree.

Chapter 20

Ace-Ace

Had anyone told me a man could sit at a table for more than three or four hours at a time without looking either to the left or the right, his eyes fixed on a pack of cards, and later that same year pass all his exams with flying colors, I would not have believed him. I saw it happen with my own eyes. The year was 1961. Once again energized by the results of the exams at the end of the previous year, with renewed determination I had begun the third year of work at the Law College.

It was a year mainly devoted to the practical aspects of the profession in terms of learning how a civil case and a criminal case would proceed through the courts of law. We were taught what actions need to be taken in each case through its various stages, including what type of evidence is relevant to a case and how to present evidence in a court of law.

Criminal Procedure was taught by W.D. Gunasekera who had taught us Criminal Law in the previous year. Civil Procedure was taught by S.R. Wijetilake, a senior judicial officer who at the time was the Secretary to the Judicial Services Commission and was appointed as acting principal of the Law College. He was later a judge of the Supreme Court and on his retirement became the principal of the Law College. Law of Evidence was taught by a brilliant lawyer, E.R.S.R. Coomaraswamy, who having become a proctor of the Supreme Court passed all three advocates exams at the same time in 1949. He was the only one to do so, until I had the honor of following him in 1962.

He later became a President's Counsel and represented the country at legal committees at the United Nations. He also authored the seminal work on the *Law of Evidence*, a textbook we used.

Another practical aspect that was important was how to prepare and execute legal documents, particularly Deeds conveying property from one person to another (the subject was called Conveyancing). It was taught by another leading practitioner of the art, Kurukulasuriya. Company Law (laws governing the formation and operation of business enterprises) was taught by S.W. Walpita, a leading company law expert with a large civil practice, who later became a judge of the Supreme Court and Chairman of the Insurance Corporation.

In the third year, there was a more relaxed atmosphere among the students. There was no examination at the end of the year. The subjects learned during the third year were included in the final examination that took place at the close of the fourth year, which was devoted to practical training under a senior practitioner.

*   *   *

Most students found various ways to use this relatively free time. Some took up part-time and even full-time jobs. I joined the Central Bank of Ceylon as a clerical hand in the Employees Provident Fund (EPF) Department. The Central Bank maintained the retirement fund for non-governmental officers in the private sector and public corporations. Both employers and employees contribute during the working years of an employee's life. On retirement, the employees have the option of either withdrawing the amount due as a lump sum, or to receive periodic payments.

At the Bank a team of us were responsible for checking the entries of incoming monthly contributions. We were happy to work at the newly-built Central Bank building on Prince Street in the heart of the financial and commercial center of the country. Although the building had no more than seven floors, it was considered a skyscraper of sorts at the time. Still later, the Bank built a more elaborate tall building on Queen's Street (now Janadhipathi Mawatha), which was the target of a terrorist bomb attack by the LTTE. The building received extensive damage but was rebuilt and now stands as a modern highrise.

The Central Bank of Ceylon was considered the star institution of the Public Service. As such, it employed the brightest economists who were sent abroad for graduate studies in the course of their duties. As a result many in the staff held Ph.D degrees. They were on the highest pay scale in the public sector. The institution was led by Governor of the Bank, who at the time was D.W. Rajapathirana. At that time, the bank had in its staff three people who later held the same post (Dr. Waranasena Rasaputram, Dr. H.N.S. Karunatilake and Dr. A.S. Jayawardana).

I came to know A.S. Jayawardane, because his brother was a fellow law student who was with me in the EPF section in the Bank. Dr. Karunatilaka was the Director of Research at the Bank and, time to time, I went to the library in search of information that would help me in my legal studies. I had a fleeting acquaintance with Dr. Rasaputram thanks to his friend and colleague Dr. Uswatte-Aratchi (who hailed from my hometown Ambalangoda), who was also in the Bank staff. Much later in life, all three were to become lifelong friends, since the days when they used to attend conferences at the United Nations. Dr, Rasaputram later became a Director in the World Bank and still later functioned as Ambassador to the United States.

* * *

There were others in my batch who took advantage of the extra time at hand to become experts at the 'cut table' (gambling table) engaged in the card game *booruwa*, (local form of poker). The largest space at the Law College was allocated to the canteen, where many spent their breaks between lectures. In one corner was the card table, always in use, where some of us sharpened our skills in playing cards. Many student- gamblers spent hours at the cut table at the expense of their performances at the exams, as well as their pockets.

The leader of the cut table, though a perpetual loser, was M.D.K. Kulatunge, who also was the President of the Students Council during my time. Among the others were Aquinas Fernando, who also served in the student body as the editor of the Law College journal; Roland Anthony, Gerry Perera and Nihal Serasinghe. They were all a close-knit group, and I consider them my close friends. They went on to become successful lawyers after completing their law examinations, although not necessarily on the time span of four years that is the allocated time to complete the course. Among them was a pair, who competed to be the head of the class each time the examinations came by. They both completed the exams with highest honors and became President's Counsels, reaching the zenith of the profession. They were D.S. Wijesinghe and Gerry Deraniyagala.

Sisira Wijesinghe (DS Wije) was a brilliant student who nevertheless spent most of his time at the cut table. Obviously, before or after his visits to the cut table, he spent long hours immersed in his studies as he was either first or second at all exams. It could be that the cut table was his way of relaxing, for he was equally adept at the table, and was often among the winners. Shortly after he took oaths as an advocate of the Supreme Court, he joined the Attorney General's Department as a crown counsel.

It was during this time that we became quite close friends as we were occupying adjacent rooms on the top floor of the newly constrcterd building of the Young Men's Buddhist Association (YMBA), at the corner of Bristol Street and Main Street, in the heart of Colombo Fort. We were the first occupants there and it took a while before it was full. This meant that the two of us spent quite some time in each other's company. When we came back to the YMBA after work, often we would have friends visiting us and we ate out in the Chinese restaurants in the area.

The YMBA Building has at its base a lovely Buddhist shrine, with a serene Buddha statue beckoning the passersby for a moment of peace and tranquility. This was in 1962 and it comes as no surprise that this architectural gem has today become a National Heritage

Site. Shortly thereafter I left the country, but my friendship with DS Wije blossomed over the years. On every single occasion I visited my homeland I have visited him at his residence at Thimbrigassyaya on Havelock Road, which is his wife Nimala's home.

Very early in his career Wije was on a train to Kandy to appear on behalf of the Attorney General in an important case, when he was struck by a heart condition requiring bypass surgery. He was young to be afflicted with such a malady, but he has survived it well for over fifty years. During his career at the Attorney General's Department, he often represented the country at the United Nations meetings in New York. This offered us the opportunity to further interact with each other. He was a very competent prosecutor and was rapidly promoted to the senior level of Deputy Solicitor General when he decided to leave the department and establish a legal practice of his own. Shortly thereafter, his services were sought by many clients including leading political and business people. He appeared almost exclusively in the Appellate Courts. Soft-spoken and highly capable, he has the ability to argue complex legal issues with clarity and competence. His incisive mind would immediately focus on the main issues involved and he would bring to bear his endless knowledge of the law to deal with the issues at hand. He is sought after by successive governments for advice on important constitutional issues, which is his forte along with complex cases that were on appeal to higher courts.

After half-a-century of legal practice at the Bar, Wije continues to appear for one side or the other, in all of the important cases in his field. I would always consult him on any legal issue that I or my friends might encounter, and often he has helped my friends without charging a fee. Whenever I enter his chambers, with or without notice, he has always found time for a chat. I immensely enjoy the banter which is also extremely informative and allowed me to get a peak at the inner workings of the officialdom. Wije and Nimala is another couple who joined our New Year's Eve group parties. In a recent publication, *Lore of the Law*, Wije has been venerated as the reincarnation of Prophet Isaiah in recognition of his prophecy on the fate of the justice system in the country, but during his law student days, he would have been anointed as the "Saint of the Cut Table!"

Gerry Deraniyagala was Wije's friend and competitor in the battle to be the first in the batch. Yet, he too spent time at the cut table, I would surmise, to relax from the arduous work he did late at night or early in the mornings. He too could not have done as well as he did, spending most of the day at the cut table, had he not burned the midnight oil pouring over his text books. He too was brilliant, and had an extremely lucrative practice in the District Courts of Colombo and outstations, appearing primarily in civil cases. Regrettably, at the zenith of his prowess as an attorney, while on a wildlife safari with his family at the Yala National Park, Gerry became a tragic victim of the Boxing Day Tsunami that engulfed the country in 2004 [1].

* * *

There were some other friends who blossomed out as outstanding practicing attorneys from my Law College days. While a few of them served their clients, most spent time in public service. Sasi S. Sahabandu, who played with me in the Law College cricket team, became a President's Counsel, as did Jayantha Gunasekare. Many others excelled in the profession and in national and international public service and academia.

There were others who took judicial appointments and had distinguished careers. Justice A.S. Wijetunge, my batchmate and President of the Law Students Union, was a close friend of mine who ended up as a Judge of the Supreme Court. So did Justice Priyantha Perera and Justice C.V. Wigneswaran (presently chief minister, Northern Province), who were also my batchmates. Justice Ranjith Dheeraratne, who was with me in Law Hostel, also ended up as a Supreme Court Judge.

Whenever I came basck to Sri Lanka I would visit them in their chambers and they always welcomed my visits. I have also visited some at their residences and even after their retirements I have kept in touch with them. Ninian played in the Law College Cricket team with me, and Dudley and Oliver were my hostelmates at the time. A motley crew, to say the least! They all proved themselves in the field of law later on. Ninian Jayasuriya rose to be a judge of the Court of Appeal, Oliver Weerasinghe a High Court Judge, and that somewhat of a rascal, Dudley Karunaratne, also became a High Court Judge.

Though senior to me, also with me at the Law College Hostel was and had very close family contacts was Justice G.D. De Silva (GD), who hailed from my hometown, Ambalangoda. He was a leading advocate in the Galle District who had served as Deputy Legal Draftsman of the Ministry of Justice. Later he took an appointment as the Legal Draftsman in Seychelles, where eventually he was made a judge of the Supreme Court. He married a teacher by profession, Indrani De Silva, daughter of a former member of parliament M.W.R. De Silva. As his family had ties to mine, we attended each other's functions (weddings, funerals and religious ceremonies). They have a son Kanishka and daughter Ishani who are physicians (professors in medical schools), and on some occasions they have readily assisted my family. Dr. Kanishka De Silva is the Consultant Oncological Surgeon, who established the Cancer Surgical Unit in the Kandy Teaching Hospital. He was President of the Kandy Society of Medicine. Presently he is on the Board of Post Graduate Institute of Medicine in Colombo. His sister Dr Ishani Rodirigo is Consultant Pediatrician and Senior Lecturer, Medical Faculty, University of Colombo.

They have a second son, Lakpriya, who lives in Tampa, Florida, United States. He used to visit us during his vacations, while he was a graduate student at New York State University in Buffalo, New York. His wife Swanthri is a physician. She is the daughter of former Chief Justice G.P.S De. Silva, who has close family connections to my hometown Ambalangoda, and he is a person well known to me as a friend and fellow lawyer. Lakpriya, graduated with a M.Sc, and he is an executive in the mercantile sector. They have two daughters. GD and Indrani have a third son, Channa De. Silva, an executive at Microsoft in Colombo, Sri Lanka. His wife Navamalika is also a physician.

Indrani's elder brother, Dr. Padmasiri De Silva, married a distant relative of mine Kalyani Saddhasena, daughter of the legendary physician of my hometown and our family doctor, M.H. Saddhasena, who later became the member of parliament for Ambalangoda. Padmasiri and Kalyani have visited me in New York on a couple of occasions, when they were at the University of Hawaii. Padmasiri was professor and head of the Philosophy and Psychology Department, University of Peradeniya, Sri Lanka, and a world-renowned expert on Buddhist and Freudian psychology. I remember having long discussions with him on Buddhism and the functions of the brain, which he explained with great clarity and expertise during the time he stayed at my home in New York. Now retired, he lives in Australia where he had also held academic positions. Indrani's younger sister, Irani, is married to Pathmasiri who operates a popular motel in Kandy in Sri Lanka, in close vicinity of the famous Buddhist shrine *Dalada Maligawa* (Temple of the Tooth). G.D. and Indrani are also retired and live in Kandy.

Another friend of long standing is Sunil De Silva, who became a crown counsel and rose to be the Attorney General. Sunil was in my class at Richmond College from the junior school to the middle school. From middle school onwards he was at Royal College, but our paths crossed again at the Law College. As Attorney General he had a very active and visible role to play because of the raging terrorist war during his tenure. He was a brilliant lawyer, a fearless fighter for causes that he represented in court, and forthright when called upon to provide legal opinions by the governmental authorities. An accomplished actor and prankster par excellence, he acted in many English plays that were critically acclaimed. He has visited me in New York when he used to visit the UN on official duty, always finding time to have a meal at my home accompanied by interesting repartee. He was a chain-smoker, and on one occasion, when we stayed up chatting late into the night, having had an ample amount of alcohol, he nearly set fire to my house with his lighted cigarette that accidently ignited the wall which my wife Shanthi had padded with fabric. He later retired to Australia.

Sunil was succeeded by Tilak Marapane, whom I came to know well while he was serving as counsel in the Iran US Arbitration Court in The Hague. He too loved to play pranks. When he arrived in The Hague he shared a flat with another person. Beginning to like the place, he sent for his wife and as her arrival drew close, he hatched a plan to get his flatmate out of his abode. He pretended that the flat was haunted and took necessary action to simulate a haunted atmosphere. His flat- mate promptly vacated the place, leaving the flat to Tilak and his wife. Later, as Attorney General, he too visited me in New York during his official visits. Once retired, he established a lucrative legal practice, and for a while served as a cabinet minister.

Preceding them, as Acting Attorney General at a very young age of thirty, was Nihal Jayawickrama, a close friend whose mother hailed from my hometown. He obtained a Ph.D from University of London for an outstanding thesis on International Law of Human Rights, an area in which he later became an internationally recognized expert on Human Rights. He was Permanent Secretary to the Ministry of Justice when the Constituent Assembly was convened in 1970, and was involved in the processes that led to the drafting and adoption of the 1972 Constitution of Sri Lanka. In 1978 he participated in the proceedings of the select committee on the revision of the constitution as legal adviser to the Leader of the Opposition in parliament. He was a member of the national delegations to the Annual Sessions of the U.N. General Assembly and representative to several legal bodies of the U.N. I used to see him often during our years in New York.

Later, Dr. Jayawickrama was a professor of law at University of Hong Kong and University of Saskatchewan in Canada, where he taught comparative constitutional law. He then served as executive director of Transparency International (international NGO on human rights), in London. Currently, he serves as the Coordinator of the United Nations Committee on Judicial Integrity – a committee of prominent judges from ten countries.

Nihal is a nephew of former Supreme Court Justice T.S. Fernando from my hometown Ambalangoda, his mother's brother, with whom he lived in Colombo. Justice Fernando's residence was off Barnes Place, just a very short walk from the Law College Hostel, and I used to visit him there fairly regularly. He married Sarojini (Saro) Amarasuriya, daughter of former President of the Senate, Thomas Amarasuriya, member of the first Cabinet of independent Ceylon, member of the Amarasuriya clan that I have referred elsewhere. Saro graduated with a degree in English, the same year as I received my degree from the University of Ceylon, Peradeniya. She went on to earn a Ph.D from the University of Hongkong, and teach literature in Universities in Hong Kong and England. Recently she published a theortical expose on the writings of Robert Knox, *Writing that Conquers: Re-reading Knox's Historical Relation of the Island Ceylon.*

My wife Shanthi and I have been houseguests of Nihal and Saro in Hong Kong, Berlin and London, where they lived in later years, and they have visited us in New York. It was on one of those occasions that Saro gave courage and helped Shanthi to walk a couple of months ahead of what the doctors had expected, after Shanthi had been confined to bed following an accident. More about Nihal and Saro are narrated in the pages ahead.

The other Acting Attorney General I had known was a fellow Alumnus of Richmond College, Percy Colin-Thomé. He was a brilliant student at Richmond, as well as at Cambridge University, and an outstanding athlete and cricketer who won Cambridge tennis colors. Drama was his forte. At Richmond and in the Drama Circle of Colombo he continued to excel as an actor. He and Sunil were both alumni of Richmond, and they both acted in several famous plays such as *He Comes from Jaffna*, written and produced by another distinguished Richmond Alumnus Prof E.F.C. Ludowyk. Percy Colin-Thomé ended up as a Judge of the Supreme Court and I have visited him on several occasions in his chambers.

There were a few who took to politics. Among them Vasu and Battie Weerakoon went on to become Cabinet Ministers. Srima Lenaduwa, who married Gamini Dissanayake, member of the cabinet under several governments and a presidential candidate. Following the assassination of her husband, Srima conteted as the U.N.P candiate at the 1994 presidential elections.

Among those from my class at the Law College who ventured into other realms was my very close friend Anil Obeysekere, with whom I spent quite a bit of time during our student days. He was one of those who joined our group of friends and enjoyed going to the popular public dinner dances of the day. He had an *Austin A-30* car, which was handy on such occasions, and he readily let me borrow it whenever I needed to. His sister Shriyani was one of the few girls in our batch. Anil went on to become a successful lawyer and a President's Counsel. He was related to the Bandaranaike family, and not surprisingly became a member of the SLFP led by the Bandaranaikes. Though he was not an active politician, he was ready to help his countrymen in every way he could. It is no surprise therefore that he held several responsible positions in the public sector during his career. He was chairman of two mega corporations. During his tenures as Chairman of the Petroliam Corporation and later Chairman of the Telecommunications Corporation he is reputed to have made major improvements in those establishments. At the time of his untimely demise, he was holding the position of Chairman of Lake House, the premier publishing house of the country. During my visits to Colombo he made it a point to see me for long chats about world affairs, and how they would impact the operations of establishments he was heading. Of course, we didn't fail to go down memory lane after many decades of different experiences we each had had by then. Early in his public career, he served as Trade Commissioner of Sri Lanka in Czechoslovakia. During his service there I had to represent the U.N. at meetings in Prague on two occasions, and we had a wonderful time in each other's company. He went out of his way to find time to spend with me during the little free time I had, particularly in offering me a very welcome 'bath curry' (rice and curry, staple diet in my homeland) prepared under the directions of his charming wife.

There were other friends from the Law College days who went along a similar route and served in public sector corporations. One was Alloy Ratnayaka, who was the President of the Law College Union during my early days there. Later, he too was a successful lawyer and became a President's Counsel. During his public sector career he became the deputy high commissioner (ambassador) of Sri Lanka in the United Kingdom, where I had the occasion to meet him after many years. On his return home, he became Chairman of the Lake House publishing firm.

Then there was Anura Weeraratna, also a prominent member of the Students Union, who became Director and Secretary of the leading firm of Lever Brothers Ltd,. Later, he became chairman of the newly-established Ceramic Corporation, where he is reputed to have pioneered modern management systems, and initiated a joint venture with the famous Noritaka Company of Japan to manufacture high-quality porcelain for export. Even today, Noritaka brand ceramics, made in Sri Lanka, are found in leading department stores in the United States and Europe. Thereafter, Anura served as Permanent Secretary in the Ministry of Industries at a relatively young age. He married a sister of my Richmond College friend and fellow athlete G.H. Amarasinghe, and migrated to Australia, where he established a legal practice. He also earned a doctorate degree there, and authored the authoritative publication on the Freedom of Information Law of Australia.

Another active member of the Law College Union and a lifelong friend is Nihal Serasinghe. We began our friendship when we were at Richmond College hostel. He entered the Law College a year ahead of me and I looked up to him for inspiration. He did not disappoint me and provided very helpful information and encouragement. He joined Carson's Ltd, a trading and plantation establishment as a legal counsel, and later served as the Chairman of the State Trading Corporation. He married the sister of our mutual friend Elmore Perera, to whom I have made reference elsewhere.

* * *

During the course of that year, and the following years at the Law College, I made some friendships that have lasted throughout our lives. My friendship with Norman Weerasooria blossomed after we had both left the country. He is the son of the legendary lawyer N.E. Weerasooria Q.C. Norman graduated from the University Of Ceylon, Peradeniya, with Honors, and joined the Law College to complete his studies as an advocate. He was an executive at the World Bank in Washington D.C. while I was at the U.N. in New York. He had earlier followed a course in New York at Columbia University, during which time we were in close contact. Over the years we continued to have constant contacts visiting each other's homes in United States and in Colombo.

After graduating, Norman established a lucrative practice but soon his time was devoted more and more to the family busines established by his father. Along with his siblings he gradually expanded the business to the level of a conglomerate dealing with management, construction, tourism, and information technology, among others. Gradually, he gave up the practice of law to manage the business empire full-time.

He used to visit me in New York every three or four months when he was in the United States to transact business. We had much fun during those visits. When we chatted about the political and other developments back home, he always displayed an uncanny insight as to what was going right and what was going wrong in the management of our homeland. When the time came for a meal, irrespective of whether it be eastern or western cuisine, he would want to empty a good half of a ketchup bottle on to his plate.

While I was in Vienna I learned that he was taken ill and was in the U.K. for treatment. He had surgery, recovered and resumed his normal life. But during a business visit to Tokyo he was taken ill again, and on return, the doctors in Sri Lanka advised him to seek the assistance of the doctors who had done his previous surgery in the UK. Regrettably, the surgeon who performed the surgery at the Royal Marsden Hospital, a leading cancer center, had not taken out the nodules as required, nor had he recommended post-surgery treatments such as radiation and chemotherapy. It was because of such tragic decisions that he suffered a relapse and was told that nothing could be done to alleviate his condition. He returned to Colombo and was at the Durdens Nursing Home when I last visited him. He was very courageous, and at the time I saw him, he was still attending to his work from his hospital bed. He was making all necessary arrangements for the family business conglomerate to continue seamlessly after his demise. When I discussed with him the unfortunate situation he was in, because of the negligence of his U.K. surgeon, he uttered one of his often used classic retorts: *Kaata Kiyannada, Kiyala Mokatada*; (whom should you complain to, and what is the point in complaining?). He was a wonderful human being, outstandingly brilliant, soft-spoken and kind-hearted, who lived a good life and left with no regrets.

Yet, for all this, it is difficult not to think Norman was cut down in the prime of his life and too young to go when he still had so much to contribute to society and the world. I personally feel a sense of sadness because I know, if at the time he first needed surgery, I was still working in New York where I had been for many years, and not in Vienna, I would have convinced him, and he would have come to the United States without much hesitation for treatment. He might have extended his rich life for decades more, if it had been so.

When I learned of his illness he sent me some reports which I sent to my friend Dr. Sunil Kumar Gulavita, an oncologist who at the time was at the Mayo Clinic in the United States. Mayo is considered a world-class medical facility. Dr. Gulavita mentioned that Norman should come to the United States for treatmant. When I mentioned to him that Norman was being treated at the Royal Marsden Hospital in the U.K., his response was that the doctors treating him were his professors as he had worked there for a decade, but the cancer treatment in the U.K. at the time was fifteen to twenty years behind the United States. He explained that was simply because of lack of funds available under the National Health System in the U.K.

Sometime after Norman's untimely demise, his brother Sarath contacted me to say that there had been serious lapses in the treatment given to Norman, and I agreed with him that he should proceed to take appropriate steps to somehow remedy the situation. Along with the rest of the family he decided to point out the lapses and request the surgeon to make amends by contributing a reasonable sum of money to the cancer hospital in Sri Lanka, which is seriously underfunded. In spite of repeated efforts, the surgeon decided to ignore the request. That was even after it was intimated to him that the family would otherwise be compelled to inform the British Medical Board and take whatever appropriate action that might be needed. His only response was to send a report justifying his treatment. Included with his response was some medical evidence to support the course of action he had taken. Serendipitously, Norman had the habit of keeping a detailed diary, and it was revealed that he had visited the Dentist on the day that the X-rays supposedly had been taken after surgery, showing that all was well. On further investigation by Norman's brother Sarath, it was discovered that the good surgeon had indeed sent the X-ray of another patient, because he had never taken an X-ray of Norman's condition after surgery.

On realizing the situation, legal advice was sought from Jim Bandaranayake. He was a schoolmate of mine at Richmond though much senior to me, and was working in a leading legal firm in the U.K. He dispatched several letters to the surgeon but without any positive response. This was rather strange, but the surgeon's defiance may have been because he was a leading surgeon, himself an official of the UK Medical Board. With his great reputation, he perhaps thought that the relatives of the deceased patient from a third world country would not have the wherewithal to successfully challenge a person of his standing.

In the absence of any positive response from the surgeon, eventually the matter was reported to the UK Medical Board.

To their credit they decided to investigate the matter through its disciplinary body. The investigations took a couple of years, but it was a serious and deliberate procedure including the visit to Sri Lanka by a member of the Board to interview and record statements and examine the evidence for the benefit of the Board. In the end, with all his reputation and skill, the Board impounded his license, forbidding him to practice medicine and levied some form of fine as redress. It is a pity that he decided not to contribute, what to him would have been a paltry sum, to a good cause-the Sri Lanka Cancer Hospital, instead of suffering ignominy that no one in his standing would wish to, and suffer heavy pecuniary losses as well.

Norman married Rani De Saram, a beauty from an eminent family in Kurunegala. Rani was a kind and gentle lady and a good friend. She was the ideal mate for Norman and good company to his friends. She was generous to a fault and admired by all. On visits to Colombo I had often stayed at their mansion-like residence in Kotte. The house they built and lived in was in close proximity to his father's ancestral home, on the rubber estate owned by Norman's father. Norman built his residence at the front end of the extensive estate. At the back end, Sarath, his youngest brother, who had married Rani's sister Ungi, built an equally spacious home. More recently, a new home was also built on the same estate for Norman's only son Nishan. He was a regular visitor in my home in New York during his vacations, while he was a student at Emery Riddle Aviation School in Florida in the United States. Nishan later became a champion race driver and a successful businessman in the family business.

Surrounding the houses they built, both sisters, Rani & Ungi created some of the best landscaped gardens in Sri Lanka. It is testimony to their great flare to recreate nature that these creative gardens were extensively featured in a recent coffee table publication: *Gardens of Lanka*, by Sarala Fernando. This unique publication brilliantly traces the diplomatic history of the country through transformation of the royal and monastic gardens from the first diplomatic encounter in third century B.C.; through the large botanical gardens established during the colonial times to the present day ecologically friendly village and home gardens, like those of Rani and Ungi. Sarala Fernando, a member of the diplomatic service of Sri Lanka, retired as Ambassador to the United Nations in Geneva. She has been a close friend for many years and is married to my former New York roommate Vijitha Fernando, who later served in the World Bank in Washington D.C. Now retired, Vijitha has taken a leading role in the local Olympic movement, and the controlling authority for the sport of swimming in Sri Lanka, as an important offic-bearer of those bodies.

After the demise of Norman, his youngest brother, Sarath, took over the management of the family business. By then, Finco and Company, which began as a finance company in the early sixties, had mushroomed with several other companies dealing in multiple areas in the commercial sector. Alpha, run by Nishan, was manufacturing security equipment, steel and wood office furniture and fittings; Finco Garments is a leading entity in the thriving garment industry of the country; RDC and Uga Escapes run by Rani's brother, Harsha De. Saram is a building and consulting firm that built major highways in Sri Lanka and abroad and more recently constructed and operates three boutique-type luxury tourist resorts. RDC also built the tallest residential complex in Colombo located at Galle Face, abutting the ocean in the best hotel area in Colombo. During our most recent visit home, with the generous courtesy of Rani, my wife and I had the luxury of spending our extended vacation in this famed 'Iceland Residences'.

Today, the Group of companies have moved away from its original undertakings as a finance company and gem exporting concern, and moved on to more current commercial aspects such as information technology (IT). This company now provides consulting and software development and telecommunications overseen by the younger generation of family members. Sarath's son Priyanjana was educated in the United States, while the sons of Norman's other brother Wickrama were educated in Australia.

Sarath's wife Ungi and Rani have both spent vacations with us in New York and Vienna. These were always very pleasant occasions. Whenever I am in Colombo I visit them, and even after the demise of Norman I have stayed at his residence. Rani offered me Norman's car for Shanthi and me to use while in Sri Lanka, insisting that I should not rent a vehicle for our use, although on one occasion my vacation lasted nearly three months. Such was the generosity displayed by her to all and sundry, particularly to her workers as well as religious establishments and medical institutions.

Finco was established by the brothers with the oversight of their father about the same time as we graduated as lawyers. At the time, Norman's brother Wickrama, having heard that I was to join a law firm, invited me to join Finco. He explained that Finco could support an establishment of a law firm that is truly indigenous as most law firms at the time were established by Anglo-Asians and others. I had no interest in remaining in the profession for any length of time, thus, I had no interest in making a long-term commitment by accepting the kind offer made by my friend Wickrama.

Wickrama Weerasooria was also a brilliant student who graduated with first class honors, both at the University of Ceylon, Peradeniya, and at the Law College, a rare achievement indeed. In spite of such outstanding achievements, he was a person with a variety of interests, and a favorite among the fellow students of the fairer sex. He later obtained a Ph.D. from the London School of Economics. He practiced law for a short period while helping his brother Norman to expand the family business. Then he went on to become a high-level civil servant, a canny political consultant, a respected diplomat and an outstanding academic. He was the Permanent Secretary to the Ministry of Plan Implementation, former Sri Lankan High Commissioner (ambassador) to Australia and New Zealand, and a professor of law at the University of Ceylon, Ceylon Law College and Monash University in Australia. He also served as Director of the Banking Law Centre set up by the National Australia Bank, and served as a legal consultant in financial sector law reforms at the Central Bank of Sri Lanka.

In his semi-retirement, he is serving as Sri Lanka's first Insurance Ombudsman and continues to be the prolific author of highly aclaimed academic and other publications. Dr. Weerasooria has published over fourteen texts most of them on banking, credit and commercial law in Australia and Sri Lanka. He is considered an internationally renowned expert on commercial law. As a political consultant and tactician with unmatched vision and guile, he is credited to have masterminded the return of the UNP at the general elections in 1978.

We kept up our friendship through the years. Once, as President of an international academic body, I was responsible for the organization of a worldwide Moot Court competition for law students, which was judged by three judges of the World Court in The Hague. He invited me to hold it at Monash University saying that he will take responsibility for the local organization in Melbourne, Australia. Knowing his skills I readily agreed, and he sought and got the approval of the university authorities. He spared no effort to make it a success and it was perhaps one of the best organized Moot Courts in its then twenty-year history.

I have visited him when I am in Colombo and at Mirigama, where he has a hide-out without radio, television, or telephone, in order that he can write his books undisturbed. He married Rohini (Gamini Dissanayake's sister) and their sons, Senaka and his brother, are as brilliant as their father. They are engaged in the family business, taking it to the next level in the IT era through their expertise in the field. Wickrama is not only one of the most brilliant products of my generation, but also a very humble and caring individual.

Sarath, the youngest in the Weerasooria family, is an accountant by profession, and Chairman of the Finco Group of Companies. He is an avid fan of wildlife and spends all his spare time travelling to wildlife parks in the country and abroad, and scuba-diving off the coasts of Sri Lanka. Once, knowing their mutual interest, I arranged for him to tour with a high-level diplomat at the United Nations, who was on an official visit to Sri Lanka. They both enjoyed each other's company, and the diplomat praised Sarath's knowledge and skills in their mutual pastime. We continue to enjoy and treasure our warm friendship with the Weerasooria family.

* * *

As usual, during the vacation between the second and third year of law school, we planned a tour. But this time it was rather a short one as we were all busy with one thing or another. Despite the fact that we were busy a quick trip over a long weekend, in the company of our usual traveling companions, was too enticing to pass. As always Vasu's *Austin Mini* was ready for our journey and so we set forth to Kandy.

Though I had been to Kandy with the Richmond College Cricket team to play with Kingswood College, I had never really come to know the place because previously we were on a regimented tour focused entirely on the cricket match. This time it was different, as the purpose was to visit and become acquainted with what the town had to offer. Kandy is a picturesque, historic town in the hill country at an elevation of 1500 ft with a salubrious climate. It is located 72 miles inland from Colombo, in the mountainous and thickly forested interior of the island, in between multiple mountain ranges (Knuckles and Hanthana), adjacent to the artificial Kandy Lake built in 1807.

In Kandy, we visited the home of The Temple of the Buddha's Tooth Relic *(Sri Dalada Maligawa)*, one of the most venerable places for the Buddhist community of Sri Lanka. The temple is part of the monumental ensemble of Kandyan architecture that was originally part of the royal palace complex of the Kandyan Kingdom, which is the last royal palace built on the island.

Kandy was declared a World Heritage Site by the UNESCO in 1988. Historical records suggest that Kandy was first established by the Vikramabahu III (1357–1374 CE), and named Senkadagalapura at the time. In Sinhalese, Kandy is called Maha Nuvara, meaning 'Great City' or 'Capital'. It is most often refered to as *Nuvara*. In 1592, Kandy became the capital city of the last remaining independent kingdom on the island after the coastal regions had been conquered by the Portuguese. Several invasions by the Portuguese and the Dutch (in 16th, 17th and 18th centuries) and later by the British (most notably in 1803) were repelled. The first time Sri Lanka fully fell into the hands of a foreign power was with the signing of the Kandyan Convention in

1815 at the Sri Dalada Maligawa. The King, Sriwickrama Rajasinha of Kandy, who was of South Indian ancestry, faced powerful opposition from the Sinhalese chieftains. The King sought to reduce their power. A successful coup was organized by the Sinhalese chieftains accepting the British King as their new King. This ended over 2500 years of rule by Sri Lankan monarchs. Rajasinha was taken as a royal prisoner by the British. He was removed to Vellore Fort in southern India, along with all claimants to the throne. By 2 March 1815 the island's sovereignty was under that of the British Empire. The treaty was not signed by the deposed King, but by members of his court and other dignitaries of the Kandyan Kingdom.

We also visited the only other remaining part of the Royal palace complex, which now houses the National Museum in Kandy. The museum holds an extensive collection of artifacts from both the Kandyan Kingdom and the British colonial rule.

Our next stop was at the Lankatilaka Temple, considered to be one of the best preserved examples of traditional Sinhalese temple architecture. Built on a rock on a scenic location, the temple is reached by a long line of steps carved into rock. A colossal seated image of the Buddha is within the inner sanctum where the walls are covered in ancient paintings. Among the other important temples, built mostly on the design of South Indian origin with a Devale (Hindu shrine), is Embakke Devale, which was also one of the places we visited on our tour.

The main attractions at Embakke are the intricate wooden carvings of the 14th century shrine dedicated to God Kataragama. Visitors to this and other shrines, like Natha Devale, could witness the Hindu religious customs although most of the worshippers today are Buddhists. It is not surprising that Hindu customs have influenced the Buddhist religious centers, because four of the last Sri Lankan kings were of south Indian origin.

Kandy is surrounded by many major Buddhist temples. On the shores of the lake are Malwaththa and Asgiri temples, the custodians of the Tooth Relic. Fine painted murals of Buddhist stories in these temple buildings are a good example of the arts in the Kandy period. Kandy is very popular due to the annual procession known as the 'Esala Perahera', in which one of the inner caskets used for covering the tooth relic of the Buddha is taken in a grand procession on a royal tusker (an elephant bearing tusks) through the streets of the city. The procession includes traditional dancers and drummers, flag-bearers of the provinces of the old Kandyan kingdom, the Nilames (lay custodians of temples and Devales) wearing their traditional dresses, torch-bearers and also the grandly attired elephants. This ceremony, which is annually held in the months of July or August, attracts large crowds from all parts of the country and also many foreign tourists. Though we did not see it on this particular trip, I have seen the perahera on several occasions in later years.

We also stopped to enjoy the splendors of the Peradeniya Gardens situated in the suburb of the city of Kandy, at Peradeniya (near the University of Ceylon, Peradeniya campus) which has over a million visitors per year. The 147- acre garden housing the national Herbarium is renowned for its collection of a variety of orchids. It includes more than 300 varieties of orchids, spices, medicinal plants and palms trees. The Commander of the Allied Forces in Southeast Asia, Earl Mountbatten, had his headquarters in the garden during the Second World War.

From Kandy we traveled further upcountry to Nuwara Eliya (the city of lights), in the central highlands of Sri Lanka with a picturesque landscape and a cool climate. Located at an altitude of 6,128 ft., the town is overlooked by Pidurutalagala, the tallest mountain in Sri Lanka (8281 ft). On the way, we made a brief stop to visit one of the several tea factories around Nuwara Eliya.

The tea lands, dating back to the days of British rule of this highland region, produce some of the world's finest Orange Pekoe tea.

The city of Nuwara Eliya was founded by Samuel Baker, the explorer of the Nile in 1846. Nuwara Eliya's climate lent itself to becoming the prime sanctuary of the British civil servants and planters in Ceylon. Nuwara Eliya, called Little England then, was also a hill country retreat where the British colonialists could engage in their pastimes such as fox, deer and elephant hunting, polo, golf and cricket, or boating and fishing on Lake Gregory. The town is a base for visitors to the Horton Plains National Park - a place we had no time to visit on this trip, though I did so in later years. This is a key wildlife area of open grassy woodland. The plains also have a well- visited tourist attraction at World's End, a sheer precipice with a 1,200 ft drop beyond the scenic Baker Falls.

Just outside Nuwara Eliya, we visited the famous Hindu Kovil (temple) and the Hakgala Botanical Gardens. Established in 1861 this is the second largest of the three botanical gardens in Sri Lanka. It is contiguous to the Hakgala Strict Nature Reserve. There are over 10,000 species of flora planted here and it is famous for a number of species of orchids and roses. The place finds mention in the Ramayana, an ancient Indian Sanskrit epic ascribed to the Hindu sage Valmiki, which says that the mighty Sri Lankan demon King Ravana, after kidnapping Sita, the queen of the Indian king Rama, kept her hidden at Hakgala, which was offered to Sita as a pleasure garden. The area was named as 'Sita Eliya' and the Hindu Temple called 'Seetha Kovil' (Hanuman Kovil) was built on the site.

As evening loomed we made our way toward Nanu Oya to stay overnight at my uncle Samarapala Amarasuriya's railway bungalow. He was then the District Railway Engineer with a spacious official bungalow situated on an attractive location near the railway station. He later became the General Manager of the Railway Department.

Though it was a short distance of less than 10 miles from the Nuwara Eliya town, the trip unexpectedly became a very treacherous one as thick mist set in. This is a common occurrence in the area at this altitude, but we had no experience of it before this. The headlights of the car were of no help. We parked off road and waited an hour, but to our dismay realized the mist was gradually getting worse. To add to our woes, darkness set in. We had no option but to try to crawl our way through. While Vasu was at the wheel Ana and I walked on either side of the car to make sure the vehicle did not fall over a precipice. After a couple of miles of trudging, thankfully, the mist dissipated enough for us to drive slowly to the town, thanking our stars that we were spared a night in the freezing cold.

When we arrived, Uncle Sam and his ever cheerful Bee Akka (Irangani) welcomed us with a fabulous dinner. Satisfied with the sumptuous meal and tired from the day's trip, we had a wonderful night's sleep.

Nanu Oya too was a sleepy town at the time. Before leaving we took a walk with Uncle Sam to the railway station. He explained that in 1885 the railroad from Colombo reached Nanu Oya, 5,300 feet above sea level. Haputale station is 25 miles past Nanu Oya and midway between the two; the line reaches what apparently is the highest elevation of any broad- gauge railroad in the world--6,226 feet at the summit. It was along that route that we traced our way back to Colombo the next day. We made a brief stop at Haputale to visit the now famed missionary house, which we were able to view only from the outside. Known as Adisham Bungalow, it was built in the 1920s for Sir Thomas Villiers, who had come to Ceylon in 1887. In the mid-1890s, he managed the Dumont Coffee Company, Brazil's largest coffee plantation. He returned to Ceylon, and by 1922 was chairman of the Ceylon Estates Proprietor's Association. He was knighted in 1933. Late in life he wrote *Mercantile Lore in Ceylon*, a study of the companies which had built the plantation economy. The elegant stone- block was modeled on Leeds Castle in Kent. To recreate his English lifestyle he added beautiful gardens and lawns amid the tropical surroundings. Adisham Bungalow, which later became a Benedictine monastery, is till known as such.

Our final stop was at the Bambarakanda Falls, the tallest waterfall in Sri Lanka with a height of 863 ft, located just a short distance interior from the road to Colombo.

* * *

Back in Colombo, the final academic year was spent as an apprentice at the legendary law firm of F.J. & G. De Sarams, mostly engaged in the subject of conveyancing. I worked along with my friend Jaffer, the only other apprentice that year in the prestigious law firm. But I had other important tasks to attend to as well. My top priority was to complete the Proctors final examination held at the end of that academic year in August 1962. I had completed the required courses for the exam in the third year of lectures at the Law College.

But, by then, my interest in law had changed from being a practicing lawyer in the court system to more academically- oriented pursuits. This was, I guess, partly because of the studies I had undertaken towards obtaining the University of London law degree. I had undertaken those studies possibly because of my changing attitude towards the practice of law. I realized that perhaps it would be advantageous to become an Advocate. I was aware that if I obtained a law degree that I was already pursuing, I would be eligible to sit for the Advocates exams. I set my goal at completing the Advocates examinations possibly in the following year.

Thus, I steered my ship changing directions according to the compass in my heart, determined to brave the storms and confident of success or at the most, of satisfaction, knowing at least I tried.

FOOTNOTE:

[1] As I was finishing this book my friend Gerry Deraniyagala's daughter, Sonali Deraniyagala, published a tragic account of the 2004 Tsunami that drowned her parents, husband and two children. It was entitled *Wave,* and was published by the well-known U.S. publisher Knopf, in early 2013. It made the prestigious New York Times Best Seller List. It is the second book written by a Sri Lankan author to be selected to the list. The only other was Michael Ondaatje's *English Patient.*

Chapter 21

Euphoria

When you are twenty-three with the whole world stretched out in front of you waiting to be conquered; no mountain seems impossible to climb, no river too difficult to cross. Thus, in early 1961, when the University of Ceylon, which hitherto had been a completely residential university, announced it would begin granting external degrees, I naturally set my sites on taking advantage of this opportunity.

It stipulated that those who had successfully completed the intermediate examination of the University of London would be allowed to register for the final examination of the Ceylon University, as long as at least a year had elapsed after registration. Having already completed the intermediate examination of the University of London (Inter-Laws), I promptly registered for the law degree (LL.B) of the University of Ceylon. This was with the hope of preparing and sitting for the exam, possibly in the year following my completion of my Proctors final and London University degree examinations.

This was no easy task as the Faculty of Laws at the University of Ceylon was a very exclusive and a particularly challenging domain. Every year no more than a dozen graduate from the law faculty. This was even less in the earlier years. While hundreds graduated from the other faculties, only a handful succeeded at law. Needless to, say the law faculty was considered a particularly demanding faculty to graduate from. The subjects had also to be approached from a very academic point of view, which is quite different to the practical approach taught at the Law College. Of course, I had already had some exposure to the academic approach when I read for my Inter-Laws examination of the University of London, an approach that appealed to me, and indeed, steered me away from being a practicing lawyer once finished with my Law College career.

I was now setting my sites on six final examinations, possibly within the two years - 1962 and 1963. A tall order, but perhaps in my naivety, I did not dwell on the difficulties that the plan presented, and simply began preparing for the tasks at hand, always buoyed by the results that I had obtained in my first and second exams at the Law College.

In much the same way I had done for the London exam, I thought of getting the assistance of a senior person from the University of Ceylon to prepare for that exam. With the pleasant experience with Nimal, without any hesitation I approached the person who, I thought, would be best to guide me. Mark Cooray had graduated with a first class honors degree the previous year, and was a junior member of the law faculty as a lecturer. I found my optimism was misplaced when he gave me a rude shock by telling me that obtaining a University of Ceylon law degree, particularly attempting to sit for the final exam without having followed the courses in person in the faculty, was a dream. He went on to say that the task was much more difficult than I could imagine, and that there was no way I could get through it, with the kind of practically-oriented training I had at the Law College. He advised me not even to try, unless I was ready to commit several years of preparation prior to sitting for the exam. He was rather certain of the advice he was giving me. Unfortunately he refused to part with any of his study notes.

Mark may have been right in his own assessment of the situation, but he was not aware of the extent of my commitment. I was naturally disappointed and was having second thoughts when I ran into my friend Wickrama Weerasooria, who had just graduated also with first class honors, and had joined the Law College to complete his Advocates' exams. On hearing of my encounter with Mark, he readily volunteered to lend me his lecture notes, and went on to encourage me. He too impressed upon me that it might be a hard grind.

I was lucky again to have Wickrama's notes that were equally immaculate and highlighted as was the case with Nimal's Cambridge notes. Mark went on to obtain doctorate degrees in law from University of Ceylon, Peradeniya, and Cambridge University. He later migrated to Australia and continued teacing law.

* * *

The incident with Mark happened on my first of many visits to the University of Ceylon and its law faculty located at the Peradeniya campus of the Ceylon University. University education had taken a long time to be introduced to Ceylon. By the end of the nineteenth century there was a well-developed secondary school system in the island, but only a few had the means to go abroad, to Britain or India, to pursue university education.

The first step in tertiary education was taken in the field of medical education with the establishment of the Ceylon Medical College in 1870, to be an 'elementary school' for Medical Assistants. It expanded rapidly, and by 1888 its Licentiate in Medicine and Surgery (LMS) was recognized by the General Medical Council of Great Britain. It became a medical school for fully-qualified medical practitioners. In 1874, a Council of Legal Education (later Law College) was formed to produce lawyers. In another development, a Technical College was established in Colombo in 1893 to train sub-professional engineering personnel.

The initiative and the sustained interest of an association under the leadership of Sir Ponnambalam Arunachalam led to the founding of the Ceylon University College on 1st January 1921 as a government institution at 'Regina Walawwa', Thurstan Road (now Cumaratunga Munidasa Mawata), Colombo,. It was renamed 'College House'. The Ceylon University College was granted recognition by the University of London to prepare students for Arts and Science external degrees. The staff consisted of five professors, three lecturers and four visiting lecturers, and the total student enrollment was 155. During its brief existence, the University College had produced 580 graduates of the University of London. According to an estimate prepared by the University of London in 1938, Ceylon had provided the largest quota of external students outside the United Kingdom.

Dr. Ivor Jennings (later Sir Ivor Jennings) arrived in Ceylon in March 1941 to assume duties as the second principal of the Ceylon University College. He stressed the urgent need to create a university in Colombo and then move it to Peradeniya, where by then the government had identified land for a future university. The university would be unitary, residential and autonomous, with its seat in Peradeniya, but until the buildings were ready it was to remain in Colombo. Dr. Jennings undertook the enormous task of establishing the university by amalgamating the Ceylon University College and the Medical College into a single unit and a residential and autonomous university was created on 1st July 1942.

The university established in 1942 changed its identity several times because of changing of its location and subsequent legislation. The first batch of students from the Departments of Law, Agriculture and Veterinary Science came into residence at Peradeniya in 1949. The major move took place on 6th October 1952, when the staff and the students of the Faculties of Arts and Oriental Studies, together with the library and the university administration, were transferred to Peradeniya.

By the time of my first visit to Peradeniya in 1961, a full- fledged university campus with faculties for most disciplines had come into being.[1] Located in a site that touches the lower slopes of the lush mountains of Hanthana, University of Ceylon, Peradeniya, is famous for its natural beauty. Its picturesque campus, known as the University Park, covers about 150 hectares occupied by buildings of the faculties, halls of residence, staff bungalows, playing fields and places of worship, surrounded by forest land.

There was a strict university rule that any student failing the first exam twice had to leave. It is noteworthy and interesting that several such seemingly unfortunate students, as well as some who failed to gain admission to the university in the first place, joined the Law College. There they later proved that their first failure was a blessing in disguise, for many went on to become successful lawyers, and serve their profession and the country well. A similar fate may have befallen me if I had not set my eyes quite early on being a lawyer. I left Richmond to join the Law College, particularly because I was paying scant attention to studies until I left Richmond, where I was wedded to sports and extracurricular activities. During my era, selections to the university were done with care and close attention to the individuals concerned. They were not judged mechanically by the scores one attained at the entrance exam, as has been the case since my days.

It was this careful scrutiny that enabled my cricketing-pal D.H. De Silva, cricket captain of Mahinda College, to be selected for admission, although he was able to secure a pass only in one of the four subjects offered at the entrance exam. Same was true in the case of Douglas Gunawardane, who captained the Richmond cricket team, under whom I played. He too was selected although had two passes. They both performed well at the oral interview following the exam. D.H. went on to captain the university cricket team and play on the national team. He became the Charity Commissioner of the Municipality of Colombo before he retired. Douglas regretfully suffered from spells of depression and met with a tragic death at a young age. Even considering such exceptional possibilities, there would have been the distinct possibility of others, like me, who were not nerds in school, of not being chosen.

As for me, a serendipitous chance came my way to kill two birds in one stone, when the Faculty of Law announced that it would grant LL.B degrees to external candidates beginning in 1961.

* * *

The Faculty of Law dates back to the Department of Law established in July 1947 under the Faculty of Arts. It was then located in 'College House' pending its transfer to Peradeniya, on completion of the necessary buildings at the new site. With the construction of a part of the buildings, the Department of Law was shifted to Peradeniya in 1950, where the first law degrees were awarded. However, the Department of Law was brought back to its original place when it was transferred to the University of Ceylon, Colombo in 1965. It continued to be under the Faculty of Arts till 1967 when it was upgraded to become the first and only Faculty of Law in the university system, a position it continues to enjoy to this day.

Sir Ivor Jennings, the founder Vice Chancellor of the University of Ceylon, was a renowned constitutional law expert. He was an advisor to the government of the first Prime Minister of independent Ceylon, D.S. Senanayake, in drafting the Independence Constitution of Ceylon. Sir Ivor Jennings was also the Lecturer on Constitutional Law for law students in the University of Ceylon. The other lecturers included Justice Soertsz Q.C., Dr. H. W. Tambiah and Professor T. Nadaraja. Prof Nadaraja was the Dean of the Faculty of Law when I registered in the faculty in 1961.

The first batch of four students was selected from those who had passed the First Examination in Arts, and they went on to do a further three years of law studies and qualified for Bachelor of Laws degrees. Those who obtained the LL.B degree from the University of Ceylon were permitted to sit for the then Final Examination for enrollment as an advocate (now attorney-at-law) of the Supreme Court of Ceylon conducted by the Ceylon Law College.

Among the leading lights produced by the Law Faculty were the pioneers who entered the university at its inception. I have had the privilege of knowing them beginning with R.K.W. (Rajah) Goonesekere from the first batch of students in the Law Faculty. He became a legendary lecturer in law in the faculty, loved and admired by all his students. He was appointed as the principal of the Law College where he had a successful tenure introducing innovative changes to the curriculum and teaching practices. He later became a practicing lawyer in the Metropolitan Bar, and is considered one of the foremost constitutional and human rights law experts whose advice was sought by successive governments.

Then there was Dr. H.L. De Silva, who also became an authority on constitutional law and commanded a rollicking practice in the courts throughout the country. He later served as the Ambassador to the United Nations in New York, where I had the privilege of meeting him.

Among the other two from that early batch were Felix Dias Bandaranaike, who served as Minister of Finance, Minister of Justice, Minister of Public Administration and Parliamentary Secretary for the Prime Minister and Defense and External Affairs (de-facto foreign minister), in successive governments. He was very active in defeating two major coups against the government that he served. One was the attempted military coup in 1962 and the other, the JVP's 1971 Insurrection.

The other classmate was his close friend John De Saram, an Olympian, who after an illustrious career as a preeminent lawyer at the United Nations, became Ambassador to the UN. From time to time I had heard a few stories about Felix from John. John's stories were always full of praise of Felix's work and I got to know of his outstanding abilities. John had joined the United Nations Legal Department just a few years before me after completing his graduate studies from Yale University in the United States. He had an outstanding legal mind with excellent political sense, a combination that is certain to provide success in the U.N. environment. If there ever was a perfectionist in drafting, he was the one.

John went on to become the Deputy Director of the Legal Division and Director of the Treaty and Codification Division with responsibilities for the United Nations International Law Commission (ILC), the premier lawmaking body of the U.N. Later on, after his retirement from the U.N. he served as the Ambassador for Sri Lanka to the United Nations. We interacted with each other servicing the U.N. Legal Committee dealing with Outer Space Matters. For many years, we spent several weeks together in Geneva, Switzerland, as the committee used to meet annually for a month in Geneva. We became friends and often spent our coffee-breaks chatting about affairs at the U.N and back home. For several years, we lived near each other in Parkway Village (a U.N. enclave), in New York City, and used to carpool to work together. He was married to Flavia, a very soft-spoken and kind-hearted person and they had one daughter (Ann). John and Flavia now live in Baltimore near their daughter and enjoy being with their grandchildren. We have kept in contact to date, and I value his advice when needed.

John has told me "Felix and I were together in Royal College and sat for what was then known as the 'university entrance examination'. We both got 'exhibitions' (which meant that we both got Rs 10 each month and spent it on lovely small bottles of the then imported beer - 'Becks', I think) and used to saunter off to various places and enjoy our 'exhibitions'. We both decided to enter what was then known as the 'Law Faculty'. I had a place in Oxford, having sat for the London Matriculation earlier, and having learned sufficient French from a lady who was one of the few in Colombo who knew French. But Felix (I was his bestman when he married Lakshmi, another later graduate of the Law Faculty) persuaded me that if I was going to practice law in Ceylon, there was no point learning U.K. law. So, instead of going on to Oxford I went into the Law Faculty with him".

I met Felix on his many visits to the United Nations and admired both his intellect and eloquence. He displayed an air of arrogance that perhaps was not intentional. I got to know more about him from my friend Nihal Jayawickrama, who was a close associate of Felix. Nihal was a much later graduate of the Law Faculty, who at the very young age of thirty-something, was Secretary of the Ministry of Justice and Acting Attorney General when Felix was Minister of Justice. Nihal used to relate many stories about the happenings in the inner-circle of the Ministry. He told me that the head of an autonomous institution in the legal field once declined to provide Felix with information that he required to answer a question in parliament. Felix was furious since the question related to a raging controversy at the time. The head had also previously ignored a request made by Felix to refrain from making certain vital changes in the institution until he had finalized his reform program. Although rebuffed in this manner, Felix decided not to retaliate at that stage. He advised Nihal that in a situation such as that, however humiliating, one should not immediately declare war. The attack should be launched only when one is fully armed and ready, and the enemy is vulnerable. Sometime later, Felix used his legislative authority to bring that institution under the control of the ministry. About a year later, when he unexpectedly spotted a chink in the enemy's armor, he launched his attack on the head of that institution. This was advice that stuck in my memory which I always tried to follow. It invariably works!

I have also been fortunate enough to know several of the other distinguished graduates of the Law Faculty. I have already noted my close association with Norman and Wickrama Weerasooria. Dr, Hiran Jayawardene, son of the distinguished Queen's Counsel H.W. Jayawardene, brother of the former Prime Minister and President J.R. Jayawardene, was one such close friend. I first met him soon after he had obtained a Doctorate degree in international law from Cambridge University working on a book based on his seminal thesis on Law of the Sea. This was when he came to New York as a member of the Sri Lanka delegation to the United Nations Law of the Sea Conference. Over the years he played a decisive role in drafting of the U.N. Law of the Sea Convention along with Chris Pinto. In doing so, he concentrated on securing the rights of small islands such as Sri Lanka, and ensuring ways and means for developing countries to benefit from ocean resources. It was those efforts that culminated in establishing and expanding an Exclusive Economic Zone (EEZ) beyond the limits of traditional territorial waters.

Not long after this, Hiran single-handedly established a national organization in Sri Lanka in 1981, for the management, conservation and development of aquatic resources, The National Aquatic Resources Research and Development Agency (NARA). He has been serving as its Chairman since its inception.

He then played a critical role, being almost the sole initiator for the establishment in 1986 of an international organization known as the

Indian Ocean Marine Corporation (IOMAC). IOMAC's mission is to protect and develop the ocean resources of the coastal states of Asia and Africa abutting the Indian Ocean. Dr. Hiran Jayawardene was elected as the founding Secretary General of IOMAC. Through these organizations he has been instrumental in expanding the utilization of the ocean resources of Sri Lanka and other countries of the region, while preserving and developing the coastal environment.

Hiran has played a leading role in other international ocean resource organizations, such as the Indian Ocean Tuna Commission, through which he ensured Sri Lanka's fishing interest in tuna, while protecting tuna as an endangered species through over-fishing in the region. He has actively participated in the International Oceanography Commission (IOC), the premier organization for ocean management, and other United Nations related agencies dealing with ocean resources and coastal management.

Remote sensing technology using satellites has become an indispensable tool in ocean and coastal management. I had worked closely with Hiran providing whatever assistance I could through the United Nations, particularly in educating and training of personnel in remote sensing technology for ocean resources and coastal management. At his invitation, I organized U.N. regional meetings under the auspicious of both NARA and IOMAC in Sri Lanka and other countries of the region. The U.N. also provided assistance for personnel from Sri Lanka to participate in international programs conducted by the U.N. and other national and international agencies.

Similarly, on his invitation, I represented the U.N. at IOMAC policy making conferences. He also was the initiator of an academic journal of significance. The *Journal of the National Aquatic Agency* has published more than fifty volumes. At his request, I was happy to have contributed to its Volume 3 an article in 1984 entitled "Remote Sensing of the Oceans from Space with Special Reference to Marine Resources". Hiran continues with his good work both at national and international levels shuttling between Australia and Sri Lanka. I am happy to have met him in Colombo on a very recent visit, when we briefly reminiscenced about our joint cooperation in the years past.

I first met Lakshman Kadirgamar, another distinguished graduate of the Law Faculty, when I sought an article for publication in *The Ceylon Law College Review* which I edited. The next time I met him was in Geneva. He was an official of the World Intellectual Property Organization (WIPO), and we met during my visits to U.N. meetings at the U.N. European Headquarters in Geneva. He became a senior official of WIPO before he retired and moved back to Colombo. He was a brilliant man, who had been the President of the Oxford Union. Once he moved back to Colombo he entered private practice and soon was nominated as a member of parliament and appointed Minister of Foreign Affairs. He distinguished himself in that capacity displaying his eloquence at the U.N. General Assembly, and other numerous international gatherings, that brought him admiration and appreciation of world leaders. I had visited him at his residence twice during my visits to Colombo. On the latter occasion, knowing of my impending retirement from the U.N., he inquired of my plans and whether I had any interest in an appointment in the Foreign Service of Sri Lanka, if the opportunity were to present itself. Not too long after that he was gunned down by the LTTE leaving a great void in the administrative service of the country.

A similar fate was to befall Neelan Tiruchelvam, yet another distinguished graduate of the Law Faculty, who was an outstanding academic and constitutional expert whom I had met in the company of my friend T.D.S.A. Dissanayake, who later became Ambassador to Indonesia, on a visit to New York, while they were at Harvard University.

The third Minster of Foreign Affairs, the Law Faculty produced, is G.L. Pieris - a brilliant academic who was Dean of the Law Faculty before he moved to the political arena. I had first met him when he was a lecturer in the Law Faculty. He occupied the downstairs apartment on Park Road, when his brother-in- law and my friend Nihal Jayawickrama and his wife Sarojini (Saro) occupied the upstairs apartment. I used to be a frequent visitor there whenever I was in Colombo. Saro's sister Savitri, married to G.L. Pieris, was a classmate of my wife at Visakha. Their elder sister was married to Ranjith Salgado, who was a senior official in the World Bank. I came to know them while they were in Washington. They lived across from G.L. Pieris on Park Road in Colombo. Pieris was a senior lecturer in the Law Faculty at the time. Much later I met him officially during a visit to Colombo accompanying the Director General of the United Nations. I have always admired his intellect, not only as an academic, but also as a diplomat during his visits to the U.N. and the United States during trying times for our country emerging from a long terrorist war. His negotiations at the time with Secretary of State, Hilary Clinton, may have been facilitated by the fact that he was a classmate of former U.S. President Bill Clinton at Oxford when he was a Rhodes Scholar there.

Of others from the Law Faculty, I have known Ranjith Abeysooria from his young days in Galle. His family lived near Richmond College. His father Dr. Fred Abeysooria was the leading physician in Galle during my student days at Richmond. I remember being taken to him on several occasions as a youngster whenever I was ill. The medication he prescribed was always some powder in a packet to be taken mixed in water. To me it was the bitterest medicine on earth that one could ever concoct. Though a very friendly and kind man, I hated visiting his clinic facing the canal by the Galle Railway Station. Ranjith's brother captained Wesley College cricket team while I captained the Richmond team. We played opposite each other for a few years. Ranjith married Indrani Amarasuriya, a relative of my step mother and a cousin of Saro. Ranjith had a successful career in the Attorney General's Department and rose to become the Director of Public Prosecution, the highest-ranking office for criminal matters. Later he started his own practice at the Colombo Bar and remains as one of the leading counsels in Sri Lanka.

There were three Amarasinghes who graduated from the Law Faculty. They distinguished themselves in different fields. I had known A.R.B. (Ranjith) Amarasinghe, who played with me in the

Law College cricket team. He went on to have a varied career ranging from academics, commercial enterprises, international organization consultant, Secretary Ministry of Justice, Head of the Law Reform Commission and Acting Chief Justice. C.F. Amarasinghe was a Legal Adviser in the World Bank in Washington, where I met him. I admired his work, particularly his expertise in the Administrative Law of International Organizations, on which he has written an authoritative book. The Third was Priya Amarasinghe, who was in the batch that I graduated with. He had a successful career at the Asian Development Bank becoming Secretary to the Board, one of the highest-level staff positions. I had met him only occasionally after graduation and that was during his brief visits to his uncle Shirley Amarasinghe, who at the time was the Ambassador to the U.N.

Then there was Faisz Musthapha, who graduated in the same batch as I did from the Faculty of Law, University of Ceylon, Peradeniya. He worked on the civil cases in the Attorney General's Department rising up to be the Deputy Solicitor General. Later he was Ambassador to the United Kingdom. I met him from time to time, including during his visit to the United Nations representing the Government of Sri Lanka.

In our graduating batch of fifteen at the Law Faculty were some who remained close friends, like I. S. De Silva, a highly regarded senior member of the legal community, Lalith Weeratunge, who migrated to Canada, and Mark Fernando, who was the only one to graduate that year with a First Class Honors degree in Law. Without doubt he was a brilliant lawyer and scholar just like his father H.N.G. Fernando who was a Chief Justice of Sri Lanka. H.N.G. used to live in very close proximity to the Law College Hostel. He resented the noise that emanated time to time from somewhat rowdy parties late into the night at the hostel. Normally he would telephone and complain to the Warden, Wagissa Perera, but on one occasion in the absence of the Warden, he decided to come and admonish us himself. Knowing that he was on the way, everyone retired to their rooms. The first room that he walked into happened to be the room of Kandiah, who after consuming an ample amount of the local brew – Arrack, had taken off his clothes to escape from the inner heat of the alcohol and the outer heat of the muggy Colombo nights. H.N.G. a prim and proper gentleman was so embarrassed; he turned around and made a quick exit to the great amusement of the hostellers. Mark was a chip off the old block, as far as his demeanor was concerned, and the great heights to which he rose as a judge of the Supreme Court. Regretfully, he was not able to reach his father's position as Chief Justice, because when his due turn arrived, for political reasons, he was bypassed and a judge junior to him was appointed as Chief Justice.

Of the rest, I already alluded to my experience with Mark Cooray, who had graduated a year before us. He went on to become a lecturer at the McConnell University in Sydney. I also knew Nirmala Chandrahasan before her marriage to Chandrahasan Chelvanayagam, son of S.J.V. Chelvanayakam Q.C., long serving member of parliament, and leader of the Federal Party. Before her marriage she was Nirmala Naganathan, daughter of a prominent member of parliament, Dr. E.M.V Naganathan, a physician. She joined the Law Faculty as a lecturer. I also knew her sister Lakshmi Naganthan who had a distinguished career in the Foreign Service and retired from the position of Ambassador to Germany. The rest of the Law Faculty graduates who distinghished themselves were mostly junior to me and only a few of them were passing acquaintances.

* * *

With modest beginnings with less than half a dozen students to about a dozen and a half during my time in the early 1960s, the faculty has grown now to accommodate nearly 200 students. A major expansion took place in the 1970s. The curriculum of the Law degree spanned three years and was taught in the English language from its inception. However, in 1971, the medium of instruction was expanded to include the teaching of Law in Sinhala and Tamil as well. From its commencement in 1947, law degree course was a three year program. It was extended to a four year program in 1981. The Administration introduced many new Law subjects in

353

the curriculum. This was a major revision which took place after ten years of teaching in the national languages. I am most pleased to note that more recently, the Faculty of Law has also expanded the breath of its curriculum with the introduction of a Department of Public and International Law and a Department of Private and Comparative Law. These subjects were not covered in any depth during my time. The Faculty of Law now also has the Master of Law, earned by research, and a PhD program. The Master of Law, program commenced in the late 1970s. These were very encouraging developments.

From 1961, the Faculty of Law introduced the LL.B degree for external candidates; however, it ceased to entertain new registration after 1985. I was fortunate to be the first registrant as an external candidate in the Faculty of Law in 1961.

I made frequent visits to Peradeniya to use the library and get other assistance. At the time it was almost a fully residential campus. I made my ventures to this hallowed place with feelings of awe. The beauty of the campus, which is as attractive as any campus in the world, overwhelmes one with its spacious environs full of fauna and flora and winding roads and walkways abutting the majestic Mahaweli river. The campus includes what was dubbed the 'Lovers' Lane'. Kandyan architecture, along with a sprinkling of the reproductions of ancient masterpieces from the Anuradhapua and Pollonaruwa periods, make it a truly imposing campus.

Sadly, it later took a downward spiral with the explosion of the numbers of students, for which the campus was not designed. The University at Peradeniya was originally planned to provide full residential facilities for the entire student body, as well as accommodation for members of the staff. This was the case when I used to spend time there during my visits in the early 60s. But the residential requirement has since been relaxed because of the increase in the intake of students in recent years. The student body of about 1,800 during my days has ballooned to nearly 9,000 now.

The once majestic campus has long past seen its best days. Because of the changing nature of the student body, from mostly elitists schools in metropolitan towns, to a new wave of students from the rural and economically-deprived areas, campus facilities were overwhelmed and lost its charm.

In the prcess it became a crowded facility that is badly in need of a complete resurrection. The Peradeniya University today is a reflection of continuity and change observable in Sri Lankan society, economy and polity.

To its credit, amidst the changes, the university has survived with some of its spirit intact. The 1950s and the early 1960s are generally considered the best years of the Peradeniya campus in many respects, when it was an orderly campus with very high standards of academic excellence. The Vice Chancellor, Sir Nicholas Attygalle, a no-nonsense educator of highest repute, led the university during that golden age. Legends of Sri Lankan academic world, such as Prof. Ediriweera. Sarathchandra, Prof. Gananath Obeysekara, Prof. Ashley Halpe, Prof. F.R. Jayasuriya, and Prof. T. Nadaraja dominated a faculty that was full of renowned scholars.

A wide range of community activities were available in abundance to complement the academic program, activities such as sports, literary and cultural events. It was during this golden era that Peradeniya gave birth to not only world- class research work and exceptional literary works, but also the revival of the Sinhala drama. Professor Ediriweera Sarathchandra's historic productions of 'Maname' and other dance dramas were first staged at the open air theater in the campus with a cast of university students.

The vicinity of the campus also provided an ideal spot for those who were romantically inclined. The mist covered Hantana hills became the regular haunt of young lovers from the university. As the years went by the place came to be romanticized by Sinhala lyricists and novelists. Many found wedded bliss from campus romances. One such shining union brought together my friend Nihal Jayawickrama

355

and his lifelong companion Saro (nee Amarasuriya). On hearing of the romance her parents contacted the Vice Chancellor, who admonished the two undergraduates never to be seen on campus together or risk expulsion from the university.

No attempts at such warnings deterred those who were determined, and so like Nihal and Saro, many not only found ways and means of continuing those romances, but also ensuring that they ended up as life partners.

The halls of residence in the campus included Jayatilleke, Arunachalam, Akbar, Marrs, Marcus Fernando, Jayatilake, James Peiris, Ramanathan, Hilda Obeysekere and Sanghamitta – named after well-known historical, social and political figures. Marrs Hall was named after the first principal of the University College, Colombo, and precursor to the Peradeniya University. During my visits to the campus I stayed at Marcus Fernando Hall, where my friend and classmates from Richmond College, Punya Illeperuma and Tissa Weerasinghe were sharing a room. I was fortunate as their guest to enjoy the meals served in the dining hall. I also enjoyed the company of their friends with some of whom I continued my friendships long after the campus days. I had several other friends, in other halls of residence particularly those I knew from school days in Galle. For instance, in Ramanathan, one of the largest men's halls, I had my friends Hema Perera, Namel Weeramuni, Wickrama Weerasooria and others, through whom I came to know several friends of theirs.

Although I was happy to have shared some of the atmosphere and life in the campus, during my many such transitory visits, I know that my friends were greatly enriched by their campus life, to which I only had a fleeting exposure. Most of my friends did not experience a student's life in the metropolitan city of Colombo and Law College in environs of the judicial center of the country. I am glad I had some of both.

*　*　*

The Peradeniya campus in those days witnessed tranquility with some sporadic disturbances of political nature. Some disturbances were almost comical and were readily handled by the authorities. The Vice Chancellor ruled with an iron fist. In later years, the campus has seen many upheavals leading even to the closure of the campus for long periods following the increase in the acceptance of students during the mid- sixties, which generated the dastardly violence of the 1980s.

Unlike the Law College, where there were no political activity, nor party-affiliated clubs and societies, the Peradeniya campus was full of such activity. Most of the students were either Trotskyites (LSSP) or Stalinists (CP), and only a handful was identified as capitalist or UNP supporters of the right wing United National Party. Though party politics were quite prevalent in the campus, they were carried out in good spirit enriching one's overall education. There were very few strikes and other political disturbances, unlike in later years, which resulted even in murder and leading to the closure of the campus for inordinately long periods. Some of these riots had national repercussions.

While I was quite interested in national and international political developments, there was precious little time to pay any serious attention to them. However, I did find time take part in one protest, the only political activity that I participated in. That was during the period of the Bay of Pigs and Cuban Missile Crisis, when there were protest marches organized mainly by the socialist-oriented political parties and trade unions. Along with a mass of people I joined Vasu and some law college friends in a couple of protest marches and demonstrations in front of the American Embassy in 1962.

These protests were the result of the developments in far- away Cuba, a small island like my homeland. Cuba in 1950's was lead by a right-wing dictator named Batista. He dealt with opponents with extreme harshness and while a few prospered under his regime, many Cubans were very poor. Batista was not tolerant of Communists and received the support of the Americans.

Batista's sole support within Cuba came from the Army, which was equipped by the Americans. By 1959, the rebels lead by Fidel Castro felt strong enough to overthrow the Government of Batista. This they easily achieved as they were aided by popular support. Castro's first task was to punish those who had abused the poor. Those found guilty were executed. He then nationalized all American firms in Cuba so that their wealth would be invested in Cuba itself rather than leave the island and go to multinationals in America. The money made from this measure was primarily spent on a national health system so that all medical treatment was free as well as on education. Castro also introduced major land reforms Some Cubans fled and to Florida. These Cuban exiles were treated by some Americans as heroes. They brought with them stories that outraged the American press. Most were false or exaggerated but this fact was ignored. America reacted by refusing to do any trade with Cuba whatsoever. This trade embargo would have bankrupted the island as her biggest money-earner was exporting sugar to America. Up to this time, there is little evidence that Castro, or Cuba had any real intention of teaming up with Communist Russia. In 1960, Castro referred to himself as a socialist - not a Communist. However, the trade embargo brought the two together as Russia stepped in to buy Cuba's sugar and other exports. Now, with a supporter of Communism less than 100 miles from Florida, the new American president, John F Kennedy, decided to give support to the anti-Castro Cubans who had gone to Florida. With CIA funding, a group of armed Cuban exiles tried to land in Cuba at the Bay of Pigs in 1961, with the sole intention of overthrowing the Castro Government. It proved a fiasco, jeeps landed without fuel; they had no maps of the island; Cuban exiles fired on Cuban exiles.

After the Bay of Pigs fiasco, Cuba obviously felt threatened by her massively powerful neighbor. Castro started to look for a closer relationship with Russia which could offer her protection. In September 1962, anti-Castro Cuban refugees reported to the CIA that there was a build-up of Russian bases in Cuba. While this was happening USA Intelligence reported that over 20 Russian ships were heading for Cuba with 42 medium-range missiles and 24 intermediate-range missiles capable of carrying nuclear payloads. These missiles had a range of 3,500 miles, while Cuba was only 90 miles off the coast of the United States. 22,000 Russian troops and technicians accompanied the missiles. U2 reconnaissance photographs showed that the bases would be fully operational in a few days, at the latest by the end of October. The threat to the USA was very obvious. On October 27th the matter was made worse when a U2 was shot down by a Russian missile and the pilot killed.

The United States considered attacking Cuba via air and sea, and settled on a military quarantine (blockade) of Cuba. The U.S. announced that it would not permit offensive weapons to be delivered to Cuba and demanded that the Soviets dismantle the missile bases already under construction or completed in Cuba, and remove all offensive weapons. Premier Nikita Khrushchev wrote in a letter to Kennedy that his quarantine of "navigation in international waters and air space constituted an act of aggression propelling humanity into the abyss of a world nuclear-missile war."

The Soviets publicly balked at the U.S. demands, but in secret back-channel communications initiated a proposal to resolve the crisis. The confrontation ended on October 28, 1962, when President John F. Kennedy and United Nations Secretary-General U Thant reached a public and secret agreement with Khrushchev. Publicly, the Soviets would dismantle their offensive weapons in Cuba and return them to the Soviet Union, subject to United Nations verification, in exchange for a U.S. public declaration and agreement never to invade Cuba. Secretly, the U.S. agreed that it would dismantle missiles recently installed in Turkey. A month later, the Soviets had dismantled and shipped back the missiles and the quarantine was formally ended. An additional outcome of the negotiations was the creation of the Hotline Agreement creating a direct communications link between Moscow and Washington.

Just one year later in 1963, both nations signed the Nuclear Test Ban Treaty. This multilateral treaty, signed later by over 100 countries, stated that neither would explode nuclear bombs during testing in the atmosphere. This was a popular treaty in America and a sign that something positive had come out of the Cuban Crisis – each having greater respect for the other.

*   *   *

While I followed those developments with keen interest, soon enough, the decisive year of 1962 rolled in, and I found myself deeply involved in preparing for three final exams: LL.B of the University of Ceylon in April, LL.B of the University of London in June, and Proctors Finals of the Ceylon Law College in August.

My Law College friends and colleagues including those at the Law hostel were equally engrossed in their studies, even though they were only preparing themselves for one of the exams to be held at the Law College in August of that year. My batchmates were of course making an extra effort to complete the final hurdle after four years of student life at Law College and become a fully-fledged proctor or an advocate. Those who were bright were trying their best to secure First Class Honors, and others, who were not so gifted, were trying hard just to pass the exams. The atmosphere was therefore very conducive to committed work over long hours.

Not everyone knew of my plans, though most had a vague idea that I was studying for more than one exam, because self- doubt kept me from revealing my plans in detail. Of those few who knew the details, some were extremely supportive and others were somewhat skeptical of such an undertaking; but because of my performances in the previous years, no one openly discouraged me in any manner.

First of the three final exams was that of the University of Ceylon. In preparation, I was reading mostly subjects that either I had already read, or was reading for the other two pending exams as well. However, there was a fundamental difference that made them practically new to me. This was because the subjects I read for Law College exams were practically-oriented and were not approached in an academic sense. Similarly, where the subjects I read for the

London exam had the same academic approach, the substance of the laws and cases involved were quite different from those of the local laws that were the object of study for the University of Ceylon exam.

As April approached I took residence at my Cousin Dayananda's wife's home in the campus at Peradeniya. Dr. Lily De Silva (Lily Akka), being a senior lecturer in Buddhist philosophy, was provided with a university bungalow within the campus premises, on the Hantana Hills. That bungalow was spacious and was surrounded by a beautiful garden, which had a green lawn, from where there was a view of the nearby hills. Thus Lily Akka's Peradeniya bungalow was an ideal place of tranquility to prepare for the exam. I was provided with meals as Akka had a household help for cooking and cleaning while the garden was maintained by the university staff. I was so well cared for that Akka made certain to give me a flask of coffee every night before she retired, so if I were to burn the midnight candle or rise before the sun, I had the necessary energizer to get on with my work.

As the exam approached a certain amount of panic descended on me because I had not experienced any of the university exams, and more so, because of the extremely high reputation of the university, particularly the Law Faculty. I also had the knowledge of the brilliant set of students with a reputation as high achievers who were sitting for the exam with me. After the first paper I was somewhat relieved knowing that at least I was able to handle it reasonably well. As time passed, with each subject I became more relaxed. At the end of the exam I left for Colombo with gratitude towards Lily Akka for her hospitality and support, but with trepidation as to what my results would be.

Back in Colombo I had little time to relax before getting down to the final preparations for the University of London exam, which was scheduled in two months. I was of course somewhat more relaxed about it, because I had passed the Intermediate Exam and was confident of what was expected, although I was not completely certain I had read all that was required. The exam came and went uneventfully in June.

Once this was over, I immediately had to settle down to prepare for what I considered my primary objective for the year 1962: successfully completing the final examination to be held in August for the admission to the Bar as a Proctor of the Supreme Court of the country. By then, panic had set in throughout the Law hostel. Many were at the edge of their nerves.

Since returning from Peradeniya, I spent most of the day either at the Law College Library or at the Colombo Public Library. The Colombo Library was located almost walking distance from the Law Colllege Hostel on Green Path next to the Victoria Gardens. Walking across the gardens from Barnes place, where the law hostel was situated, to the other end of the park, one could reach the Public Library. The walk to and from the library across the park was very pleasant and provided most of the exercise and relaxation that I got during those heady days. My reason to spend the time in the libraries was most reference material was not otherwise available. We continued the drudgery of study at night. My roommate Aelian and I had similar study habits. It worked out well when we retired simultaneously for a few hours of badly-needed sleep.

August came and the exam was over before we knew it. Everyone was elated that it was done. Though anxiety about the results was to return in due course, no one cared just then, whether they were successful or not. Everyone was happy that it was all over at last.

In due course, the results of the exams arrived. Results of the Ceylon University LL.B exam were published in the *Ceylon Daily News* in mid-1962. To my greatest delight I happened to be the first of two external candidates to receive the LL.B degree from the University of Ceylon (Peradeniya Campus), thus earning the first external degree of the University of Ceylon. There were twelve internal candidates who graduated, with one First Class awarded to Mark Fernando, who went on to become an Acting Chief Justice of the Supreme Court before his retirement.

University of London results were published in the *Ceylon Daily News* later the same year. I was thrilled that I was lucky enough to be the first among the half a dozen or so successful candidates who passed the final exam for the LL.B. degree. By the time the Proctors final results were posted, on the basis of my law degrees, I had already been offered a position in the prestigious law firm of Julius and Creasy in Colombo. I was offered the princely sum of Rs. 650, which at the time was considered an attractive one, considering the coveted post of crown counsel in the star institution of the government, the Attorney General's Department, was paid Rs. 750.

The sweet bliss of success was upon me. Having felt throbbing within me the power to scale the hurdles I had set for myself, and having scaled them as well as it could possibly be done, I doubt that anyone would begrudge my belief that I genuinely earned this sense of immense satisfaction.

FOOTNOTE:

[1] During the decade of 1954 to 1964 new Departments of Science, Medicine and Engineering were started in Peradeniya and a new Arts Faculty was started in Colombo. In 1967, in order to cater to the increasing demand for higher education, the University of Ceylon which had existed as two campuses (Peradeniya and Colombo) of the single University of Ceylon, was divided into two Universities: University of Ceylon Colombo and University of Ceylon Peradeniya as separate entities. In 1972 they were again amalgamated as one university – University of Sri Lanka, with five campuses with the addition of Vidyodaya and Vidyalankara, for Oriental and Buddhist Studies and the Ceylon College of Technology, Katubedda, for Engineering. Since 1978, they all became independent Universities. Still later, two other universities have been established (University of the South-Ruhuna and University of the East; while Vidyodaya became University of Sri Jayawardanapura, and Vidyalankara became University of Kelaniya).

— ❖ —

Part 4

Westward Bound

"Life is either a daring experience or nothing at all"

– Helen Keller (Open Door)

Chapter 22

Fortune Favors the Brave

In December of 1962 I embarked on the biggest and last challenge in my life as a law student. Having completed the LL.B final exam of the University of Peradeniya in April of that year, the LL.B final exam of the University of London in June, the Proctors' Final exam of the Law College in August, I decided to sit for all three exams required to be an advocate (preliminary, intermediate and final) in one sitting in December of the same year.

Hardly three months remained before the exam. Luckily, with several exemptions I received for subjects I had passed which were common to both proctors and advocates exams, I was able to limit the number of total subjects to be taken for the three combined exams. Of the rest, I had studied some of the subjects either for the University of Ceylon or University of London LL.B degree exams. Of course, their content varied to some extent. Where the content was somewhat similar, the methods of approach for the exams were quite different. University exams emphasized an academic approach, while the Law College exams had a practical approach.

There were also a couple of subjects that were not offered by me for any of the previous exams. 'Digest' is a subject taught in the first year, and 'Voet' in the final year only to students registered to qualify as advocates. They were two archaic subjects taught by a leading practitioner, A.H.M Ismail, which had to be studied in Latin, which forms the basis of Roman Dutch Law. It was considered important to know Latin to understand the full import of the Roman Dutch

367

Law concepts. The subject "Voet" was named after Johannes Voet, the great Dutch jurist who was a professor at Utrecht University and Leiden University in Holland. The most famous work of Voet is his *Commentarius ad Pandectas* expounding legal humanism, and it still is an important source of law for the South-African system of Law, which is Roman Dutch Law similar to that in Sri Lanka. Voet and Digest are subjects that lend themselves more to cramming, rather than understanding. It was a difficult task to learn the concepts, written in a dead foreign language, particularly at short notice. Fortunately, in those young days I was endowed with a photographic memory. Cramming came somewhat more naturally to me than to some others who were endowed with more incisive minds.

The whole project was a greater challenge because by then I was starting my first legal appointment at the Julius and Creasy Law Firm. Popularly known as J&C it was one of the two most prestigious Law Firms in the country. The other was F.J. & G De Sarams, which was where I had apprenticed.

Julius & Creasy was established in 1879. After 125 years, it is the largest and second oldest law firm in Sri Lanka. Its reputation has been built on rich tradition, as well as the caliber of the professionals passing through its corridors. Harry Creasy was the son of Sir Edward Creasy, who was at one time Chief Justice of Ceylon and a member of the legislature. V.A. Julius, then Senior Partner of the firm, worked long and hard hours along with Harry Creasy. They carried out their functions and duties with meticulous care and detail. In a few years their reputation for honesty, integrity, industry and precision grew to such an extent that they were respected unfailingly throughout the business and civil communities, as well as, by the government of the day. History records that despite being Englishmen, the two founding partners showed a deep attachment to their adopted country and were great benefactors. They functioned with a sense of independence and fairness, which endeared them to their adopted local community.

Recognizing the potential of homegrown lawyers, the British solicitors opened the doors of the senior partner's rank to Sri

Lankans. The first Ceylonese partner of the firm was Mr. J.F. Martyn in 1944. He was the senior partner when I joined the firm in 1962. J.F. Martyn was followed by H.T. Perera and subsequently, by J.A. Naidoo and A.R.N. de Fonseka, who were all junior partners when I joined the firm.

Julius & Creasy was also responsible for the first female Senior Partner in the annals of legal history in Sri Lanka. Mrs. L.C. Fernando was one of the first two women to qualify as proctors in Ceylon, and was subsequently the first Senior Partner in an otherwise male-dominated profession. It was a sign of events to come, as over the years Julius & Creasy have admitted, and is now almost dominated by the fairer sex that Mrs. Fernando represented. It was Mrs. Fernando, a Junior Partner at the time, who invited me to join the firm and I worked under her supervision.

Traditionally, most of the work of the firm was related to property and family law. In the more recent years the Senior Partners of Julius and Creasy have been striding the commercial and litigation landscape of Sri Lanka manifesting their commitment to the development of the firm, and the consequent development of their clientele. Mr. Berty Amarasekera was responsible for a large number of property transactions in the country and was a conveyancing practitioner of repute. Mr. R.H.S Phillips, who was well known for his work in the field of intellectual property law, also helped draft the pioneering Intellectual Property Act of 1979. Mr. N. Ratnasabapathy was synonymous with the practice of commercial law as was Herman Perera. These gentlemen, who later became Senior Partners of the firm, contributed enormously to the value added by Julius and Creasy to the legal environs of Sri Lanka.

I had the privilege of working with all three. Later we became close personal friends. During my days, I was engaged in conveyancing and in some commercial matters assisting Berty Amarasekare and Herman Perera, who were Senior Assistants at the time also working under Mrs. Fernando. Since the days of the two highly-respected Englishmen, Julius & Creasy has evolved and expanded into the largest, and one of the most highly-respected and sought-after legal firms in Sri Lanka.

As December and my exams drew closer my employers rather reluctantly granted me a few days of study leave. They knew that if I were to succeed, I might not remain in the firm as very few advocates made a career in law firms, which was the exclusive domain of proctors (solicitors). It helped me that I was resident at the top floor, Room 13, of the newly completed Y.M.B.A. Building, which was a very short walk away from my office. I could study till the last minute in the morning before I walked to the office, and continue my studies almost as soon as the office closed in the evening.

The three exams were held in December 1962 with a slightly-adjusted schedule to accommodate me; and I managed to complete them satisfactorily, so I hoped. When the results were announced I experienced the most exhilarating sense of accomplishment in my young life. Before me there were only two proctors who had accomplished the task of completing the three examinations to become an advocate. Arthur Amarasekare, who was a proctor, had passed the preliminary, intermediate and final exams within one year. He went on to become a President's Counsel and later Ambassador to Myanmar. The other was my teacher E.R.S.R. Coomaraswamy, who was the only one to have completed all three advocates' exams at one sitting in 1949. He later became a President's Counsel, represented the country at legal committees at the United Nations, and was a highly respected author.

*　*　*

Even before the results of the advocates exam were released, I had set my sights on continuing postgraduate studies in international law abroad, with a view to having an academic career or a career in an international organization. I had applied for a Commonwealth Scholarship, a government to government scholarship program within the countries of the Commonwealth (former British colonies). Along with the Colombo Plan scholarships and the U.S. Fulbright

Scholarships, the Commonwealth Scholarships were one of the three annual award programs in the country at the time. There were of course a very limited number of opportunities under private sponsorship such as the Rhodes scholarships and those granted by the U.S. Rockefeller Foundation.

At the time, most scholarships were awarded to medical doctors, who were in great shortage and required specializations that were not available in the country, but were essential for the health of the nation. The remaining scholarships were awarded to a sprinkling of engineers and members of the university academic staff.

I was lucky to be chosen among the many applicants to be called for an interview. On the interview board was Prof. O.E.R. Abhayratna, Dean of the Medical Faculty at the University Medical College, along with the Director of Education, S.F. De Silva, who later became Ambassador to China. At the final interview it was made very clear to me where the priorities were. Prof. Abhayratna mentioned to me that the country's need was greater than mine (reference being to the need to train doctors), and wanted to know why they should consider me for a scholarship. I mumbled a response the content of which is best forgotten, because I did not consider it as a smart or logical answer. Although the rest of the interview went well, I walked away from the board with the distinct impression that I would not be selected for one of the half a dozen scholarships for which there were a large number of applicants.

By then, I had received an offer of employment to a post for which I had applied and had been interviewed. I decided not to accept the post. I was well settled at Julius and Creasy. But after the interview for the Commonwealth Scholarship, which I felt had not gone well, I began to reconsider my decision. The reason was my feeling that it might open a door for me abroad, as it was from the Asia Foundation, which also granted a few scholarships to America.

The Asia Foundation was led by an American Director, Dr. Richard Haggie, and a Deputy Director who was also an American. There were two local Program Officers and an assortment of clerical and technical staff. I was selected as a Program Officer. The other was T.B. Illangansinghe, a few years my senior, and designated as Senior Program Officer.

The Asia Foundation is a nonprofit, non-governmental organization committed to the development of a peaceful, prosperous, and just, Asia-Pacific region. The Foundation collaborates with private and public partners to support leadership and institutional development to improve governance, law, civil society, economic development and international relations.

With 18 offices throughout Asia, and its headquarters in San Francisco, annually, the Foundation at the time provided an average of 100 million dollars in program support. The Foundation distributed nearly one million books and journals valued at nearly $50 million, to help educators and communities enhance English-language capacity and give young people the gift of literacy. Strengthening the rule of law is an important component of the Foundation's work to address the problems confronting the criminal justice system, including a lack of adequate legal representation, delays in administration of justice, and overcrowded prisons. This program included training and support for volunteer lawyers and paralegals. I was to support the latter program which was not very extensive in the country at the time.

The Foundation's book program was extensive and included distributing the books, mostly to libraries in Buddhist temples, and other rural educational centers. The program included support for refurbishing or extending the facilities to house the books in those locations.

Whenever a donation took place the recipient institutions organized an elaborate ceremony and expected the representative of the Foundation to be present to make a statement. Because I was a Buddhist, the Foundation found me to be a suitable person to deputize for the Director and the Deputy Director who rarely attended such ceremonies. My colleague Illangansinghe also had had enough of the ceremonies, having being employed at the Foundation for some time. He gladly let me handle the task.

Being young, I found it a fascinating job. It allowed me to travel to rural villages. It also gave me the opportunity to hone my skills in public-speaking, though with great reticence at the beginning. I also had the opportunity to work with two Americans, which eventually gave me confidence to work with foreign nationals, which was helpful especially once I went abroad. I was tempted to take on the appointment also because I had at my disposal a chauffeur-driven car to take me back and forth from work, and to all my official engagements. This was quite a luxury for a young man barely an adult.

Leaving Julius & Creasy after such a short stint left somewhat of a bad taste among my colleagues at the firm, particularly my boss, Mrs. Fernando, who had been kind enough to recruit me. I did not visit J & C or Mrs. Fernando for many years out of embarrassment, but when I eventually had the courage to do so, they greeted me quite cordially. It was perhaps because by then I was a United Nations official and my J&C Colleagues appreciated and admired my position. They readily understood that I would have left the firm eventually. Since that first visit there was no bitterness of any kind, and colleagues like Berty Amarasekara, who later became the senior partner, in the firm remained lifelong friends.

*　　*　　*

I was thoroughly enjoying my work at the Asia Foundation when the Commonwealth Scholarship awardees were named. To my great surprise I had been chosen as one of the candidates to proceed to Canada for postgraduate studies on a Commonwealth Scholarship. I thought that the only reason for selecting me would have been one simple fact that they could not have ignored; I had received the equivalent of four academic degrees by passing six examinations in one calander year, a feat not achieved before or since that time.

It was a euphoric period as I had now obtained the opportunity I wanted: to pursue postgraduate studies in my chosen field. At the time, there were no possibilities for such studies in the field of law in Sri Lanka, and the only option was to proceed abroad. To do so, I had to obtain one of those elusive scholarships as the financial commitment otherwise required was beyond my family short of disposing most of my parent's assets.

Chapter 23

Tears in Paradise

Even as I made the preparations to begin the next phase of my journey I could not help but look back at the years I had spent in Colombo pursuing my law studies and recollect how my dreams were almost shattered in the late 1950s.

In 1957, when I had reached the last few days of my life at Richmond Collage, my education had taken place in a relatively stable and peaceful environment. These were the years when the country was still under British rule, or in its immediate aftermath.

Though it stymied national resurgence and culture, the British rule in Sri Lanka in many ways was salutary. Among the most positive legacies that the British left behind were the system of education and the administration of law and justice, both of which, benefited me enormously. They also left behind a wonderful network of railways. My father and some other family members benefited by serving the Railway Department, where they made their careers. Similarly, the British left an extensive road network which was hardly supplemented, just as the railways, until about two years ago. The tea and rubber plantation industry that the British left behind was the nation's main source of revenue till recently. Even today, plantations are a substantial foreign currency earner. Thanks to the railway and road network, I roamed around the country in my youth, soaking up the history and beauty of my land. It was the British national pastime, cricket, which I enjoyed most in my childhood. Playing cricket taught me the value of intensive preparation and team work, and inculcated in me leadership qualities and important ingredients of group interaction. These were the essential tools for success in later life. Of course, cricket still remains one of my favorite pastimes.

There was a downside to the British rule as it dominated the local culture. The British displayed a sense of superiority that made much of the local society feel and act subservient to the rulers and their way of life. Their rule also ignited several riots which were controlled with much brutality. The policy of divide and rule among the Sinhala and Tamil communities was very much apparent during the British rule. Thus, they may have left behind the seeds of an ethnic conflict that would erupt decades after the colonists have left. But most of the obvious drawbacks were experienced mainly by a generation before mine. By and large, I grew up during the early years of my education in relative tranquility in terms of the social and political environment in the country under mostly British rule, and benefiting from the legacy left behind.

The same could not be said of the period during my final years of education. In fact, it was just the opposite. It was a time when the country was moving towards one of the most volatile periods in its recent history. I nearly did not make a start to my legal career, due to communal disharmony that began to manifest itself in the mid-fifties. By mid-1957, a rupture began in the amicable community in which I grew up. With the formation of the Sri Lanka Freedom Party (SLFP) by Mr. S.W, R.D. Bandaranaike, who advocated a Sinhala only policy, and its electoral victory in 1956, the Tamil Community in the North began agitating for a federal system of government to replace the unitary form of government that we had inherited from the British, who ruled until 1947. There followed serious threats of Satyagraha and other forms of civil disobedience by the Federal Party. The Federal Party had been formed by the Tamil politicians, led by S.J.V. Chelvanayagam, in response to the policies of the SLFP.

These developments which threatened the political stability resulted in a pact signed between Bandaranaiyke and Chelvanayagam in July

1957. The intention was to set up a system of Regional Councils in the North and the East that would give control to the Tamils over local issues, without having to form a Federal System of government. The pact was accepted and the threatened Satyagraha campaign was called off. But it was only a stopgap measure to the Tamil leaders, who expressed their definite desire for a Federal System with equal language and other rights as known to the majority Sinhala community. In fact, neither community was happy with the arrangement. One thought too little was achieved, the other thought too much was conceded. Agitations on both sides continued calling for the abrogation of the pact.

In that atmosphere, among other actions carried out to implement the National Language Act, the government changed the lettering of motor vehicles from the English alphabet to the Sinhala letter 'Sri'. In March 1958, when public vehicles bearing the new lettering started arriving in the North, there began a campaign of civil disobedience. Led by the Federal Party politicians, people began covering the Sinhala lettering with tar and replaced it with its Tamil equivalent. This led to an ugly reaction in other parts of the Island where thugs and hooligans went on the rampage defacing Tamil signs wherever they were found. It ultimately spiraled out of control, because provocative acts by both sides. It became a nightmare that began in the eastern cities of Trincomalee, Batticaloa, Gal Oya and Amparai, eventually engulfing the entire Island. Many were killed and maimed on both sides with Sinhala mobs relentlessly attacking every Tamil they could lay their hands on. Such acts were intensified on both sides by mostly unfounded rumors.

During these dark days my father volunteered to house the Tamil grocery store owner in the town of Galle. My father had bought household provisions on credit, paying him at the end of each month. It is an understatement to say that people of our age were terribly frightened of the critical dangers we felt all around us. We were confined to our homes, because the government had declared an Emergency and proclaimed a dusk-to-dawn curfew. That was in May 1958, an ugly period in our history.

When all this began, we were happily ending our annual cricket season in school, and I was personally looking forward with anticipation to begining my law studies in Colombo later that year. Instead, it turned out to be a period of uncertainty for many of us. Shortly after the riots had been brought under control, the Government introduced new legislation to give reasonable use of the Tamil language in the North and East. It was a measure that was agreed to be implemented as a result of the Bandaranaike-Chelvanayagam Pact. Once again an uneasy calm returned and life became normal. Thankfully, this was in time for me to begin my studies as planned in August 1958.

In spite of the assassination of Prime Minister Bandaranayaike in 1959 by the disillusioned Sinhala extremists, and a spate of political agitations of lesser proportion, life continued in relative peace. We had generally assumed that the level of violence unleashed during the riots of 1958 was sort of an aberration and we could carry on in our merry ways.

It turned out to be a misplaced assumption. Under the Official Language Act of 1956, the final date for the switch over to Sinhala as the state language was designated as January 1961. That date came and went. A civil disobedience campaign of Satyagraha was begun by the Tamils in the Northern and Eastern Provinces in February 1961. In spite of the provisions that had been made for the reasonable use of Tamil, the Tamils saw the Official Language Act as a draconian piece of legislation that would violate their fundamental rights of equality. They had previously enjoyed equality when English was the language for state transactions.

Led by the Federal Party, the campaign of sit-ins to disrupt the functioning of the state institutions escalated. Later the Federal Party issued its own stamps, opened Post Offices, and threatened to organize their own Police Force. In April 1961, the government, led by Mrs. Bandaranayaike, dispatched the Army to control the situation and declared an Emergency once again in the North and the East. That resulted in a spate of violence on both sides which was confined to the North and the East, though for the first time, the upcountry Indian Tamils in the central province joined the fray to support the Federal Party. This time, there was relative calm elsewhere, particularly in the South, where perhaps the lessons of 1958 were still fresh in everyone's memory. [1]

This was the time when we were in the midst of our third year lectures. I was personally in the midst of undertaking the challenging task of completing a series of examinations. Once again, uncertainty set in as far as the immediate future was concerned, though life in general in Colombo continued as usual.

Mercifully, the situation in the North and the East was brought under control rather expeditiously. With that, relative peace existed until I had finished my education, and a brief period of employment, and left the Island in 1963 for further studies in Canada. My stay abroad was much longer than was expected. But I continued to regularly return home. I was present in the Island on many occasions when the brewing storm of my student days slowly but surely engulfed the country in an inferno that lasted the next half-century.

* * *

It was on one such visit that I was present to see and experience the beginning of the most brutal part of the conflict. This was on the first occasion on which my wife Shanthi and I visited Sri Lanka together. Along with son Amal, we had returned for a vacation, and were residing at my sister's home in Nawala. Amal later joined his mother at her residence.

While we were there, on an eventful Monday in July 1983, I had gone to the Ministry of Foreign Affairs, opposite the Queens House, the residence of the President. Unknown to me, the National Security Council was convened that morning, and President J.R. Jayewardene and Prime Minister Ranasinghe Premadasa were meeting with the Cabinet. While I was at the Ministry, a dawn-to-dusk curfew was announced and there was a rumor that shots were heard and 'Koti' (Tigers) have descended on Colombo. Panic broke out and everyone began rushing out of the ministry. I drove my brother-in-law Douglas' Audi, the wrong way up York Street to Laksala, the local curios shop, to collect Shanthi and my sister who were shopping there. We headed home as fast as we could. Even as we left the area, flames were coming out of the historic Bristol Building, and we later learned, that the Tamil owned Ambal Café in the building was the first of many to be set on fire.

All was well, until we passed the national cemetery at Kanatta, when we felt something was really wrong, because from there on the entire road was filled with hooligans in riot mode. First, we found that some of the waiting bus passengers were making requests to be transported to their destinations in view of the impending curfew. Others were demanding to siphon off petrol from vehicles so they could fill theirs. Others were inspecting each vehicle for Tamils. They would come up to you and make demands with knives to the throat, and insist that Sinhala prayers be recited to ensure that no Tamils were travelling in any of the vehicles. I dread to think of what happened to any they found.

By this time, my vehicle was full with people sitting on laps of Shanthi and my sister. Using all my wits, I managed to get home; after depositing the passengers, with much persuasion, at the turn off to my sister's house near Nawala junction. Some were not so lucky. One van driver who was behind us stopped to argue and challenge the mob. In short order he found his vehicle going up in flames, while he was still arguing. Once home, I found both Shanthi and my sister rather hysterical after the experience and Shanthi was running a high fever.

The curfew by then had been advanced to 2 p.m. We arrived home in good time. It was then we began to learn the background to the incident. The evening before, on Sunday, 13 army personnel had been killed in Jaffna, and on Monday morning the remains were being brought to be interred at the National Cemetery. Although the authorities had tried to keep the news under wraps and make it a low key event, the word got out, and the rumor mill had begun to churn juicy stories, inflaming the Sinhala mobs. In the next few days thousands of innocent civilians, including children and elderly, suffered relentlessly. More than 64,000 took refuge in temples and other guarded locations. Many were killed or maimed. What first began in Colombo spread to the hinterland, and while Tamils as a group were victimized and suffered heavily in the North and the East, in the process of retaliation, many Sinhala people in those areas lost their lives and property.

By August, far later than should have been, order had been restored. We flew back to New York to watch from the uneasy comfort of distance, the ghastly story of the recent history of our country, as it unraveled during the next three decades [1]. It is with great relief and excitement, though a sense of sadness is never too far, that we now return on our visits to the homeland, where peace at last has been restored. Pray, we shall, that it will last and last for generations, never to experience the past again, and for it to remain in our memory only as a lesson well learned that is never to be repeated [2].

FOOTNOTE:

[1] The first ethnic conflict of course was in June 1956 that lasted a week. Gal Oya settlement scheme begun in 1949 was planned to settle landless peasants in formerly jungle land. By 1956 there were over 50 new villages where over 5,000 ethnic Sri Lankan Tamil, Muslim, Indigenous Veddha and Sinhalese were settled. Settlement of large numbers of Sinhalese peasants in what Tamil nationalists considered their traditional environment, was a source of tension within the settlement area. That tension led to the Gal Oya riots which were the first ethnic riots between the Sinhalese and Tamils in post independent Sri Lanka. The riots were localized to the settlement area, but it is estimated that over 150 people lost their lives due to the violence. The Police and the Army were eventually able to re-take control of the situation and brought the riots under control. There were no immediate repercussions.

[2] There were many implications internationally that influenced the course of the conflict throughout the decades as recounted in detail in a recent publication: 'Gota's War', by C.A. Chandraprema. As far as the initial impetus was concerned, none as important as the events

in Tamil Nadu, in India,. Interestingly, it was a time that Tamil Nadu politicians had been agitating for independence from the Hindu led Central Government of India. Throughout the course of the struggle of the Federal Party, events were dictated by the politics of Tamil Nadu and its politicians, who encouraged the Federal party to seek a separate state through agitation. Federal party demands were based on the language issue, self rule in the North and the East within a Federal System of Administration, but the underlying thread has always been the establishment of a separate state in the North, and at least in parts of the East. This was apparent from the beginning, when the Bandaranaike-Chlvanayagam Pact was signed. Immediately following the conclusion of the pact, the Federal party declared it as an interim arrangement that would not affect their fundamental objectives. In later pronouncements, among the stated objectives of the party, was the establishment of a homeland for the Tamils. The time that the Federal Party received the support of Tamil Nadu was when Tamil Nadu was agitating for a homeland of its own, separating from the central government of India. But, with the passage of the 6th Amendment to the Indian Constitution, in 1963(the year I left Colombo for studies abroad), mandating all Indian politicians to take an oath upholding the sovereignty of the country, effectively banned any separatist propaganda. If violated any violator would forfeit the right to sit in any of the central or local legislatures. The dream of Tamil separatism was nipped in the bud in India.

With that, the Federal Party in Sri Lanka also lost steam and negotiated a deal with the UNP government of Prime Minister Dudley Senanayake. The Federal Party joined the government as a constituent party. That was shortly after I had left Colombo. After a period of relative calm, the Tamil agitation gradually turned violent, led by the Tamil youth, who took advantage of any provocations such as the language based standardization for university admission promulgated in 1971, the adoption of a new constitution in 1972 which included provisions affecting Sinhala, the state language, and Buddhism, the state religion. That was until the radicalized war began with the LTTE led by Velupillai Prabhakaran.

Since 1980, India ruled by Indira Gandhi, under the pretext of Indian security considerations, covertly helped the terrorist movement by providing training camps in India and with other assistance that radicalized the conflict. This time it was not driven by Tamil Nadu pressure. Prime Minister Gandhi claimed that minority citizens were being killed in droves and over 40,000 refugees have landed in India.

She made it an Indian issue. The real reason behind Gandhi's intervention however, was the shift from non-alignment towards the west by the Jayewardene regime and Gandhi's personal dislike of President Jayewardene partly because of his treatment of her friend, Mrs. Sirimavo Bandaranaiyke, whose civic rights were abrogated by Jayewardene. When Rajiv Gandhi became Prime Minister he carried on the policies of his mother in promoting terrorism and fighting a proxy war in Sri Lanka, even to the extent of surreptitiously providing arms. In mid-1985, India brokered the 'Thimpu Talks' in search of a settlement, which Gandhi claimed was not meant to divide the country. Such division would clearly have negative repercussions in India. By early- 1986, LTTE managed to maneuver India to be their spokesman, by getting India for the first time to lodge a complaint with the Human Rights Commission in Geneva on the violation of Tamil minority rights in Sri Lanka. Nevertheless, after the 'Thimpu Talks' broke down, India was no longer able to control the LTTE, which claimed that it had become the sole representatives of Sri Lankan Tamils. Indeed, the intransigencies of the LTTE and the realization through LTTE propaganda that Prabhakaran was leading India by its nose, for the first time gave the Indian government a clear warning that Tamil separatism had gone far enough and had to be terminated. In fact, the contagion would infect Tamil Nadu as well. But following the Vadamarachchi operation in early 1987, which allowed the Sri Lankan government to take the upper hand, once again India, claiming that the horrific loss of life is not acceptable, intervened on the side of the LTTE. By forcibly dropping food parcels from aircrafts, against the wishes of the Sri Lankan government, India gave a strong warning to the Sri Lankan government to heed its call for a ceasefire. This action had its desired effect. The Sri Lankan government halted its operations, and was forced into a peace accord that would internationalize the conflict by bringing an Indian peace-keeping force (IPKF) to Sri Lanka. It did not take long for Prabhakaran to renege on the agreement and force the withdrawal of the IPKF, after inflicting over 2,000 casualties left in its wake. This was facilitated with the somewhat surprising help given to the LTTE by President Premadasa, who from the beginning was against the Indian involvement in the conflict in Sri Lanka. In spite of that experience, and the later assassination of Rajiv Gandhi by the LTTE in 1991, the Indian support continued apace. Even two years after the end of the war, the Indian support for the Tamil cause still continued. Once again led by Tamil Nadu, minority governments in New Delhi are beholden to Tamil Nadu politicians to keep holding the reins of power at the center. Some have cogently argued that successive Indian Governments have supported and tolerated the LTTE, claiming it to be a liberation force rather than a terrorist organization, simply to change the geopolitics of South Asia, possibly the rest of Asia for its own strategic reasons.

Thankfully, the bedlam that lasted nearly three decades ended eventually in peace, which prevails now, since the war ended with the defeat of the LTTE under President Mahinda Rajapaksa in May 2009. One wonders however, what is still in store, because even at this writing, three years after the devastating war ended, the leading Tamil Nadu politician DMK President, one time Chief Minister of Tamil Nadu who had been a shadow figure behind the cause throughout the struggle, declared that: "we have not dropped the demand for Tamil Eelam, a separate homeland for Tamils in Sri Lanka, which remains an unfulfilled dream." Chief Minister Jayalalitha, who Succeeded the former is continuing to make similar belligerent threats to disrupt the unitary nature of Sri Lanka. These are not threats that can be ignored.

Chapter 24

Number 13

On a cold morning in January 1963, just as the Northeast monsoon season was beginning to descend on Colombo in the form of heavy showers and clouded skies, I made my way to the parliament building in the Colombo Fort. In spite of the cold weather, my heart was beating faster than it should; my brow was glistening with perspiration. I knew whatever that transpired within those hallowed walls in the course of the next hour would have a tremendous impact on the rest of my life.

I sat in front of Sam Wijesinha in his office at the imposing colonial building housing the parliament complex and lay bare my future in front of him. A heavy silence fell between us when I gave him the copy of The Ceylon Law College Review I had taken with me. After reading the editorial I had written, entitled "The Case of Law vs. Space", he looked up at me through his glasses and said "You seem to have a strong inclination towards international law". "Yes Sir," I replied, relieved to hear someone else saying out loud, the wishes nestling deep within my heart.

The reason I sought his advice was I knew Sam had done graduate work in Canada. Having worked as a senior crown counsel, at the time I met him he had just joined the parliament as an official where he later became the Secretary-General. "As you already know, I studied in Canada and specialized in aviation law" said Sam. "I hear that my university has recently added courses in space law to the subjects they teach. I think this is the best university for you."

He went on to point out that since space law was still evolving, I could possibly become an expert and a pioneer in the field. Furthermore he explained, the particular institute was based in the law faculty of the most prestigious university in Canada. I also learned from him that the then Attorney General, A.C.M. Ameer Q.C., had also studied there and was fully supportive of the institute for the quality of the education standards it upheld. Apparently both of them were responsible at different times in dealing with aviation related cases and aviation agreement negotiations in the Attorney General's Department. Although Sam mentioned a few other possibilities as well, he was not as enthusiastic about them as he was about his first suggestion.

I was most grateful for his kind advice. Sam later became the first Ombudsman of Sri Lanka, and even today, at the age of 90, serves as the Chancellor of the Open University. I recently had the opportunity to read the Festschrift published on the occasion of his 90th birthday. Reading it I realized that he had helped countless people who are indebted to him, as I was, for the advice and assistance that Sam had so generously provided to advance the careers of dozens of people. He must be unique to have touched the lives of so many in such positive ways. My own saga did not end there. While abroad, for some time I thought of returning to work in my country.

Once, I saw a vacancy announcement for the post of Assistant Clerk in the parliament, a post that Sam had previously held. I applied for the post and informed Sam. The letter he wrote to me in response in 1966 is still in my files. Early this year, I made a courtesy visit to him in the company of my law hostel buddy, Bertram Tittawella, and I showed the letter to Sam. In the letter, he had informed me that Bertram, who was at Harvard at the time, has also applied for the post. He had then gone on to advice me to remain in the U.N., because I would make a successful career there; and that he would be recommending Bertram for the post, because he would do well back home at the parliament. How true it all turned out. Bertram later served as Secretary General of the Parliament, the post that Sam had earlier served in. His astute advice served us both well. Later in life,

I visited him in his office in the parliament on several occasions, and he never failed to detain me to have lunch or tea before I left him. It was on one of those occasions that he related to me the news, how my father had complained to him, that because of Sam's advice, he would lose his son once I left the country.

Having received Sam's advice concerning my graduate studies, I immediately began researching the field of study he suggested, as well as the Institute he had mentioned. This was of immense importance to me, because once a Commonwealth Scholarship is granted it is the responsibility of the scholar to gain admission to a university in the country granting the scholarship. Usually, they had no difficulty finding a place. This meant I had to decide on a subject that I wished to read and then select an appropriate university in which to enroll. This was where Sam's advice was immensely helpful.

It is the custom of the Embassy of the country concerned to assist in directing scholars on the procedures concerned. Having been briefed by the Education Officer at the Canadian Embassy in Colombo, I made an application to the Institute of Air and Space Law at McGill University in Montreal, Canada. This was now my first choice, and though as required, I had to make at least two other applications, I held them back as I still had time to turn to the other options should my first application fail.

Before long, I had a positive response from McGill. Later I learned that the prompt acceptance was partly because of the great reputation left behind by Sam and Ameer, who had been recognized as outstanding students from my country. To my delight, much later, I found out that one of my professors there, Ivan A. Vlasic, happened to be a classmate of Ameer several years prior to my admission. A couple of years later, Vlasic served as the supervisor of my thesis. He and I became close friends and he served often as a U.N. consultant on my projects.

* * *

Working at the Asia Foundation was quite a blessing in preparing me for the trip to Canada. The Foundation had many resources I could consult. This was because the Foundation made arrangements for its own scholars proceeding to the United States on scholarships they sponsored.

The academic year in the Canadian universities began in late September. I had noted that there were many short term summer programs to which the Foundation scholars were sponsored. I decided it would be useful to take advantage of such programs in Europe on the way to Canada and set about researching them.

Within a week or two, I identified two summer programs in Europe that I wanted to attend. One was a course at the prestigious Hague Academy of International Law, based at the World Court in The Hague. It was and still remains the most prestigious program for International Public and Private Law, where the most well-known professors from universities around the world conduct lectures. The other, was the World Federation of United Nations Associations (WAFUNA) Summer School for university students, held at the United Nations premises at the Palais des Nations, in Geneva, Switzerland.

The two programs followed each other with a short interval between them. Of course, in order for me to attend them, I had to apply for financial support from the programs. In the back of my mind was the possibility of a travel grant from the Asia Foundation. I was lucky to be accepted for both programs with financial support. Thus I started planning my journey to Canada.

The ticket to Canada was provided by the Commonwealth Scholarship Program and I decided to see as much of Europe as possible within the time available and to the extent my airline ticket would allow. Those were the days when certain amount of miles are allocated to a ticket between two points, and any number of stops may be made within that mileage, as long as one does not backtrack. Having finalized my itinerary, I set about getting my passport and necessary visas and completing other formalities. Canada is a member of the Commonwealth of Nations, as is the United Kingdom. Thankfully, I was spared of the drudgery of obtaining visas to travel to Canada through London. But I had made arrangements to be in Switzerland and Holland and to tour a few other European countries. I had to obtain a visa for Switzerland. The other countries did not require a visa as I was travelling through Switzerland.

All this was at a time when, due to the scarcity of foreign exchange, the government had rationed rice and other commodities including milk powder for infants and clothing material. Coupons were issued for limited quantities of rice, Maldive fish and a meter or so of clothing which could be purchased by a coupon-book holder each week from the government Cooperative Wholesale Establishment (CWE). Rice in fact was the crucial issue on the political scene. Elections were won or lost on the "rice policy". Mrs. Sirimavo Bandaranaike won the elections and was appointed as the Prime Minister having famously declared that, if elected, she would bring rice even from the Moon to ensure its availability. But, during her tenure as head of the government, even flour was scarce. Long lines formed early morning in front of bakeries to purchase the daily quota of a loaf of bread. The rice ration book and coupons were therefore highly valued. Those leaving the country had to ensure that no one else used their coupons by surrendering the ration book to the authorities, and obtain a seal to that affect on their passports.

Another formality was to collect the limited foreign exchange that was allowed to those traveling abroad. Due to the Foreign Exchange scarcity, only three U.K. Pounds were allowed per person, at the then exchange rate of around Rs. 11 per Pound, unlike today's high rates. To collect the three Pounds, one had to first go to the Exchange Control Department in the Central Bank with a bundle of evidence to show one was entitled to it. Then one had to fill out another bundle of forms before the meager amount was authorized. Then one could go to a travel agency to collect the traveler's checks worth three U.K. Pounds.

Today, there are Banks on every corner and ATM machines to transact business 24 hours a day. In those days there were only a few Banks and almost all of them were located within the Colombo Fort. They transacted business with the public between 10 am and 1 pm, just for three hours, five days a week. One would go to a travel agency because you needed to go there to collect the airline ticket as well. That is where I next headed with passport in hand, with all necessary seals of authority permitting to travel stamped thereon.

I went to the Office of Thomas Cook's & Sons on Prince Street, which was then the leading and about the only travel agency in the country. There I met a distinguished looking man with an imposing mustache on whose desk was the equally imposing name plate that read, Wing Commander Noel Fernando. He was in-charge of the section with which I had to transact business that day. Each time I visited the country in the next two or three occasions, I went through the same routine and came to know that the imposing looking man was indeed a gentle person who soon became a friend. Noel Feranando had been in the Air Force and had taken an early exit to join Cook's agency. Later, he established what is today one of the leading travel agencies in the country, 'Finley Travels,' which he now owns. His firm is housed in the prestigious colonial building, where Cook's office was then located, James Finley Building, next to the Colombo Port.

The first stop was to be in Geneva for the 17th Annual WAFUNA Summer School, 3-23 July 1962. The next event I was to attend was the 1963 Session of The Hague Academy of International Law 29 July to 27 August. In between I planned to visit Paris and Berlin (West). After the two programs were completed, I planned to spend several weeks in the U.K., where I had friends and had made arrangements for a brief internship at the Council of Education in World Citizenship, in London. The Council, along with organizations such as the Parliamentary Group for World Government, vigorously promoted the concept of global citizenship where individual's awareness, loyalty, and allegiance can and should extend beyond the borders of a nation to encompass the whole of humankind. But my primary intention in the U.K. was to see the famed country, where most of my compatriots went for education and pleasure in those days. In addition, I confess, I wanted very much to witness a Cricket Test Match in England, where the game of cricket originated and is venerated.

* * *

One evening, after returning home from work at the Asia Foundation, I lay on the bed in my room at the YMBA, listening to the familiar sound of the evening traffic outside my window. My days here in this room were numbered. I wondered about the next occupant of my room. Would a young man more superstitious than I, worry over the room number? Would he have doubts if number 13 would bring him bad luck? I wished I had some way of telling him not to worry. This room, in spite of the two digits considered unlucky, had helped me realize the biggest dream in my life so far – the dream of pursuing postgraduate studies combining my interests in law and outer space.

My musings were short lived. A sharp knock on the door brought me back to the present. In walked G.P.T Karunaratne and Hema Perera. "Before you take to the skies, let's fly around our own country" said GPT. He was referring to his *Hillman Minx*, and a trip to the East coast as a kind of a farewell to me, for it was doubtful if the three of us would ever go on other journeys in the *Hillman* ever again. "For old times' sake" added Hema, thumping me on the back. I needed little persuading. I wanted to cherish my last days in my homeland in the company of friends whom I would not be seeing for a long time to come.

Our first stop was at Kataragama, where we attended the pooja (ritual of religious offering) at the Kataragama devale (Hindu temple). The next day saw us "flying" on the newly constructed Siyambalaanduwa road to Gal Oya and Ampara. This was my first visit to this remote city, on the East Coast of the Island, about 360 km from the capital of Colombo, which was once a part of the domain of King Kavantissa (2nd century BC). In developing the Gal Oya scheme in 1952, by damming the Gal Oya river at Inginyagala, the first Prime

Minister of the country, D.S. Senanayake, transformed Ampara into a town. Initially, the residence for the construction workers of the Inginiyagala Dam, Ampara, later became the main administrative hub of the Gal Oya Valley. Gal Oya National Park was established in 1954 and serves as the main catchment area. An important feature of the Gal Oya National Park is its elephant herd, which can be seen throughout the year. It was exhilarating to breath the fresh air and feel the wind ripping through our hair as it swept toward us across the Senanayake Samudra, the largest reservoir in the history of Sri Lanka (7,680 ha), that created 40,000 thousand acres of irrigated land.

As we sped past acre upon acre of paddy land, stretching in front of us like an endless ocean dyed with green paint, it was easy to realize why Ampara is called the largest paddy harvesting district in the country. Dusty and wobbly after the long ride in the car, we were more than happy to see my Cousin Sarath waiting to greet us at the hostel of the German- sponsored Hardy Institute of Technical Training. We were graciously granted lodgings there for the night. After a good dose of galcoffee (coffee laced with ganja), we spent an enjoyable night in the company of Sarath.

The next day we meandered along the coast to Batticaloa. Our destination was the home of Ranjini Devanayagam, who had been at Law Colleage with us. Ranjini's father, Bill Devanayagam, was a prominent lawyer in the town, who later became a member of the Cabinet and at one time, the Minister of Justice. He was married to Ruby, the sister of Sir Lalitha Rajapakse Q.C., who had himself been a former Minister of Justice and later Ambassador to the U.K. I had already planned to stay with aunt Ruby during the London stop, and Sir Lalitha became a close friend much later in life. To our secret delight, when we landed on Ranjini's doorstep we found she had already invited a group of her friends to holiday with her at her home. When she saw us she greeted us warmly. "If you are having visitors we don't mind leaving" said GPT, while Hema and I stood behind him nodding vigorously to show Ranjini we really didn't mind finding somewhere else to stay. To our relief Ranjini said she would have none of that nonsense. "The house is so big the whole town can live in it", she assured us.

When a domestic aid showed us to our rooms we realized Ranjini had not been exaggerating about the dimensions of her father's house. Built on an extensive amount of land, it was perhaps the best and the largest residence in the town. But what was most attractive to us was the lagoon abutting the front garden. Though the Baticaloa lagoon is famous for its singing fish, try as we might, none of us could hear this orchestra of the water nymphs on that first night we spent basking in Ranjini's and her father's hospitality.

Perhaps if we had made our way to the lagoon on other nights we would have heard the singing, but this was not to be. My two companions left me the next day. GPT had an appointment to keep in Colombo, and Hema returned with him. I stayed behind for a couple of days. My friends Kumar Amarasekare and Sunil De Silva were already there as Ranji's guests. I wonder if there have ever been so many Law College students staying under one roof in a colleague's house as there were on those few days we were in Batticaloa. The friendships we made and the bonds we formed have lasted throughout our lives.

One of the strongest among these staunch friendships was the one I formed with Ranjini. I was happy to assist her when she sought my help in preparing for her exams at the Law College. Ever since then we have been close friends. She married a Law College colleague, Shanthi Fernando, a distant relative of mine from Ambalangoda, who had also been at Richmond College with me. He was a couple of years my junior. Ranjini and Shanthi later migrated to Canada and built lucrative legal establishments in Toronto. They purchased a mini- mansion to which I was a frequent visitor from New York and elsewhere. They too were my guests from time to time in the United States. Their daughter, Gayani, graduated in international relations and took up residence in the UK after her own marriage. Shanthi and Ranji have a granddaughter Larissa. They also have a son Kusal, who was a champion tennis player and ended up being one of the most sought after tennis coaches in Toronto.

Many years later, after a wonderful life together, they separated. Ranji continued to live in their house, while Shanthi set up a home office in a fancy apartment in the center of Toronto. I continued to visit them for this did not strain our amicable friendship. Whenever my wife Shanthi and I visited them, Ranji always graciously hosted a dinner party for our mutual friends. of course, the former head of the household was now the chief guest occupying the chair he had always occupied. More recently, Shanthi has been visiting us in Los Angeles, where he likes to play golf, his favorite pastime. He has joined us on many a trip in Sri Lanka and abroad.

Ranjini's classmate Kusum Kalawila was also there on that trip to Batticaloa, as was their batch-mate Nihal Pieris. Several years later, Kusum married Nihal. Apparently, they had connected while they were working on the editorial committee of the Buddhist Brotherhood Magazine at Law College; despite romance being not part of religious pursuits! They too migrated to Canada and worked as lawyers for some years in Toronto, but they felt more at home in Colombo and returned there to establish the thriving law firm of Peiris & Peiris in Hultsdorf. Whenever we visit Colombo we are entertained at their four storey mansion in Nugegoda, Colombo. They have also visited us in the US several times and joined us on trips both in Sri Lanka and abroad. They have a son Kanchana, a successful lawyer himself, who married Himali, an attorney in the Law firm of Paul Ratnayake Associates, a leading law firm in Colombo. Paul has been kind enough to entertain us at his elegant home on several of our visits to Colombo.

Hema Perera, who left us after a day or so in Batticaloa, later married his Law College colleague Mallika and went to the Caribbean. I have already recorded their saga. It remains to say that they are now on the verge of retirement from their lucrative practice as legal advisers to foreign investors. With their newly found freedom, they are enjoying frequent visits to their two daughters in the United States and their extended weekend visits to the 'Waluwa' (mansion) at Mankidiwela. There they manage the tea plantation that surrounds the 'Walauwa' in the salubrious climate of Kandy. During our visits to Colombo we are well entertained by them. They never fail to invite us to the 'Waluwa'. I enjoy the bath from the well in the compound, where you draw buckets full of refreshing water from the deep well to shower yourself, getting the necessary exercise and clean-up simultaneously. It also takes me back to the days when my Seeya used to bathe me buckets full of river water.

A few years ago, when their daughter Enoka, an Aerospace Engineer, married Hiran Fernando, a connoisseur of good wine in Los Angeles, her parents were unable to be present at the wedding. I was honored to be asked to give her away. Enoka now works for the Boeing Company in Everett, Washington, engaged in the production of the Boeing 787 'Dreamliner', the next generation aircraft.

We were also happy to attend her sister Rohini's wedding when she married Dinooka at a lavish wedding at the Hilton in Colombo. There, I was honored to be asked to propose a toast to the couple. With Dinoo being a professional chef, and Hiran a connoisseur of wine, I feel Mallika and Hema who are great lovers of good food and wine have arranged things very well for themselves with the two sons-in-law to provide great evenings of relaxation.

Like Hema and Mallika, Shanthi and Ranji, Nihal and Kusum, there were several other contemporaries who married their Law College colleagues, although this was not the norm at the time. Among the others, of course, were our close friends Vasudewa and Wasanthi Nanayakkara, to whom reference has been made already.

Perhaps partly because both husbands and wives were Law College colleagues, this core group of friends, Shanthi and Ranji, Nihal and Kusum, Hema and Mallika, along with another pair of Law College colleagues, Namel and Malini have continued to be one family for over half a century. Whenever we get together in the United States we always take trips or cruises to various tourist sites such as Alaska, Mexico and the Caribbean. We do the same whenever my wife and I visit Sri Lanka. Our latest excursion was to the North and the East, the war torn areas of the Island. For many years we have continued to enjoy these gatherings and trips which we consider a great blessing. We enjoy the company of good friends from many years past. On all these trips, Shanthi Fernando, being the only bachelor among us, becomes the focus of many jokes, which keeps everyone including Shanthi in a good mood. He is a good sport and enjoys a good laugh, even when it is at his expense.

It was on one of those trips from Los Angeles to San Francisco that we began to be concerned about an incessant cough Shanthi seemed to have. It became worse day by day. He was a chain smoker and the cough had been dismissed as a 'smoker's cough,' but on this occasion everyone insisted he should give up smoking. He readily agreed and stopped the habit when he was in our presence, but we knew he was continuing the habit. It was shortly after this trip that to our great distress we learned he was being treated for lung cancer.

Everyone rallied around him. Most of all, Ranji, who by then was separated from him, but who made daily visits to see him with food and other necessities, to ensure that he would get over the ordeal. In spite of the odds against him, miraculously, he beat the odds and made a complete recovery to the great relief and joy of all of us. He joined us on our next trip. Retired, he now lives in Colombo and spends the summers in Toronto. Let me now go back to Batticaloa. Present during our holidays there was Surangani Premis, who married Gamini Marapane, also a lawyer. She joined the Bank of Ceylon and ended up as the Legal Adviser and Secretary to the Board of the Bank. Also there was Sunil De Silva, my friend from Richmond College, who became the Attorney General and later migrated to Australia, and Kumar Amarasekare.

Kumar was a gifted orator who won the Gold Medal for oratory at the Law College. He was the nephew of the famous Zoysa brothers: Stanley, Minister of Finance, Sydney, Inspector General of Police, and Bunty a leading criminal lawyer. Kumar lived with his parents and sister at the official residence of his father, who was the General Manager of the Wellawatte Weaving Mills, the premier textile establishment in the country. They used to party often and Kumar used to invite me to join them. Among those I met there were his cousin Roma De Zoysa. Roma celebrated her seventy-fifth birthday recently in Los Angeles, where she is now resident. My wife and I were guests along with many acquaintances from our bygone days.

I also met there Nihal Fonseka, an accomplished tenor who used to sing for us. He later joined the Toronto Opera Company in Canada, one of a very few Sri Lankans who became international opera stars. Kumar became an advocate and was a member of the Colombo bar for a while. He then obtained the LL.B degree from the University of London and proceeded to Monash University in Melbourne, Australia, where he obtained his Masters degree in law and joined its teaching faculty. I have had constant contact with him. He has visited me in New York and I have visited him in Melbourne. Regrettably, in the prime of his life, he succumbed to a bout of cancer which he fought with courage.

We spent a couple of pleasant days in Batticaloa and visited the Batticaloa fort, built by the Portuguese in 1628. It was the first fort to be captured by the invading Dutch in 1638. One of the most picturesque of the small Dutch forts of Sri Lanka, it is situated on an Island, and still in good condition. There is also a 1st century CE Buddhist Stupa (shrine) inside the Dutch fort.

We went swimming at the heavenly beaches of Pasikudah and Kalkudah. Pasikudah, a bay (Van der Loos's Bay), is protected from the ocean. This location is significant in that its bed is flat and sandy and it has a pleasant effect on the feet. This sandy bottom extends to nearly 150 or 200 meters from the shore. Pasikudah is an ideal location for those who wish to learn swimming. Many among us enjoyed the opportunity of learning to swim there without the fear of drowning. Being a good swimmer, with a life saving certificate from the Royal Life Saving Society to boot, I was in great demand when it came to swimming lessons, particularly among the lady-folk who showed a keen interest in learning to swim, or to put it more accurately, being taught to swim. As I look back, I believe that it must have been most reluctantly and under great pressure that I would have obliged, particularly on those moon-lit nights when we went swimming at Pasikudah. More recently, Pasikudah has become a faorite resort town with many luxury hotels turning it into a tourist heaven. There were no lodging places at the time we visited and hardly a visitor came by except those from local towns who came for an occasional dip in this magnificent bay.

After a relaxing holiday, we travelled back to Colombo by train, in luxury coutesey of Ranjini's father who bought us first class tickets. Many years later, the memories of this first visit came back to me with deep sorrow, when I heard Batticaloa was one of the worst hit areas during the Boxing Day Tsunami of December 26, 2004. The water rose up to 15 ft within 90 minutes of the beginning of the 2004 Indian Ocean earthquake off the coast of Indonesia causing the Tsunami.

*   *   *

All my law studies in Sri Lanka culminated in my taking oaths before Supreme Court Justice Sri Skanda Rajah, in the court presided over by him in the hallowed court complex in Hultsdorf, Colombo, on 2 December 1962. Thereafter I had the license to practice as a lawyer in any court of law in the country.

This was quite naturally considered as a significant event in any young person's career. The oath taking was therefore followed by a big celebration in the evening. Whether invited or not, all your friends would attend the party. Mine was no different. It was held at my aunt Dotty's place at Laurie's Road in Bambalapitiya. My aunt had ordered all sorts of food from the nearby 'Green Cabin' restaurant.

But the main fare for the day at oaths parties is always plenty of liquor. At the time, with the austerity measures taken by the socialist government of the day, foreign liquor was highly taxed and was beyond the reach of young lawyers. Its use was confined to the elite. So the local brew, Arrack, was the drink that was consumed in great quantity. At about that time, due to the import restrictions, locally made Rockland Gin and Beehive Brandy had appeared in the market, but they were not yet quite trusted for consumption by most. Besides, Arrack at Rs.8 per bottle at the time, it was more affordable.

Arrack is a traditional Sri Lankan spirit, distilled from the sap of the coconut flower. It was once accessible only to the Royal Family, and believed to be a 'gift from the gods'. The coconut flowers' sap can only be collected by hand and aged in Sri Lankan oak casks. Collecting the sap (toddy) is a timeless art handed down from one generation to the next. Containing its own yeast, the sap starts fermenting naturally once collected. Therefore, Arrack is one of the rare spirits in the world which is a distillate of a 100% natural fermentation. Plenty of it was available that memorable night, as was the case in all such parties. Several friends were in great spirit by the time they concluded a noisy musical evening.

* * *

It was on one such occasion, at my friend Rowland Anthony's oaths party, that I met Leighton Jayasekera. That evening everyone's attention was directed towards him as he was in attire we had rarely seen before. He had a belt around a smartly cut trouser and shirt of the type that was not available in the country at the time. We soon learned that he was indeed new to the country, having returned from America after graduating from a university in New York.

I later met him during my first trip to New York in 1964. He had just married and was working as a social service officer for the City of New York. He lived in a highrise building near Columbia University on the periphery of Harlem. It was a pre-war era building with an interesting feature. It had several towers but only one had an elevator. If one wanted to reach the upper floors of one of the towers without an elevator, such as the 21st floor where Leighton lived, one had to take the elevator to the roof, and walk across the roof to the tower in which he lived, and then walk down a few floors to his apartment. That is unless one is fit enough to walk up 21 floors! This was how I reached his abode, when invited to dinner on my first visit to New York. On that occasion, I found our mutual friend Wickrama Weerasooria was visiting him and because of the limitation of space, Wickrama had spent the previous night on the kitchen floor.

Leighton was a modest person who was always in good spirits. He had broad interests in politics, history, and almost anything else worth knowing. A prolific reader, a good cook, he loved the theater and enjoyed a good drink, and everyone around him enjoyed his company.

He literally married the girl next door, Chrisanthi Talagala, a very attractive young teenager who was his neighbor on Jambugasmulla Road, Nugegoda, and a suburb of Colombo. In an intriguing tale of heartwarming romance, Leighton being a neighbor and older than Chrisanthi was trusted with the task of bringing her home from school whenever no one else was around to do so. Chrisanthi had at first called him Uncle Leighton, but with each trip in each other's company they formed an intimate bond which grew and blossomed into a lifelong love affair. Chrisanthi is a wonderful person and they were a popular couple wherever they lived. Since my first visit to their apartment in New York, I have forged a lifelong friendship with Leighton and Chrisanthi. It was providential that after half a century, I was present this year along with Shanthi, to celebrate their golden anniversary.

At the time I arrived in New York, Leighton was planning to dispose of his *Mercedes Benz 190*. I had just begun my employment at the United Nations when he offered it to me at less than the market price. This was my first automobile in the United States and, thanks to Leighton; I was the happy driver of a Mercedes at the age of 27 and the envy of my friends back home. After a few years in New York, Leighton decided to return to his native land. By that time he owned one of the first *Volkswagen* cars that were imported to the United States. It was a bright red shiny new vehicle and again he parted with it at less than the market price. I was once again the lucky buyer. Just recently, I had to trade in my decade-old *Jaguar*. The businessman that he is, Leighton told me I should sell it to him for considerably less than the market value. He explained, it would make up for the losses he incurred on my behalf, when he sold me his cars for less than their real value, because I was just starting life. Needless to say I had no choice, but to comply with his seemingly cogent argument!

He had a phobia which prevented him from getting on a plane most of his life. So he returned to Colombo on freighters, which were less costly than passenger ships. Once he got to Europe on a freighter he drove overland to Basra, a port city in Iraq, from where he caught another freighter. He took a good part of the year getting to and from Colombo but he enjoyed it all and soaked in the experiences in doing so.

When I came to Colombo after they had returned, I found Crisanthi was expecting their first child, a son, Leshan. I invited them on a trip to Diyatalawa in the hill country. We traveled along the winding mountainous roads and throughout the half-day trip Crisanthi would throw up every few miles. But as always, she was a great sport and we had a good time once we reached Diyatalawa. At the time Leighton worked as the Secretary to the Supreme Court Justice Christie Weeramantry.

After a few years the travel bug beckoned him to a trip on yet another freighter. This time he sailed via Japan, to the West Coast of the United States, from where he was planning to take a Greyhound Coach to New York. After he had left Colombo, for a few months I had not heard from him though by that time he was supposed to have reached the United States. I was particularly concerned, because when he returned home, he had left the funds he had here in my charge. At the time, exchange regulations were so tight and it was uncertain whether any funds taken to Sri Lanka could ever be repatriated. That was why he left behind part of the savings he had. Eventually one day I received a post card from him informing that his freighter had broken down and he was stranded in a port city. The parts needed to repair the freighter had to come from a distant port in another passing freighter. He did not really mind all that, as long as he had a supply of cigarettes, because he had no particular hurry to get to his destination.

Finally, when he arrived, he was met at the Los Angeles port by a mutual friend, Mil Gooneratne. Mil was in New York when I met him in Leighton's company, and he later moved to the West Coast with his wife Jayanthi.

In New York, Leighton had worked as a Social Services Officer for the City of New York, and his old job was available on his return there. Mil forced him to join the Social Service Department in the City of Los Angeles, which Leighton agreed to as a temporary measure. But as time passed, Leighton decided to settle down in Los Angeles, and Chrisathi who patiently tolerated Leighton's schengans joined him there.

Mil and Jayanthi were staying in a small apartment complex behind the house of one of the early Sri Lankan settlers on the West Coast, Mr. Sam Hathurusighe. Unlike today, where there are over 25,000, at the time, there were only a few Sri Lankans in Southern California. Several of the few were lodging in the same complex. Among them was Sara Saravanabahvan, an accomplished cricketer of my vintage and his wife, Travis and Barbara Willenberg, and a Muslim couple, a motley crowd, but representing the ethnic amity that prevailed among my generation; before the ethnic enmity generated by the tragic terrorist war that engulfed their native country in the decades that followed.

On one occasion, I visited Leighton and Crisanthi for a week- end at that location, which they called the 'colony', while others called it the Sri Lankan Ghetto! I had the opportunity to meet some of Leighton's friends and observe that their week-ends were consumed by lots of fun around board games and the like. When Leighton and Chrisanthi were previously in New York, in the early sixties, there were even less Sri Lankans on the East Coast. Perhaps, there were just a handful, other than the U.N. and the Embassy staff. They spent the week-ends mostly in the apartment of Lawrence Goonatilake, the doyen of Sri Lankans there. He was a good cook and welcomed his friends as he was a bachelor for long years. We mostly spent the time consuming inordinate amount of liquor that Lawrence reveled in, and his gourmet food, unlike the more sober pasttimes of board games that occupied the members of the West Coast 'colony'. The friendships that were forged among the Sri Lankans on both coasts continue to date.

After a few years he had enough of a career in the Social Services Department and took the plunge into the private sector. By then Crisanthi had qualified as a Montessori teacher and Leighton established a school for her. This was such a success, he opened two more. He then purchased a gas station and a car-wash and found himself to be a full-time business operator. As time passed, Leighton ventured into investing in real estate for rental purposes, and began managing rentals on a full-time basis. By then, he had moved to a distant suburb of Los Angeles, San Bernardino, considered then to be a remote outpost which later blossomed into a large and vibrant satellite city of Los Angeles. In due course, Leighton disposed of the gas station and leased out the schools. In the meantime, Crisanthi's school flourished. During this period I used to visit them whenever I happened to be on the West Coast of the United States on official work or give guest-lectures at some universities in the area.

On some of those visits Leighton used to drive me to nearby attractions such as Las Vegas. My first visit there in the late sixties was in his company. We stayed at the famed Tropicana hotel, where the world-famous Moulin Rouge show was featured. Built in 1957, it was one of five or six hotels in Vegas, which now sports more than fifty casino-hotels. Tropicana was a relatively small 300 room facility then. Today the revamped and extended casino-hotel features nearly 2000 rooms, a golf course, spas, tennis facility, pools, theaters, night clubs and other amenities. The historic hotel had hosted such stars as Frank Sinatra, Dean Martin, Sammy Davis, Elvis Presley, and was the location for several films including the Godfather series, James Bond and Elvis Presley movies. It was a very pleasant trip across the Mojave Desert.

Leighton took me to other popular places, like the top of Arrowhead Mountain, which features a large lake at an elevation of about 6,000 ft. That lake happens to be only an hour's drive away from where I now live, more than 25 years after that visit. We also visited friends in the Los Angeles area and I remember a particularly pleasing visit to the seaside resort town of Santa Maria for a weekend visit with my friend, Dr. Hemal Fernando. He is a cardiologist, whom I had met during the time he lived in the New York area. Shortly after Hemal returned to Sri Lanka and established himself as a leading cardiologist in the country. I consider it a privilege to still continue my friendship with Hemal and Sundari.

Once, Shanthi and I visited Jayasekaras in Los Angeles on our way to Sri Lanka on vacation. We were going to make a stop in Hawaii. We invited, or better to say, dragged Leighton as company to Hawaii. Even with our support it was most reluctantly that he boarded the aircraft after emptying a packet of cigarettes in short order. Those were the days when airlines had smoking sections. Once there, Leighton discovered a long lost nephew. Since then he has been flying many times to visit his nephew. Eventually, he bought a home in one of the outer islands with the intention of retiring there. The frequency of his visits to Hawaii increased with his son being later employed in Honolulu. Though he has been to Sri Lanka many times, he has not seen the inside of a freighter since he accompanied Shanthi and me to Hawaii. Gone was his fear of flying in airplanes.

Much later towards my retirement in the late-nineties, it was on one of those visits to see Leighton and Crisanthi, that my wife Shanthi decided to purchase a retirement home in Southern California. It was Leighton and Crisanthi's endearing friendship and their presence in Los Angeles that made us decide eventually to retire there in 2000.

Their son, Leshan went to Bard College, an exclusive liberal arts college very near New York City. On the first occasion he went there I drove him from my home to Bard with his bag and baggage. Leshan used to live with us in New York during holidays and visit us on week-ends. He became very close to my family. It was on one of those week-end visits that he brought along his girlfriend Thushani. Shanthi and I took to her immediately to the delight of Leshan as we heartily endorsed his choice, at the time unknown to his parents. Leshan graduated as a lawyer and married Thushani. They have a son, Kona, who was named after the Big Island in Hawaii. It was in Honolulu, Hawaii that Leshan began his legal career as deputy district attorney.

He spent a good part of his early years there. Later he moved to New York, where he now works as an attorney for the giant multinational company AIG. His sister, Renuka, also became a lawyer and worked for the leading US and European legal firm of Sherman and Sterling in New York City. She married Garfield Drummond from Jamaica, and has a son Theo.

Sherman and Sterling, founded in 1873, is one of the largest law firms in the world headquartered in New York City. The firm has 20 offices located in major financial centers around the world. Since 2005 it has been headed by Rohan Weerasinghe, who became the first non-white head of a major American law firm. Rohan is son of Oliver, and Cristobel Weerasinghe. Oliver, an architect, had been the Town Planner in Colombo, but at the time I joined the United Nations, he was working at the United Nations Office for Urban Planning in New York. He was a relative of former President of Sri Lanka J.R. Jayewardene. Christobel was a cousin of former Prime Minister Sir John Kotalawala. They were most kind to me and invited me for meals at their home. As I was a young bachelor at the time, they were also anxious to find a partner for me. Later, Oliver was appointed Ambassador of Ceylon to Washington, D.C., where he served for several years. On his retirement, the couple returned to Sri Lanka. When I saw him at his parents' home in New York, young Rohan was attending the United Nations International School before he went off to Harvard University to earn M.B.A. and J.D (a law degree). Rohan joined Sherman and Sterling in 1977. He is currently the head of the firm as its senior partner. As a fellow Sri Lankan and as a lawyer, I take pride of his uniqe achievement.

* * *

It was fortuitous for me to meet Leighton at my friend's oaths party. The day I took my oaths as a lawyer, I celebrated the occasion at Aunty Dotty's place. That event marked the end of my days of growing up on the Island. I was scheduled to leave the country shortly thereafter.

— ❖ —

Ending Student Days

▲ *Law College Graduate (1962)*

▼ *McGill Graduate (1965)*

▲ *Our Wedding Top of the World Trade Center (New York)*

Part 5

My Own Universe

"It is not flesh and blood but the heart which makes fathers and sons"

–Johann Schillar

Chapter 25

Meeting Expectations

On my last visit home before I left my homeland, I sat in the front verandah of my father's house in Ambalangoda, and described to him the two programs I would be attending in Geneva and of my intentions of visiting England as well, before flying to Canada. My father listened with his eyes on the sea, glistening in the light of the setting sun in the far distance. It was only when I mentioned that I hoped to watch a cricket match while in England that he turned his face away from the sea to look at me. I saw a glitter of excitement in his eyes. For a moment the features of the young "Prince," who had played cricket for his school, took over his wrinkled, wizened face. But the moment was short lived. He turned his attention once more to the sea and the waves as if seeking solace from a companion he had known all his life. When I reached the end of my monologue, for he did not even once make a response regarding the plans, he cleared his throat and said "Isn't it high time you settled down. One never knows what might await one in these foreign countries".

I cast my eyes on the cement floor of the verandah. Though newly built, slight cracks had begun to appear on the middle of the floor. An ant scurried along one crack pausing every now and then searching for that ever elusive tidbit.

"There are many respectable families I know of, who wouldn't mind joining our family."

I did not oppose my father, but remained silent, my eyes still on the ant looking for food. When he realized I was not going to break the silence, my father said "Hmm, better think about it" and left the verandah. I watched him walking towards the small grocery store he ran, in the corner of the front garden.

I thought about it long enough to realize I needed help from Aunty Dotty if I were to persuade my father that an early marriage before I completed my graduate studies abroad was out of the question. To my relief Aunty Dotty thought as I did and together we convinced my father this was not the best of times for me to enter the holy enthrallment of marriage.

He continued to remind me of his idea in several of his letters, and often sent me the names of prospective brides. Once I concluded my graduate work in residence at McGill University in Canada, and just prior to assuming duties at the United Nations, I made a visit home for a month during the Christmas holidays. When my father, once more brought up the subject of seeing me "settled down", I no longer had any excuses to give him.

Although I had ignored his requests till then, I was intensely aware that my father had sacrificed much as a single parent to raise my sister and me. Deep within me I knew I was not going to disappoint him in anyway, particularly in his 'old age'. I confess, by then the romantic involvements I had formed in my younger days had also receded from my heart. I had no reason not to acquiesce to his request. Accordingly, simply to please him, I made a couple of hurried visits to the homes of several prospective brides, none of which led to a satisfactory conclusion. But my father was happy. At long last I was abiding by his wishes, and at least I was looking.

These visits to prospective brides had their special charm. The young man accompanied by his parents and a few close relatives would visit the young lady's home. An awkward atmosphere would prevail throughout the visit while the two families and the prospective young couple tries to feel each other out to ascertain their compatibility, both in terms of the couple to be and the suitability of each other's families that would eventually become one, if the visit culminates in a marriage. Usually, the host family would entertain the visitors with a feast of the best of food and drinks. The young lady would be the last to join the company of those present with an invitation to the feast. All eyes would naturally be on her though the eyes of the couple would not meet till much later as a sense of shyness would descend on them to do so in the presence of their families. Eventually, the families would find an excuse to leave the couple alone for a moment of banter that normally goes nowhere. It is in subsequent visits usually without the family in attendance that they would get to know each other, if they were to proceed towards marriage.

On these occasions it is also usual for the young man to be accompanied by a close friend or two to keep company in the midst of the awkward atmosphere that follows. They also serve as sounding boards for the young man concerning the suitability of the prospective bride because one's friends know you best. Among friends, there are some who are known not to miss any such opportunity. Among our friends, Hema and one affectionately called Bola Cooray were ever ready to be companions. They relished the idea of enjoying a good feast and never missed an opportunity. Generally on return they would discourage the young man, so that they can make additional visits for yet another feast!

Arranged marriages have been an accepted practice in Sri Lanka for ages. This is the case in the neighboring countries (India, Pakistan, Bangladesh), as well as other Asian countries (Iran, Iraq, Afghanistan, Malaysia, Indonesia and Japan), and some other Muslim and African countries. An arranged marriage is a practice in which persons other than the couple being married select the persons to be wed (usually parents of the couple often with the help of a marriage broker, a relative or a priest). Such marriages have deep roots in royal and aristocratic families around the world including Europe (British Royal family followed it without exception). They are established traditions in many cultures. While some marriages are forced, generally parents ensure that their sons and daughters are satisfied with their parents' choices. It is based on the premise that parents know their children best and have the wisdom and wherewithal to select the best candidates. Such a marriage would benefit from the support and encouragement of the elders and hence would be more durable and permanent.

Arrange marriages were more prevalent also because of the nature of the society at the time. It was a period when girls in particular were heavily protected. It was a handful, who would venture out on their own without a family escort, except to and from school. It would not be a common scene at all to see a young boy and a girl together except in the company of family members. It would for instance be shocking to see a couple in their mid-twenties to be seen in a movie house. This was so even during their university days, or even in the early stages of their working life. The only exceptions were among the highly westernized families particularly in the Eurasian community. It was therefore natural that young people had to depend on arranged marriages. Some of my Law College and University friends were in the forefront of a change that began particularly in the sixties with the expansion of the university system. The beginning of a radical change started only in the mid-seventies. Today, the roles are reversed with arranged marriages being the exception, although still quite prevalent even among the expatriate Sri Lankan communities around the world.

In some cases however, even during my time, a prospective partner may be selected by the son or daughter instead of by the parents or by a matchmaker. In such cases, the parents will either disapprove of the match and forbid the marriage, or approve the match and agree to proceed with the marriage. They are distinct from love marriages, because courtship is curtailed or absent and the parents retain the prerogative to forbid the match. This was the case with my parents, as noted earlier.

In such cases, even if the couple does not love each other at first, the expectation is that a greater understanding between the two would develop, aided by their often similar socio- economic, religious, political and cultural backgrounds and the strong support of parents and family. Among the cultural factors that are almost always considered important is that both parties should belong to the same caste. For my father, it was important that his children were married from his caste (Karava caste: traditionally they were fishermen, naval warriors, seafaring traders, boat-builders, carpenters; and, more recently, many were pioneering renters and landowners). When it came to marriage of his children, all those factors were of importance to my father and in his own case they happened to coincide with those of my mother. I knew very well that he did not look favorably upon marriages that were not blessed by him from the experience of my Aunt Dotty, who ran away with the love of her life (her cousin), and did live happily ever after though she was, for quite sometime, completely cut-off by my father's family.

After a year of employment at the United Nations, I visited home at Christmas, to hear the same demand from my father, but this time in a more intense manner. He seemed to indicate that he would consider it a disappointment if his request was not taken seriously. This was particularly so because he had, by then, begun to suspect I might be romantically involved with someone in New York, and that this could be the reason for my rejection of the proposals he brought to me. In the end, it was clear that I would have to relent or go against my own intentions of not seeing him disappointed. This time not only my father but the whole family zeroed in on a person they considered to be the best partner for me. She and her family in general met the criteria of an arranged marriage.

Among the cultural criteria before marriage is considered was horoscope matching, a tradition in some of the Asian countries like India and Sri Lanka. When a baby is born, parents used to consult an astrologer and a horoscope was made according to the alignment of planets on the date and time of birth. This tradition is deep rooted in Sri Lanka. When it comes to marriage, seeking a potential couple with matching horoscopes is considered a basic requirement for a successful marriage. It is believed that if the two horoscopes of the potential pair do not match they risk their peace, health, wealth, prosperity, happiness and even the lives of unborn children. The horoscope is also supposed to indicate if a separation or divorce is predicted and in the event of such a prediction, marriage is not recommended. In my case my horoscope and that of the potential partner found by the family were supposed to have matched.

* * *

The young lady, Mangalika Jayasuriya (Mangali), was from a well-known family 'down-south'. Her father was a prominent lawyer, a landed proprietor and race-horse owner, E.M.W. (Edwin) Jayasuriya. He had married Mangali's aunt who had died young, leaving four young siblings. He then married his former wife's only sister, Dora Jayasuriya (nee Fernando), who by then was divorced from her first husband, Wilmot Perera, a prominent politician and the first Ambassador to China. At St. Bridget's Convent, a leading girl's school in Colombo, Dora J was a classmate of Mrs. Sirimavo Bandaranayke, who became the World's first lady Prime Minister. The only offspring from Edwin and Dora's marriage was Mangali, but the family grew up together as one family, because they were all half-brothers and half-sisters.

Mangali's eldest half-sister was Kusuma, who married Senarath Dias, a lawyer who became the Public Trustee of Sri Lanka. He hailed from the famous Dias family of Panadura. They lived in Senarath's inherited three-storey mansion 'Silumini,' next door to his aunt, the grandmother of Prof G.L. Peiris, Professor of Law and Cabinet Minister. They were a very warm couple who treated me as a close friend than a relative by marriage. Senarath was a debonair person who enjoyed a good drink and conversation and welcomed my company. He was an avid wildlife fan who introduced me to the beauty and charm of the wild by taking me along to Yala and Wilpattu National Parks. Their only son, Vimal, was a bright lad. After his schooling days at Royal College, he proceeded to the UK and obtained an Industrial Engineering degree from Loughborough University. Thereafter, he came to the United States and spent a year living with us in New York, while he earned his Master's degree in Industrial Engineering from Columbia University. Later in life he worked at the National Institute of Business Management (NIBM) in Colombo, and still later as an international consultant in several Asian countries. He also managed the Beruwela Arrack Distillery, which was a family concern.

Next to his mother Kusuma, was her brother Sena, who after his studies at Royal College, Colombo, proceeded to the UK and graduated from Manchester University. He later earned a Masters degree from the University of the Philippines. For a short while after his return home, he worked at the Lake House as a sub-editor of the 'Daily News' paper. Shortly thereafter, his father passed away and he took over the management of the family plantations and the distillery. He occupied the family house on Turret Road (now Dharmapala Mawata), Kollupitiya, in Colombo. He had a large circle of friends who visited him there, and never felt the need to marry, and remained a lifelong bachelor. He was a voracious reader and had an exceptionally large library of books and western music, which included the family collection that he inherited. I used to be a regular visitor to his library and enjoyed the variety that it offered. He was also a compulsive conversationalist particularly on political issues around the world. He would not release me easily whenever I visited him, but I truly enjoyed chatting with him.

His two younger sisters too remained as spinsters spending most of their adult life on religious and philanthropic affairs. They lived together in a spacious house on Horton Place, Colombo. The younger of the two, Ranjini was the tennis champion of Ceylon for several years and won the Asian Games Gold Medal in Bangkok in 1960. They were both very religious and philanthropic to a fault.

This was the family I was to join through my marriage to Mangali.

Today, as I retrace my steps to those decisive days of my life nearly fifty years ago, I realize I cannot, in all honesty, claim I had stepped into this union blind-folded and unaware of where I was heading. In the end, no matter what the motivations were, no matter how young I was, the decision to marry Mangali was mine and mine alone.

Our engagement was announced in December, 1965. I returned home in June the following year, to be married. About a week before the wedding, my Aunt Dotty questioned me as to whether I was sure that I was ready to get married to Mangali. Mangali's brother, Sena, told me he wondered how one could just jet in from New York and at relatively short notice get married. Though the latter comment, coming from a lifelong bachelor, was not surprising, both were obviously expressing some doubts about the impending union. I paid no particular attention to their comments, though naturally, I may have had concerns about an arranged marriage, just as much as Mangali would have entertained such concerns. But arranged marriages were the norm of the day. Some people fell in love and married and others marry and fell in love. No one had chartered a sure course as to how life would unfold in a marriage.

My father, on the other hand, was most pleased and went ahead with all the arrangements to make the wedding ceremony of his only son a great success. The formal part of the wedding was held at Mangali's home on the morning of an auspicious day, with relatives and close friends present from both families, followed by a reception at the Mount Lavinia Hotel by the sea with a larger gathering. The Mount Lavinia Hotel was built to be the weekend house of the then British Governor Sir Thomas Maitland. It is said that he lived there with his mistress, a native gypsy girl and flamingo dancer named Lovina, and the hill on which the hotel stood was named after her. It is a magnificent colonial building with large rooms and great halls. It became a hotel in 1877. It is now a thoroughly modernized hotel much in demand because of its location surrounded by the Indian Ocean with a fabulous beach front.

A mentor of mine and a distant relative from Ambalangoda, Supreme Court Justice G.P.A Silva, was my attesting witness, while my Richmond College principal E.R. De Silva, proposed the toast. In the wedding party were my close friend Bandu and my Cousin Sarath, along with the twins Dayamini and Dayanthi Fernando, and Sherine Peiris. Dayanthi married Diva Sandrasagara in New York after she joined the United Nations. They are both now retired and live in Princeton, New Jersey, in close proximity to their son Mitra and his family. Dayamini, who became a dietician remained single and lives in New York City. Sherine married Moritz Fernando, an accountant, and lives in London where their two daughters, Shamira, a psychologist and Shehani, a television producer at BBC, are based. Over the years, we have all been as close as friends could be and it is a blessing that we are all in contact to date.

After the wedding, we proceeded to New York. We used to return home once a year for a long vacation. It was during one of those vacations that we accompanied Mangali's mother to the Buddhist pilgrimage sites of India, (Bodh Gaya - The site of the Enlightenment of Gautama Buddha; Sarnath, outside Varanasi - The site of the First Sermon; Kushinagar - the site of the Buddha's paranibbana (death); Nalanda, - site of an ancient Buddhist university).

As her mother was living in their home at Havelock Place in Colombo, often Mangali used to spend at least three months with her, particularly after our son was born, while I returned to New York to resume my work at the U.N. Towards the end of the seventies, the differences which my Aunty Dotty and Mangali's brother Sena had possibly sensed before the marriage, became more and more apparent. Slowly but surely, by the early eighties, it became obvious that Mangali and I were not destined to live together as man and wife for the rest of our lives.

As fate would have it, about this time I also heard from Aunty Dotty that our horoscopes had been difficult to match, as several horoscope readers had given different interpretations with regard to our union. My father was not deterred. He gave credence to the positive aspects of the interpretations. It is possible that meeting Shanthi, my present wife, just about the same time, would have precipitated the situation. Towards the latter part of 1982, Mangali returned to Colombo with her mother who was visiting us at the time. Shortly after, I was divorced from her.

— ❖ —

Chapter 26

Making a Choice

In the year 1982, on a memorable day I met my wife Shanthi. I had known her for some years simply as an acquaintance. We met mostly at the Buddhist temple or at a few social gatherings. But that year, when we met as our eyes clinched across the room, so did our hearts. It was as if destiny was telling us we were made to spend the rest of our lives together, holding each other's hands, to share the laughter and the tears that lay in the years stretched before us.

When I met her, Shanthi Nanayakkara was married to Ananda De Silva who, as luck would have it and though I did not remember, had been my classmate in the primary school at the Dodanduwa Buddhist Mixed School. He was a civil engineer, who had come to the United States on a Fulbright scholarship in the late-sixties. He married Shanthi in 1970. By the early-1980s he had become a partner of an engineering firm and was resident in Englewood, New Jersey. By then, they had two sons Chaminda and Janaka. In the late-seventies, due to the complexities of her own marriage, Shanthi had twice departed with her children to the U.K., where her two sisters were then resident. She had no intention of returning home to New Jersey.

Shanthi's two sisters, Brenda (Chitra) and Princy (Sujatha) were long-time residents in the United Kingdom. Elder of the two, Chitra, just like Shanthi, was educated at Visakha Viddyalya, Colombo. Sujatha was educated at Devi Balika Vidyalaya. Chitra, a batch-mate of Ananda at the University of Ceylon, was a graduate in Chemistry and worked as a chemist for a technological firm in London. She married Dr. Nanda Wijewardane, a physician who had been an officer in the Department of Health in Colombo. He later was practicing as a physician in London. She had no children. She purchased a house in Isleworth, London, near the airport, and her choice of location was solely because Shanthi and I were visiting or transiting through London several times a year on official U.N. duties, and also on vacation trips to Sri Lanka. Later, when she retired, she purchased a spacious apartment near the beach in Mount Lavinia, where we were invited to spend vacations. Today, in her retirement, she lives partly in London and partly in Colombo. She is a soft-hearted person who now spends her time with friends enjoying and helping in social and religious activities.

Sujatha, who obtained a Nursing degree in the U.K., was employed at the Chichester Hospital, and was resident at Bognor Regies. She married Nihal Wickramatunge, a refrigeration engineering technician. They have two sons Robert (Bobby) and Amal. Bobby earned a degree in aerospace engineering from the University of London. He spent several internships in my United Nations Office for Outer Space Affairs in New York and Vienna, and eventually was employed as a technical specialist in the Vienna Office. He is in charge of the United Nations registry of spacecraft, satellites and other objects launched into space. While we were in Vienna, he resided with us for some time, and remains quite close to us. More recently, Bobby purchased an attractive home with a spacious garden within walking distance of where Shanthi and I live in Corona, Los Angeles.

Sujatha's second son, who married Anshu Wedamulla, is a partner in an IT company which has an office in Sri Lanka to carry out work outsourced from the U.K., Australia, and the United States. Amal unlike his elder brother is an outgoing person which helps him to run a successful business. They live in London with their two sons Anu and Anik.

On two vital occasions, when Shanthi needed assistance while recovering from two different accidents, one in New York and the other in Los Angeles, her sister Sujatha willingly came over from the U.K. to nurse her through long days of recovery. Though separated by distance the bond of love between the three sisters Shanthi, Chitra, and Sujatha, is indestructible.

Sujatha is now remarried to a relative and her childhood sweetheart, Ranjith Kumarage. Ranjith is an irrigation engineering assistant. He was trained at the German Hardy Institute of Technology in Amparai, and worked in the Department of Irrigation for many years. Thereafter, he was employed in a civil engineering firm overseeing road building projects in the dry zone of Sri Lanka, until he left to reside in the UK. Sujatha, in her retirement, returned to Sri Lanka along with Ranjith. She completely renovated the family home which their parents had built fifty odd years ago on Maligawa Road, Kotte, overlooking the parliament. She also added a self-contained two-room apartment to the original building for her sons, who live abroad, to occupy on their vacations to Colombo. Shanthi and I were one of the first guests in her apartment during our vacations in Colombo. Sujatha now circulates between her home in Sri Lanka, her son Amal's home in London, and spending vacations with us and her son Bobby in Los Angeles.

Shanthi's father, Nanayakkarage Justin Ernest Reginald Perera, was a well-known educator and had been the principal of several government schools before he migrated to Malaysia, where he was the Principal, Prince of Wales College, in Kuala Lumpur. Shanthi's two sisters were born in Malaysia, while her parents were there. During one of our visits to Malaysia, Shanthi and I visited the school and were pleasantly surprised to see a picture of the Prince of Wales College staff hanging on the wall. He was seated in the center. By the time I married Shanthi he had passed away. He was from Kandy, married to Margret Chandraratne of Matale.

She was a kind and religious lady who was immaculately dressed. She had multiple talents, and an accomplished seamstress who enjoyed the art of crochet. She passed on those traits to Shanthi. She lived at the family home in Kotte, and looked forward to visits by her children. She always gave us a hearty welcome during our visits to Colombo. Regrettably, she passed away in her golden age, suffering a heart attack on hearing of Shanthi's car accident in the United States.

Shanthi, the youngest in the family, also had three brothers. I have never met two of them, Sarath and Anura. They passed away before I ever had the opportunity of meeting them. Their daughters Damayanthi and Roshini have been close to Shanthi and the family, and I have had occasion to meet Shanthi's two nieces during my visits home. Her elder brother Amitha, who had qualified as an Assistant medical Officer, resided in Pennsylvania in the United States. He was married to Yvonne and had several children. The eldest, Iroshana, has been in contact with us. He lives with his family on the outskirts of Washington, D.C. The second son is extremely talented and persevering; he was a member of the United States Basketball Team which won the gold medal at the Special Olympics. Amitha and Yvonne visited us in California while Shanthi's sisters Chitra and Sujatha also were visiting us, and they all had a grand old family reunion. Regrettably, shortly after this visit Amitha passed away.

* * *

Shanthi is a caring and friendly person who is ever ready to be of assistance not only to family members but also to her friends and anyone who needs her help. Most of all, through good times and rough times, she has been able to be a loving wife and caring mother, and now a doting grandmother. Obviously, over thirty years, Shanthi's companionship has not only enriched my life, her naturally-gifted talents have served me well both professionally and socially.

Among her many talents, two that have been abundantly displayed by her are interior decoration and entertaining. Whether in New York, Vienna or Los Angeles, where I have worked and lived, she has been able to create a magnificent ambiance in our home. She has designed and constructed the interior decoration in each of our abodes, as labor of love. Her superlative work has been the admiration of every visitor, and for me, it has provided an extraordinarily-attractive place to relax and work.

She also mastered the art of enjoying the pleasures of entertaining. This has been especially important to me. My functions at the United Nations entail social interaction among the officials of the organization and representatives of governments and institutions with whom I happen to work. Social interaction between colleagues at the United Nations becomes essential, because important business tends to be transacted in friendly social environments. Personal relationships built through those occasions invariably become handy in one's daily work. During the last decade of my work at the United Nations I was attending such social gatherings, often multiple ones, most days of the working week. This meant one was obliged to reciprocate. To do so one has to have a presentable and pleasant environment. Shanthi was an expert, who never failed to rise to the challenge. Most diplomats and government officials who represent their countries are provided residences that are suitably appointed for social entertainment at the cost of their governments. The Officials of International Organizations, who interact with those governmental representatives, have to fend for themselves. Over the years, Shanthi had to entertain ambassadors, ministers and other high government officials. It is a matter of pride that Shanthi's interior decor was admired consistently by all our guests. On such occasions her culinary talents were also well displayed, along with the variety of table decors she presented as the occasion demanded. I remember fondly that on more than one occasion Dr. Kurt Waldheim, former Secretary General of the United Nations and former President of Austria, and his gracious wife appreciably commented on Shanthi's multi-talents. My Austrian friends also greatly appreciated that Shanthi had mastered conversational German, which of course was essential for her to be functional in her daily life while we lived in Austria.

Social gatherings of course extended beyond the official milieu to the friends in the Sri Lankan community in the locales, where we resided. By nature, I have always enjoyed social interaction and have had a great circle of friends and family. Consequently, adding to Shanthi's many obligations was the constant flow of friends and family that visited us as house guests. Many friends from my home country and others were welcomed by her, mostly because she knew how much I enjoyed their company. It is fortuitous that she enjoyed or tolerated all such social obligations that were thrust upon her, and of course, without doubt, they enriched our lives immensely.

Shanthi has extended her god-given talents in interior decoration to serve the communities whereever we have lived. In Austria, a close friend, Dr. Alexander Trost, a dermatology specialist at the Vienna Hospital had visited our home. He called upon Shanthi to refurbish the Vienna Sai Center, where he was serving as the President at the time. Shanthi gladly complied with the request and the members of the center were most pleased.

Similarly, in Los Angeles, Venerable Aluthnuwara Sumanatissa Thero, the Abbot of the Lankarama Temple, invited her to do the interior decorations of a new building which was constructed in the Buddhist Temple premises. Shanthi obliged with great enthusiasm. That work was later followed by an invitation from Venerable Wathugola Saranasiri Thero, the Abbot of the Sambuddholoka Vihare in Los Angeles, to undertake the interior decorations of the new buildings at the temple. Once again, she willingly volunteered to comply with the request.

On all such occasions Shanthi did what was required with dedication, devoting many hours of labor to complete what was asked of her to the satisfaction of all concerned. Such activities have brought her many friends who admire and support her work, and we are both blessed to have their friendship which continues to enrich our lives.

Looking back today, I realize Shanthi's gentle, caring ways have touched not only the lives of those living in close proximity to our home in Los Angeles, but of those in our motherland as well. On every visit to homeland she helped the needy and the elderly, often distributing large numbers of reading glasses which she carried from the United States to the villagers. On the last occasion she was home, she donated a few artificial limbs to several disabled servicemen who are still in the service. To our surprise, the army authorities organized an elaborate ceremony at the Panagoda Army Camp on the day Shanthi planned to make the donation. When the presiding officer asked me to say a few words, I said, it was her idea and Shanthi should be the one to speak. Moved beyond words when she was invited to address the gathering of about hundred disabled army personnel still in service and stationed at the camp, she broke down and cried openly in the middle of her speech. All of us in the audience that day, felt the warmth and love that surges within her heart for all living beings, heralding peace and tranquility to the lives of whoever comes her way.

She could not have owned a more suitable name. As it happens, Shanthi, derived from Sanskrit 'santhi', means peace, tranquility or bliss.

* * *

Shanthi and I have been together 30 pleasant years. On that memorable day we were married, with our close friends in attendance on the 110th floor of the World Trade Center in New York City, if we were not in the seventh heaven, we were pretty close to it!

As surrogates for the occasion, Arnold and Joyce Korokian, with whom Shanthi was living at the time in New Jersey, represented Shanthi; while Irwin and Adrienne Ranasinghe represented me. Adrienne served at the United Nations and Irwin was Station Manager for Kuwait Airlines at the John F. Kennedy Airport. Shortly after our union, Shanthi and I purchased a home in Jamaica Estates in New York City, in close proximity to Adrienne and Irwin. We continued our close relationship enjoying each other's company and friends. On their retirement, they too followed us to Southern California and today live not far from us. We are delighted to continue our long and intimate relationship often reminiscing about the good old days in New York.

Our marriage ceremony was followed by a dinner reception at the 'Windows of the World' entertaining area, on the same floor. With its floor to ceiling glass windows, it provided a magical view from the sky of the entire New York area from the southern tip of Manhattan, where the Hudson and East Rivers meet. Viewed from there, were the shimmering necklaces of Pearl the famed Brooklyn, Verrazano, and a host of other bridges that span out of the Island of Manhattan. They seem to compete with one another, each with its own unique beauty. Right below was the great Statue of Liberty, welcoming the many ships from around the world that were docked in the New York harbor, reminding us of the vast lands that were to be explored and experienced in our new life. Yet, the conglomeration of skyscrapers, lit at night like a scene from wonderland, reminded us that this is unlike any other place on earth.

Indeed, the 'Windows of the World' offered Shanthi and me a magical night that began a marvelous journey through life, working, wandering and living in many parts of the world. After many eventful years, we have put down our anchor on the opposite coast of New York, in Los Angeles. We were eagerly looking forward to celebrating our 20th wedding anniversary on top of the World Trade Center, when a few months before that date, the Center suffered a terrorist attack on 9/11, demolishing the behemoth to ashes and rubble. By the time Presidents Obama and Bush recently inaugurated the first of the newly built replacements of the 'Twin Towers', our 30th wedding anniversary was just around the corner.

The years gone by have been a time of great joy. But such are the travails of life that we too have had our share of bad weather, particularly during the two occasions when Shanthi suffered severe injuries from a car accident in New York and a freak accident at home in Los Angeles. She had to undergo extensive surgeries and the recovery periods were long and arduous, but thankfully no permanent effects remained. There were other occasions of grief we had to endure through loss of family and friends.

Thus, life has brought us joy and anguish that it inevitably brings all mortals. Like every married couple, we have faced disappointments of one kind or the other, and had to make compromises where there were differences of opinion. But whatever impediments and challenges we have faced, and are likely to face, given the choice, neither of us would ever trade the life we have been fortunate to enjoy together. Most of all, she remains an indispensable partner to me.

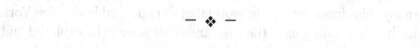

Chapter 27

Indescribable Joy

As I held the bundle wrapped in blankets in my hands and stared at the tightly closed eyes, the ruddy cheeks, the clenched fists, I thought to myself, this is surely the most beautiful baby in the world. I will protect him with all my life, may nothing, nothing ever happen to my baby..... In short, I am sure every thought a first-time Father has ever thought since the dawn of mankind, sailed through my mind during those first few minutes when I held Amal in my arms.

21 July 1970, is etched in my mind as a day that brought me immense joy of the type that I had rarely experienced. My son Amal saw the light of day just after twelve noon, at the New York Cornell University Medical Center abutting the East River in Manhattan, New York; while I was pacing up and down the walkway by the river, in anticipation. At that time I was living in Kips Bay, a highrise building, situated within walking distance to the United Nations, which could be seen from the window of my apartment. The building in which I was living had twin towers of 30 floors each, with a big lawn between the two. It was also abutting the East River on 34th Street in Manhattan, facing the New York University Medical Center.

Though I would not have believed it possible the day Amal was born, six months later, I was on the verge of losing my temper with him. From the end of July to December of that year, Amal kept yelling at the top of his voice whenever he was not being rocked in his pram. This meant someone had to be around to rock his pram almost nonstop throughout the day and late into the night. Luckily, his

431

grandmother was living with us at the time and happily volunteered to oblige him. Amal's pediatrician had advised us not to give into his tantrums, just let him cry. After awhile, he will surely get the message and stop the crying, said the Doctor. But with the mother and the grandmother around, this was impossible.

One day, when Amal was about six months old, I had to follow the instructions of the pediatrician by sending his mother and grandmother away. The first day he was left alone with me he cried for well over an hour. During the next two days the bouts of crying became radically shorter, and on the fourth day he stopped his tantrums altogether.

In later life, Amal grew up to be a listener rather than a talker, and silence was what he observed most. From his birth through his College days, Amal spent about three months of the year in Sri Lanka; his ancestral country (first, during the winter months of New York and later during his school holidays in the summer). These visits helped him to acquire a good conversational knowledge of his native language, Sinhala. He was also able to learn the language and be attuned to the culture of Sri Lanka because of the many Sri Lankan housemaids we were fortunate to have, courtesy of the facilities provided to the United Nations officials. They were most-caring of him as he grew up, and spoke the native Sinhala to him at home and often read story books from Sri Lanka. Roslin, Piliyandala Daya, Leela, Chandra, Padma, Rajangane Daya, Kamala, Nayana, and Damayanthi, served us well, and tended to the children, and the multitude of guests that pass through our home during nearly four decades of service. It is a matter of great satisfaction, that all of them were able to lead a more comfortable life when they returned home, than they had, before they left to join us. Some had saved enough even to build or renovate their modest village homes. Though, sadly, few of them later became prey to the shenanigans of the men they married on return.

Amal began schooling in London in 1975, under the watchful eyes of his first teacher Ms. Sandra Lemmon at Fox Primary School in

Kensington. That was while I was in the U.K. on sabbatical as a Fellow at the University of London, Institute of Advanced Legal Studies. Following that year, Amal attended the United Nations International School, in New York City. His primary years were spent at the Queens campus of the school, near where I had purchased a residence shortly after his birth. Once he reached secondary school, he had to commute by school bus to the main campus in Manhattan.

The United Nations School main campus was a new spacious building coinstructed on stilts over the East River. It had plenty of open space. The rooftop was utilized for recreation in addition to the indoor gym. While most students were children of U.N. and embassy officials, there were some internationally oriented American academics, writers and artists who sent their children to the U.N. school to acquire their education in a broader setting. Among them were children of people such as Dustin Hoffman, the acclaimed Hollywood Actor. As Amal was attending the school, for a while I served on the Board of Directors of the school, along with Kofi Annan, UN Secretary General, whose children were there, too. It was an institution of excellence with both students and teachers being thoroughly international. The school prepared students for admission to universities both in the United States and through the International Baccalaureate Diploma for universities in Europe and other countries. A greater part of its student population typically went to the upper tier universities in the US, including the Ivy League schools and Oxbridge in the U.K.

Amal was a good student and developed excellent writing and computer skills, although his real interest was in the sciences. During his early educational period, desk-top computers first became popular. Amal started work very early on an Apple computer in the beginning of the eighties.

Later on, he used that computer to write a brilliant thesis for his Baccalaureate Diploma entitled "Mind and Buddhist Phillosaphy". I still have a hard copy of the thesis. During his summer vacation visits to Sri Lanka, he took the opportunity to make himself useful.

One year he carried out research work on Malaria under a professor at the Sri Lanka Medical College. On another ocassion, he edited the publications of the Sarvodaya Shramadana movement, a voluantary self- help organization headed by A.T. Ariyaratne, who founded it emulating the movement of Vinoba Bhave in India. While in school, Amal also played soccer and attended the summer soccer camp conducted by world-famous soccer star Pele, who was a member of the World Cup Winning Brazilian team. At the time Pele was playing for the New York Cosmos team. Amal was also interested in martial arts and continues to be interested in it in his adult life.

His other interest was helping to manage the environment. Along with his schoolmates, he was involved in a major environmental project in the New York city area. The work he did on the project won him an award from Ronald Reagan, President of the United States. The plaque he received, which commends him for "Outstanding Achievement in Environment Protection Service", is hanging on the wall of my home office. His interest in the environment continued through his university days, and he majored in Environmental Modeling for his Ph D program at the State University of New York at Stony Brook (SUNY-Stony Brook) in the Department of Ecology and Evolution. During his graduate work he spent one year in the World Heritage Site Sinharaja Forest (one of the few extensive rain forests in the world), working on a Harvard University research project, directed by famed Harvard Professor Peter Ashton, and funded by the Smithsonian. He worked with outstanding botanists Prof. Nimal Goonatilake and his wife Savitri. They are professors in the same faculty at Peradeniya University, and they jointly shared responsibilities for the Harvard University project in Sri Lanka.

A renowned Ornithologist and Conservationist, T.S.U. de Zylva, in his enthralling book, *SINHARAJA: Portrait of a Rainforest*, has described the uniqueness of the forest where Amal spent a year living and working. The author says: looking at the mind-blowing extent of the stupendous wilderness of the Amazon, aptly described as the 'lungs of earth', it is extraordinary that Sri Lanka, a mere fleck in the Indian Ocean, has its own tract of Vanishing Treasure.

He goes on to say, that the difference in scale is graphic, but what is elating and remarkable is the biodiversity of Sri Lanka's Sinharaja, which is varied and wonderful as the amazing Amazon. Shanthi and I had the occasion to visit Amal at the forest station where he was based. He took us on a short tour, and we were fascinated by what we observed. It reminded me of a visit to the Costa Rican rain forest, which I had the opportunity to visit while I was in San Jose, Costa Rica, for a United Nations workshop. After the brief tour given by Amal, we ended up with leeches hanging on all over our feet. Having shared a cup of tea back at the station while getting rid of the leeches, Shanthi and I left the place with full of admiration for Amal, and his American friends, who were roughing out in Sinharaja.

In 1996, he served as a member of the coordinating team for forest dynamic project as a Field Assistant Tropical Biology in Costa Rica, for the Organization for Tropical Studies in the United States in 1996. It was a part of his Ph.D. program at SUNY. Earlier in 1991 he had served the same organization in an ethno-biology field program in Ecuador.

Amal did his undergraduate work at Swarthmore College in Pennsylvania which is considered one of the three leading liberal arts colleges in the United States. In 1988, the year he entered Swarthmore, it was the number one rated liberal arts college in the annual survey of institutes of higher education. It was founded in 1864 by the Religious Society of Friends (Quakers) as one of the nation's first co-educational colleges. Swarthmore currently is non-sectarian, but still reflects many Quaker traditions and values.

Like all liberal arts colleges, Swarthmore has a small student population, under a thousand, with a student-faculty ratio of one to eight. Being a small college the opportunities were very high for individual attention from the faculty. Amal had the opportunity to work on research projects with his professors while still an undergraduate. One such study was published in a scientific journal. It was co-authored by Prof. David Heart, Professor Brian Clark and Amal Jasentuliyana. The study was titled, *Fine Scale Field*

Measurement of Benthic Flow Environment Inhabited by Stream Invertebrates (see: www. also.org).

Amal's interest in biology became more apparent in the final years at Swarthmore. He selected Swarthmore because he wanted to enter a small engineering faculty. Swarthmore is one of the very few liberal arts colleges that have an engineering faculty, and it had less than 100 students. But after one term, Amal decided to major in physics with mathematics as a minor. Later on, he added biology as a minor. By the time he graduated from the United Nations International School, he had acquired excellent skills in writing, math and computer applications. Thus, while at Swarthmore, he wrote some very perceptive term papers in his English and Philosophy classes, which received excellent grades. I still have several of these papers in my possession.

However, once in the university, he was quite temperamental in his academic work. When something interested him, he completed assignments at the highest level. On other occasions, no amount of prodding would make him complete his assignments. He was always good at taking tests. For, instance, at the SAT and GRE tests for College admission, he scored quite high in both Math and English, and this was so throughout his education. Even when he completed course work and took the final comprehensive exam for his Ph.D. exam, he was placed third among dozen students. Because he lost interest in teaching and research, which he was previously inclined towards, he did not complete writing the thesis that was required to obtain a doctorate degree. At the time he wrote to me, "I enjoy nature and being in wild places, hearing frogs and insects, and to some extent, learning about all this. But I don't think I am so passionate about knowledge that I want to dissect nature and discover its secrets. It is enough for me to watch and read about them"

Amal was always academically-inclined. This is apparent from the fact that throughout his adult life he continued taking certification courses in biology and environmental issues, just for his interest and edification at Columbia University long after his formal education had ended. He had other interests as well. When he was at the university, he participated in cross-country races and he has continued jogging as an adult. While at the university he also took to roller-skating and Shanthi and I were delighted to be present on the occasion of the university annual variety show, where he and three other colleagues performed a brilliantly choreographed dance on roller-skates. He continued to roller skate as an adult for exercise and relaxation.

Amal graduated in 1992. I wrote him a rather long letter expressing how proud I was and what I expected of him. My Secretary who did the mailing always filed a copy. Thanks to her, I went over it recently and here is some of what I wrote him. "When I said I am proud of you, I have in mind not only your academic work, but more importantly, the qualities that you have cultivated as a person; a critical mind, balanced way of evaluating what you see or hear, interest and knowledge of the environment, religion and ethics, all of which I trust will help you see life in its proper perspective. Speaking for myself, I wish I had the skills and outlook in life you have at your age. Like most others, I had to face many adversities, I hope you were spared, and had to strive constantly very hard to arrive where I am, I guess with the grace of providence.

... So as you graduate, and about to start a new phase in life, let me wish you success, and once again say I am proud of you. ... Do please keep in touch and never fail to write, call or visit as often as you can, and I want you to know that nothing is important or exciting to me than hearing from you over the next few years when we will be separated by the Atlantic Ocean". Reading it today, I can fully appreciate my father's yearning for me to leave the United Nations and return home to be a country lawyer in his hometown!

I moved my office from New York to the European Headquarters of the United Nations in Vienna, shortly before my sister moved to New York, purchased a residence and established a business in New York. My sister invited Amal to be a guest at her residence, as he had just started working at the Education Alliance in Manhattan after his graduation. A well-established charitable foundation, the Education Alliance is working primarily in the education field, assisting disadvantaged and disabled youth and conducting other related projects in the state of New York. Amal joined its Information Technology Unit as a computer specialist.

Though Amal is a person with a wide variety of interests, and knowledgeable on many fronts, he is very much a service-oriented person who is content with whatever life has to offer. More recently, he has turned his attention to the field of physiotherapy and follows courses at SUNY. He explains his interest by way of his desire to assist the physically-disabled to be functional. At the time he lost interest in researching about the envioranment and wanted only to enjoy its beauty, he also wrote to me, "I am willing to undergo any academic or physical hardship in order to gain the ability to heal and administer to the sick".

In the first place, it came as no surprise when he joined a charitable organization and shunned the corporate world, which was what many in his generation preferred. By nature he has always been inclined towards a minimalist life style, but it is difficult not to wonder whether or not the influence of his longstanding interest in the technique of *Vipassana* (insight) meditation has played a major role in the way he prefers to lead his life. Having committed an appreciable amount of time over the years to this form of meditation, Amal still considers it important to attend one or two ten-day meditation retreats every year, to which he devotes his vacation time. With all his commitments, whenever he finds time to visit us in Los Angeles, it is always a welcome occasion, as we now live in opposite coasts of the United States. With his interesting and complex personality, he remains very much an enigma in the best sense of the word.

— ❖ —

Chapter 28

Circles of Love

I remember how Shanthi closed her eyes and kept her wrists tightly clenched together. I cheered and played an imaginary game of my own as Chaminda wrestled with his opponent in the middle of the ring. "I wish he'd stop. Tell him to stop." Shanthi kept telling me. "Come on son, give it to him" I shouted enjoying myself thoroughly. As much as his mother disliked watching her eldest son in the middle of a wrestling ring, involved in such a combat sport, fighting, throwing, grappling, I enjoyed watching him provided he came to no harm. Wrestling fascinates me. It is one of the few sports I had not participated in during my youth.

Shanthi's two sons Chaminda and Janaka, along with my son Amal, were a close-knit trio, who grew up as one family. Growing up, all three provided Shanthi and me a great sense of responsibility as well as immense joy.

Chaminda and Janaka spent weekends and holidays with us. During the weekdays, they lived with their father, who by then was remarried, because they attended Englewood High School in New Jersey, where the father lived.

They were both good students. Chaminda was the Englewood School and New Jersey State Champion in wrestling. Janaka's interest was in theater. He actively participated in the school productions and enjoyed being involved in set-design.

On completing his education at Englewood, Chaminda attended Case Western University in Cleveland, Ohio. He was a good student and made the Dean's Honors list during his days at the university. He graduated with a degree in English and psychology, Janaka attended Westchester University in Pennsylvania and Rutgers University in New Jersey. They both, like Amal, were very proficient in the field of Information Technology (IT) and, like many in their generation, grew up with computers. It was no surprise therefore; that all three worked in the IT field, though none of them majored in that field.

Chaminda took time off after graduation to live in Germany, while we were in Vienna. Since then he has continued to be engaged in the IT field, first in the insurance sector of 'Progressive,' a large group of companies in Cleveland, and now, in the banking sector. While he worked hard and is very successful in his profession, his interest is in fast cars. He invested his earnings in sports cars. He is very kind to his mother and me, often spending generously on birthday and anniversary presents. Recently, he got engaged to Nicolay Benson, a pretty damsel with a caring disposition. A graduate of special education, she is a member of the teaching staff of the School for Students of Special Needs in Cleveland, Ohio.

Janaka, who was interested in motorcycles invested in one and enjoyed riding it to the consternation of his mother. For a while he worked in an establishment that specialized in them in Philadelphia. He later moved on to the County Office of Investigation in Delaware, and then into the trucking field. He married his university sweetheart, Jai Lo, an accounts executive in the investment management team of the PNC Bank in Delaware. She is an incredible person with great ability to focus simultaneously on her family and her work. Shanthi and I feel Janaka is blessed to have her as his wife and the mother of his three children.

Our granddaughters Nina and Kara and grandson Kai have brought a lot of joy to the family. On special occasions such as the birthdays of our grandchildren, Shanthi and I travel to Newcastle, Delaware, where Janaka and his family are settled.

We always look forward to seeing them there, and when they travel to be with us in Los Angeles. Their birthdays have also been occasions for the family to get together. Amal would come down from New York and Chaminda would drive down from Cleveland. Though we are not with them most of the year, we are blessed to follow the young ones growing up with the help of the modern technology of video-conferencing.

* * *

My adopted family does not end there. My wife Shanthi had many friends of her own before I met her. Among them two were special. Apparently during their school days at Visakha Vidyalaya, the trio was inseparable. They tell me Shanthi, who was the creative one among them, wrote the love letters that the other two sent to their boyfriends. Perhaps it was the charm of Shanthi's prose that made both her friends end up marrying their boyfriends to whom those letters were addressed. As the trio remained lifelong friends, my wife's two special friends and their families became very much a part of my life as well. I am grateful for their loyal friendship.

I consider Ranjila and her family as a part of my own adopted family. Ranjila married Priya Batugahage. He was a senior executive in the mercantile sector, serving in the leading commercial firms in Sri Lanka, including Finco Group of Companies; Brown & Co; United Motors Ltd; Mercantile Credit, Ltd; and ended up as a Director of Andrews Travels. I had a casual acquaintance with the Batugahages before I met my wife. This was because my sister and her husband Douglas had rented one of the two houses in Ranjila's family compound, while they spent time in Colombo in between two of Douglas's diplomatic appointments abroad.

It was during my first visit home from New York after I married Shanthi that I came to know them well. Ever since then we have been like a family and we have spent much of our subsequent visits to Sri Lanka in their company.

Whenever we were free in the evenings, we would spend time in the company of close friends and the Batugahages were always present. Priya had a good vehicle and was an excellent driver who could be completely relied on, even after consuming an inordinate amount of any sort of brew. That is no mean achievement. Together, we made many trips to places of historic importance, as well as venues of leisure along the sandy coast and in the beautiful hill country of Sri Lanka. Many of these were places I had first visited in my student days.

* * *

Those trips were all enjoyable because of the beauty and historical or religious significance of the places we visited. But one was particularly memorable. On that occasion, we accompanied our Austrian friends Gerti and Ernst Fasan, who were visiting us in Sri Lanka. We had taken them to the historical cities and ended up visiting the Udawalawe National Park. The national park was created in 1972 to provide a sanctuary for wild animals displaced by the construction of the Udawalawe reservoir on the Walawe River. It is most famous for the nearly five hundred elephants that live there. During a visit, it is possible to see whole herds of adults and young elephants– feeding in the grasslands or bathing and playing in the water. In addition to this main attraction, the park is home to many water buffalo, sambar deer, monkeys and the occasional Sri Lankan leopard and bear, as well as being an exciting location for bird enthusiasts. There is also the Udawalawe Elephant Transfer Home established by the Sri Lanka Department of Wildlife Conservation. It is a facility within the park to rehabilitate abandoned orphaned elephant calves for ultimate release back into the wild. I had seen nearly fifty being cared in the premises at a considerable cost.

During our trip with the Fasans, we camped inside the park by the river. We had a great barbeque night, laced with good wine, by a campfire that was set up by the tour company. We then went to sleep to the sounds of nature, with occasional trumpeting by elephants on the opposite bank of the river. As the dawn broke, we were on a safari jeep traversing the park observing the animal world, in its entire splendor. As the sun got hot, we were on our way back to the camp for breakfast, when we were surrounded by a heard of elephants. Our experienced driver and the tracker were not perturbed, and we were asked to be silent while the vehicle was stationary.

One particular beast seemed more agitated, and the tracker whispered that it had a young calf alongside. We were stranded for nearly an hour, and time to time, we feared the agitated one was about to charge towards us. Through the ordeal, the Fasans in their own usual relaxed manner seemed to enjoy it all. Eventually, enough of the large heard moved in to the thicker forest for us to drive away. As we moved to safer ground, Ernst inquired from Ranjila how she was able to speak to the elephants to get them to move away. It so happened, that Ranjila had been reciting all the prayers that she had ever known, and Ernst had been intently watching her performance. On his return to Austria, Ernst wrote a narrative of his experiences during the visit to Sri Lanka in order to circulate it among his family and friends. The most hilarious part of it was how Ernst assumed that Ranjila spoke to the elephants to give way, so we would not miss our breakfast!

Another such trip took us to several places that I had not visited during my student days. It was a trip to the East coast of the Island. Our first destination was Trincomalee, commonly called Trinco. On the way, we drove up the massive rock in the shape of an elephant (Athagala), in Kurunegala, to see the giant modern Buddha Statue that can be seen from many miles away. From the top of the rock, we also had a wonderful view of the whole region. We had a good view of the ruins of the 13th century citadel of the Sinhala kings during their reign in the Kurunagala era. Four kings ruled from this royal capital for 50 years, from the end of the 13th-century to the start of the 14th century. The beautiful lake that was part of the moat of the citadel was clearly visible in the distance.

Our base was the Nilaweli Beach Hotel by the pristine East coast beach. We took a short cut along an unpaved road across the neighboring jungle, which connects the villages of Kanniya and Nilaveli. A jumbo was cited and there was excitement among some of us, but we made it without incident. Once settled at the hotel, our usual fellowship-hour followed. We were lounging on the patio with a view of the ocean and enjoyed a glorious sunset. We bantered along fueled with Arrack and Ginger Beer, reminiscing of our experiences.

Next day we visited the nearby Piegon Island by boat. It is virgin surroundings full of rare fauna and flora enriching the biodiversity of the East coast of the Island. It is bordered by a coral reef making it a maritime sanctuary. Piegon Island is designated a National Park and it is one of two marine parks in Sri Lanka.

We then set out to explore Trinco city and its environs. First stop was the Koneswaram Kovil (Hindu Temple), a site built in the 5th century. The Temple is situated within the Dutch Fort, originally built by the Portuguese in 1623. It is on the gigantic Swami Rock (a rock of that size on the coast is in itself a wonder, because the Sri Lankan coast is otherwise flat and sandy everywhere). Koneswaram kovil is also known as the Temple of a Thousand Pillars. The primary deity worshipped here is Lord Shiva in the form of Koneswar. During the conflicts between the Portuguese and the Dutch, the original Kovil, which is over 2,000 years old, was destroyed. Several statues were recently discovered submerged in rubble and the sea. They are displayed and venerated now inside the temple.

We observed the religious rituals taking place and offered the inevitable "panduru" (coins) to the Hindu gods, seeking their blessing, as did the multitude of pilgrims and visitors. Many are Buddhists, who are supposed to refrain from such rituals and dependence on any external force for ones wellbeing! Next we moved with the crowd to the back of the temple to see the "Lovers Leap". This rock has a sheer drop of 350 feet. Legend has it that a Dutch Officer's daughter jumped off this rock after a broken love affair, hence the name Lovers Leap. Some of the best and most breathtaking views of the ocean and town can be seen from this area.

Passing the well-kept World War II British Military Cemetery, we proceeded to China Bay Naval Headquarters. The cemetery was established for soldiers of the British Empire who were killed or died during World War II.

Trinco, which is the world's second largest natural deep-water harbor, has attracted seafarers like Marco Polo, Ptolemy, and sea-traders from China and East Asia, since ancient times. It has been a seaport since the days of the ancient Sri Lankan Kings. Prior to the Second World War, the British had built a large airfield to house a Royal Air Force base, and a base for the Royal Navy. After the fall of Singapore, Trinco became the home-port of the Eastern Fleet of the Royal Navy, and submarines of the Dutch Navy. The harbor and airfield were attacked by a Japanese carrier fleet in April 1942 in the Indian Ocean raid.

The naval and air bases were taken over by Sri Lanka in 1957 from the British; today the Dockyard is used by the Sri Lankan Navy, while the Sri Lanka Air Force is based at China Bay. In the early 1950s the British built bungalows for the officers of the Royal Forces. Now some of the old buildings in the Trinco Fort, including the one previously occupied by The Duke of Wellington, are used as residences for senior officers of the two Sri Lankan Forces.

On the way back to the hotel, we visited the hot water wells at Kanniya. It is considered the "8th wonder" of Sri Lanka, and has seven hot water wells of varying temperatures. According to *Ramayana* (Valkami's Epic), Ravana, adventurous king of Lanka is reported to have been responsible for these hot wells springing forth. It is also believed that these natural hot water springs hold therapeutic healing powers for ailments such as arthritis. Our next stop was at the ancient Velgam Vihara. Formerly known as the Velgam Rajamaha Viharaya, it was built by King Devanampiyathissa and later renovated by succeeding Kings. This temple was a place of worship for both Sinhala and Tamil Buddhists. That is one of the reasons that Vilgam Vehera was not destroyed by south Indian Chola invasions in 10th century. The temple suffered destruction during LTTE terrorist war. A few yards away, towards the jungle, are located excellent ruins of a complex built by King Devanampiyatissa in 240 BC, during his reign in

Anuradhapura. According to the priest who guided us, ironically, this was a temple complex protected from Chola invasions by Tamil Buddhists who had come from India preceding the South Indian Chola invasions in the 10th-century, and were living in the nearby villages.

After a good night's rest, we headed south along the East coast, passing Passikudah and Batticaloa, which brought back memories of an earlier visit to my Law College friend Ranji's residence, on vacation during law school days, described in a previous chapter. We were on the way to our destination for the night at Arugambay. On the way, we passed through many small towns, primarily populated with Muslims and a sprinkling of Tamils and Sinhalese. This area later became a hot-bed of LTTE activity for decades. It was also the area that the government was able to take control of first, in its eventual successful campaign to eliminate the terrorist control in the North and the East of the country. It did so with the help of a breakaway group of the LTTE, so-called the 'Karuna Faction'. The leader, Karuna, who had a change of heart concerning the utility of terrorism in attaining their goals, survived many assassination attempts by the main LTTE during the height of the war in mid-2,000. He is now a member of the Cabinet.

We stayed the night in the only reasonably-good hotel in the area. It was on the beach facing the beautiful bay. But the lodges had thatched roofs. During a heavy shower that night, one of our fellow travelers was drenched by the leaking roof. Next morning, we had to travel rather slowly on a yet unpaved, but newly-built road south of Arugam Bay. We were motoring towards Kumana (the bird sanctuary) and Yala (largest Wildlife Park in the country), which offered a feast to wildlife lovers. These locations were not easily accessible on that road. We were headed to visit the historic Panama Rajamaha Vihare. When we arrived, we found the ancient stupa was under repairs. We were informed that the priest who is in meditation does not wish to be disturbed by visitors. We approached the premises carefully and heard a group of Buddhist nuns chanting. From there we back-tracked past Arugam Bay to Potuvil

In Potuvil we visited Samudra Maha Vihara (ocean temple). It is here that King Kavantissa met Viharamahadevi. The legend has it that people who saw a princess landing ashore in a gold-gilded canoe reported it to the King, who hastened there to meet her. The King was informed that the damsel in the canoe was Princess Devi, daughter of king Kelanitissa, of Maya Rata, who was offered as sacrifice to appease the wrath of the sea-gods as the sea-waters threatened to drown the villages of his kingdom (first known tsunami in Sri Lanka). At Samudra Maha Vihare, there is a complex with the well-preserved statues of the King and Princess, along with a statue of the Buddha blessing them. It is near the sand dunes of a deserted beach of endless beauty, with no one in site.

It is believed that the canoe with the Princess was first sited near the shore in the village of Kirinda, several miles to the south. The boat could not land there due to rocky environment, and sailed on to a place north of Potuvil. King Kavantissa, who heard the news and hastened to meet the princess, was ruling near Lahugala, several miles in the interior. When he arrived, the boat was gone. "Ko Kumari" (where is the Princess), inquired the King? He was told that she went to the next village (ara gama ta giya). The King then went to the spot where Samudra Maha Vihare is, and met her there. The place the King went first is a town now known as Komari, just north of Potuvil, and the next village became Arugambay!

We then proceeded through jungle road towards Lahugala and Monaragala. Near Lahugala we visited Magul Maha Vihare (wedding temple), an unbelievable complex of palace and temple premises of King Kavantissa. This complex is similar to the complexes in Polonnaruwa, but not as well known. The most impressive are the size and the carvings of the ornate magul poruwa (marriage platform). In keeping with traditional customs, it is on that impressive platform on which the King married Princess Devi. She is known as the legendary queen Viharamahadevi, highly respected for her scarifies to save the people of her father's kingdom. At the entrance to the Poruwa is the largest Sandakada pahana (moonston) used as a guard stone in Sri Lanka. The entire Vihara complex had covers an extent of about

10,000 acres where ruins of a palace, monastery, stupas, ponds etc. were found scattered all over. According to a pillar inscription there, the history of this temple goes back to King Dathusena who ruled Anuradhapura in the 6th-century AD, and a stone inscription there testifies him as the founder of the Vihare.

Past Lahugala, traveling towards Siyambalaanduwa, we diverted about 5 km towards the jungle to visit Thalengala or the Tharuthengala Cave Temple. It is the largest cave temple in Asia (180 ft x 150 ft), accommodating 3,000 people, and housing the only known prehistoric paintings in Sri Lanka, which were discovered only recently. Fossils of pre-historic man who lived 37,000 years ago were found here. To get to the largest caves one must climb a steep rock. Though the resident priest had built railings to aid the climb, it is one that only those in good physical condition can attempt. Although only one of us climbed the entire way, every one of us was able to see the impressive caves with pre-historic paintings. We also saw the cave housing one of the longest ancient images of reclining Buddha made of mud bricks (about 10 meters), still pretty much intact, though treasure seekers of the years gone by had dug into it. It was also affected by the terrorist war in later years. Those caves were closer to the location where the resident monk lives.

I was thankful to my friend Suneth Rajawasam, nephew of my Richmond College friend T. Rajawasam, for having directed me to this almost unknown historic monument. Suneth, a physician served in a hospital in Kalmunai, not far from these sites. He is an extremely bright young man with an inquisitive mind. On his off-days he explored the jungle area and observed many little-known historic places. When he first visited the caves he sent me pictures of the paintings, asking me whether I would know anyone who might be aware of them in some detail. I sent his message over to Prof. Gananath Obeysekera, Professor of Anthropology, at Princeton University. He wrote back to say the information was so fascinating that he was going to visit the place forthwith. Gananath was a professor at Ceylon University, Peradenia campus during my student days. He is now an acclaimed specialist in the field of anthropology. Suneth was a student at St. Thomas' College, Mt. Lavinia. Just as he left college to pursue medical studies, he wrote a charming book on his experiences at school titled, *Sainted Blue, Painted Black* (his school colors). It is a masterfully written, extremely witty account of his years at St. Thomas'. Having been awestruck by what we had seen, we left the historic caves and headed home.

On the way, near the town of Balangoda, we diverted on a village road about 5 km to see the Bambarakanda Falls (also known as Bambarakele Falls), which is the tallest water-fall in Sri Lanka, with a height of 863 ft. The waterfall was formed by Kuda Oya, which is a branch of the Walawe River. It is certainly a sight to behold. From there, we were on the way now back to Colombo, but not before finding our way to my law hostel friend Palitha Wanasundar's waluwa in Rathnapura, where a sumptuous lunch was served.

* * *

While taking trips with Priya, Ranjila along with other mutual friends such as Chandrani and Ranjith, were something Shanthi and I looked forward to whenever we returned home for vacation. Priya was an enthusiast of the local brew and we carried plenty on our trips. He introduced me to the absolutely refreshing Sri Lankan drink Arrack with locally-manufactured Elephant House (Cold Stores) brand Ginger Beer as a chaser. Ceylon Cold Stores had its modest beginning in 1866 as the Ceylon Ice Company, which imported and used the country's first ice-making machine. Aerated water was included in the Company's product line in 1932 by a German Engineer and bottles were stamped with the distinctive "Elephant" trademark. The leading brand of carbonated drinks was Ginger Beer, which competed favorably in international fairs of the time, and won awards in Melbourne and Calcutta. I still remain faithful to the drink to which Priya introduced me whenever I am back home in Colombo. Our Austrian friend Ernst also adopted it with enthusiasm while he was in Sri Lanka.

Priya and Ranjila visited us in New York and Vienna. On those occasions we toured around, in the United States and in Europe. They were enormously helpful to us whenever called upon for any assistance we needed in Sri Lanka while we were resident abroad. On instances such as when Shanthi met with her accidents, Ranjila would perform religious and other social rituals for the well being of her friend, Shanthi.

When we moved to our home in Los Angeles in 2,000, we moved along with Priya who was visiting United States on business. Ever since we moved to our new home, we have had a stream of nonstop house guests and we feel this is all due to the positive or negative vibes, depending on how one sees it, of having Priya as our first guest.

A few years back Priya and Ranjila migrated to the United States. As we were in Los Angeles at the time, it was natural for them to end up where we were. On coming to the United States as immigrants, Priya and Ranjila rented a lovely apartment not far from us. It was in walking distance to the Montessori School, in which Ranjila was offered a position as she arrived in the United States. It had to be in walking distance to her place of work, because Ranjila never fancied driving a car in her entire life. The school was owned and run by Chandrapala and his wife Lalitha, who had helped many Sri Lankans settle down in the United States by offering them employment and other assistance.

Ranjila and Priya moved to the United States along with Ranjila's mother who had been living with them in Sri Lanka, and their son Gayana, who at the time was in an Indian University in Bangalore. Little more than a year after they moved to the United States, Ranjila's mother, who had been the rock of their family, passed away after a very short bout of cancer. Gayana registered at the local university to continue his education, while holding down a part time job.

At first, for Priya the move was unsettling. It was not easy to obtain a position such as he held in his home land. This was particularly so because they came in the midst of the unprecedented down turn in the U.S. and world economies. Most mornings I would accompany Priya to interviews through out Los Angeles, and return late in the day. After a while, he lowered his expectations and was ready to accept a position that would bring him a living wage. He was very lucky to be called for an interview by Fedex Corporation, for a managerial position. After a couple of interviews, contrary to both our expectations, Fedex offered him a position as Manager of their branch in Corona Hills where we lived, and within short distance from their apartment. After a period of two month's training he started his new job.

By then their daughter Erangi, who was in Washington, D.C. had dispatched her car to Los Angeles for her parent's use. Now the family was well settled in our vicinity and once again we began enjoying each other's company almost every free evening and on weekends. Within a few months, Fedex offered Priya a senior position as supervisor of their twenty branches in the San Francisco area. It was an offer too good to turn down, and they soon moved to San Francisco, where Ranjila also obtained a position at a Montessori School. Their son moved along with them and registered in a local university. He held a part-time position in one of the Fedex centers in the area. They later purchased a spacious home in Sacramento, California, and are now settled there. Whenever there is a possibility, they come down to visit us or we go up to see them.

* * *

Ranjila and Priya are proud parents of their daughter Erangi. From her very young days she displayed a variety of talents. At Museus College in Colombo she was not only a good student but also showed her talent in drama, dance and music. She was the leader of the school band and Deputy Head Girl of the school. Her main interest was in the Japanese art of Karate. At a very young age, while still in school, she became the first woman 'Black Belt' in Sri Lanka. It is a most commendable achievement. Unlike other girls her age, Erangi was so skilled she used to spar with the boys. One burley chap in her training group thought he would have the better of her, but he was floored to the ground in double quick time. Whether out of sympathy or for other reasons, they later fell in love and were married.

Whenever I was in Colombo I used to admire Erangi's achievements, particularly her dancing skills. She was a great fan of Michael Jackson. At the same time, she was a very devout girl, who was respectful of her parents and elders. Before she left home each day she would say a prayer at the little shrine they had in their home.

The family had planned that after finishing school in Sri Lanka Erangi would proceed to the United States for her university education. When I was in Vienna, Priya wrote me a letter announcing the plans. I wrote back discouraging the move because I believe that girls in particular, and boys as well, should have their university education in Sri Lanka and then proceed abroad for graduate studies. My belief is based partly on my own experience, and because, once graduated back home, they are mature enough to deal with the rough and tumble of the environment of the youth abroad, particularly in the United States, with all its distractions. More importantly they would have laid down solid roots in their motherland. The social structure of the youth in the West, and in the U.S. in particular, can be challenging to the uninitiated, who might be easily led astray. While thanking me for my views, the family decided to send Erangi to the University of Iowa, where she had obtained placement with a scholarship. Little did I know that she was by then engaged to the lad she floored at the Karate training class, and that he also would be going to the same university? In any case, once the decision was made I was glad to send her an air ticket to travel to the United States to begin her university studies.

She went to the United States accompanied by her fiancé Sreshta Wickramasinghe. Sreshta was the only son of a Cabinet Minister. His father Wimal Wickramasinghe was a professor of economics and Director Economic Research at the Central Bank of Ceylon before he became the Minister of Environment. His mother, Daya, also was a professor in comparative religion. Both of his parents have authored several books. It is no wonder then that Sreshta turned out to be a brilliant student and an accomplished expert in information technology. After a year in Iowa, Erangi decided she had had enough of the cold winters in the mid west of the United States. Together she and Sreshta arranged a transfer to Arizona State University in Phoenix, where it was nice and warm throughout most of the year.

Now they were not far from Los Angeles, where we had moved from Vienna. Route 10, which goes east-west from coast to coast in the United States, goes via Arizona and California. In that section of the Highway 10, it is mostly a desolate highway through the Mojave Desert. Although the distance is several hundred miles, Erangi used to visit us on weekends whenever she was free. I admired her tenacity in driving back and forth to see us, particularly during the time my wife Shanthi was confined to bed for several months after an accident. Erangi used to visit and load our fridge with enough food to last for a while for the two of us. She bathed my wife and generally helped around the house. I learned that the trip was not particularly challenging for her. She used to drive at 100 mph on that desolate highway. At the time highway patrols were rather rare.

We were always close to her. With such caring attention as she showered on us when Shanthi was recovering, we consider her the daughter we never had. She and my wife Shanthi became as close as any two friends could be. They would not hesitate to confide and seek each other's guidance on anything that concerned them. While Ranjila was still a friend to whom Shanthi would turn to for guidance and help when needed, the closeness that Ranjila and Shanthi have from their childhood is now being reflected in the relationship between Shanthi and Erangi.

We had already attended an impressive engagement party held in Colombo, during one of our visits home, when Erangi and Sreshta also had returned home to Sri Lanka. Not long after that we attended their graduation ceremony at their university in Phoenix. On graduation, Sreshta received an excellent offer from one of the world's most prestigious consulting firms, Deloitte & Co. He and

Erangi, who had also graduated with a degree in Business, moved to Sacramento, California where his new employment was based.

There, they purchased a lovely home but shortly after they did so, had to rent it and move to a company-rented apartment in Maryland, where Sreshta was assigned a project for more than a year. From there they were moved to Pasadena, California, Oregon and later to Michigan. Wherever they went, they had a large community of Indian friends. That was natural because they had many during their university careers and Deloitte employed many tech-savvy Indians. In the community of their Indian friends and associates, Erangi was a live wire in organizing their social events. It was with admiration that I watched how, even among the Indian community, it was Erangi who directed and trained her friends in Indian dances that were staged during Indian festivals such as 'Divali' celebrations.

It was during the time when they were in Pasadena that Erangi gave birth to her first child, Dhilena. My wife and I were there on that eventful day to welcome her. That was just about the time they were transferred from Pasadena to Maryland. Sreshta went by himself to his office in Maryland commuting back on weekends, while Erangi spent several months with us. As Erangi's parents were still in Sri Lanka, we gladly acted as surrogates. The beautiful baby Dhilena spent much time in my home office-room. I enjoyed feeding her, sometimes every two hours. During this period we became very fond of the baby and as she grew-up she has been very close to me, her 'Loku Seeya' (Big Grandfather). We have been visiting each other as often as possible and have been as one family.

During the World Cup cricket competition in the West Indies in 2008, we were visiting them in Michigan, where they were based when Erangi had her second child, a son. On the day of his birth, the Sri Lanka team did very well with the star player Sanath Jayasuriya scoring a century. It was that event that prompted the proud parents to name the baby boy Sanith, after the great player, who excelled on the field on the day of his birth.

Of course, both Erangi and Sreshta are avid cricket fans, as I am. Sreshta and I have travelled together to the Caribbean, when the Sri Lanka team played against the host West Indian team at the legendary Queens Park cricket grounds in Port of Spain, Trinidad. Sreshta in particular enjoyed meeting and chatting with the team members at the hotel. He was overjoyed to have joined me when I had a long chat with Mahelala Jayawardane late into the night, and the next day, with Kumar Sangakkara. They were the Captain and Vice- Captain at the time, both of whom I knew well by then.

Erangi and Sreshta built an attractive little mansion with a wonderful view in Eldarado Hills, Sacramento, California, where his Deloite home office is located. They have finally setlled there, not far from her parents home.

My wife and I consider ourselves blessed to have Erangi and her family as part of ours.

* * *

The third of the trio was Chandrani, who also married her childhood boyfriend, Ranjith Gunatilake. Ranjith was a British-trained technical officer. He specialized in the field of Intellectual Property and Industrial and Commercial Standards established by the International Standardization Organization (ISO) based in Geneva, Switzerland. He worked as a specialist consultant to several industries in Sri Lanka and Bangladesh.

They have two daughters Ruchira and Hemamala, who are the same age as Erangi. They also attended the University of Arizona in Phoenix and graduated in Business. They both went back to Colombo after their graduation and now serve as executives in the garment industry.

Chandrani and Ranjith visited us in New York and in Vienna. We never fail to socialize with them and enjoy their kind hospitality whenever we visit Colombo. Often, the two of them joined us on our trips around Sri Lanka with Ranjila and Priya.

We also came to know their extended families intimately. We have known Ranjith's younger brother Lalith and his wife Ranmali, who were living in Vienna at the same time as we did. Lalith, an industrial expert, was an officer at the Vienna based United Nations Industrial Development Organization (UNIDO).

But our association was closest with Ranjith's elder brother Susantha and his wife Hema. Susantha Gunatilake is an intellectual par excellence. He is an engineer who earned his doctorate in socio-economics. He served as the Director of Research at the People's Bank in Colombo and later had many research and teaching appointments with universities and research institutes abroad. He also served for many years as a consultant to United Nations agencies. He is a member of several prestigious academic and professional organizations and served as President of the Sri Lanka Association of Advancement of Science. He is currently serving as President of the Sri Lanka Branch of the Royal Asiatic Society.

Together with Judge Christie Weeramantry, I consider Susantha to be two of the most erudite and prolific authors of our generation. The range of topics on which both have published books is indeed mindboggling, most of which were considered as seminal works. Some of his internationally recognized publications range from anthropological and scientific evolution to socio-political issues. His wife Hema was a professor of Buddhist philosophy and later she worked as a consultant to United Nations agencies dealing with womens' affairs and related issues. She now publishes the *Buddhist Times* News Paper, and is the President of the Sri Lanka Social Scientists' Association. At times, their outspoken views have been politically controversial, though they were always courageous enough to express their points of view fearlessly.

Susantha and Hema have been close friends and have visited us in New York and Vienna. We have also met each other elsewhere such as in Cambodia where, at one time, Hema was based on a United Nations assignment. On all those occasions we have enjoyed their company and their wealth of knowledge on a broad spectrum of subjects.

* * *

Back to my own children who are now adult men. Every one speaks of parenting as though it is the most natural thing in the world. Rarely does anyone explain how it actually works. It is not as natural or simple as it sounds, and doubly complex for a step parent. In spite of the distances and the pressures of modern day life in America, I am happy that our family has stayed together to the extent possible in today's environment. I was always happy to receive a note, card or telephone call on my birthday or Father's day from the children, and more recently, from the grandchildren. This sense of pleasure is heightened by some thoughtful notes that I have received from time to time such as when Chaminda wrote:

> *"I just want to thank you both for the opportunity to come visit you in Vienna. I had a lovely time and I am looking forward to coming again. Thank you also for the beautiful watch and the camera. I look forward to many years of use and pleasure from both. But, the greatest gift you have given me is my education, for which I thank you both from the bottom of my heart. I hope you both take the same sense of pride and accomplishment in my achievements that I do – for you both gave me the key to making them come true. I hope I will make you very proud. Love, your son, Chaminda".*

More recently, on last year's Father's Day, Janaka sent me a card that read, "to the man who has all the answers!" In his frank, forthright manner he wrote on it:

> *"I'll always take pride in the fact that you chose to be my dad. You gave me truth, guidance and love; I only hope I can be ½ as good a father as you are."*

What he wrote in the first sentence of his note, he had already proven when his son was born two years before he send me the card. The ultimate satisfaction and an unexpected gift of appreciation was received when he named his son after me. I had clearly suggested that he should not do so, because the mere thought was sufficient satisfaction for me.

Today it is a pleasure to travel back in time to my own childhood whenever I am with my grandchildren or Erangi's children. To have them come running to me shouting "seeya," flinging their arms round my neck, and giving me a hug, gives me indescribable joy.

With United Nations
Secretary Generals

◀ With
Dr. Kurt
Waldheim,
Secretary
General
& Former
President
of Austria

With
Secretary ▶
General
Javier Perez
De Cuellar,
(2nd from
left)

▲ *Welcoming Secretary General Boutros Boutros-Ghali, with Under Secretary General Giorgio Giacomalli.*

▼ *With SG Annan*

▲ *With SG Annan (Right)*

▲ *With SG Annan (Above)*

With Head of States

◀ With U.S.
President
Jimmy Carter

With President ▶
of China Jiang
Zemin

◀ With President
of Uruguay
Julio Maria
Sanguinetti

With Austrian ▶
President
Thomas Klestil

◀ *With Prime*
Minister
of Sri
Lanka Mrs.
Sirimavo
Bandaranaike

With President ▶
of Sri Lanka J.R.
Jayewardene
& Foreign
Minister A.C.S.
Hameed

▲ *With President of Sri Lanka Ranasinghe Premadasa*

With Prime ▶
Minister
of Ceylon
Dudley
Senanayake

With Renowned Personalities

▲ With Sri Sathya Sai Baba &
Shanthi at Puttaparthy.

▼ With Crown Prince Hassan
BinTalal of Jordan

▲ With Rev. Desmond
Tutu

With US▸
Secretary
of State
Madeleine
Albright

▲*With Vice President of the World Court*
Judge Christopher Weeramantry

◂ *With US Astronomer Carl Sagan*

Accepting Credentials
from Ambassadors

▲ *Sri Lanka Ambassador to the U.N.
C.S. Poologasingham Presenting
Credentials (unique occasion of a Sri
Lankan presenting credentials to another
Sri Lankan)*

◀ *Ambassador of Saviour Borg of Malta Presenting Credentials*

Ambassador of Ivory Coast Claude Stanislaus of Cote d Ivoire (Ivory Coast) Presenting
▼ *Credentials*

With Astronauts & Cosmonauts

▲ *With Astronaut Buzz Aldrin & Wife (Aldrin, was Pilot of Apollo 11 which made first landing on the Moon and he was second person to walk on the Moon in 1969)*

▲ *With Astronaut Dr. Mae Jamison (First Black Woman in Space on Shuttle Endeavour in 1992)*

◄ *Shanthi with Astronaut Buzz Aldrin & Cosmonaut Valeri Polyakov (Polyakov completed the longest space flight in human history staying 14 months aboard Mir Space Station in 1988)*

With Astronaut ▶ *Thomas Stafford, Commander Apollo 10 & Alexi Leonov, (First Man to Walk in Space on their 20th Anniversary of the handshake in space on the occasion of the Apollo Soyuz docking in 1975)*

◄ *Chairing a conference with Astronutes and Cosmonauts in Vienna*

Part 6

Awakening

"Yesterday is dead, tomorrow hasn't arrived. I have just one day, today, and I am going to be happy in it"

—Groucho Marx

Chapter 29

Carpe Diem

As he grew older, my father looked forward more and more to my visits home. As I made my way through several foreign countries, at first studying, then working, he wrote me letters at least once a month. In every letter the one constant was the perennial question: when would I be coming home? One day he visited Sam Wijesinha in parliament. My father knew that it was Sam who advice me regarding my graduate work in Canada. He had asked Sam "what have you done to my son"? Obviously, the visit was with the hope of enlisting Sam's help in my father's quest in having me return home.

At first, my father encouraged and cajoled me to return home and begin work as a lawyer. Then he urged me to come home to get married. After my marriage which took place exactly according to his wishes, the query would be about the date of my next vacation.

I have in my possession a collection of over one hundred blue color aerograms, written in his attractive hand writing, penned with the multi-color Parker fountain pen he always sported in his breast pocket. Even as I write today, a photograph of my father with his pen in place is staring down at me from atop my computer console. I often wonder why I did not inherit his wonderfully attractive hand writing, and how I ended up with the most illegible handwriting. Thanks to the process of dictation mastered by my most competent Secretaries Imelda Bacolod, Pacita Montanez, Kapilnath Natarajan, Khatun Jivraj and Penny Liang, who served me diligently over the years; and of course, the typewriter and now the computer, many others were spared the task of deciphering my awful script. I have always been grateful to the army of examiners who suffered through my scroll over the years and were somehow dissuaded from giving up on me.

I would return home to see my father at least once a year, often two or three times when I had the opportunity to be in a nearby country for official work. That was never enough for my father, particularly as he advanced in age.

Yet, no matter how much we urged, encouraged and pleaded, it was not easy to get him to visit us. That was because he loathed spending even a single night away from his home, particularly in later years. When my sister was in Karachi, where her husband functioned as the Sri Lanka Trade Commissioner, my father visited them twice. The only other visit was much later in his life to New York, when he came to stay with my family and to Ottawa, Canada, to stay with my sister and family.

By then, he had three grandsons to dote over in North America, as my sister also was living in Ottawa, where her husband was functioning as a senior diplomat at the Sri Lanka High Commission (Embassy). My father had a very pleasant visit. I was able to show him part of the east coast of the United States, and my son Amal had time to get to know his grandfather. While he was shuttling between Ottawa and New York, my father saw a good part of North America. He admired the natural beauty of the place such as the Niagara Falls, but was not so enamored with the crowded cities with skyscrapers.

By the time he came to visit us, he had been the victim of two heart attacks but had recovered well. About a year after he returned from New York, he suffered a series of such attacks. Dr. George Handy, one of the leading cardiologists of the time, was a family friend and as such, would immediately motor down to Amabalangoda from his Colombo base and treat him. Those were the days when physicians visited patients in their homes, and on occasion, even traveling considerable distances from their base. This may seem strange today. But not compared to the life of physicians in early part of the twentieth century as related by Dr. Peter Peterson in his memoires: "In March 1925, I was back in a planting district, as D.M.O. Watawala, the wettest station in the island. I was in charge of the dispensary with an apothecary to assist me. We had lots of patients but most of them were far away on estates. We had to walk to see them. Estate district means walk - eighteen, twenty miles. Very often you had to do that. And there were no roads, either, in front or behind the dispensary. Often it was a case of walking and doing practically nothing because these patients didn't get anything that we recommended. Except for medicine - medicine, they would get from the hospital or the dispensary".

Whenever Dr. Handy would see my father, I would phone him to inquire about his condition. Invariably he would assure me that there was no reason to worry. On one occasion, however, when my father was admitted to the National Hospital in Colombo and was in the intensive care unit under the care of Dr. Walupillai, the other most prominent cardiologist of the time, Dr. Handy advised me to return home to see my father, if I could. I rushed to Colombo, and was with my father until a week after he was moved to the Wycherley Nursing Home, also in Colombo, for recuperation.

Shortly after I returned to New York, my father too returned home to Ambalangoda. While back home he suffered yet another attack. In spite of the best efforts of his younger brother Chandrapala, who by then was practicing medicine nearby, my father passed away on his own bed at age 69; a number of which I have since become wary!

When the news reached me my first thought was how lucky I had been to have seen him just before his demise. Though an immense sadness engulfed me, at the same time I felt a sense of contentment. I had grown up under his wings: loved and disciplined, acquiring the essential tools needed in adult life. I felt I too had served him well. Though I had disappointed him in his wish to make me a physician, but had relented to please him by marrying the girl of his choice. Though I had not returned home to settle down as he desired, I had made use of my stay abroad to provide him some minor pleasures.

At a time when importation of vehicles was banned in the country, except where they are purchased with funds earned abroad, and import duty exceeding hundred percent of the value of the vehicle was paid. I was delighted to have sent him an early edition *Morris Cooper* automobile from the UK manufacturers, to replace his Czech *Skoda* that had seen better days. He was delighted, not because he had a new car, but because his son had thought it fit to send it to him. I know that, because soon after he received it, he would visit family and friends and first thing he would do was to announce that his son had sent him a new car.

Upon hearing of his death there were many thoughts that crossed my mind going back to my childhood. But in the end, I was quite content to accept the inevitable, though it came much earlier than one would have expected.

At the time of his demise, my sister was resident in Colombo. Her husband was serving his home assignment as the Deputy Director in the Department of Trade and Commerce. My sister has always been an overly emotional person. She had cried and mourned the death of her dog for months. So it was no surprise that she was uncontrollably emotional at the death of our father, who had always been close to her. Part of this demonstration resulted in incessant hourly calls to me in New York urging, demanding, and ordering me to return for his funeral.

While I felt the loss deeply and grieved his demise, I was more circumspect of the situation. Long before then, I had realized the futility of demonstrating one's grief when the inevitable strikes and the moment of truth has to be faced in situations which are completely beyond one's control. To me, what was left was to celebrate the life my father, which I knew he enjoyed to the hilt. He worked beyond the call of duty to bring up two motherless children, but always enjoying what he did. Naturally, part of that celebration would be, to provide a fitting farewell. I knew my sister and her husband Douglas, who was treated as a son by my father, would be more than capable of doing the needful along with the large extended family and friends back home. I had spoken to Douglas and requested that the best possible arrangements be made, not sparing any costs which I would bear.

The determining factor in not returning home for the funeral was my great desire to keep the happy memories I had of my father. I wished more than anything else to keep the cherished recollections of seeing him as his normal cheerful self. The desire to avoid seeing him in a coffin was overwhelming. The memory of seeing my mother in that state, when I was hardly three years old, was then and is now a perplexing image in my mind. Perhaps for this reason, I have always avoided funerals, and when compelled to be in attendance, I would have only a fleeting moment when my eyes would meet the departed. In fact, after my father had been cremated, my sister was kind enough to send me a big packet of photographs, expecting that I would find solace in viewing them. Even as of this writing, she is not aware that the unopened package rests in the steel cabinet in my office.

Well past the dreaded age of 69, as I began this retrospection of my own life, my perspectives have begun to change radically. It first began with the reading of Dr. Elisabeth Kubler-Ross's seminal work *Death: Final Stage of Growth*. She notes that ours is a death-denying society, and I could very well relate to this feeling as much of my life I had been part of that. She goes on to expound that death is inevitable, and we must deal with the issue of how to address it. Coming to terms with our finiteness helps us discover life's true meaning. She also explains why we treat death as taboo, what the sources of our fears are, how we could express our grief, how we should accept the death of a person close to us, and how we should prepare for our own death.

All of these are issues that were addressed many centuries ago, in the minutest detail in the most profound philosophy that Buddha expounded. I was exposed to the teaching of Buddha from a very young age. That knowledge was intensified in more recent years, with Shanthi's deep interest in the study and retreats of the technique of Goenka tradition of *Vipassana* meditation (insight meditation - mindfulness).

To know is one thing, but to have been exposed to the issues in sociological terms that Dr. Kubler-Ross explored, was another. Thus, I continued to read her books like *To Live Until We Say Good-Bye*, as well as other related sociological studies like *Many Lives Many Masters* by the famed Yale University Psychiatrist Dr. Brian Weiss, who explored rebirth through a spellbinding case study, breaking barriers of conventional psychology through past life therapy, combining science and metaphysics.

I found the book *The Last Lecture* most meaningful to me concerning how one should deal with death. This book contains a lecture delivered by the recently departed IT Professor Randy Pausch. The lecture followed his being diagnosed with terminal cancer. The lecture he gave entitled, "Really Achieving Your Childhood Dreams," wasn't about dying, but about overcoming obstacles, enabling dreams - yours and others, and seizing the moment. It was about living.

And so with my new introspection of life and death, I might even open the package my sister mailed me nearly thirty-five years ago!

Chapter 30

Puttaparthy

One morning I was finishing breakfast before leaving for work when my wife Shanthi described a dream she had the previous night. She related how 'Swami' came to her in a dream and raised his palm in a manner you see as a stop sign on a pedestrian crossing. I had only a very vague idea of who she was speaking of. The only familiarity she has had with Swami was from driving my cousin Malini to the Hindu Temple in Flushing, New York. Shanthi would drive on odd Sundays when Malini needed a ride, because Malini did not drive. On most such occasions my wife would take my cousin to the Temple where she attended weekly Bajan recitals (devotional services) by the devotees of Sri Sathya Sai Baba (Swami to his devotees). Shanthi would attend to her own errands until it was time for them to return home when the service ended.

That eventful day Shanthi was not feeling well, and told me she would stay at home and rest. It so happened though, that Janaka our youngest son, was to leave for London the next day. He had left his sneakers behind and needed them to be delivered to him. Shanthi drove from our home in New York City to meet Janaka in New Jersey, where he was schooling. She was accompanied by Daya, who was our housemaid at the time. On the way, Shanthi realized that sneakers were in my car and called me in my office to inquire whether I could meet her to hand over the sneakers. By the time I was able to catch up with her, she was already not far from Janaka's school, and I decided to follow her in my car.

In the most terrible, nightmarish moment of my life, as we neared Janaka's school, I saw Shanthi's car meeting a head-on crash. Apparently, the driver of the other car had fallen asleep at the wheel, after consuming a considerable amount of alcohol. When the two cars collided, such was the impact: Shanthi's car ended up on the lawn of Janaka's school, while the other car rolled in the opposite direction, hit a tree, and turned upside down, with the engine resting on the hood. I drove between the two cars, which were lying on either side of the road leaving a clear path for me to drive through, though not a clear head, because of the shock of what had just taken place!

I rushed to Shanthi's car, which was on fire, and frantically searched for a way to get both of them out before the car blew up altogether. I got in the car through a rear door and was relieved that Shanthi gained consciousness within a few seconds, though it felt like light years to me at the time. Then we both did our best to revive Daya who was slumped over the dashboard, completely unconscious. Then the firefighters and the police arrived and cut the front doors to take them out.

They were both in deep shock, momentarily dazed and badly injured. To this day, Shanthi has no memory of what occurred and the ordeal that followed until after the surgery when she was brought to her hospital room. Shanthi suffered from two crushed ankles and a broken humorous; Daya with a life-threatening liver laceration that required eight hours of surgery and a week of intensive care. Shanthi had three surgeries in two hospitals, and three months of rehabilitation before she could walk freely again. It was a traumatic time for the entire family, but with her courage Shanthi thankfully recovered completely, as did Daya.

All through the ordeal, Shanthi was thinking of her dream and what it all meant in the context of what she had to endure as a result of the accident.

* * *

Shortly after her recovery, we moved from New York to Vienna, Austria. My office was moved from New York to the United Nations Office at Vienna. There, Shanthi came across a Swami devotee who persuaded her to attend the weekly Bajan recitals at the Vienna Sai Center. It was a well-organized center that had a good following of Austrians. The local people were mostly professionals including several physicians and academics, who later became our good friends. The Center's President, Dr. Alexander Trost, became a particular friend of ours. He made annual visits to see Swami. It was following this initiation that Shanthi wanted to visit Swami in Puttaparthi, where he lived and carried out his spiritual work.

About this time, Dr. U.R. Rao, the Chairman of the Indian Space Research Organization (ISRO), visited our home during an official visit to the United Nations. He had been a professor of Astronomy at Massachusetts Institute of Technology (MIT), a leading engineering university in the United States and a scientist who was highly acclaimed in India. During dinner, I asked him about his views on Swami. He explained that he was not a devotee, but knew of Swami's work. He said that ISRO had assisted in some of Swami's charitable projects. On one occasion Dr. Rao was seated in the front of the audience when Swami delivered a sermon. He was impressed beyond his expectations at the discourse given by Swami, though he had not completed his primary education. Prof. Rao found him expounding complex philosophical themes that would be appreciated by people of highest intellect; and yet, Swami was addressing an audience of common people. He said Swami somehow had the capacity to communicate with all sorts of people at the same time. Prof Rao had nothing more to say about Swami and his spiritual work. He was never a devotee. Impressed by what my friend Dr. Rao said, whose views I deeply respected, I agreed to visit Puttaparthy during our year-end home leave in December of 1993. While we were holidaying in Colombo, we flew to Bangalore, where the ISRO Headquarters are located. As usual on our many visits to India, Shanthi and I were warmly welcomed by our friends and colleagues at ISRO, although on this occasion it was not an official trip. ISRO officials had made arrangements for our stay at the famed colonial era Windsor Hotel in Bangalore, as well as arrangements for our visit to Puttaparthy. ISRO is an organization with which I have had close association from its very inception, when it was created through the vision of Dr. Vikram Sarabhai who was its founding head. Dr. Sarabhai also initiated the Indian atomic energy program and managed both of them during their infancy. The first ISRO sounding rocket launching range was created in the early sixties under auspices of the United Nations. A UN team, of which I was part, visited the range annually in its early years.

After a pleasant day in Bangalore, several friends from ISRO and their wives joined us for the trip to Puttaparthy.

We left in a convoy of three cars and after nearly a half-day trip we arrived in Puttapathy. There, we were welcomed by the Collector of Andhra Pradesh, the highest government official in the province, where the town of Puttatparthy is located. Among those who travelled with us were the Scientific Secretary of ISRO, Dr. M.G.R. Chandrasekhera, his wife Sheela and their two daughters, Shruthi and Sriya; Sridhara Murthy, who headed the ISRO's commercial arm, the Antrix Corporation, and his wife; M.Y.S. Prasad, who headed the Indian Space Launching Center in Sriharicota; and of course, the Andhara Pradesh Collector, T. Kripanandan and his wife. Over the years, we have continued to meet each other in many parts of the world wherever official work took us. We always cooperated closely in our mutual work and enjoyed each other's company. They all became lifelong friends, who could be considered as family, and we are most thankful for their continuing friendship.

On arrival at the sacred premises of Swami in Prasanthi Nilayam, we had two surprises. First, the Administrative Secretary of the establishment informed us that Shanthi and I were to be housed in 'Sai Sree Niwas,' the Guest House reserved for Swami's special guests, while the others were to lodge in the accommodations provided for the general public. We later learned that several Presidents, Prime Ministers and other high-ranking guests had occupied "Shanthi Nivasa". Indeed, the visitor before us who occupied it happened to be the former Prime Minister of Italy, Carlo Ciampi. The other surprise was much more welcomed. We were asked to hurry and be seated in short order at the public hall, because Swami was to address the gathering that afternoon. This was an auspicious occasion for the devotees. It was a surprise gift because it is not often that Swami would address public gatherings, and it was the only occasion we have witnessed him doing so.

The hall was full and crowds that numbered in the thousands spilled on to the lawns on all sides of the large structure that was the hall. He spoke for about an hour and it was translated to English by a very competent devotee. But Swami often corrected words or phrases used by the translator, that Swami thought did not convey the exact meaning of what he was saying. The main discourse was centered on the theme – The unity of religious philosophies. He explained, that all religious leaders preached the same message which he summarized as "Be Good, Do Good". He pointed out that renowned professors of philosophy in great universities around the world are spending time and energy to find the differences between religions. He said, the world would be a better place, if everyone looked for the commonality in various religious teachings than their differences.

Swamy spoke in a soft gentle voice, but he moved rapidly from topic to topic and you find your mind racing to catch up with his thoughts. He explained that the idea of God, which he defines as 'goodness,' is imminent in all of us. Each person should realize the God in you. Besides high philosophy, he spoke of the evils and temptations that abound in the society, but pointed out that a determined person can overcome these and achieve anything through his own will-power. He gave examples and returned to some topics for emphasis. He spoke of the need to have a pure mind. He said that less luggage, more comfort, made travelling a pleasure. He explained that, by luggage he meant the weight of desire and by travel he meant the journey that is life. Thoughts and ideas, blending with humor, poured down like a cascade of clear cool water from him. He spoke with such sweetness and affability that his simple and direct words made his profound messages stimulating to everyone present.

Dr. Rao's impressions came to my mind as I scanned the hall to note young and old, poor and rich, intellectuals and commoners were all equally mesmerized by the message he was delivering. At the end he recited a few Bajans in a very deep and melodious voice, which resonated throughout the building. What was also amazing was that thousands of people waited in pin drop silence, spellbound by the proceedings, for well over an hour.

The rest of the evening, my mind was on what he said and what Buddha had preached. The Buddha's revelation, two thousand five hundred years before, was to give eminence to the individual. He for the first time attributed to the individual a potential power to rise to his or her full stature through self- realization. I wondered, that what Swami was saying also is essentially the same, when he said the Divine is in you. The way to the relief of one's suffering is within oneself. Buddha's teachings have also emphasized that the effort for one's self improvement should not be restricted to one's own realization and advancement towards Nirvana (salvation). It should be used to help and serve others as well. As I fell a sleep that night, I wondered whether his simple words of "Be Good and Do Good' did not echo the *Dhamma* (the teachings of the Buddha).

After a good night's sleep we were awakened just before four in the morning, in order to attend the *Darshan* (sighting), where Swami can be seen by those gathered to witness him and receive his blessings. On each such occasion, that takes place twice a day, a few are selected for a private audience with him. Thousands lined up at pre-dawn to enter the 'Mandir,' the audience hall. On special occasions, such as his birthday, Christmas and New Year, or other religious occasions such as Deevali, crowds numbering in millions, mostly European and other non-Indians, descend on Prashanthi Nilayam to receive the blessings of Swami. No matter whether it is the daily routine with a few thousand devotees and visitors, or the special times when the attendance grows to mindboggling numbers, all are fed and accommodated for a very nominal fee. The proceedings throughout the day are very well organized and disciplined, making Prasanthi Nilayam a most serene place for contemplation and reflection.

We were lucky to be called for the private audience that morning. It is the custom that if one is chosen, the entire accompanying family or group also could see him in a private chamber. He exchanged ideas with several present. Chandra was asked what his profession was. When he explained that he was Scientific Secretary of ISRO, Swami asked him "what is science". Each of the people in our party gave our own concept of science. Then with his hand he drew an imaginary circle and divided it in half, and explained that both science and spirituality begin as inquiry; and while quest of science reaches the half circle stage quest for spirituality comes full circle, because scientists with limited vision cannot see all things or comprehend them. He noted that the part that is science is understandable, while the part that is spiritual is something we have to seek, and much of it, might not be perceptible to many.

After he invited those present to speak of anything they had in mind, and following a few others, Shanthi tried to explain why she was there. As she began saying "Swami I had an accident" he interrupted her, saying "Yes I know;" and went on to say you broke here, here and there, pointing to the three places that she had broken. And then, he startlingly said, "I was there in the Operating Theater". He made a few circular movements with his right hand and instantaneously there was a shinning pearl and gold necklace in the hollow of his palm. He gave it to Shanthi and asked her to wear it for her protection and wellbeing. He then turned toward Chandra, and in similar manner materialized from thin air a gold ring with a large green emerald stone. He gave it to Chandra and asked him to pass it around. It ended up with me and Swami blew at it and it became a gleaming diamond. He said that green symbolizes peace while diamond signifies prosperity. He then asked me to place it on my finger. Having worn it, I was trying to make it rest more comfortably on my finger while he continued responding to others. Suddenly, he turned to me and said "so it is too tight". I had not thought he had even noticed what I was doing. He asked me to take it off my finger which was rather difficult, as it was tight, but eventually when I got it out, he blew on it and the ring fitted my finger perfectly.

Similarly, he materialized Vibhuti (holy ash) that he gave to everyone present. Having done so, he wanted to impress upon us that he was not a simple magician to behold, and he said "this is only my visiting card and if I do not demonstrate such powers, people will not come to listen to me; the visiting card is not what is important, but the message - Be good and Do Good". That is when the skeptic in me vanished, even though I had been most favorably impressed by the oration I had heard the previous evening from someone who has had no formal education. I had taken the trouble to come to Puttaparthy only as a gesture of support for my wife and carried with me loads of questions and doubts. Thereafter, I was much more receptive to what was happening around me.

He then invited people individually to an inner chamber for a private discussion. When our turn came Shanthi and I sat at his feet and he spoke to us of the importance of looking after each other, and asked whether we had any specific issues to discuss with him. As we had nothing specific except the welfare of our children, which he assured would be fine, he continued to speak of the importance of spirituality. And suddenly, while gesticulating with his thumb placing it on his lips, indicated to Shanthi, in an inquiring manner, that I consumed alcohol. Shanthi gleefully confirmed by nodding and smiling, fully expecting him to ask me to stop imbibing in alcoholic drinks. To her surprise, he said it is fine, because I had to do so, in view my social obligations which were a part of my official functions. This we later learnt was a rare nod to alcohol by him as a story of a different nature was related to us by one who was serving in the dining hall. He had been an alcoholic when his father took him to Swami for advice. Swami had told him not to touch alcohol again, or the next drink he takes will turn to poison. Apparently, he had gone into convulsions with his next drink that he had dared to take in desperation after a week of abstinence. Swami ended the interview telling her to look after her husband well. It so happened that his birthday and mine are on the same date. Whether for that reason, or for other reasons, he took a liking to me, and later, I had several other opportunities to meet him. On those occasions he materialized various items for Shanthi and me, which remain in our precious possession along with one of his robes that he gave us and an album with pictures taken with him.

Following that wonderful and rare experience, we had an unexplainable uplifting of our spirits. During the interview we were asked to visit the other establishments at Prasanthi Nilayam. Arrangements were made by his staff for us to attend the School, the Museum and the hospital built by him. The modern edifice and facilities at the hospital are indeed very impressive, and it is exclusively for the treatment of the poor. No fees are charged. Many physicians and surgeons from around the world, some world famous, come to serve there for two weeks at a time. The waiting list for a place to serve is two years long. The school is equally impressive and the student body is most efficient, spiritually learned, and devotees of Swami. On a later visit, I had the opportunity to lecture to them, an opportunity that I always cherish.

Some of the visits we made thereafter were in the company of friends, such as Ranee, my friend Norman's wife, after he had passed away following a bout of cancer. On a previous visit with Norman, when he was afflicted with the malady, Ranee had sought his help. Swami had said it is his Karma and there is no remedy to what is caused by the Karmic force of one's actions. On every occasion, we had the good fortune of meeting him and discussing issues, except the last when we saw him in a wheelchair and he had by then discontinued seeing people individually because of his advancing age. He would always ask me about the work of the United Nations and I would bring up the issues concerning my country. He used to say that the terrorist war raging at the time in my country, which he always called 'Lanka,' is like a passing cloud and it would dissipate in time.

His teachings are the same as those of the Buddha, but through his work, I feel he was making Dhamma alive to people who throng to Puttaparthy. He often said that troubles and difficulties are part and parcel of human life. They are the results of your 'karma'. There is no point in praying to God to wipe away such troubles; the right prayer would be to ask God for courage and strength to bear all the difficulties, problems and tragedies with equanimity. It is essential he said for a man to live a good life with good thoughts and good actions; only through such a life can he realize the divinity in him. One thing he often said that struck in my memory was that man must understand that everything he does has a reaction and a reflection; it is he who writes his own destiny by his own actions. But above all, I admired him for urging large international gatherings of devotees who come to pay homage, to emphasize on the unity of religious teachings and not their differences, which as we know, have fueled many national and international conflicts in our times.

Since he passed away a couple of years ago, we have not returned to Puttaparthy; but we feel that our experiences during our visits have enriched us, and for that, I am thankful for Shanthi's dream.

Speaking At International Conferences

▲ *Addressing a U.N. Meeting in Graz, Austria.*

◀ *Speaking at a Regional Meeting in Santiago Chile*

◀ *At Asian Regional Meeting in Seoul, Korea.*

U.N. Meeting ▶ *in Rio de Janeiro, Brazil*

◀ *Addressing the Association of Space Explorers (Astronauts) in Washington, D.C.*

Working At U.N. Meetings

As Executive ▶
Secretary at the
World Conference
on Nuclear
Energy in Geneva.
SSwitzerland
Switrzerland

◀ Addressing
IAEA
Meeting in
Vienna,

Serving as ▶
Secretary
of U.N.
Outer Space
Committee,
New York.

▲ *Seated with Space Agency Heads at the Opening Ceremony of International Astronautical Congress in Montreal.*

▲ *U.N. Work Shop In Colombo (seated with Arthur Clarke & Ministers Bernard Soysa & Srimani Athulathmudali).*

▲ *Speaking at UN Workshop in Beijing (Head of Chinese Space Agency, Liu Jiyuan and Canadian Space Agency, Karl Deutsch are seated).*

At the Inauguration ▶ of IOMAC Meeting in Colombo with Minister Gamini Dissanayake & Arthur C Clarke.

Part 7

Ad Astra

This is my Island in the sun.
Where my people have toiled since time
begun, Though I may sail on many a sea,
Her shores will always be home to me.

(A Caribbean calypso)

Chapter 31

The Old Order Changeth

1961 was a year filled with milestones, not only for those of us on planet earth, but also for the stars and galaxies of the entire universe. This is the year outer space first beholds a human being in its midst. In April 1961, Yuri Gagarin went down in history as the first man in space, followed a few weeks later by the American - Alan Shepard. Gagarin's Vostok spacecraft managed one Earth orbit along a preset course, while Shepard's Freedom 7 went up and came back down on a suborbital flight. Both were magnificent accomplishments. In that year also, barely six weeks after Shepard's flight, President John F. Kennedy proclaimed "I believe that this nation should commit itself to achieving the goal, before this decade is out, of landing a man on the Moon and returning him safely to the Earth."

For one earthling, located at Latitude: 06°54'N, Longitude: 079°52'E, 1961 proved to be as eventful a year as it did for outer space. This was the year I had decided with youthful bravado to sit for multiple examinations, conducted by the University of Peradeniya, the University of London and the Ceylon Law College. It was also the year I was elected Editor of the *Ceylon Law College Review*.

Previously known as the *Ceylon Law Students' Review*, it was a law journal, published annually, which contained scholarly articles by well-known lawyers, academics, as well as a selected number of law students, who were encouraged to engage in scholarly publication. It also contained a summary of activities in the law college during the year under review, such as sports, elocution, and debating.

Looking back, I realize it was mainly because of this assortment of simultaneous pursuits, that I had a fair experience in multi-tasking, which became immensely useful in my later years. During my Richmond College days I was also involved in multiple activities. This experience stood me in good stead later through my postgraduate work, and more particularly, during my career at the United Nations. At the UN I always handled an assortment of official and semi-official duties, in addition to the functions of my primary job. And, indeed, it helped me in the final five years before retirement to hold two senior appointments, which entailed a variety of responsibilities. That is a rare occurrence in the U.N. system.

The election at the Law Student Union in the 1960-61 academic year including the post of the Editor, was held before I had decided to sit for the multiple exams. I had thought I would have enough time to edit the Review as I would be finishing my lecture courses and commencing my apprenticeship during the last quarter of 1961.

I had always been interested in the *Law College Review* and considered it an honor to be elected as its Editor. In my intermediate year, I had written an article on the law relating to "Promise of Marriage" in Sinhala, which was published in the 1959-1960 issue of the Sinhala law journal *Neethiya* (The Law). In the same journal of 1961-1962, I published another article in Sinhala entitled "Landlord and Tenant: Rent Control Act of 1960.' Later, two more articles I wrote were published in the English journal. The article on "The Structure and Operation of Trial-at-Bar in Ceylon and England" was published in the 1961-1962 issue; and the article on the "Aviation Law of Ceylon" in the 1962-1963 issue of the journal. There was a third journal that published articles written in all three languages (English, Sinhala and Tamil) and that was the 'Law College Buddhist Annual'. I contributed an article in English to the 1960-1961 issue entitled "Buddhism and the Welfare State".

While researching and writing legal articles were enjoyable and instructive, the responsibility of editing the 1960-1961 issue of the Law Review was demanding and quite challenging. The Editor was not only responsible for the content of the journal, but also for raising the funding for its publication. On the one hand, you have to solicit articles of good quality from prominent jurists and outstanding law students, and ensure that they are of a high standard and suitably written for publication in the journal. On the other hand, you have to solicit funding from commercial establishments by selling space for advertisements in the journal. As far as the articles were concerned, the Editor had to take sole responsibility, but for funding, the Editor could call on the members of the Students' Union and other willing volunteers. Once all these aspects are taken care of, the Editor had to supervise the printing process of lay out, proofreading, and other aspects of printing, to ensure that the finished product is of high quality both in content and appearance. It was indeed, a time-consuming task.

In compiling and editing the 1960-1961 Law College Review, I wanted to limit the advertising space and therefore decided to limit the number of pages for advertising by getting major funding from leading commercial establishments. I therefore sought and received the help of the Law Students' Union Business Manager, Maithri Aturupana, Asistant Treasurer, Oliver Weerasinghe and the President A.S. Wijetunge, to assist me in raising the required funds. They were all my friends and batchmates. Maithri went on to become a leading advocate at the Kegalle Bar, Oliver became a judge of the High Court and Wije became a judge of the Supreme Court. With their help and the sponsership of Elephant House, Nestle, Shell, M.D. Gunasena Publishers, and Baur & Co, where the Chief Accountant was my uncle Weeraratne, we were able to collect major funding. Cheaper, smaller-size advertisements were accepted only as page-fillers where an article ended leaving a blank space at the end of a page. This precedent was followed for few years after me, making the journal more attractive and academic-looking.

* * *

Although it was time-consuming, I relished working on the content of the journal. Most of all I enjoyed the opportunity it gave me to meet giants in the law profession. I made appointments and met several leading lawyers, judges, and academics to seek contributions to the Review. Though some declined, and others disappointed me, the experience of meeting and discussing the plans for the journal, irrespective of their brevity, gave me the needed confidence early in life to interact with people of stature. Eight eminent jurists consented to provide articles. They were submitted in due course, and published in the journal that I had the privilege to edit.

As Norman and Wickama were my friends, it was not difficult to see their father N.E. Weerasooria Q.C. But what was fascinating was to see him in his old Walauwwa (mansion) in the middle of a rubber estate in Kotte and to speak with this giant of a figure in the legal annals of the country, although he was diminutive in size. He was a soft-spoken, kind man who listened to me patiently as I made my pitch for a contribution to a student journal. He noted my comment that an article from him in the journal would be of great encouragement to the law students.

After being lost in thought for long seconds, leaving my throat dry with anticipation, he agreed. Eventually he warmed up to the idea and mentioned he would write about an important legal personality. He added that writing about the travails and accomplishments of a great jurist might add fuel to the burning ambitions of aspiring law students.

Mr. Weerasooria then agreed to write an article on Sir Thomas de Sampayo. The final text which was published in the Review was indeed great encouragement to students. It related the long and patient wait Sampayo experienced, while briefs started only trickling in, in spite of his brilliant career at Cambridge University. Mr. Weerasooriya quoted Sampayo in his article: "I had no outside support. I had nobody to back me or exercise any influence on my behalf. So I had simply to work on my own account. I did not think of the fee I got. They were not very high fees either. I used to spend sleepless nights, go through the papers and next morning give over the papers to the Solicitor or Proctor. The fee came afterwards and that was a guinea." He went on to write not only about Sampayao's great learning and wisdom, but also of his humanism and humility, particularly how he encouraged his Juniors, complimenting on their "great effort" even when the case was lost, provided his junior had done his best. Mr. Weerasooria also quoted from Sampayo's farewell to the Bar on the occasion of his retirement. "I am but a learner in the science of Law which is not only noble but exacting. I may, perhaps, say that I am one of those who look into a deep well and think they can see the bottom without being aware that beneath the deepest depth there is a deeper still". Sir Thomas de Sampayo went on to become a Queen's Counsel and a Senior Puisne Judge, a rare honor for a Ceylonese during the British era. N.E. Weerasooria in writing of Thomas de Sampayo imparted many lessons to law students.

Another giant of the Bar whom I had the privilege of meeting in his chambers at his residence one Sunday morning was N.K. Choksy Q.C. He had that magic of giving me the courage required to approach him and speak my mind, which he instilled in me with just a nod and a smile. Such power, such grace, I was humbled. In the course of the discussion he mentioned that while it is important to learn the law, it is equally important to know the procedures and ways and means of taking your case to a successful conclusion, even when one had a bad case. He asked whether he could contribute a piece to the Review with some pointers from his experiences. I readily agreed. In due course he handed me a text with the title 'Random Reflections and Recollections', which contained a brilliant lesson in the art of presentation in court. He had a good memory, and through the reminiscences of not-so- pleasant experiences of his junior lawyers, he conveyed many important messages. His understudies, who in time learned useful lessons, later became effective lawyers with successful careers. "Random Reflections" was both a humorous and highly educational article.

Of course there were several analytical articles as well. These were contributed by prominent lawyers: R.K.W. (Rajah) Goonesekere, lecturer in Law at the University and later principal at Law College; Dr. H.W. Tambiah Q.C. and later Judge of the Supreme Court; J.A.L.

Cooray. These prominent constitutional experts were among those who contributed learned articles in fields of their specialization. When I first met them, they were all extremely courteous, and I was happy to meet them at the time. Our mutual cordiality helped in continuing my association with them in later years. It was also the first occasion I met Lakshman Kadiragama, then a prominent civil lawyer, who later became an official of the United Nations Agency for the protection of Intellectual Property (WIPO) in Geneva, Switzerland. I used to meet him during my visits there or on his visits to the U.N. in New York. The association continued when he became the Foreign Minister of Sri Lanka. I visited him in his official residence only a few months prior to his unfortunate assassination by the LTTE. He inquired of my plans for my impending retirement. Dr. M.J.L. Rajanayagam, Legal Adviser of the Central Bank, whom I had met during my temporary employment at the Central Bank, contributed a scholarly article outlining a case for "Reform of the Banking System in Ceylon".

My interests at the time were very much on international affairs, and I wanted the Review to carry articles on international aspects of law. I approached Austin Gunesekare, who had just returned after completing his Masters Degree in Law (LL.M) from New York University Law School in the field of international law. He readily agreed to write a summary article on the more extensive work he completed for his LL.M. on the subject of 'Jurisdiction Obtained in Violation of International Law'.

I then turned to foreign sources and the obvious choice was Prof. Dr. (Mrs.) Gesina Van Der Molen, a prominent Dutch jurist who had just visited us at the Ceylon Law College. She was a professor of international law and relations at the University of Amsterdam, and had been the Dutch delegate to United Nations legal conferences. I was delighted to receive an article from her, on 'Law, Politics and Ethics in International Relations.'

In her brilliant article she argued for a strengthened system of international law and organization in the wake of the changing dynamics of the world order. She pointed out that: "In the turmoil of international life which is daily forced on us, we are becoming more and more aware of the interdependence of all nations and states. What is going on in one part of the world may have its effects on any other part, directly or indirectly. In a sense no country, no state is independent. They are all dependent on each other, not only economically, but also politically. Even the big Powers are not fully free. They have to reckon seriously with conditions, circumstances and even ideologies that prevail in other countries. Even more than that, our national life may at any time be disturbed by forces from abroad we can neither control nor stop. The whole world-picture has changed rapidly and profoundly within a quarter of a century, whether we like it or not we all are closely bound together for better and for worse. Economically, culturally and politically the entire world has shrunk into one great coherent unit". She lamented that "The development of the legal world structure has not kept pace with this dynamic evolution. The result is a very dangerous situation. On the one side, a closer contact between peoples and states than ever before, which easily may lead to frequent clashes of interests; on the other side the legal structure of the world staying considerably behind. No political institution has been created that can direct international life in good channels". Finally, she pointed the way forward by asking the question: "Can we agree on an international ethos that is acceptable to all peoples of the world whatever theory, religion or philosophy?"

I have no doubt that her article had an indirect but definite influence on my later career. Moreover, the thoughts expressed by her were those that I was grappling with throughout my career at the United Nations, and later as head of an international organization dealing with law and policy.

I tried and failed to get a contribution from the other distinguished international visitor to the Law College that year, Judge Philip Jessup of the United States. He had just been appointed to the International Court of Justice (ICJ) on the nomination of John F. Kennedy, who had been just elected as the President of the United States. Later, I had the privilege of knowing Judge Jessup after he had retired from the World Court and was lecturing at the Colombia University Law School, where, at his invitation, I had the opportunity of delivering some lectures as a visiting lecturer.

Next, I turned to the Embassies of the United States and the U.S.S.R. seeking assistance in securing articles relating to their justice systems. Officials of the embassies were most kind, and though it took a considerable amount of effort and time I was able to get two articles through their efforts. An article on 'The Administration of Justice in the U.S.S.R' written by Yuri Todorsky. Candidate of Juridical Science was published along with an article entitled 'Criminal Justice in the United States', by Professor George W. Stengel, Professor of Law, at Washington University. These articles described the authors' respective legal systems.

Finally, there were the contributions from my fellow law students which were selected for publication. They were contributed by Palitha Wanasundare, Vasudewa Nanayakkara, Nawaz Dawood, Ananda Grero, S.S. Sahabandu, Cecil Wickramanayake, Dasooki Mohamed, and Mohamed Yehiya. They wrote on subjects of local interest at the time, such as the effectiveness of the jury system in Ceylon, constitutional safeguards of minorities, and Quran as a source of law in Ceylon.

The Editorial I wrote was entitled 'The Case of: Law Vs Space'. Obviously instinctively, almost as a premonition of what my career would be, I had combined in my editorial, the two areas (law and space) that later became the focus of my life. At the time, the real reason was that it was the year when the Russian Cosmonaut Yuri Gagarin became the first human to venture into space on April 12 1961, as the Vostock 1 spacecraft made a complete orbit around the Earth in 108 minutes reaching a latitude of 203 miles in a flight that lasted 1 hour and 48 minutes. It was also the year that the first American astronaut, Alan Sheppard was launched in to space in his Mercury capsule on a sub-orbital flight that lasted 15 minutes. Even as the euphoria of these astounding scientific feats dazzled the world, the fear of a new arms race in space was very much in evidence in the midst of the cold war. In the editorial I wrote:

"The year 1961 has been momentous, Man has finally done it! In defiance of the law that what goes up must come down, he has gone there and stayed there. We are assured that the sight is beautiful, no doubt it must be so. For, the further we get away from things the prettier the look. But we could no longer afford to view things from far and dwell on their prettiness.

The time is most opportune when we should view them as they are. We should learn to live on Earth our own mother planet before we can live on Moon, Mars or Venus. We tend to forget this fact far too often. The regular interference in satellite countries by the big powers may well prove the nucleus of a world catastrophe. In the face of all this we engage ourselves in making wild guesses as to what altitude will be reached by the next test rocket, hoping perhaps of establishing a society of saints or a model political system of the ideal—"ism". It seems ridiculous that man should blind himself to the need to live at peace with his neighbor today before he strikes out on a new adventure of peaceful coexistence with strangers never met.

Governments may go bankrupt in the South East and others may be overthrown in the Middle East, but the two space kings Russia and America, will go on building the monsters they are so proud of. To some of us the whole business seems like watching some gigantic fireworks display, for little do we realize that the day may be at hand when these, instead of moving vertically upward turn their course to the horizontal, Man will surely then rue the hell he has loosed around him with his own work.

It is our tragedy that we are chiefly aware of the glamour and glory, and yet strangely blind to the terror and madness of it all. The next time THE PRESIDENT speaks ill of THE PRIME MINISTER we may find an I

C. B. M. labeled "Washington C. O. D", hurtling over us,
destination—definitely known. We wonder who will reply.

It is incumbent on us as lawyers, and lawyers- to-be,
to ascertain our function today in relation to this state
of affairs. The Law always has had as its object the
reconciliation of divergent and conflicting interests. The
problem today is that human ingenuity has created forces
of tremendous power, and the need for their control is
not only urgent but is of absolute necessity for the very
existence of man. On the one hand the personality of the
individual has been built up and each individual thinks
of himself as a superman today. Consequently there is
greater conflict with his fellowmen. Therefore the need
of law to reconcile their interests is never more urgently
felt. On the other hand, the powerful forces built up by the
great nations threatens the annihilation of mankind. The
need for a more effectual system of international law has
become no more a luxury but a necessity. Hence it is left to
the lawyers and jurists to balance the conflicting interests
among the peoples of the world, by working towards a
more effective form of International Law instead of Inter-
National Law".

By June 1962, I had received in the country of my birth, a sound education and good academic credentials, most of it free (I had to pay fees at Law College, though winning scholarships lightened the burden), along with opportunities that turned out to be character-building experiences. Armed with all this valuable baggage, I was ready to go abroad seeking further education, and eventually, as it turned out, a career that was immensely enriching. A career, that later led me to be named by the prestigious Washington-based United States National Space Society, in special Collector's Edition of its Journal *AD ASTRA*, - as one of "THE 100 STARS OF SPACE: ONE HUNDRED SPACE PEOPLE WHO HAVE HAD THE GREATEST IMPACT ON OUR LIVES".

The editorial of the journal noted that: "It was said that we go to the Moon not because it is easy, but because it is hard. That same spirit and desire to accomplish great achievements in space drives hundreds of thousands of individuals every day to exceed others' expectations - and sometimes even their own - to move the people of the Earth closer to the ultimate goal of understanding and conquering space. Space age is still in its infancy, but already individuals have played critical roles in bringing us to where we are today. This special issue of *Ad Astra* highlights the 100 people we feel have had the greatest impact on the space program up to date. These 100 men and women have undeniably shaped the way the world perceives and participates in space."

Among those honored were astronauts, space scientists and engineers, visionaries, and political leaders mainly from the United States, Russia and Europe. The list began with Cosmonaut Yuri Gagarin and included among others Neil Armstrong, Buzz Aldrin, John Glen, Valentina Tereshkova, Werner Von Braun, James Van Allen, Carl Sagan, John F. Kennedy, Nikita Khrushchev, H.G. Wells and our own Arthur C. Clarke. To be listed with such illustrious names was an honor of which I never even dreamed. My own citation in part read:

> *Everybody talks about peaceful international cooperation inSpace, butNandasiriJasentuliyana actually does something about it. "His vision has always been that though only a few nations have space faring capability, somehow all nations should benefit." Says Montreal-based international air and space lawyer Lucy Stojak who calls him "very pragmatic and astute to political realities."*
>
> *Although Jasentuliyana sees a positive role for treaty-verifying satellites he has taken a strong stand against making space into a battlefield, saying that "a growing militarization of space could increase the risks of international conflict and divert important resources from more productive uses." The native Sri Lankan is outspoken against space-based weapons.*
>
> *Since 1965 Jasentuliyana has been on-staff at the United Nations Outer Space Affairs Division (which provides*

year-round support for the UN Committee on the Peaceful Uses of Outer Space) and currently serves as division director. He has had a hand in drafting all five UN space treaties that govern space activities, from the 1967 Outer Space Treaty to the 1979 Moon Treaty.

Jasentuliyana holds advanced degrees in law and international relations from the University of Ceylon, the University of London and McGill University in Montreal, and he authored the Four-volume Manual of Space Law. A strong proponent of environmental research from space, Jasentuliyana argues it is one of the most critical areas that will need international cooperation in the future."

In some ways, even more satisfying is to have received the following reference made by the most outstanding Sri Lankan jurist of our time, Deshamanya Dr. Christie Weeramantry, Judge of the International Court of Justice, former judge of the Supreme Court of Sri Lanka, and professor of Law at Monash University in Australia, at the convocation address of the Bandaranaike Center for International Studies:

International law is as yet in its infancy and the main contours of its response to the new world situation will be laid down in the next few decades. I have referred in the preceding sections to many areas of significance to the future. In all of these, international law would need to adapt its concepts and its principles to take stock of new situations and to make itself a more useful instrument of global service. In all of these changes every country must participate, or else its vital interests could tend to be overlooked, not through any bad faith on the part of other countries but sometimes through sheer lack of appreciation of the problems involved.

There is today a vast amount of learning and writing on the law relating to outer space, for soon there will be increasing activities in space including manned colonies in outer space. Law is required to regulate, all of this and international law has been responsive to the need. Indeed

Sri Lanka could well be proud that one of the world's foremost authorities on outer space law is a Lankan –Dr. Nandasiri Jasentuliyana – who is not only the Head of Outer Space Affairs Office of the United Nations but is also one of the most prolific and authoritative writers on contribution to this most forward-looking of all areas of international law. We are thus making a very substantial contribution to the develoment of law in this area.

In June 1963, after the usual farewells to family and friends, it was with great expectations that I boarded the British Airways newly-minted Viscount jet to begin an eventful journey. Little did I know it would be 50 years long!

During the half-a-century that I have been abroad, it was a blessing not only to have broadened my education and have a satisfying career, but also to have had the opportunity of being in over 125 cities in nearly seventy-five countries in all the continents including the Antarctic, to be enriched by people of all levels from the common people on the street to Astronauts, Heads of States and Nobel Laureates. That though, is another journey, another story, to be told another day.

— ❖ —

Chapter 32

From a scribe's pen

"NANDI" - THE SOUTHERN STAR IN SPACE *
H.L.D. Mahindapala,

(Former Editor, Ceylon Observer, Secretary-General, South Asia Media Association and President, Sri Lanka Working Journalists' Association).

The route from an obscure Sinhala-Buddhist mixed school in Dodanduwa, Sri Lanka to the Outer Space Affairs Office of the United Nations in New York and Vienna was inevitably long, winding and arduous, with usual quota of diversions and pitfalls on the way. But nothing en route - not even the English alphabet unknown to him in his early education - daunted Nandasiri (known to his friends as "Nandi") Jasentuliyana. His upward movement from the Sinhala-Buddhist village school in the south to the heights of the Director of the United Nations Office for Outer Space Affairs and Deputy Director- General of the United Nations in Vienna is an untold saga known only to a few who had known him.

The story of the boy from the south, who climbed the dizzy heights of international mountains, overcoming all obstacles on the way to the top at the UN, can be told only in superlatives. This is inevitable because Nandasiri Jasentuliyana has left behind an outstanding academic and professional track record. Despite this and despite his international status he has studiously kept out of the limelight without sharing honors at home with the other towering Sri Lankan celebrities like His Excellency Christopher. J. Weeramantry, the

Vice-president of the International Court of Justice, or Shirley Amerasinghe or Jayantha Dhanapala. There is a reason for this. He deliberately cultivated a low-profile ever since Mr. Sam Wijesinghe, former Secretary-General of the Parliament, told him sometime in the 60s': "Young man, success attracts jealousies! If you want to succeed keep away from publicity in Sri Lanka." He followed his mentor's advice with such tenacity that not even a dental surgeon could pry open his mouth all these years.

He was quite content to go about his work without any fuss. But he took care to leave an indelible mark with every step he took. He walks the corridors of the UN with an easy familiarity - almost like a home away from home. In those corridors his reputation has grown as a leading authority on the laws governing the new frontiers of outer space, which at the time of the Reaganite "star wars" threatened to be the theatre for the next cosmic wars. His achievements parallel that of Shirley Amerasinghe, Sri Lanka's distinguish Ambassador to UN, and Jayantha Dhanapala. Shirley Amerasinghe plumbed the depths of the sea, Jayantha Dhanapala drilled deep into the core of atoms, and Nandasiri Jasentluliyana scaled the heights of space at the UN. Both are internationally recognized authorities in these two critical areas vital for the future of humanity. It is, indeed, a remarkable coincidence that two Sri Lankans should be acknowledged as leading authorities on the two extremities of the earth that determines its survival.

In the post-Gagarin era outer space assumed a greater significance as a vantage-point for political and military purposes. The open spaces out there assumed a new political, economic and military importance. Outer space was viewed as the new colonial territory needed for supremacy on earth. The jockeying for positions in the administration of outer space reached a critical stage at the height of the Cold War when the super-powers were competing for strategic places in space as a means of dominating terrestrial landscape.

One key position was that of the Executive Secretary to the UN Conference on the Peaceful uses of Outer Space 1982 (UNISPACE II).

In the early eighties at the height of the cold war UN was deadlocked over who should be appointed to this post. Soviet Russia and United States were competing for 10 months to grab this key position. US had wanted the job for an American (Marvin Robinson formerly of NASA) who has temporarily been heading the UN's outer space affairs division. The Soviet Union and the Communist bloc had been pressing the candidacy of a Czechoslovakian official who had joined the division in February 1981. In January 1982 Kurt Waldheim, the departing Secretary-General of the UN, broke the deadlock by appointing Nandasiri Jasentuliyana. The news of breaking the deadlock grabbed the headlines of the international media. It was Waldheim's last act before he ended his term as Secretary-General of the UN.

It could be argued that Jasentuliyana was the ideal non-aligned candidate acceptable to both sides. But it is more than that. He was already in the Outer Space Affairs Division (OSAD) with the requisite credentials behind his name. Ambassador Jean J. Kirkpatrick, the Permanent Representative of the USA to the UN, in her letter to Waldheim, commending his appointment, wrote: "While we continue to believe that Mr. Robinson was the logical choice to be Executive Secretary for UNISPACE '82, we know that Mr. Jasentuliyana is an able and experienced officer of the Outer Space Affairs 'Division (OSAD) and would surely be an effective Executive Secretary for the Conference." This was written in April 1981. Since then Nandasiri Jasentuliyana's record as a suave and cool-headed diplomat, maneuvering his way through Cold War warriors, has earned him a commendable reputation among international civil servants, starting from Kofi Annan downwards.

The Washington-based National Space Society honored him with the rare distinction of being one of the 100 "Space people who have had the greatest impact on our lives". In this exclusive club he is in the company of celebrities like John F. Kennedy, astronauts Yuri Gagarin and Neil Armstrong, movie director Stanley Kubrick exploring futuristic themes, movie producer Steven Spielberg etc. All these are shining stars of space exploration. They are the

Columbuses of the new age going in search of the unknown space that is most critical to the next stage of man's evolution. The first was in the Silurian Age when the fish and algae came out of the sea and established colonies on land. The second was when man went out on voyages exploring the unknown parts of the earth. The third - and perhaps the final stage — was when man stepped out of the earth and moved into space.

Yet it is this virginal space that is fraught with complex issues, if not danger, for the survival of mankind. International cooperation in space projects is a prime need. Space wars projected in science fiction – genre in which yesterday's fiction becomes today's reality — can threaten the survival of our blue planet. The world went to the brink of total annihilation under the Strategic Defense Initiative (Star Wars) program of Ronald Reagan which pushed Soviet Union into a rival program with both super powers competing for supremacy in space. Both were engaged in research and development of space-based offensive and defensive weapons. The theory was that those who conquer space would conquer the earth. Jasentuliyana works at the legal and political frontiers of this space with consummate ease. He works with a tireless commitment to turn space into a non-military zone. Commenting on this Jasentuliyana told the Space society magazine that "a growing militarization of space could increase the risks of international conflict and divert important resources from more productive uses".

Faced with the potential threats as well as the immense possibilities for the future welfare of mankind, the UN went into top gear to explore the peaceful uses of outer space. Nandasiri Jasentuliyana became the key figure in coordinating, directing and organizing this program from way back as the 1960s. The UN Conference on the Peaceful Uses of Outer Space (UNISPACE) has become a regular forum for the international community to discuss and initiate new programs for the peaceful uses of space. This could range from a World Weather Watch collecting data from satellites to sorting out overcrowded airwaves from the communication satellites thrown into space like balloons. Last but not the least, is the threat of one of the millions of stray meteorites hitting the earth with an explosive power strong enough to send it into another ice age.

The future, therefore, is in space and everybody's talking about it. In the collector's issue of the Space Society magazine honoring the new stars of space it was said: "Everybody talks about peaceful international cooperation in space but Nandasiri Jasentuliyana does something about it His vision has always been that though only a few nations have space faring capability, somehow all nations should benefit." Turning space swords into planetary ploughshares is not an easy task. He has to bring together diverse and competing interests and harmonize them for peaceful purposes. Even though the political contest for lebensraum in space has not yet reached critical proportions the legal aspects have to be spelt out to accommodate rival claims and to prevent future space wars. As the grim and grave scenarios of science fiction draw nearer Jasentuliyana will have to work harder to define the legal space within which the rival claimants - whether they be states or gigantic corporations ~ will have to settle for peaceful solutions. It is a daunting task but he works at it unfazed by its complexities. But at the back of his mind lurks a fear of the future in space. Behind the publicized camaraderie of international astronauts embracing in space stations there is a threat that can turn nasty and hit the earth with devastating power.

The militarization of space took a new turn with Bill Clinton reviving the Star Wars program investing, initially, $10 billion — a massive injection of funds partly to please the Right- wing and partly to maintain the military superiority of the United States. Once again the Reagn era Star Wars is back on the international agenda with countries like China and Russia bristling with resentment. Against this background, his impending retirement (he passed the three-score and ten on November 23 last year) has the UN corridors buzzing with fears for the proposed UNISPACE III (scheduled to be held in Vienna between June 19 and July 30). It is the uncertainties of the future in space that makes him a man much in demand in the UN circles for his diplomatic skills and his expertise in space law.

Now as he moves into the proverbial three-score-and-ten, without the claws of time leaving any discernible scars, the U.S. delegate Kenneth Hodgkins has expressed his country's "serious concerns" over the future staffing of the Office with the intended departure of Jasentuliyana. The IPS Daily Journal (November 2, 1998, Vol. 6.No.209, page 6) quotes Hodgkins as telling the Special Political Committee of the General Assembly: "We now understand that changes in the senior leadership of the Office might take place this year. This is a disturbing development, since it has the potential of disrupting preparations for UNISPACE III." He added that if UNISPACE III is to be a success "the people doing this work must be experienced, hard working and deeply knowledgeable about international space cooperation."

Hodgkins was supported by Ambassador Raimundo Gonzalez of Chile, the Chairman of the United Nations Committee on Peaceful Uses. The IPS Daily reports that Ambassador Gonzalez himself had heard about upcoming changes in the staff of the Office for Outer Space affairs, beginning with its director. He commented: "The United Nations could not afford the luxury of dispensing with the valuable contribution of that division, especially at such a crucial state. It would be unrealistic to press ahead (with UNISPACE III) without the support of the Secretariat in the preparations for a world conference of such scope, magnitude and importance, particularly to developing countries...."

Following these appeals, the Secretary-General Kofi Anan promptly requested Jasentuliyana to continue his services beyond the mandated age of retirement for United Nations Officials, in order to organize and direct the United Nations World Conference on Space (UNISPACE III). The conference was considered a great success and drew up a blue print for nations to follow in the next decade as they explore outer space and utilize its practical applications. It was a fitting farewell to the long and successful career of Jasentuliyana at the helm of UN space program.

Unlike Shirley Amerasinghe and Jayanatha Dhanapala, it must be emphasized, that Jasentuliyana did not break into the international diplomacy through the Sri Lankan Foreign Service. He worked his way up through sheer dint of his own efforts. When he left Sri Lanka on a Commonwealth scholarship to McGill University in Canada he was determined to study space law. It was virgin territory, virtually unexplored unlike the other branches of the law. To him it was a new and adventurous field. He envisaged the potential dangers and the possibilities of the conflicts in space even as a law student in Sri Lanka. As if foreshadowing his future career he wrote in 1961, when he was the editor of the Ceylon Law College Review: "This year 1961 has been momentous. Man has finally done it! In defiance of the law that what goes up must come down, he has gone there and stayed there. It is our tragedy that we are chiefly aware of the glamour and glory, and yet strangely blind to the terror and madness of it all. The next time THE PRESIDENT speaks ill of the PRIME MINISTER we may find an ICBM labeled "Washington C. O. D", hurtling over us, destination - definitely known. We wonder who will reply." That is a question that continues to haunt him. His career has been devoted since then to prevent it happening.

Once again it was Mr. Sam Wijesinghe who put him on the right track when he was casting around for a direction in his future career path. It was Mr. Wijesighe who told him to specialize in space law, and gave him the exact location where he could find the ideal avenue for his métier.

In Vienna protocol demands that newly appointed ambassadors should present their credentials to the head of the UN Office in Vienna as representative of the Secretary-General of the United Nations, and it happened to be Jasentuliyana as Acting Director General of the United Nations Office in Vienna when Sri Lanka's newest ambassador, Mr. S. Poolokasingham called on him in January this year. This is, indeed, a rare occurrence where one Sri Lankan diplomat presents his credentials to another Sri Lankan representing the UN.

For a pioneer sailing in the uncharted territories of space it was inevitable that it would be filled with star-studded celebrities of space. A routine part of his career was to rub shoulders with Neil Armstrong and Buzz Aldrin who went to the Moon, Valantina Tereshkova, the first woman in space, Cosmonauts Valeriy Polyakov and Vladmir Titov who spent over a year in space, Sally Ride and Dr. Mae Jamison the lady astronauts are among the many legendary stars of space whom he met. The Austrian Cosmonaut Frans Viehboch of Austria and Cosmonaut Dumitri Prunariu of Rumania are among his family friends.

Dealing with outer space drew him naturally into the universality that envelops space. Though he did spin in space he never lost the touch of the earth under his feet. For instance, assembling five Nobel Laureates -- President Jimmy Carter, Archbishop Desmond Tutu, Mrs. Elena Bonner and Poet Wole Soyinka – to a public discourse on their own personal experiences was a part of his public duty. The lives of these Nobel Laureates under totalitarian regimes that had robbed them of their own human rights for many years, or as activists speaking out on behalf of those still suffering from discrimination, servitude and other forms of modern day oppression kept his feet firmly on earth.

At the end of his career NASA Administrator Daniel Goldin signed and presented as a memento a framed U.N. flag that was flown aboard space shuttle Columbia (STS-90) along with a crew patch worn by the astronauts on board the spacecraft and a signed photograph of the crew. This symbolic memento is a fitting tribute to his mission in space. The inscription in it went further. It read: "Presented to Nandasiri Jasentuliyana in recognition of his support for furthering the peaceful uses of outer space for all nations."

That says it all. What more can a boy from an obscure village do than serve all nations – and that too from outer space!

* Original text dated March 1999.

517

Presenting and Receiving Awards

Receiving ▶
IISL Annual
Award for
Excellence at
the Versailles
Palace in
Paris, France
in 1982.

◀ *Receiving*
International
Astronautical
Federation
Book Award
from Head
of German
Space
Agency in
1993.

▲ *Receiving and Acknowledging NASA Award of Recognition from Astronaut Franklin Cheng-Diaz (a framed citation with U.N. flag flown on the space shuttle Columbia STS-90 & the Crew Patch worn by the Astronauts on board the shuttle).*

◀ *Presenting the Distinguished Service Award of the Institute of Space Law to Judge Gilbert Guillume of the World Court.*

Epilogue

"Life is a journey not a destination"

—Ralph Waldo Emerson

Epilogue

GLIMPSES OF MY UNTOLD STORY

You now know everything about the first twenty-five years of my life, and thereafter, the important milestones of my personal life. But the journey that continued, after I left my motherland until it gradually started to crawl towards its inevitable destiny, which was when I started to write this memoir, has much that has not been recorded here.

In addition to the first lap of the relay that has been my life, narrated in detail within these pages, the second leg has been sketched by the hand of a journalist, H.L.D Mahindapala, in broad brush, leaving ample space on the canvas to etch further details. The third lap, covering a decade and a half of service in the international milieu and the final leg that is still limping towards the inevitable finishing line are not touched upon within these covers.

What is not written here belongs to the second half of my journey, to be recorded one day in the future. Yet, in order not to leave in midstream, the reader who joined me in retracing my journey, I have recorded here, in brief, what is intended to be recounted in due course.

*   *   *

When I left the shores of my motherland for North America to pursue my graduate studies, I planned to spend a summer of education and travel in Europe before I reached my final destination. My studies began with a summer program on international relations conducted by the World Federation of United Nations Association (WAFUNA), which was then headed by the Sri Lankan historian and educationist Horace Perera. It was held at the European Headquarters of the U.N in Geneva giving me my first glimpse of the World Organization. Then I made my way to the summer session of the prestigious Hague Academy of International Law at the Peace Palace in the Netherlands, where the World Court is located. In between the two programs, I was able to undertake a sojourn savoring the first tastes of the great European cities of Paris, Berlin, Bonn and Brussels. The summer in Europe ended with a tour of the U.K., to visit important sites of London and great campuses of Cambridge and Oxford, which bred a good number of leaders and intellects of Sri Lanka. The highlight was the opportunity to witness a historic Test Match between the famed West Indian and English teams at the high temple of the game of cricket, the 'Lords' cricket grounds.

Next was the maiden trip across the Atlantic, which has since been crossed countless times. My final destination on this maiden voyage was Montreal, Canada. The city was drenched in the glorious colors of autumn when I first arrived to begin my challenging but deeply satisfying years of graduate studies. The prestigious Institute of Air and Space Law at McGill University was the home where I took my first steps in the field of aerospace law and policy, which has since then been the universe of my career.

Internationally recognized jurists of the caliber of Prof. Maxwell Cohen Q.C. directed the Institute, while Prof. Ivan Vlasic, a pioneer author of space policy spearheaded supervision of my research work. The demanding schedule of seminars and research was carried out in the company of a small collegial group of highly motivated lawyers from around the world. Among them several became lifelong family friends and many distinguished themselves in their own careers.

In our group was Stephen Doyle, who went on to become an attorney policy adviser to NASA, the State Department, and later worked in the senior staff of the White House under two Presidents and the U.S. Congress dealing with space and telecommunications policy, before entering private industry and retiring as President of a technology firm; Langhorne Bond who served as Assistant Administrator of the Department of Transportation and became Head of the U.S. Federal Aviation Administration; Paul Larsen and Frank Lyall who became distinguished professors of aerospace law in the Universities of Georgetown, USA, and Aberdeen, Scotland. Others held high posts in international organizations, national airlines and aerospace agencies. We were a close-knit group, and surprisingly, many still keep in touch after nearly half-a-century since we first met.

I also enjoyed the social and cultural life on the campus making many friends from around the world. I was elected the President of the International Student's Association (ISA), under which many national organizations carried out their activities. During my tenure I organized a successful International Week beginning with a parade of nations carrying their national flags through the town of Montreal. The week that was coordinated by my colleague Stephen Doyle, Chairman of the Organizing Committee, featured Discussions of international issues, music, dance, literary activities and a food festival featuring the cultures of different countries that were represented in the campus. As part of the celebrations the English Department staged E.M. Fosters "Passage to India" in which I took part alongside Tandy Cronyn (daughter of famed actors Sir Hume Cronyn and Jessica Tandy) who went on to become a Broadway and T.V. star. The tradition set that year for the festival is being continued to date. Eventually, I was elected to the Scarlet Key, the Campus Honor Society for the contributions made to campus life. Many memories of these and other activities come to mind to be told another day.

Montreal is the biggest city in the Francophone Province of Quebec, which was experiencing a momentous time, when I first started to live there. The political party Quebecois was fighting a separatist battle, seeking to secede from the rest of English-speaking Canada. Long before I came in contact with the JVP and ethnic conflicts and the separatist movement of LTTE in my own homeland, I had a firsthand experience of what it means to live in an atmosphere laden with the psychosis of fear. Anxiety and fear reigned in the town of

Montreal with mail box bombs exploding in the city center and in the suburbs.

*   *   *

Summer vacations paved the way to broaden my horizons. I travelled extensively, delving into new areas of knowledge and skills. The first of these experiences began when I took part in a special program on American and Comparative Law in Dallas, Texas. This was only a few months after the turmoil that ensued following the assassination of President John Kennedy in Dallas (I write this epilogue in the 50th year of his death anniversary, and just prior to my 75th birthday). There were also memorable Internships, like the one at the United Nations. All these summer events offered new perspectives of places, people and the opportunity of making lasting friendships. In Dallas I was glad to have shared a room with Jayakumar Shunmugam who became a professor at the National University and later became Foreign Minister and Deputy Prime Minister of Singapore. Tommy Koh was my mate at the internship program. He later became President of the United Nations General Assembly. Jaya came to the Dallas program from Yale University and Tommy came from Harvard, where they were pursuing their graduate work. Jaya, Tommy and some others I met at these programs continued to stay in touch. We visited each other during our travels. These visits were always holidays to look forward to, for their homes soon became home away from home to me.

It was in the midst of the intense civil rights campaign that I found myself in Dallas. There I tasted the bitterest part of the racial discrimination in America. Travelling in the Deep South from Dallas to New Orleans and back through places such as Little Rock, Arkansas and Atlanta Georgia, beholding 'Whites Only' signs when I only wanted a meal of any kind to satisfy my hunger or a Motel bed to put down my weary body for a few hours. They created ineffaceable visions that would change one's perspectives of humanity.

*   *   *

At the end of it all, as my student days receded to the background leaving bitter sweet memories, it was unquestionably providential to have been beckoned to the epicenter of world affairs, while I was still in my late-twenties. Thus began an enduring voyage through a life full of multifarious experiences. United Nations became the home from where I observed the world events from the cold war years to the dawn of the twenty- first century. It was home from where I lent a hand to ensure that man traversed the space age safely to create the global village. Our goal was to create a mission using the historic advances in space technology and its practical applications to alleviate the human condition and not annihilate nations and their civilization.

This was a time when fortune smiled on me so brightly, I moved among world leaders, met and got to know them. Images roll by of the days when special moments of drama, unfortunately most of them filled with the human tragedy of war and peace, took center stage at the greatest theater of all times in the glass house besides the East River in Manhattan, New York. There, I had an orchestra seat to soak up all the tensions of world affairs and occasional moments of comedy. Some that readily come to mind were the dramas and lead actors of the Suez Crisis, Conflict in the Congo, almost non- stop multiple wars in the Middle East, Vietnam War, Soviet- Afghanistan War, Iran-Iraq War, India-Pakistan Wars, Sino-Soviet War, Gulf War, Yugoslav and Bosnian Wars, multiple African wars from Western Sahara War, Uganda Tanzania War, Somali-Ethiopia War; and civil wars with international implication in Angola, Biafra, Somalia, Mozambique Liberia, Sierra Leone, Congo and Rwanda.

There was also the drama surrounding the radical political struggles in Africa in the decades of decolonization, as scores of countries gained independence from the European colonial rulers; the saga of eradicating Apartheid regimes in Zimbabwe, South Africa and Namibia; and other significant political events like the oil crisis and conflicts involving liberation movements in Eastern Europe, Central America and Asia.

The spells of oratorical prowess displayed by the lead actors that shaped those events, justifying or opposing the rationales that prompted their actions, were no less fascinating, and often awe-striking, as the many facets of the real world tensions which were enacted in the hallowed halls of the United Nations. From Yasser Arafat, the Palestinian leader, to Fidel Castro, President of Cuba; great European leaders from General Charles de Gaulle, President of France to Chairman Mikhail Gorbachev of the U.S.S.R; Adlai Stevenson of the United States and the Asian oratorical giants from Krishna Menon of India to Zulfikar Bhutto of Pakistan, and Abba Iban of Israel; to name a few in the vast ocean of great speakers who thundered in the halls of the United Nations. There were also many others who argued their cases in softer tones, but in an intellectually cogent manner that captivated the onlooker. They include Secretary of State Henry Kissinger, Ambassador Arthur Goldberg who later became a Judge of the Supreme Court of the United States, Ambassadors Andrei Gromyko and Yaakov Malik of the Soviet Union, who were later the Foreign Ministers of the U.S.S.R. Their polished and precise presentations, often laced with sharp wit, made it educational, intellectual and entertaining to behold.

There were several moments that come to mind even as I write, which illustrate the drama created almost as part of these eminent leaders' oratory: when Arafat to emphasize his revolutionary credentials, appeared to address the General Assembly wearing his gun belt and holster, reluctantly removed his pistol before mounting the rostrum. He told the world body, "Today, I have come bearing an olive branch and a freedom-fighter's gun. Do not let the olive branch fall from my hand."

I had the great fortune of listening to Mandela at the United Nations in New York, on two occasions; both prior to his being the President of South Africa. First, at the Special Session of the Committee on Apartheid in 1990, and two years later, when he addressed the Security Council. It was shortly thereafter that the Nobel Prize was awarded to him in 1993. On each of those occasions the atmosphere was electric in anticipation with every inch of the council chamber being occupied. On those occasions he recounted the history of Apartheid and the importance of peace with justice. On Apartheid, he said that it will forever remain an indelible blight on human history, and that future generations will ask how the crime of apartheid came to pass in the wake of the Universal Declaration of Human Rights adopted by the United Nations. On broader issue of peace, what remains in my memory is his frequent calls for unity within diversity; as expressed in his statement that, "Peace is not just the absence of conflict; peace is the creation of an environment where all can flourish, regardless of race, color, creed, religion, gender, class, caste or any other social markers of difference. Religion, ethnicity, language, social and cultural practices are elements which enrich human civilization, adding to the wealth of our diversity. Why should they be allowed to become a cause of division, and violence? We demean our common humanity by allowing that to happen." With Mandela one has the sense of being in the presence of a very wise man, with charisma of extraordinary humanity.

No less fascinating was watching other leaders make their case before the General Assembly or the Security Council at times when their countries were in the brink of war or peace.

Abdul Nasser, David Ben-Gurion, Anwar Sadat, Golda Meir, Ben Bella, Nkrumah, Indira Gandhi, Gorbachev, Zhou Enlai, Sukarno, Harold Macmillan, Vaclav Havel, Bruno Kreisky, Konrad Adenauer Helmut Kohl, Deng Xiaoping, Lester Pearson, Margret Thatcher, Haile Selassi, Mummer Gaddafi, Ayub Khan; and a host of others.

Then there were those with whom I had worked when they were young diplomats who later went on to become leaders in their countries over the years. Two come to mind readily as they were leaders of the recent Arab Spring: Mohamed El Baradei and Abu Moussa, who was the Presidential Candidate in Egypt after the recent Arab Spring. Abu Mousa was the Secretary General of the Arab League. His successor and currant Secretary General Nabil El Araby former Foreign Secretary was yet another with whom I grew up in the U.N. milieu. I was fortunate to grow up with them in the U.N. system from our young diplomatic days. Dealing with the subject of space, a realm where the United States sought international leadership, I also had the privilege of being present in meetings with the likes of President George H.W. Bush while he was the U.S. ambassador to the United Nations.

* * *

It was also a great privilege to work under five of the eight distinguished Secretaries-General of the U.N. who were great humanists and visionaries like U Thant, Javier Perez de Cuellar and Boutros Boutros-Ghali, or those simply working with great commitment to make the world a better place like Kurt Waldheim (Austrian diplomat who was chair of the U.N. Outer Space Committee of which I served as Secretary before he became the Secretary General, and later President of his country), and Kofi Annan (we joined the U.N. together and were promoted together to higher levels, until he was elected the Secretary General).

Many impressions and experiences of these outstanding leaders come to mind. So too, do the experiences from interacting with countless diplomats and international civil servants with whom I had the privilege to work, and from whom I learned.

* * *

My country too had notable moments of glory throughout most of my U.N. career. It is a matter of pride that for decades two intellectually-gifted orators from Sri Lanka were looked upon by the whole of the Middle East and Africa to represent their causes in the United Nations. Ambassador Neville Kanakaratne championed the cause of decolonization in the sixties and early-seventies, at a time when Africa did not have the clout in the world body nor the able speakers to espouse their causes, as they had in later years. Ambassador Shirley Amarasinghe served as an effective spokesman of the Palestinian cause for a long time when they had no representation in the world body. He was also a reliable ally and leader to whom

Middle East countries turned when it came to arguing their cases in a more neutral voice.

Sir Senarath Gunewardene, the first Ambassador to the U.N. after Ceylon became a member in 1956, was an acclaimed leader among the non-Western countries. He supported the cause of the Asian and other small nations. He was concurrently Ambassador to the United Nations and Canada and a father figure to me, when I arrived in New York as a young official of the United Nations in the mid-sixties. It is providential that I can consider as friends towering figures such as Shirley Amarasinghe, Neville Kanakaratne, Sir Senarath, and a host of others of their caliber.

It is a matter of pride that over the years, able men represented Sri Lanka as Permanent Representatives to the United Nations, who mostly had to support the causes advocated by the Non-Aligned Movement. Many in the latter years had to explain and defend the interest of Sri Lanka during more than a quarter century of turmoil in our land. Ceylon-Sri Lanka was often called upon to serve in United Nations bodies established to find solutions, or to be arbiter of delicate issues that arose. Whether it was on the occasion of the burning of the Al Aqsa Mosque in Jerusalem, or the inspection of Saddam Hussain's palaces for weapons of mass destruction, it was Sri Lanka, as a nation trusted by the membership of the U.N., which was often called upon to lead. In addition to those already mentioned, several well-known Sri Lankan lawyers (H.L De Silva, Daya Perera, B.J. Fernando, and John De Saram); prominent academics (Prof. Gunapala Malalasekare, Prof. Stanley Kalpage); and able Civil Servants and Foreign Service Officers (M.F.de S Jayaratne, Nissanka Wijewardane, Ben Fonseka, Charley Mahendran, Bernard Goonetlleke H.M.G.S. Palliakkara, Prasad Kariyawasam and Palitha Kohana), most competently and skillfully represented my country during their respective tenures as Ambassadors to the United Nations. Of these gentlemen, who I consider my friends and colleagues, many stories remain to be told.

* * *

The United Nations itself is a fascinating place because it is the crucial center of world affairs in war and peace. While most of its political work is well known around the world, and widely reported in the media, its work in other areas is less known, and rarely occupies the headlines. Yet, its work in saving lives, whether in peacekeeping missions in hot spots around the globe, or in eradicating malaria, polio or containing the spread of aids and HIV and other diseases, are of vital importance to populations everywhere. Its essential work in the economic and social development in areas such as food security, agriculture and forestry, environmental protection, population control, and disaster relief is not well known or recognized. There are a host of technical areas that affect all nations where the United Nations has been bestowed the responsibility of ensuring international order. They include aviation and maritime safety and security, regulation of international telecommunications and broadcasting, ensuring the safe use of nuclear energy, and the establishment of uniform labor standards and trade agreements among states. Among the tasks that have taken center stage in more recent times at the United Nations are prevention of trans- border crime, the menace of drug control and international terrorism. The development of international law and the settlement of international disputes are preeminent tasks of the United Nations under its charter. The establishment of legal regimes to govern the newest environments of human exploration: the sea bed, the ocean floor, and outer space, was also entrusted to the United Nations, so that the benefits of new natural resources of these global commons will be shared equitably by all nations.

Thus, The United Nations work ceaselessly in all areas of human endeavor to make the world a better place, and the life of citizens everywhere more sustainable and meaningful. United Nations however, is not devoid of inherent weaknesses and glaring failures, particularly where it had failed or delayed to intervene to avoid conflict and human disaster. Much of it is consequent to political disagreement among Member States, particularly the great powers, as the United Nations can only mirror the will of nation states that are its members. Nevertheless, it remains an indispensable tool in managing world affairs, and alleviating the human condition. Reflecting this truism, when the founding fathers of the United Nations met in San Francisco in 1945, an American banker named Beardsley Ruml made the remark:

> "At the end of five years, you will think the United Nations is the greatest vision ever realized by man. At the end of 10 years, you will find doubts within yourself and all throughout the world. At the end of 50 years, you will believe the United Nations cannot succeed. You will be certain that all the odds are against its ulitimate life and success. It will be only when the United Nations is 100 years old that we will know that the United Nations is the only alternative to the demolition of the world."

The drama that incessantly unfolds within the ambit of the United Nations, keep those within its walls continuously engulfed in the excitement that is generated by events, which are more often than not, of worldwide interest.

* * *

While much of what I mentioned so far was occurring around me in the halls and corridors of the 38-floor tall glass building, I was putting in long hours on my 33rd floor office, in the Outer Space Affairs Division of the Department of Political and Security Council Affairs. First, as a junior officer engaged in intense research work and preparing draft papers and speeches for senior officers and officials of the Intergovernmental Committees dealing with Space Affairs. Soon, I was servicing those committees as Assistant Secretary and later as Secretary, with full responsibilities for the conduct of the committees assisting their Chairmen and other officers. Real satisfaction came as the United Nations Committees in which I was involved began drafting International Treaties and Declarations of Legal Principles creating a regulatory framework for the conduct of space activities of nations. Initially, in the midst of the Cold War, it was arduous work as every word and every sentence had to be negotiated among competing interests of the two space powers: the

United States and the Soviet Union. Then it was the task of balancing the interests of space powers and non- space faring countries that were keen to protect their still unknown future interests, and ensure that space would be used exclusively for peaceful purposes. At times, negotiations over a single phrase would take many meetings over a period of months or even years. But in the end, it was all worthwhile to have successfully concluded five International Treaties and five Declarations of Legal Principles. Thus, collectively creating a solid legal framework for nations to carry out their space activities in a peaceful manner and avoiding an arms race in space. That is a story worth narrating in great detail and I look forward to doing so in due course.

In parallel to such legal and policy determinations, the United Nations also established a program to assist countries in the developing world to benefit from the practical applications of space technology. Many national and regional programs were designed, funded and administered through the UN sponsorship. They were particularly focused on educating and training people in the developing countries to be able to take advantage of the vast and unlimited potential benefits of space technology. Training operationally included satellite communication and TV broadcasting, weather and climate monitoring, education and health care programs, agriculture and resource management, health and entertainment, environment and disaster management; thus virtually touching every facet of human endeavor.

Soon it was apparent that developing countries, constantly plagued by poor infrastructure, were to benefit enormously, and eventually, they benifitted even more than developed countries from this new technology, which, by shrinking both time and distance, provided us a totally new tool to accelerate socio-economic development. It is in this context that I referred earlier to the collaboration of the United Nations with the National Aquatic Resource Agency and the Arthur Clarke Center for Modern Technologies in Sri Lanka. They are examples of the type of United Nations activities under this broad program relating to space applications to promote development.

Several Regional and World Conferences were organized periodically by the United Nations, to bring together all nations to review the state of affairs and agree on an agenda of activities to be followed by individual countries, individually and collectively to benefit from the practical applications of space technology. It was a great honor and privilege for me to have led the organization and conduct of such global events. There again, the negotiations required to agree on a program of work was always tedious and much preparation was needed. The effort required to ensure that what was agreed was indeed carried out was equally demanding. All those efforts left a slew of memories which are certainly worth detailing in due course.

*　*　*

Those were the major areas of focus of my official work, first, as a member of the supporting cast, and later with full responsibility for them as head of the United Nations Office for Outer Space Affairs. Along with those official responsibilities, I was actively involved in academically-related work which I cherished. I took great pleasure in interacting with the academic community, from whom I always received a different perspective, which I brought to bear on my official work. I particularly liked the interaction with the younger generation of students in the field, and I have watched many of them blossom into leaders in the space community around the world. I delivered several university lectures, and participated in a number of academic seminars and meetings each year. Participating in such activities led me to author and or edit a number of books, book chapters, and articles relating to space law and policy and the United Nations. Six young colleagues, Ralph Chipman, Bruce Schonfeld, J.T. Thaker, Mathew Sanidas, Takemi Chiku and, George Puthupalli, assisted me at various stages in my academic work and publications. I also served on the editorial advisory boards of several American and European Journals. In pursuing such activities, I was able to meet a wide variety of academics, which enriched my horizons. Many of them are involved in the personal stories that come to mind.

Particularly satisfying is a story with a long tale in this context, which began in 1982 at a U.N. global conference. I was able to make the connection between three young visionaries, who had just finished their university education and the eminent space personality Sir Arthur Clarke to explore the possibility of establishing an international space university. Not long after that, an annual summer program at the Massachusetts Institute of Technology (MIT) started, which later culminated in the establishment of the International Space University (ISU), with an interdisciplinary Masters program in Space Studies. Eventually, a permanent campus was established in Strasbourg, France. From its inception, I had the privilege of serving on its Board of Directors, while Arthur Clarke served as the Chancellor, through the establishment of the permanent campus, with an international faculty, and student body of whom many were already employed in the space industry. One of the three young pioneers was Peter Diamandis, who went on to initiate several other visionary projects, including the Ansari X Prize which gave impetus to designing some of the later commercial sector launch services. Those initatives have already resulted in launching the Dragon spacecraft that ferries cargo to the Space Station, under contract to NASA. Other projects including designing spacecraft to carry tourists to space are well underway. Little did I realize those baby steps taken during the 1982 conference will result in such giagantic developments in my lifetime.

* * *

Three decades in the vibrant city of New York cannot but leave an indelible mark on the life of anyone thrust upon the many facets of the melting pot of America.

From the financial center of the world on Wall Street to the center of classical and modern theater, dance, drama and music on Broadway; the world's leading shrines that preserve centuries of culture and civilization within the walls of its great museums; from the opulence of Fifth Avenue and the shimmering skyscrapers to burnt-out hovels of the Bronx and Harlem; from the exalted halls of academics of Ivy League schools of Columbia and Cornell, to the subculture art and literature in Greenwich Village; the sights and sounds of the spirit of the city that never sleeps remain like indelible pictures in my mind. The journey in itself of the village boy from Ambalangoda, who makes it to this enchanting city, is surely like the plot of a play enacted on Broadway.

The era was dominated by civil rights agitation led by Martin Luther King, Jesse Jackson, Rev. Al Sharpton, and the violent world of Malcolm X; as well as the silent few led by Rosa Parks who made a difference in the life of many. Their agitations cast a continuing shadow in the life of America as it did with the protests over the Vietnam War that followed, dividing the American society. The defining social evolutions driven by the Women's Liberation movement led by Gloria Steinman and Jane Fonda, and the Gay and Lesbian rights movement, led by Harvey Milk and Sylvia Rivera, were part of the historical context of my personal odyssey in America, that is worth revisiting.

*　*　*

Almost as if to give a respite from the cauldron of New York, ever so often my work took me to different parts of America, where I saw a patchwork of cultures, scenery and people that are somehow unique to each region and city. Often such travel took me to far-off lands overseas, of people and cultures that represent centuries of history with little or no resemblance to what relatively young New York and America represent. Often on those missions I met with Heads of State of the countries visited, academics and scientists and countless officials. Some were fleeting encounters with high-ranking officials at opening ceremonies or official receptions; others were substantive discussions concerning policy and technical assistance. Even if they were only ceremonial occasions, to sit besides the likes of Jiang Zemin, the President of China, King Hussein of Jordan or

Princess Chulabhon Walailka of Thailand, they were humbling and exhilarating experiences.

International travel has its own unique hazards and I have had my share of incidents, including the time I was on a plane that had to make an emergency belly-landing in Beirut; or the time I was over the Atlantic when the British Airways flight to New York caught fire and returned to London, with only a single engine functioning, which ignited into a stream of fire on landing, necessitating emergency evacuation. As hazardous as those situations happened to be, there were numerous more interesting and even comical situations I had to endure and even enjoy. I had an eventful trip to the Antarctica courtesy of the Chilean Air Force. Shanthi and I also made a memorable trip crossing the Arctic Circle and entered the region where midwinter darkness descends upon the frozen land for night on 30 days of sunless gloom, but where on the longest summer day the sun shines without setting and warms the earth for fully 720 hours. They are certainly trips to places worth narrating.

When back at the U.N., there was always challenging and enthralling work to be carried out laying the foundations for the peaceful exploration of the new frontier of outer space. Many were intergovernmental meetings of governmental representatives, and regional and global conferences of diplomats, Ministers and even Heads of State. Such meetings were to be intricately prepared and conducted in New York or other parts of the world. There were also special commemorative events, which had to be immaculately orchestrated, often as public events, all of which were truly challenging and beguiling.

Whatever spare time that was available melted away in many assignments in different areas of governance, assisting in the internal mechanisms of administrative justice dealing with perceived injustices of unfair treatment, discrimination and breach of contractual rights. I was representing those affected before internal tribunals, or serving as members of those bodies. They were tasks which although arduous, gave me much personal contentment as well as interesting diversions. They permitted me to apply whatever skills were left in me of a practicing lawyer.

Most of what occurred in the context of my own work during my time at the U.N. in New York followed me as I moved to a new locale, from New York to Vienna. But in Vienna, it was with greater responsibility for a wider spectrum of activities. Home now was the newly minted triple tower that housed the European Headquarters of the United Nations by the Blue Danube that accommodated 4,000 U.N. employees. Once there, on the specific request of the Secretary General Kofi Annan, I was appointed to be his Deputy Representative in Vienna, with additional duties relating to the U.N. programs based in Vienna. They were mainly in the realm of social development covering narcotic drugs and criminal justice. I was assigned expanded administrative functions, including host country relations and responsibilities to deal with many external organizations, which interacted with the U.N., both governmental and non-governmental groups dedicated to making the world a better place.

I also carried out responsibilities to oversee the organization of special events. The last such event which I organized and coordinated in 1998 was the 50th Anniversary Celebrations of the adoption of the Universal Declaration of Human Rights. It is a matter of pride that I was able to assemble five Nobel Laureates (President Jimmy Carter, Archbishop Desmond Tutu, Mrs. Elena Bonner and Poet Wole Soyinka) for a day- long event, combining a seminar on 'Human Rights and the Rule of Law,' and a celebrative Public Assembly in the evening. Under the leadership of the Secretary General Annan (a Nobel Laureate himself), the Nobel Laureates gave moving accounts of their own experiences, whether under totalitarian regimes that had robbed them of their own human rights for many years, or as activists speaking out on behalf of those still suffering from discrimination, servitude and other forms of modern-day oppression. It was an unforgettable opportunity that allowed me to taste the intellectual prowess and humaneness of such great men with whom I have had the honor of maintaining continuing contact.

In spite of the profound discourses of the Nobel Laureates, perhaps because of my lifelong commitment to the cause, I was most struck by a brief comment made from the floor during the seminar by Michael Douglas, the famed actor. I had invited him to narrate parts of the Human Rights Declaration during the Public Assembly that evening. In a very perceptive manner he treated the most horrible danger we face in our times as the most critical of Human Right when he noted:

> The human right to security is challenged by global threats that ignore national boundaries and a new level of cooperation is needed. That level of cooperation can best come, I believe, through the United Nations, an organization that has time and again riveted global attention to a succession of evolving threats to our rights as human beings: the ticking environmental time bomb threatening not only those of us alive today but also future generations; that as long as women lacked power over their own lives, no serious inroads against dehumanizing overpopulation could be made; and giving birth to a new world criminal court to deal with present and future crimes against inhumanity. But even as the world rises to the United Nations call to come together to face those challenges, we are still living under a continuing threat: our basic right to life itself. That is the all too current threat of nuclear annihilation, which is compounded by the danger that nuclear weapons might be used not only in war but also as a result of human or mechanical error. The very existence and gravity of that threat breeds a climate of suspicion and fear between countries, which is in itself antagonistic to human rights and fundamental freedoms. The basic human right to security and peace can never be taken for granted. And thus as a citizen of one of the world's nuclear Powers, and as a citizen of this sacred planet, I ask each of you here today to work with your fellow human beings across the world to make nuclear weapons a horror of the past. We must eliminate all such weapons before they render the human right to life-and thus all human rights irrelevant.

* * *

There were a plethora of other events and meetings of United Nations and organizations outside of it, which were of a more public nature, where I was required to represent the United Nations, or the Secretary-General, and often, to speak on their behalf. They included events such as those organized by the Inter Parliamentary Union, or the International Association of Lions. Often they were of a different nature. They provided different experiences as those events were attended by people who were intensely committed to the causes represented by their organizations. They were uninhibited by strict governmental positions, such as those under which the diplomatic community functioned.

There were also times when I had to negotiate internal and external crises that occurred from time to time. One such particularly sensitive issue that comes to mind is the situation when the Kurd leader Abdullah Oclan was arrested in Turkey, a large group of Kurds, representing the cause of an independent Kurdistan, tried to occupy the United Nations Office at Vienna, having already occupied the Geneva office for over a week. At some personal risk, I had to stand in their midst to dissuade them from carrying out their intentions. The international press carried the news and the Austrian Papers said "As part of worldwide demonstrations by Kurdish supporters of Abdullah Oclan, Kurdish demonstrators forced their way in to the U.N. Office in Vienna and occupied a section of the ground floor. About two hours later the Deputy Director General Nandasiri Jasentuliyana persuaded them to hand him a petition, which he agreed to transmit to New York for action, and the group left peacefully." These experiences will be worth detailing at a later time.

The official social functions which were numerous in New York, followed us to Vienna, but there they multiplied exponentially. They were mostly enriching experiences, where both official business was transacted and enduring friendships were made with fascinating people from every part of the world. Often these functions were challenging because of the tiring routines that had to be performed out of courtesy and protocol. To have besides me an ally in Shanthi who extended her support and shared the unique experiences hand in hand, made the challenges easier to manage, and the pleasures, relished to the hilt.

* * *

Vienna the undisputed capital of opera, music and art offered a gourmet menu of opportunities to absorb the best of western classical culture, provided in the magnificent historical edifices of the Austro Hungarian Empire. It was quite by accident that we ended up in one of the historic buildings dating from the turn of the century. We were located just round the corner from the famed Vienna Opera, and within walking distance to every jewel of Austrian culture that the city offers. These included the Hofburg Palace of the Hapsburgs, the Maria Theresa Museum, and the hallowed European houses of worship - St. Stephens Cathedral and Karl Kirsch (church). The decade spent in this elegant city, in the center of historic Europe, undoubtedly sharpened and enriched the mind and spirit of the now matured man traversing towards his golden years.

Austria is a small country with half the population of my motherland. It offers the intimacy among people that is very much akin to that of Sri Lanka, a natural trait I guess in small nations. If you knew a few, you knew everyone else that mattered from the President to the local officials, making life very cozy and convenient. We left behind many friends when we bid farewell to Vienna. Two couples in particular became part of our family: Dr. Hans Ortner, former Head of the Austrian Space Agency and his wife Martina, who owned and lived in the building in which we resided, and Prof. Ernst Fassan, a prominent lawyer and his wife Gerti, whose lakeside holiday home, next to that of Chancellor Helmut Kohl of Germany, was always open to us and many of our visiting friends.

With the backdrop of mountains and many large lakes, called seas, dotted all over the country, Austria is a god-given land, filled with beauty. The historic cities of Salzburg and Innsbruck, nestling at the foothills of the European Alps, are the playgrounds of Royalty even today. Surrounded by seven western and European countries if one drives two to three hours through Austria, one will cross an international boundary.

Needless to say, Austria provided a wonderful springboard for us to explore Europe. Whether we were driving down the Amalfi Coast, passing Capri and Sorrento, or the Costa de Sol, passing the historic cities of Seville and Granada, we imbibed the beauty of the countryside of neighboring Italy, Spain and Switzerland as well as the Adriatic, Mediterranean and Baltic coasts. The quaint little towns and villages, the vineyards and olive fields we passed through were awe-inspiring and exalted our spirits. The grandeur of the great cities of Leningrad, Moscow, Prague, Paris, Rome, Madrid and Budapest left indelible impressions which will be shared in due course.

* * *

As my dual U.N. responsibilities began to recede, new opportunities and responsibilities appeared on the horizon. The first was a telephone call from a Doyen of space law and policy in America, Mrs. Eilene Galloway, inviting me to be a candidate to fill the position of President of the only international professional organization dealing with space law and policy. She was the author of the U.S. Congressional Act that created NASA and a senior congressional adviser on space policy to the US Presidents Dwight Eisenhower, John Kennedy and Lyndon Johnson. The vacancy was created by the demise of Judge Manfred Lachs, President of the World Court who had simultaneously been the President of the International Institute of Law and Policy (IISL). Following a spirited election against Prof Carl Christal, a distinguished Professor at the University of Southern California, who had just published a seminal work entitled the "Modern International Law of Outer Space," I was elected as IISL President (Prof. Christal became a dear friend in later years, and lived to his nineties in the same city as me, Los Angeles).

I had the privilege of being reelected to five terms, and leading the Institute for fifteen years, until it was time for me to be elected as

President Emeritus, providing me with ample time to begin work on my memoire.

During my tenure, I had the support and encouragement of the distinguished members of the Board of Directors composed of Judges, Academics, and practitioners, as well as the invaluable assistance of the Secretary to the Board, Tanja Masson Zwaan, member of the faculty of Leiden University in the Netherlands.

As the President of the IISL I made many friends from around the world. Every one of them was deeply involved, as I was, in a field that they loved: to ensure that space activities are regulated in an orderly manner to serve humanity including those in the developing nations. Research and educational work, including a publication program, took priority in the work program of the Institute. It worked closely with United Nations and regional and national space agencies in carrying out its mission. The Institute worked closely with its two sister organizations the International Astronautical Federation (IAF) the membership of which was mainly space engineers, and the International Academy of Astronautics (IAA), the members of which were mainly space scientists, academics and administrators. I had the high honor of serving on the Board of Trustees of both organizations and the honor of being elected as an Academician. All three organizations have their Headquarters in Paris adjacent to the premises of the European Space Agency (ESA), requiring me to make frequent visits to that city.

During my leadership, promoting opportunities for young people to be engaged in space endeavors was a mission that was energetically pursued. I promoted their participation in the annual congresses and other seminars and workshops conducted around the world. I strongly supported development of an international Moot Court competition among universities conducted within the ambit of IISL. I arranged for judges from the International Court (ICJ) to judge the finals of the competition. I also arranged them to address the university students in diverse cities where the Competition was carried out each year. In carrying out this task I came in close contact with many of the preeminent judges of the Court, who are elected jointly by the United Nations General Assembly and the Security Council. Some I knew already, through academic or U.N. activities before they were elected, including the pride of Sri Lanka, Judge Christie Weeramantry, who retired as Vice President of the Court. I came to know others through my activities in the IISL. These contacts continued over the years, including the occasion when several contributed to a book on International Law, which I had the privilege of compiling and editing, with an introduction written by U.N. Secretary General Boutros Boutro-Ghali who was also a distinguished professor of international law. Abundant memories of my final working years in pursuit of the mission of IISL are very much alive in my memories, waiting to be recounted in due course.

* * *

A life-time of work covering space activities naturally brought me in close contact with leaders in the field of space who were great thinkers as Nobel Laureates Prof. Subramanyan Chandrasekhar and Dr. Abdus Salam. They hosted workshops in their institutes which I had organized, or in which I participated. On such occasions I learned to appreciate the depth of thought that comes naturally to such great people, and others like Prof Carl Sagan, Dr. Vikram Sarabhai, Prof Yash Pal, to name a few with whom I had the great privilege of working closely over the years. I consider such interaction a blessing that is of indescribable proportions.

Among the friends and acquaintances made in the context of my work in the space field which I highly value, are the contacts with heads of space agencies and their officials, heads of aerospace companies and their staffs, but most of all the shining symbols of space exploration: the astronauts and cosmonauts. They are, of course, among the brightest scientists and engineers that the world has to offer. It was my great fortune and privilege to know many of them from almost all the countries that sent a person to space.

Among them were Aleksei Leonov and Thomas Stafford, the duo who shook hands in space in the Apollo-Soyuz Docking, as a significant event during the era of US – Soviet Détente. Astronaut Stafford later participated in the 20th anniversary celebration of the event which took place with a ceremonial handshake at the World Space Congress in Washington, DC. I was a proud recipient of a crew patch they wore on board, which the duo presented to me. Neil Armstrong and Buzz Aldrin who went to the Moon, Valantina Tereshkova, the first woman in space, Cosmonauts Valerie Polyakov and Vladimir Titov, who spent over a year in space, Sally Ride and Dr. Mae Jamison, the lady astronauts are among the many I had the pleasure of knowing. Cosmonaut Frans Viehboch of Austria and Cosmonaut Dumitri Prunariu of Rumania are among the space people I count as family friends. I have had contact with several of these space men and women during projects carried out in developing countries using space technology, or when they participated in UN workshops which I was responsible for organizing. An outstanding example of their collaborative work is that of Astronaut Mae Jamison, who devoted her time and energy for vector control on malaria in Africa, using remote sensing techniques from space.

Perhaps, the most satisfying of those contacts was being invited to the Congress of the Association of Space Explorers (the exclusive professional organization of astronauts and cosmonauts) in 1992, to address their annual congress in Washington, D.C. The speakers were: Astronauts Wubbo Ockles, Michael Griffin (NASA Associate Administrator), Thomas Stafford, cosmonaut Valantina Tereshkova, Professor of Astronomy Carl Sagan and I, as head of the U.N. space program.

At the time, I considered it a singular honor. But to my great surprise I had two other such honors. First was given to me as an appreciation of a global conference that I had the privilege of organizing shortly before my retirement which formulated an agenda for nations to follow in carrying out space activities in the decade to come. On that occasion I was presented a copy of the Outer Space Treaty that I had a hand in helping to draft which had been carried into space in the U.S. Shuttle Atlantis (STS 74) which docked with the Russian Mir spacecraft and which was signed and sealed in space by the five astronauts on the shuttle, two Russian and one European cosmonauts who were present at the docking. The other was a presentation by NASA on the eve of my retirement from the United Nations in 1999. NASA Administrator Daniel Goldin signed and presented, as a memento, a framed U.N. flag that was flown aboard space shuttle Columbia (STS-90) along with a crew patch worn by the astronauts on board the spacecraft and a signed photograph of the crew. The inscription read: "Presented to Nandasiri Jasentuliyana in recognition of his support for furthering the peaceful uses of outer space for all nations."*(see annex)*

There are many stories of these wonderful individuals known as astronauts and cosmonauts, the best of the best, humanity have to offer. They are brilliant men and women who have travelled in space, but have their feet firmly grounded on Earth. Their stories also remain to be told from my persoective on another day.

* * *

While all of this occurred in my life in the international milieu, a part of me was always tightly tethered to my motherland. Much of Sri Lanka has changed over the years from the nostalgic days of my youth. In the era of globalization such changes are inevitable and are experienced by all nations. Sri Lanka has developed a vibrant industrial base, particularly in the garment sector. The remittances of the large number of migrant workers abroad have become the highest foreign- exchange earner for the country. There is growing interest in the tourist sector. These developments have considerably improved the standards of living of a significant portion of the populace. Most of all, the strains of insurrection, terrorism and war, have receded to the background. Nevertheless, there have been most discouraging developments on several fronts.

Years of neglect and mismanagement of the plantation sector which was the backbone of the country's economy; the roads and railway system that were allowed to deteriorate unabated, and being resurrected only in the recent days; the state of the towns and villages

547

outside of the capital city, such as my home town of Ambalangoda, which remain in the state that they were decades back; the decline of an excellent educational system that produced a literary rate second to none; equally declining state of the legal and justice system; the malaise that has crept in to the administrative service; and above all the lamentable state of the political discourse; are some of the maladies that will keep the nation from emerging as strong as it should be. One must not despair, for there are signs everywhere, however minute they may be, to be optimistic that the country is resilient enough to meet the challenges before it, and emerge as a strong and thriving nation.

The experiences of growing up in that emerald island are narrated in the earlier chapters of this publication. I was able to sustain the spirit of those experiences over half a century of life abroad, partly due to the constant contacts I had with my fellow compatriots, who also were living abroad. Working in the United Nations, I came across many compatriots. They worked in the organizations affiliated to the U.N. Others were assigned to the Missions to the United Nations and as Embassy officials in countries which I visited. Being at the United Nations gave me the opportunity of knowing all Presidents and Prime Ministers of my country beginning with Dudley Senanayake, as they visited the U.N. at one time or another and, of course, when I went home on occasional visits. Among the Foreign Ministers, Shahul Hameed and Lakshman Kadiragama (whom I have referred to elsewhere in the book) were special friends. Minister Hameed, who was the longest serving Foreign Minister, never failed to mention that I helped draft his very first speech to the General Assembly, which he made on the occasion of the adoption of the Outer Space Treaty.

Then there were the members of the Sri Lankan Diplomatic Service. Arthur Bassnayake was a member of the very first batch of Foreign Service officers of the independent Ceylon. He was serving as the Deputy Ambassador to the U.N. when I arrived in New York to assume my duties. He, along with others who followed, served the country for decades as diplomatic officers eventually rising up to

Ambassadors carrying out the foreign policy of Sri Lanka. They were a circle of friends that I always treasured. We had much in common in terms of our professional interests.

There was yet a related circle of friends who served in international organizations. Among them were such legendary figures as Raju Coomarasswamy (Roving Raju), who was a senior official of the United Nations Development Program (UNDP), and Gamini Corea, Secretary General of the United Nations Conference on Trade and Development (UNCTAD), whom I consider it an honor to have known as friends. Then there were colleagues of my generation who worked together and advanced up the ladder together, such as Jayantha Dhanapala, Under Secretary General for Disarmament, and Dr. Lal Jayawardane, Secretary General of World Institute of Development Economic Research (WIDER), with whom we forged a close friendships. There were many others with whom I had the privilege of being friends with many interesting tales to be told.

For instance, the day Jayantha Dhanapala and I flew a Russian Tupolev propeller aircraft and force-landed in Almaty, Kazakhstan is unforgettable. We were quarantined for hours with no explanations, and with nothing but bread to eat. We did finally end up at our destination in Ulan Bator for a meeting on space-related disarmament. Luckily the Swiss expert had brought his own packet of cereal. We ended up eating everything made of fatty mutton and yogurt in different forms for breakfast, lunch and dinner, and nothing else for the three days we spent there. Those were the days gone by.

There were others from my country who were associated with the U.N. and who worked for other intergovernmental and non-governmental organizations (IGOs and NGOs). These folks included Thalif Deen, an astute political columnist, who has written on almost all subjects covered by the U.N. and reported from many parts of the world. Having been a journalist covering the U.N. affairs for variety of news establishments including the well known military affairs journal Jane International, he now serves as U.N. Bureau

Chief and Regional Director, Inter Press Service (IPS) news agency. He was awarded the journalist of the year award from the U.N. Correspondents Association. Anytime I wished to get the inside story on any issue, I would turn to him. He and his wife Lucille have remained longstanding friends. There are several such individuals with whom I have interacted who deserve detail description.

*   *   *

I also had the opportunity to have a collegial interaction over the years with several Sri Lankans who were celebrated in various fields of space science. Arthur Clarke, who was an honorary Sri Lankan living in Colombo, was foremost among them. I never failed to visit him whenever I was back at home and we met at conferences around the world. As a member of the Board of Trustees of the International Academy of Astronautics, I had the honor to present an award to him at the International Astronautical Congress in Beijing. I had worked with Prof. Cyril Ponnamperuma in providing U.N. support for the training programs at the Institute he built in Kandy, Sri Lanka (Institute of Fundamental Studies), when he was leading an Institute on Chemical evolution at the University of Maryland. I was happy to have counted him among my friends. His interest was exploring the origin of life. Having been selected as the principal investigator for analysis of lunar soil brought to earth by project Apollo while at NASA's Exobiology Division, he later headed the Chemical Evolution Division at NASA Ames Research Center, where he worked on the Viking and Voyager programs.

I also count as close friends internationally recognized Astronomer and Director of Astrobiological Center at the Buckingham University in England, Prof. Chandra Wickramasinghe and his wife Priya, whom I had invited to some U.N. meetings of world famous space scientists. He made impressive presentations on his specialty of evolution of life and the Big Bang Theory. Physicist, Prof Asoka Mendis, an expert well known for his work on solar system physics and cometary, worked on several important NASA projects. I came in contact with Dr. Ray Jayawardhana when, as a graduate student at Harvard; he led a team that discovered a dusty disk around a young star with a large inner hole, possibly carved out by planet formation processes. He is now an internationally recognized astronomer at the University of Toronto, and is an award-winning science writer.

I first learned of Dr. Sarath Gunapala from my friend Ed Stone, President of the International Academy of Astronautics, on whose Board of Trustees I served. Dr. Stone was the Director of NASA Jet Propulsion Laboratory in Pasdedena, California and was the team leader of many deep space scientific missions, including the team of the Voyager 1 spacecraft which made news recently, when after travelling for 35 years, became the first man-made object to leave the solar system and enter interstellar space. At the time, Sarath was working on the team headed by Dr. Stone. Sarath is a well recognized space scientist who now heads a Group working on Infrared Photo Detecting systems at the Jet Propulsion Laboratories. Since we moved to California, Sarath and his wife Vajira have been very close friends. I have also had interactions with younger generation of space scientists working in the next stage of space exploration. This group includes young Avionics Design Engineer Melony Mahaarchchi, working on the Dragon spacecraft at Space X, the pioneering commercial cargo shuttle which ferries cargo to the International Space Station.

* * *

Apart from friends I made within official circles, Shanthi and I always had much interaction with the Sri Lankan community in the cities where we lived and worked. Many of them became family friends and often assisted us whenever needed. But most of all, they were there enabling us to link ourselves to the culture, and social and political developments back home. The local Sri Lankan Associations and temples served as the locales for connecting us with the members of the Sri Lankan community. Some of those contacts were nurtured over the years and we benefited greatly from these friendships.

Finally, in semi-retirement, we moved to Los Angeles, California, which has been home to us for the last decade. Southern California has offered us most of what we were used to in Sri Lanka. Blue skies and warm weather, with the landscape dotted with palm trees. Los Angeles is very much akin to the Dry Zone back home. Nine Buddhist temples, alumni associations of all major schools in Sri Lanka, and several cultural organizations offer a rich menu of events that no one can ever taste fully. A community of over 25,000 expatriates provides us with the possibility of making our own circle of friends and associates, as well as interacting with a variety of others in the broader community, whom the reader will meet in the next volume. Many are the experiences of living in the community, as well as, the life in the mega city of Los Angeles, which offers a social and cultural atmosphere second to none.

I have attempted to give the reader a glimpse of the different facets of my life which were constantly enriched by the places where I lived and visited, and the people whom I have met and befriended. The list is too long to include here of those about whom I plan to write in a second volume, with a narration of events and memories that they engendered. [1]

That said, what is left for me now is to wonder what an eventful journey this has been. A journey with many uncertainties and hurdles, etched with dreams and aspirations, that required much effort and ambition to realize. In the end, I feel the path laid by destiny, was travelled with the support and love of many, abundant luck, and sheer hard work. I feel grateful to the universe that offered me the opportunity to make that marvelous journey.

Annexes

ANNEX A....Prominent Professionals of My Home Town (Ambalangoda)

ANNEX B....Author's Publications

Annex A

PROMINENT PROFESSIONALS OF MY HOME TOWN (AMBALANGODA)

Ambalangoda produced a significant number of educators, scholars and professionals who were prominent in their fields of endeavor. Among them were those who reached the pinnacle of their chosen profession such as Cabinet Ministers, Chief Justice and Judges of the Supreme Court, Heads of Armed Forces, Heads of Government Departments, Professors of Medicine, Engineering, Accounting and other disciplines, as well as nationally recognized cultural leaders and sportsmen. Most of them were known to me through my own contacts or through my parents and grandparents contacts, and with few exceptions, I have had the good fortune of meeting them. Ambalngoda, being a small town of closely connected families, almost all of them happen to be my relatives by birth or through family marriages. Growing up, I looked up to many of them and through the inspiration they provided; they are instinctively part of what I am today. A full list of eminent personalities of Ambalangoda is provided below, with apologies to inevitable, but unintended omissions.

EDUCATORS: P.de S Kulatatna (Minister of Education, Principal Ananda College), C.W.W. Kgara (Minister of Education), L.H. Mtttananda (First Principal of Ananda College, Principal Dharmaraja College), S. Thomas De. Silva (Founder and first Principal of Dharmasoka College); G M de Silva (Principal Dharmashoka college, Commissioner of Assizes - Supreme Court, Principal Ceylon Law college); L.L.K. Gunatunga (Director of Education); K.T. Wilson Sumanasuriya (Commissioner of Examinations and President All Ceylon Buddhist Congress); Professor C. Patuwathavithana (Vice chancellor University of Moratuwa); Professor G T F de Silva (Vice chancellor University of Moratuwa); Professor Narada Warnasuriya (Vice-Chancellor Sri Jayawardanapura University); Professor Sabarathne Kulasooriya (Emeritus Professor of Botany University of Peradeniya; Abeseela Ginige (Professor of Geography, Peradeniya University; Professor M W Padmasiri de Silva (Professor and head of Department of Philosophy University of Peradeniya); E. R. De Silva (principal Richmond College); D.T. Wijeratne (Principal Dharmasoka College); Jasentuliyana. Piyasena (Principal Teachers training College, Balapitiya); P.de S. Jasentiliyana (Principal Dharamasoka College); Wlifred de Silva (Princhipal Dharmashoka college); M.D. Wimalasuriya (Principal Dharamasoka College); A Godvin de Silva (Principal Dharmashoka college); M.W. karunananda (Vice Principal Ananda College & Principal Nalanda College); S.K. Vintha de Silva (Principal Prajapathi Girls School); Harron De. Silva Kularatna (Manager, Prjapathi Girls School); E.P. De Silva (Principal Devananda Maha Vidyalaya); G.K. Gunawathie De Silva (Principal Gramini Balika maha Vidyalaya); D.T. Fernando (Principal Devananda College); S.K Nethananda (Principal Ananda College); K.T. Solomon Sumanasuriya (Principal Deniyaya Central College and Dickwella Vijitha Madya Maha Vidyalaya); Dayawanse Ginige (Founding Principal P. De S Kularatna Viddyalaya); C.M. Weraratne (Deputy Principal Ananada College); Jinapriya Ginige (Vice-Principal Mahinda College); Abeyatunge Ginigae(Vice-Principal Mahinda College); Arthur Perera (Well-known scientist and science teacher); Kumar De Silva (Pioneer teacher of the French Language, recipient of Chevalier dans l'Odre des Arts et des Letters' – Order of Arts and Letters);

ERUDITE SCHOLAR MONKS: Venerable. Vilegoda Dhammananda (Viharadhapathi Sunandarama, Ambalangoda); Ven. Ambalangoda Sri Devananda (Viharadhapathi Puranasubadraramaya, Ambalangoda); Ven. Dr. Pollwatte Buddhadatta (Professor of Buddhist Studies, Viddyalankara University); Ven. Polwatte

Panchaloka (Vice Principal Viddyaloka Pirivena); Ven. Ambalangoda Dhammakusala (Mahanayaka of the Amarapura Nikaya and Professor of Sanskrit at the Vidyodaya University and Viharadhipathi, Sunandaramaya, Ambalangoda); Ven. Panditha Polwatte Sudharshi; Ven. Ambalangoda Chandrasiri (Viharadhapathi Lankaramaya in Singapore and Purana Subadraramaya Ambalangoda); Ven. Ambalangoda Sumangala (Mahanayaka of the Kalyanawansa sect of the Amarapura Nikaya); Ven. Poramba Dhammadhara (Professor, Shanthinikethana, India);

WRITERS AND ARTISTS: Ananda Rajakaruna (national poet, composed scores of poems and published books used in schools); P. Dunstan de Silva (First Sri Lankan graduate of Shanthinikathan Music school- In India and a colleague of Ravi Shankar and later Director of Classical Music programs- Radio Ceylon); Swarna De Silva (original singer of the National Anthem accompanying Ananda Samarokoon); C. De S. Kulatilake (Professor of Fine Arts, Music Composer, and Director Music, Broadcasting Corporation); D.T. Fernando (Dramatist, Lyricist and composer of film music); Kanthi Gunatunge (Leading Movie Actress); Kalasuri Ariyapala Wijesuriya (Ariyapala Gurunanse -national leader of sculpturing masks); S.M. Somadasa (Award winning mask craftsman); Tukkuwadu Gunadasa (Pioneer mask maker); Kalasuri Jayasiri Semage and Bandula Lokuge (Renowned Painters); Bandula Fernando (leading Batik artist); M W Lairis de Silva (renown and prominent art teacher); Chandrasoma Binduhewa (Dramatist); Sunanda Deshapriya and Bandu Karunasekara (Recognized Journalists); A.G. Iman Perera (Popular Singer);

POLITICAL LEADERS: P.de.S. Kularatne (Cabinet Minister); C.W.W. Kannangara (Cabinet Minister); P.H. William Silva (Cabinet Minister); Jasentu Liyana Sirisena (Cabinet Minister); M.W.R. de Silva (Member of Parliament, Deputy chairmen of Committees of Parliament, Crown Proctor, Gampala); Dr. M.H. Saddhasena (Member of Parliament); L.C. De Silva (M.P.)., Buddhika Kurukularatne (M.P.); Ryter Thilakasekara (M.P.); Jagath Saddhasena (M.P.); Dr. Harsh de Silva (M.P.); Sajin de Vas

Gunawardena (M.P.); Shan De Silva (Chief Minister Provincial Council); R.M.M. De Silva (Chairman Urban Council); T.C.P. Fernando (Chairman U.C.); S.G.A. De Silva (Chairman, U.C.); P.A. De Silva (Chairman U.C.); G.M. Sumanatilake De Silva (Longest Serving Chairman U.C., Ambalangoda-18 years); Anura Pradeep (Chairman U.C.); W.O. Ananda De. Silva (Chairman U.C.);

NATIONAL DEFENCE FORCERS: General Rohana Daluwathe (Army Commander); General Sarath Fonseka (Army Commander); General Jagath Jayasuriya (currant Army Commander); Commander Solomon Fernando Navy Commander); Vice Marshal Jayalath Weerakkody (Commander of Air Force); P. S. Osmond De Silva Inspector General of the Police (IGP); Indra De Silva (IGP); Mithra Ariyasinghe (Deputy IGP); Major General M.D. Fernando; Major Gen. Lalin Fernando; Major General Devinda Kaluphana; Brig. Sanath Karunaratne; Group Capt. G.M.U. De Silva (Air Commodore); Major Malraj De. Silva; Ganendra Vas Gunawardena (Senior Superintendent of Police);

MEDICAL & DENTAL DOCTORS: Dr. W.A.S de Silva (Professor of Medicine and philanthropist who established the first hospital at Pollwatte in Ambalangoda); Dr G Kanishka de Silva (Consultant oncological surgeon, who established the Cancer Surgical Unit in the Kandy Teaching Hospital, President Kandy Society of Medicine and Secretary, Oncosurgery board Post Graduate Institute of Medicine); Professor Mohan de Silva (Professor of Surgery University of Jayawardenapura); Dr Ishani Rodirigo (Consultant Pediatrician, Senior Lecturer, Medical Faculty, University of Colombo); Dr Manilka Sumanatilleke (Consultant, Teaching Hospital Karapitiya, Galle); Dr Amal Harsha de Silva (Director Private Hospitals, Ministry of Health); Dr.K.T. Samathapala De Silva; Dr.M.H. Saddhasena; Dr. A. Rajapakse; Dr Susil Manukulasuriya, (Chief Psychiatrist Department of Prisons, UK); Dr Damen Kularatna; Dr. T.G.D.S. Kularatna; Dr. J.G.R.H. De. Silva; Dr. J.C. De Silva; Dr. P.H.D.H. De Silva; Dr. Shan Ariyasinghe (USA); Dr. Vipula Ariyasinghe; Dr. J.L.L. Fernando (USA); Dr. K.T. Nihal De. Silva (USA); DR. Ananda Nimalasuriya (USA); Dr. Chula Withana (USA); Dr. Pujitha Egodage (USA); Dr.

Nirosha Nimalasuriya; Dr. Saroja Ginigalgoda-Siriwardene; Dr Srilal De Silva; Dr. Pushpa Jasentuliyana; Dr. Inoka Jasentuliyana De Silva; Dr Nalika de Silva; Dr. Prasantha Gange; Dr. Wimalasiri Gange Jr (UK); Dr. Dharshan Fernando; Dr. Ruwanthie Fernando; Dr. A.K. Sarath De. Silva (U.K.); Dr. S.R. De Silva; Dr.M. Muinandradasa, (oral surgeon, NATO at Stuttgart, Germany, with a rank of Lt.CL,); Dr.G.G. De Silva (dental surgeon and chairmen Conciliation board Ambalangoda); Dr. Susil Jasentuliyana (oral surgeon, Sri Lanka Army with rank of Lt. CL,); Dr. Harendra Kularatna (Dental Surgeon, established Roseth Hospital, Ambalangoda); Dr. Harsha Santiago (Dental Surgeon, USA), Upali De. Silva (Medical Representative) Ranjith Santiago, (Medical Representative, USA);

LAWYERS: P.de. S Kularatne; C.W.W. Kannangara; G.C.T.A De Silva (Senator and Minister of Justice); G.P.S De Silva (Chief Justice of the Supreme Court); T.S. Fernando Q.C. (Judge of the Supreme Court); G.P.A. De Silva (Chief Justice of the Supreme Court); G.G.D. De Silva (Legal Draftsman & District Judge, Sri Lanka; Judge of the Supreme Court, Seychelles); G M de Silva (Commissioner of Assizes, Supreme Court); K.T. Chitrasiri (Judge of the Court of Appeal); J.W. Samaraweera (Judge of the Court of Appeal); Tudor Gunaratna (Judge of the High Court); Kumar Ekaratna (Judge of the High Court); Sunil Rajapaksa (Judge of the High Court); T.C.P. Fernando (District Judge); Harrot Gunawardena (District Judge); K. T. P. Fernando (District Judge); G C W de Silva(District Judge); S M H de Silva (Deputy Legal Draftsman); Donald Wickramasuriya(Deputy Legal Draftsman); Norman Waidiyaratne (MP and Speaker of the House); M W R de Silva (member of Parliament, Deputy chairmen of Committees of Parliament); Kapila Widyaratne (Deputy Solicitor General); Tudor Jayawardane; D.P. De Silva; Doyle Kularatne; A.M. Bandularatna; Piyadasa De Silva; A. Welaratne; K.T.P. De Silva; G.L.H. Dharmawanse; Chula De. Silva; Wimalasiri Gange; Buddhika Kurukularatne (M.P.); Nandasiri Jasentuliyana; K.D. Fernando; Kamal Jayasekare; W.O. Ananda De Silva; Anura Pradeep; Saroja Jasenthuliyana Silva; Enoka Jasenhtuliyana; Mahinda Deshapriya; Yenuka Premaratne; Lumbini De. Silva;

ACCOUNTANTS: B.R. De Silva (Founder of the leading accounting firm in the country-B.R. De Silva & Co; and pioneered accounting education at Peradeniya and Viddyodaya Universities, Ceylon Law College, and the Ceylon Technical College; and founder member of the Institute of Chartered Accountants of Ceylon-ICSC); D.S. De Silva (Auditor General of Sri Lanka and First President of ICSC); D.O. De Silva (Past President of ICSC); Bandu Manukulasuriya (Management Account and former Chairman of a several Corporations); D.S.P.S. De Silva, A.C.D.S. De Silva, Ranjan De Silva, Sunil Santiago (USA), G.H.G. D. De Silva, D.S.P. Sirisena, G. Hewawasam, Dhammika Gunaratna, and G.D. Upasiri (Chartered Accountants);

ENGINEERS: Dr. A.G. Unil Perera (Regent's Professor, Department Of Physics and Astronomy, Gerogia State University, Atlanta, U.S.A.); M.W. Chandrasoma; Lal Premanath (General Manager, National Water Supply and Drainage Board); Ranjith Patuwathavithana (Chief Engineer, Sri Lanka Ports Authority); K.J. De. Silva (USA); Dr. Sandya Malliyawadu (Australia); Upul Jasenthuliyana (Australia); Tissa Warusawithana (Australia); Kamal Fernando (Australia); Ranjan De Silva (Australia); G Channa De Silva (Director Public Sector, Microsoft Sri Lanka); G Lakpriya de Silva (Enterprise Consultant, Largo, Florida, USA);

CIVIL SERVANTS: Chandananda De Silva (Secretary Ministry of Defense); L.L.K. Gunatunge (Permanent Secretary Ministry of Education); P.A. De. Siva (Permanent Secretary Ministry of Transport); Dayani De Silva Commissioner of Inland Revenue and Chairperson Bank of Ceylon); Dr P H D H de Silva (Director General; National Museum); G. P. S. Harsha De Silva (Director General, National Archives); Mahinda Deshapriya (Election Commissioner); K.T. Ramya De. Silva (Deputy Director of Commerce); Sajin Vass Gunawardane (Senior Adviser to the President);

UNITED NATIONS OFFICIALS: G.W. Ussawattw-Aratchi; Chandra Kodikkara; Nandasiri Jasentuliyana.

NATIONAL SPORTSMEN: Mahela jayawardene (Captain Sri Lanka Cricket team and ICC World Team); Ajith De Silva, K. M. Nelson, Upul Tharanga, and Chandimal De Silva (Members of the Sri Lanka Cricket Team); W.N. Neil De Silva (Captain National Athletic Team); Damith De Siva (Captain National Athletic Team); Oswald Rajapakse (National Athletic Team); R.M. Pradeep Chanditha (National Swimming Champion and Member National Athletic Team); T.H.M. Chandralal (Captain National Swimming Team); Jayalaith Weerkody, and R.M. Dhammika, Members of the National Swimming Team); W. Werasena, G.W. Chandrasena, and Osmond De. Silva and L.R. Ariyananda (Members of the National Badminton Team); Sarath Gunaratna, Dhammika Gunaratna, J.G.Y.C. Tilakaratne, and Namal Manoj Gunasekara (Members of the National Table Tennis Team); Lionel Mendis, and NelsonMendis (Coach- National Cricket Team)

— ❖ —

Annex B

AUTHOR'S PUBLICATIONS

Publications - Books: Space Law and the United Nations, Kluwer Law International, UK (1999); Perspectives on International Law, Kluwer Law International (1995); Manual on Space (four volumes), Oceana, New York (with Roy Lee, 1979); International Space Programmes and Policies, North-Holland, New York (with Ralph Chipman, 1984); Maintaining Space for Peaceful Purposes, United Nations University, Tokyo (1984); Space Law: Development and Scope, Praeger, New York (1991); Foreign Policy of Sri Lanka as reflected at the United Nations, Kluwer Law International, UK (Forthcoming).

Chapters in Books: The Future of International Telecommunications Law (Chapter 4), in Anthony Anghie and Garry Sturgess (Ed), Legal Visions of the 21st Century: Essays in Honour of Judge Christopher Weeramantry, Kluwar Law International, The Hague (2001); The Development of Space Law from a Third World Perspective (Chapter 7), in V.S. Mani and S. Bhatt, Recent Trends in International Space Law and Policy, Lancers Books, New Delhi (1997); Future Perspectives of Space Law (Chapter 3), in Karl- Heinz Böckstiegel, Perspectives of Air Law, Space Law, and International Business Law for the Next Century, Carl Heymanns Verlag KG, Cologne (1995); The International Regulatory Regime for Satellite Communications: The Meaning for Developing Countries, in Ko Swan Sik et at, Asian Yearbook of International Law, Vol. 2, Kluwer Academic Publishers (1994); International Law of Outer Space, in Cambridge University Encyclopedia, Cambridge (1991); Remote Sensing and the Role of the United Nations (Chapter 15), in Michael Krepons, Commercial

563

Observation Satellites and International Security, St. Martin Press, New York (1990); Priorities for International Protection of the Space Environment (Chapter 14), in Karl- Heinz Böcstiegel, Environment Aspects of Space Activities, Carl Heymanus and Verlag, Cologne (1989); Development of Peaceful Uses of Space Technology and International Law, in Josef Mrizek, The Role of Scientists in Preventing an Arms Race in Outer Space, Academia Press, Prague (1988); Satellite Remote Sensing in Developing Countries: The Experience of West Africa (Chapter 16), in A.S. Bhalla, New Technologies and Development: Experience in Technology Blending, Lynne Rienner Publishers, London (1988); Conflict Resolution in Outer Space: New Approaches - Old Techniques (Part II, Chapter 1), in Rene Jean Dupuy, The Settlement of Disputes of the New Natural Resources, Martin Nijhoff, The Hague (1983); Implications of Space Surveillance: Strategic and Political Aspects (Chapter 8), in Mateesco Matte, Space Surveillance for Arms Control and Verification, Crasl, Montreal (1987); Space Weapons and International Law: A Critique of Existing Treaties (Chapter V), in Mateesco Matte, An Arms Race in Outer Space: Could Treaties Prevent It?, Crasl, Montreal (1985); Third World Perspectives of Space Technology, in Mateesco Matte, Space Activities and Implications at the Threshold of the 80's, Carswell Co., Ltd., Toronto (1980).

Selected Journal Articles: Basic Space Science and Developing Countries, Space Policy, May 1998; Space Futures and Human Security, Journal of Space Policy, August 1997; The Role of Developing Countries in the Formulation of Space Law, Annals of Air and Space Law, Vol. XX-II (1995); Ensuring Equal Access to the Benefits of Space Technologies for All Countries, Journal of Space Policy, February 1994; Regulation of Space Salvage Operations: Possibilities for the Future, Journal of Space Law, Vol. 22, Nos. 1&2 (1994); Celebrating Fifty Years of the Chicago Convention Twenty-Five Years after the Moon Landing: Lessons for Space Law, Annals of Air and Space Law, Vol. XIX, Part II (1994); Space Commerce on Global Scale, Journal of Law and Technology, Vol. 5, No. 2 (1990); Article I of the Outer Space Treaty Revisited, Journal of Space Law, Vol. 15, No. 2 (1989); United Nations Principles of Remote Sensing:

An Agreement in Economic Relations, Journal of Space Policy, Vol. 4, No. 4 (1988); Space and International Organizations, Proceedings of the American Political Science Association, Chicago (1987); United Nations Space Treaties and the Common Heritage Principle, Journal of Space Policy, Vol. 2, No. 4 (1986); Treaty Law and Outer Space, Proceedings of the American Society of International Law, Washington, DC (1980); United Nations and Space Weapons, Harvard International Review, Vol. III, No. 4 (1985); Developing Countries and the Geostationary Orbit, Journal of Space Policy, Vol. 1, No. 3 (1985); Space Communications - Issues and Policies, Proceedings of the American Society of International Law, Washington, DC (1983); Potential for Solar Power Satellites in Developing Countries, Solar Power Review, Vol. 4 (1983); Institutional Aspects of International Cooperation in Space Manufacturing, Proceedings of Princeton, University Conference on Space Manufacturing, Princeton (1980); Direct Television Broadcasting in the Third World, Columbia Journal of Transnational Law, Vol. 13, No. 1 (1974); Regulatory Functions of ITU in the Field of Space Telecommunication, Journal of Air Law and Commerce, Vol. 34, No. 1 (1968); International Space Law and Cooperation and the Mining of Asteroids, Annals of Air and Space Law, Vol. XV (1990); Multilateral Negotiations of the Use of Nuclear Power Source in Outer Space, Annals of Air and Space Law, Vol. XIV (1989); Civilian and Military Space Activities: A Third World Perspective, Annals of Air and Space Law, Vol. XII (1987); Treaty Law and Outer Space: Can UN Play an Effective Role?, Annals of Air and Space Law, Vol. XI (1986)

Honours and Awards: Selected by the United States National Space Society to its unique worldwide list of "100 space people who have had the greatest impact on our lives" (1992); Elected as an Academician of the International Academy of Astronautics (IAA) whose worldwide membership is limited to 1000 members (1990); Testimonial Award of the International Astronautical Federation (IAF). Award given annually in recognition of important contributors to space law and policy (1982); Book Award of the International Academy of Astronautics (IAA) (1989); 1996 Elected Academician of the Russian Academy of Cosmonautics (1996); Commonwealth

Scholar McGill University, Canada (1963-1965); Editor, Ceylon Law College Review (1961); Ceylon Law College Scholarship for Standing First of the Order of Merit (1959); Who's Who in the World (1998); Who's Who in International Organizations (1992); Who's Who in the United Nations and Related Agencies; All Round Student of the Year, Richmond College (1958); Captain, Richmond College Cricket Team (1957 & 58), Captain, Combined Schools' Cricket Team Vs. Australian Schools' Team (1958), Captain, Richmond College Athletics Team (1957), Member Richmond College Debating Team (1957).

— ❖ —

Printed in the United States
by Baker & Taylor Publisher Services